Table of Contents

INTRODUCTION
Breakfast
- Meat Sandwich
- Keto Cereal Bowl
- Butter Crepes ... 12
- Soft Eggs ... 13
- Cabbage Hash Browns ... 13
- Meat Muffins with Quail Eggs ... 13
- Cinnamon Pancakes ... 14
- Paprika Eggs in Pepper Holes ... 14
- Stuffed Pepper Halves with Omelet ... 14
- Bacon Egg Cups ... 15
- Zucchini Meat Cups ... 15
- Green Hash ... 15
- Breakfast Avocado Bombs ... 16
- Spiced Hard-Boiled Eggs ... 16
- Minced Beef Pancakes ... 16
- Ham Roll ... 17
- Fluffy Eggs ... 17
- Bacon Eggs with Chives ... 17
- Avocado Boats with Omelet ... 18
- Breakfast Egg Hash ... 18
- Bacon Tacos ... 18
- Mason Jar Omelet ... 19
- Cauliflower Bake ... 19
- Cauliflower Toast ... 19
- Sausage Casserole ... 20
- Frittata with Greens ... 20
- Cheese Egg Balls ... 20
- Breakfast Crustless Quiche ... 21
- Breakfast Taco Omelet ... 21
- Keto Shakshuka ... 21
- Morning Bacon Bombs ... 22
- Egg Muffins ... 22
- Egg Sandwich ... 22
- Keto Oatmeal ... 23
- Oregano Egg en Cocotte ... 23
- Hot Jalapeno Poppers Mix ... 23
- Morning Pudding ... 24
- Breakfast Stuffed Avocado ... 24
- Layered Casserole ... 24
- Chili Casserole ... 25
- Breakfast Hot Cacao ... 25
- Zucchini Cheese Fritters ... 25
- Cauliflower Fritters ... 26
- Breakfast Spaghetti Squash Casserole ... 26
- Sweet Porridge ... 26
- Bacon Salad with Eggs ... 27
- Classic Breakfast Casserole ... 27
- Low-Carb Flaxseed Brule ... 27
- Mini Frittatas ... 28
- Egg Benedict Sandwich ... 28
- Nutritious Taco Skillet ... 28
- Wontons ... 29
- Breakfast Kale Bread ... 2?

Egg Scramble 29
Parmesan Chicken Balls 30
Blueberry Muffins 30
Chicken Fritters 30
Crustless Egg Pie 31
Mini Casserole in Jars 31
Salmon Balls 31
Spinach Casserole 32
Chicken Salad 32
Broccoli Toast Spread 32
Green Egg Bites 33
Breakfast Sausages 33

Lunch 34
Provolone Chicken Soup 34
Jalapeno Soup 34
Aromatic Lasagna with Basil 34
Keto "Potato" Soup 35
Egg Soup 35
Beef Cabbage Soup 35
Bacon Chowder 36
Butternut Squash Soup 36
Tortilla Soup 36
Asian Style Zucchini Soup 37
Chili Verde 37
Keto Taco Soup 37
Chicken Enchilada Soup 38
Creamy Cauliflower Soup 38
Kale Soup 38
Bone Broth Soup 39
Buffalo Chicken Soup 39
Sausages & Vegetable Stew 39
Keto Lunch Bowl 40
Cobb Salad 40
Lobster Salad 40
Italian Style Salad 41
Egg & Cheese Salad with Dill 41
Crab Salad 41
Chicken Paprika 42
Sour Cauliflower Salad 42
Warm Radish Salad 42
Crack Chicken 43
Salsa Chicken 43
Lemon Carnitas 43
Smoky Pulled Pork 44
Chicken & Dumplings Soup 44
Zoodle Soup 44
Hot Sausages Soup 45
Fajita Soup 45
Kalua Chicken 45
Southwestern Chili 46
Clam Chowder 46
Parsley Meatloaf 46
Pepper Pork Chops 47
Meat & Collard Greens Bowl 47
Spinach Saag 47
Chicken & Mushroom Bowl 48

Cheddar Soup 48
　　Lunch Pot Roast 48
　　Green Beans with Ham 49
　　Spiral Ham 49
　　Coconut Soup 49
　　Corned Beef with Cabbage 50
　　Lazy Meat Mix 50
　　Shredded Chicken Salad 50
　　Beef Curry Soup 51
　　Pork Roast with Sauerkraut 51
　　Cheesy Pork Rinds 51
　　Manhattan Chowder 52
　　Ancho Chili 52
　　Seafood Soup 52
　　Tuscan Soup 53
　　Winter Soup 53
　　Reuben Soup 53
　　Avocado Chicken Salad 54
　　Lettuce Chicken Salad 54
　　Zuppa Toscana 54
　　Broccoli Soup 55
　　Low Carb Zucchini and Eggplant Soup 55
Side Dishes 56
　　Cauliflower Mac&Cheese 56
　　Brussels Sprouts Casserole 56
　　Rosemary&Butter Mushrooms 56
　　Bacon Brussels Sprouts 57
　　Spinach Mash with Bacon 57
　　Mashed Cauliflower 57
　　Fried Cauliflower Slices 58
　　Mashed Brussel Sprouts 58
　　Cauliflower Rice 58
　　Soft Spinach with Dill 59
　　Mexican Style Keto Rice 59
　　Kale&Parmesan Bowl 59
　　White Cabbage in Cream 59
　　Cauliflower Cheese 60
　　Cauli-Tatoes 60
　　Butter Spaghetti Squash 60
　　Sliced Zucchini Casserole 61
　　Green Beans Casserole 61
　　Squash Casserole 61
　　Cheesy Zucchini Strips 62
　　Turmeric Cabbage Rice 62
　　Turnip Creamy Gratin 62
　　Parmesan Onion Rings 63
　　Rosemary Radish Halves 63
　　Sweet Baby Carrot 63
　　Feta and Zucchini Bowl 63
　　Herbed Asparagus 64
　　Cheesy Radish 64
　　Turnip Cubes 64
　　Cilantro-Kale Salad 64
　　Thyme Purple Cabbage Steaks 65
　　Smashed Cauliflower with Goat Cheese 65
　　Low Carb Fall Vegetables 66

Steamed Broccoli 66
Cheddar Tots with Broccoli 66
Vegetable Fritters 67
Steamed Asparagus 67
Roasted Cauliflower Steak 67
Cayenne Pepper Green Beans 67
Marinated Red Bell Peppers 68
Broccoli Nuggets 68
Yellow Squash Noodles 68
Oregano Fennel Steaks 69
Butter Shirataki Noodles 69
Asiago Cauliflower Rice 69
Spaghetti Squash Mac&Cheese 70
Sichuan Style Green Beans 70
Cauliflower Tortillas 70
Gouda Vegetable Casserole 71
Warm Antipasto Salad 71
Eggplant Gratin 71
Beet Cubes with Pecans 72
Jalapeno Popper Bread 72
Baked Green Beans 72
Garlic Bread 73
Parmesan Broccoli Head 73
Side Dish Cauliflower Ziti 73
Cauliflower Salad with Provolone Cheese 74
Spiced Asparagus 74

Snacks and Appetizers 75
Zucchini Fries in Bacon 75
Bacon Bites with Asparagus 75
Bacon Onion Rings 75
Oregano Keto Bread Rounds 76
Cabbage Chips 76
Soul Bread 76
Tender Jicama Fritters 77
Spiced Chicken Carnitas 77
Cheese Almond Meal Bites 77
Zucchini Parsley Tots 78
Paprika Deviled Eggs 78
Parmesan Tomatoes Slices 78
Mini Cheese Pepperoni Pizza 79
Keto Queso Dip 79
Keto Jalapeno Bread 79
Turnip Fries 80
Butternut Squash Fries 80
Popcorn Chicken 80
Crunchy Green Beans 81
Keto Breadsticks 81
Mini Chicken Skewers 81
Parmesan Cauliflower Tots 82
Aromatic Swedish Meatballs 82
Kale Wraps 82
Bread Twists 83
Cheese Chips 83
Butter Coffee 83
Pumpkin Spices Latte 84
Salty Nuts Mix 84

Heart of Palm Dip 84
Taco Shells 85
Mini Margharita Pizzas in Mushroom Caps 85
Keto Guacamole Deviled Eggs 85
Hot Tempeh 86
Garlic Aioli 86
Pesto Wings 86
Bacon Avocado Bombs 87
Bacon Sushi 87
Ranch Poppers 87
Keto Taquitos 88
Chicken Celery Boats 88
Keto Nachos 88
Edamame Hummus 89
Crab Spread 89
Bacon-Wrapped Shrimps 89
Tuna Steak Skewers 90
Marinated Olives 90
Chicharrones 90
Keto Spanakopita Pie Slices 91
Dog Nuggets 91
Keto Cheetos 91
Cauliflower PopCorn 92
Cheese Pops 92
Chocolate Bacon 92
Chocolate Shake 93
Egg Yolk Spread 93
Chili Pumpkin Seeds 93
Cheese Meatballs with Greens 94
Wrapped Chicken Cubes 94
Keto Crackers 94

Fish and Seafood 95
Fish Saag 95
Brazilian Fish Stew 95
Fish Casserole 96
Salmon Pie 96
Pesto Salmon 96
Tuna Salad 97
Tandoori Salmon 97
Cheese Melt 97
Prosciutto Shrimp Skewers 98
Lime Salmon Burger 98
Curry Fish 98
Fried Salmon 99
Spicy Mackerel 99
Salmon in Fragrant Sauce 99
Shrimp Salad with Avocado 100
Seafood Omelet 100
Shrimp Tacos 100
Shrimp Cocktail 101
Mussels Casserole 101
Skagenrora 101
Butter Scallops 102
Cajun Crab Casserole 102
Crab Melt with Zucchini 102
Baked Snapper 103

Salmon Salad 103
Butter Cod Loin 103
Cod in Cream Sauce 104
Salmon and Kohlrabi Gratin 104
Mussel Chowder 104
Paprika Salmon Skewers 105
Tuscan Shrimps 105
Parmesan Scallops 105
Seafood Bisque 106
Lobster Bisque 106
Tarragon Lobster 106
Mussels Mariniere 107
Tuna Cakes 107
Salmon under Parmesan Blanket 107
Salmon Poppers 108
Tuna Rolls 108
Fish Sticks 108
Crab Rangoon Dip 109
Coriander Seabass 109
Dill Halibut 109
Bacon-Wrapped Cod 110
Spinach and Tilapia Casserole 110
Fish Pie 110
Mackerel Pate 111
Crab Rangoon Fat Bombs 111
Crab&Broccoli Casserole 111
Tuna and Bacon Cups 112
Halibut Ceviche 112
Parchment Fish 112
Poached Cod 113
Light Shrimp Pad Thai 113
Coated Coconut Shrimps 113
Steamed Crab Legs 114
Salmon with Lemon 114
Zingy Fish 114
Thyme Cod 114

Poultry 115
Chicken Tonnato 115
Paprika Chicken Wings 115
Garlic Chicken Drumsticks 115
Chicken Provencal 116
Chicken with Blue Cheese Sauce 116
Flying Jacob Casserole 116
Chicken Caprese Casserole 117
Cajun Chicken Salad 117
Caesar Salad 117
Hoagie Bowl 118
BLT Chicken Wrap 118
Pizza Stuffed Chicken 118
Chicken Patties 119
Mozzarella Chicken Fillets 119
Bruschetta Chicken 119
Greek Chicken 120
Chicken Rendang 120
Chicken Zucchini Enchiladas 121
Chicken Cacciatore 121

Coconut Chicken Tenders 122
Balsamic Roast Chicken 122
Chicken & Snap Pea Salad 123
Spinach Stuffed Chicken 123
Chicken Scarpariello 124
Chicken Divan Casserole 124
Orange Chicken 124
Chicken Stroganoff 125
Pecan Chicken 125
Cayenne Pepper Chicken Meatballs 125
Chicken Cheese Calzone 126
Butter Chicken Stew 126
Chicken Cauliflower Rice 127
Chicken Crust Pizza 127
Asiago Chicken Drumsticks 127
Chicken Stuffed Avocado 128
Chicken Cordon Bleu 128
Herbed Whole Chicken 128
Ground Chicken Mix 129
Bacon-Wrapped Chicken Tenders 129
Chicken and Spinach Bowl 129
Keto Chicken Burger 130
Chicken Liver Pate 130
Coconut Chicken Cubes 130
Chicken Lettuce Rolls 131
Turkey Bolognese Sauce 131
Turkey Stuffed Mushrooms 131
Cornish Game Hens 132
Blackened Chicken 132
Anniversary Chicken 132
Ajiaco 133
Ground Turkey Chili 133
Ethiopian Spicy Doro Wat Soup 133
Chicken Fricassee 134
Chicken Steamed Balls 134
South American Garden Chicken 135
Chicken Moussaka 135
Chicken with Black Olives 136
Indian Chicken Korma 136

Meat 137
Rosemary Barbecue Pork Chops 137
Kalua Pork 137
Parmesan Pork 137
Garlic Pork Loin 137
Fragrant Pork Belly 138
Parmesan Pork Tenderloins 138
Keto Ham 138
Jalapeno Pulled Pork 139
Char Siu 139
Chili Spare Ribs 139
Taiwanese Braised Pork Belly 140
Korean Style Pork Ribs 140
Pork and Turnip Cake 140
Kalua Pig 141
Greek Style Pork Chops 141
Curry Pork Sausages 141

Sage Pork Loin 142
Spinach and Fennel Pork Stew 142
Garlic Smoky Ribs 142
Ground Meat Stew 143
Pork&Mushrooms Ragout 143
Mesquite Ribs 143
Keto Pork Posole 144
Hoisin Meatballs 144
Tender Pork Satay 144
Ham and Cheese Dinner Casserole 145
Blackberry Pork Chops 145
Pork and Celery Curry 145
Beef and Squash Ragu 146
Beef Loin with Acorn Squash 146
Beef Tips 146
Onion Baby Back Ribs 147
Beef & Cabbage Stew 147
Tender Salisbury Steak 147
Cumin Kielbasa 148
Prosciutto and Eggs Salad 148
Mississippi Roast 148
Keto Oxtail Goulash 149
Italian Beef 149
Thyme Braised Beef 149
Butter Lamb 150
Coriander Leg of Lamb 150
Dhansak Curry Meat 150
Mint Lamb Cubes 151
Pork Chops in Sweet Sauce 151
Kalua Pork 151
Spoon Lamb 152
Rogan Josh 152
Chipotle Lamb Shank 152
White Pork Soup 153
Lamb Pulao 153
Meat&Cheese Pie 154
Burger Casserole 154
Cauliflower Shepherd's Pie 155
Big Mac Bites 155
Zoodle Pork Casserole 156
Ground Beef Skewers 156
Pastrami 157
Pork Salad with Kale 157

Vegetable Meals 158
Garlic and Cheese Baked Asparagus 158
Brussels Sprouts in Heavy Cream 158
Wrapped Bacon Carrot 158
Caprese Zoodles 159
Cauliflower Florets Mix 159
Balsamic Brussels Sprouts 159
Tender Sautéed Vegetables 160
Spaghetti Squash Nests 160
Lemongrass Green Beans 160
Cucumbers and Zucchini Noodles 161
Eggs and Mushrooms Cups 161
Kale Skillet with Nuts 161

Shredded Spaghetti Squash with Bacon 162
Green Peas Salad 162
Cauliflower Risotto...162
Collard Greens with Cherry Tomatoes 163
Cauliflower Gratin 163
Scalloped Cabbage 163
Hash Brown Casserole 164
Stuffed Mushrooms...164
Green Beans Salad...164
Tuscan Mushrooms Sauce 165
Thyme Cauliflower Head 165
Stuffed Spaghetti Squash 165
Shallot Mushrooms...166
Baked Kabocha Squash 166
Sautéed Kohlrabi 166
Butter Edamame Beans 166
Marinated Tomatillos Paste 167
Tender Rutabaga 167
Zucchini Goulash 167
Cheddar Mushrooms 168
Garlic Eggplant Rounds..168
Vegetable Soup 168
Cream of Celery...168
Steamed Rutabaga Mash 169
Fragrant Artichoke Hearts 169
Steamed Broccoli Raab (Rabe) 169
Avocado Pie...170
Zucchini Pasta with Blue Cheese 170
Lemon Artichoke...170
Zucchini Boats...171
Zucchini Fettuccine...171
Keto Club Salad 171
Bell Pepper Pizza...172
Peppers & Cheese Salad 172
Bok Choy Salad..172
Avocado Pesto Zoodles 173
Collard Wraps...173
Portobello Toasts...173
Spinach and Jarlsberg Pie 173
Low Carb Falafel 174
Keto Ratatouille...174
Mushrooms and Tofu Scramble 174
Sautéed Arugula Mash 175
Masala Cauliflower...175
Pesto Zucchini Bake..175
Baked Eggplant Mash 176
Cabbage Dippers 176

Desserts 177
Chocolate Pudding 177
Pumpkin Pie Cups 177
Keto Custard..177
Pumpkin Spices Pudding 178
Molten Brownies Cups...178
Almond Tart..178
Chocolate Pudding Cake 179
Spice Pie 179

Keto Cheesecake	180
Butter Cake	180
Cinnamon Mini Rolls	180
Lava Cake	181
Rhubarb Custard	181
Chocolate Mousse	181
Cocoa-Vanilla Pudding	182
Keto Carrot Pie	182
Pecan Pie	182
Keto Crème Brulee	183
Lavender Pie	183
Blueberry Parfait	183
Pandan Custard	184
Mug Cake	184
Coconut Cake	184
Walnut pie	185
Keto Chip Cookies	185
Keto Vanilla Crescent Cookies	185
Vanilla Muffins	186
Fat Bomb Jars	186
Blueberry Clusters	186
Strawberry Cubes	186
Avocado Brownies	187
Cheesecake Bites	187
Coconut Crack Bars	187
Keto Blondies	188
Low Carb Nutella	188
Cheesecake Fat Bombs	188
Peanut Butter Balls	189
Cinnamon Muffins	189
Keto Fudge	189
Fluffy Donuts	190
Coconut Muffins	190
Raspberry Pie	190
Mint Cookies	191
Coconut Clouds	191
Shortbread Cookies	191
Lime Bars	192
Peppermint Cookies	192
Macadamia Cookies	192
Keto Pralines	193
Blueberry Crisp	193
Chocolate and Bacon Bars	193
Poppy Seeds Muffins	193
Lemon Muffins	194
Lime Chia Seeds Pudding	194
Phirni Kheer with Almonds	194
Tagalong Bars	194
Keto Marshmallows	195
Tiger Butter	195
Coffee Panna Cotta	195
Almond Milk Pudding with Nuts	196

CONCLUSION 197
Recipe Index 198

INTRODUCTION

The keto diet attracts millions of people these days. It is impossible to find a person who has never heard about it. Without any doubt, it is trendy now. The very idea of a diet is quite simple and involves the consumption of a high amount of fats and a minimum amount of carbohydrates. Let's go back to the origins of the Keto diet and understand when and by whom it was invented.

It happened back in the last century, and more precisely in 1923, Dr. Mayo Clinic developed a nutrition plan that would help people fight epilepsy. During that time, the keto diet wasn't used for weight loss. The diet started to gain popularity after the hyping of butter coffee. Since then, the diet has gained credibility around the world as one of the most effective diets in the "fight against excess weight".

Over the years, the diet has changed and improved. The classic diet involved eating 90 percent of fats and only 4 percent of carbohydrates. Today, the golden mean of the keto diet means consuming 8-9 percent of carbohydrates per meal. However, it should be noted that for every human the keto diet should be adjusted individually. That's why it is recommended to make full examination before starting a keto diet and also ask the opinion of your doctor about it. Otherwise, it can lead to irreversible bad consequences in your body and health in general.

Let's consider the good sides of the keto diet! The biggest and the most important advantage of a keto diet is fast fighting with extra weight. Reducing of eating carbohydrates helps to get rid of excess water in your body. As a consequence, you lose weight faster. Scientifically proved that the Keto diet is more effective in comparison with another weight-loss diet. A keto diet will reduce your appetite. It happens thanks to the minimum consumption of carbs. The positive sides of the Keto diet also are increasing the level of "good" HDL (high-density lipoprotein), reducing the insulin level and blood sugar level, and maintain the cholesterol level.

The disadvantages of the keto diet can be keto "flu" (feeling sick and fatigue), diarrhea, decreasing metabolism, and lean muscle mass.

All of these symptoms are individual and depend on your tolerance and proper diet. If you are not sure that you can correctly distribute the number of calories that should be consumed per day - it is highly recommended to consult a nutritionist. The doctor won't only be able to choose the right nutrition, but will also monitor your health throughout the diet.

Breakfast

Meat Sandwich
Prep time: 10 minutes | Cooking time: 12 minutes | Servings: 2

Ingredients:
- 1 cup minced beef
- ½ teaspoon chili flakes
- 1 tablespoon water
- ½ teaspoon garlic powder
- ¼ teaspoon salt
- 2 eggs, beaten
- 2 cheddar cheese slices
- 1 teaspoon butter

Directions:
In the mixing bowl combine together the minced beef, chili flakes, water, salt, and garlic powder. Then make 4 meatballs and press them gently with the help of the fingertips. Wrap every ball in paper foil. Pour water in the instant pot and insert the steamer rack. Place the meatballs on the rack and cook them on Manual (high pressure) for 8 minutes. After this, remove the meatballs from the instant pot and remove them from the paper foil. Clean the instant pot and remove the steamer rack. Preheat the instant pot on Saute mode and add butter. Melt it. Add beaten egg and cook them for 2 minutes. Then flip on another side. Place the one slice of cheese in the center egg and wrap it. Repeat the same steps with remaining cheese and egg. Then place the first wrapped cheese on 1 meatball and cove rit with the second meatball to get the sandwich. Repeat the same steps with the remaining ingredients. Pierce the cooked sandwiches with toothpicks if needed.

Nutrition value/serving: calories 353, fat 20.9, fiber 0.1, carbs 1.2, protein 38.5

Keto Cereal Bowl
Prep time: 10 minutes | Cooking time: 10 minutes | Servings: 2

Ingredients:
- 1 tablespoon flaxseeds
- 1 tablespoon sesame seeds
- ¼ cup walnuts, chopped
- ¼ cup almonds, chopped
- ¼ teaspoon ground cinnamon
- ½ teaspoon vanilla extract
- 1 tablespoon coconut oil
- 1 egg white, whisked

Directions:
In the mixing bowl combine together flaxseeds, sesame seeds, walnuts, almonds, ground cinnamon, and vanilla extract. Then add coconut oil and whisked egg white. Mix up the mixture. Preheat the instant pot on Saute mode. Then place the nut mixture in the instant pot bowl and flatten it gently. Cook the cereals for 10 minutes. Stir them every 2 minutes. Then cool the cereals well.

Nutrition value/serving: calories 281, fat 25.3, fiber 4.2, carbs 6.6, protein 9.5

Butter Crepes
Prep time: 10 minutes | Cooking time: 15 minutes | Servings: 4

Ingredients:
- ½ cup of coconut milk
- 1 egg, beaten
- 1 tablespoon butter, melted
- ½ teaspoon baking powder
- 1 teaspoon lemon juice
- 1 teaspoon vanilla extract
- ½ cup almond meal
- 4 tablespoons ground coconut flour
- ½ teaspoon coconut oil, melted
- ¼ teaspoon salt

Directions:
In the mixing bowl mix up together coconut milk, eggs, melted butter, baking powder, lemon juice, vanilla extract, and salt. Then add the almond meal and ground coconut flour. Stir the mixture until you get the thick liquid. Grease the instant pot bowl with coconut oil. Preheat the instant pot on Saute mode for 3 minutes. After this, ladle 1 ladle of the crepe batter in the instant pot bowl in the shape of crepe. Cook the crepe on Saute mode for 1 minute from each side. Cook the crepes additional time if you prefer the golden-brown crust. Repeat the same steps with the remaining crepe batter.

Nutrition value/serving: calories 204, fat 17.8, fiber 2.8, carbs 8.4, protein 5.2

Soft Eggs

Prep time: 10 minutes | Cooking time: 4 minutes | Servings: 2

Ingredients:
- ¼ teaspoon ground black pepper
- ¼ teaspoon salt
- ½ teaspoon butter, melted
- 2 eggs
- 1 cup water, for cooking

Directions:
Pour water in the instant pot and insert the steamer rack. Place the eggs on the rack and close the instant pot lid. Cook the eggs on Manual mode (Low pressure) for 4 minutes. Then cool the eggs in the ice water and peel them. Cut the eggs into halves and sprinkle with salt, ground black pepper, and melted butter.

Nutrition value/serving: calories 72, fat 5.3, fiber 0.1, carbs 0.5, protein 5.6

Cabbage Hash Browns

Prep time: 10 minutes | Cooking time: 16 minutes | Servings: 2

Ingredients:
- 1 cup white cabbage, shredded
- 1 teaspoon onion powder
- 1 egg, beaten
- ¾ cup onion, minced
- 1 teaspoon ground paprika
- ½ teaspoon coconut oil, melted

Directions:
Mix up together cabbage with onion powder, egg, minced onion, and ground paprika. Then preheat the instant pot on manual mode. Brush the instant pot bowl with coconut oil. With the help of the spoon make the small hash brown fritters from the cabbage mixture and place them in the instant pot. Cook 2 hash browns per 1 time. Cook the meal for 4 minutes from each side.

Nutrition value/serving: calories 74, fat 3.6, fiber 2.3, carbs 7.8, protein 4

Meat Muffins with Quail Eggs

Prep time: 10 minutes | Cooking time: 22 minutes | Servings: 4

Ingredients:
- 4 quail eggs
- 1 cup ground pork
- ¼ cup onion, diced
- 1 teaspoon garlic, diced
- ½ teaspoon salt
- ½ teaspoon chili flakes
- ½ teaspoon ground turmeric
- 1 teaspoon dried dill
- 2 tablespoons coconut flour
- 1 tablespoon ketchup
- 1 teaspoon olive oil
- 1 cup water, for cooking

Directions:
In the mixing bowl combine together ground pork, onion, garlic, salt, chili flakes, ground turmeric, dried dill, coconut flour, and ketchup. Then brush the muffin molds with olive oil gently. Fill every muffin mold with ground meat mixture and flatten the surface of prepared muffins well. Then pour water in the instant pot and insert the steamer rack. Arrange the muffins on the rack and close the lid. Cook the meat muffins for 20 minutes on Manual mode (high pressure). Then make a quick pressure release and open the lid. Crac the quail eggs on the surface of every muffin and close the lid. Cook the meal for 2 minutes more on Manual mode (high pressure). Use the quick pressure release.

Nutrition value/serving: calories 144, fat 8, fiber 4.5, carbs 9.1, protein 8.8

Cinnamon Pancakes

Prep time: 10 minutes | Cooking time: 45 minutes | Servings: 3

Ingredients:
- 2 eggs, beaten
- 1 teaspoon matcha green tea powder
- 1 teaspoon vanilla extract
- 1 teaspoon ground cinnamon
- 1 teaspoon baking powder
- 1 tablespoon apple cider vinegar
- 1 tablespoon Erythritol
- 1 tablespoon sesame oil
- 1 cup almond flour
- ¼ cup cream

Directions:
In the big bowl mix up together eggs, vanilla extract, apple cider vinegar, baking powder, and cream. Then add matcha green tea powder, ground cinnamon, Erythritol, and almond flour. Whisk the liquid until smooth. Brush the instant pot bowl with ½ tablespoon of sesame oil and pour the 1/3 part of all liquid inside. Cook it for 15 minutes on Manual mode (low pressure). Cook the pancake for an additional 5 minutes for the golden-brown crust. Repeat the same steps with the remaining batter. In the end, you should get 3 pancakes.

Nutrition value/serving: calories 157, fat 13.3, fiber 1.5, carbs 9.5, protein 5.9

Paprika Eggs in Pepper Holes

Prep time: 20 minutes | Cooking time: 5 minutes | Servings: 4

Ingredients:
- 2 bell pepper
- 4 eggs
- 4 Cheddar cheese sliced
- ½ teaspoon salt
- 1 teaspoon olive oil
- 1 cup water, for cooking

Directions:
Slice the bell pepper into the rings. Then pour water in the instant pot and insert the steamer rack. Brush the instant pot pan with olive oil and insert the pepper rings inside. Crack the eggs in the pepper rings. Then sprinkle every eg with salt and top with cheese slice. Place the instant pot pan in the instant pot. Cook breakfast for 5 minutes on low pressure.

Nutrition value/serving: calories 172, fat 12.7, fiber 0.8, carbs 4.8, protein 11.2

Stuffed Pepper Halves with Omelet

Prep time: 15 minutes | Cooking time: 6 minutes | Servings: 4

Ingredients:
- 4 bell peppers
- 2 eggs, beaten
- 1 oz Mozzarella, shredded
- ¼ teaspoon chili powder
- 1 cup water, for cooking

Directions:
Cut the bell peppers into halves and remove the seeds. Then in the mixing bowl combine together eggs, chili powder, and Mozzarella cheese. Pour water in the instant pot and insert the steamer rack. Pour egg mixture in every pepper half and transfer the vegetables in the instant pot. Cook the meal for 6 minutes on low pressure.

Nutrition value/serving: calories 90, fat 3.8, fiber 1.7, carbs 9.5, protein 6

Bacon Egg Cups
Prep time: 15 minutes | Cooking time: 15 minutes | Servings: 2

Ingredients:
- 2 eggs
- 4 bacon slices
- ¼ teaspoon dried parsley
- 1 teaspoon butter, soften
- ¼ teaspoon salt

Directions:
Brush the muffin molds with butter. Then place the bacon slices in the muffin molds to cover the muffin molds sides. Crack the eggs in the muffin molds and sprinkle them with parsley and salt. Cover the molds with foil and arrange it in the instant pot. Cook the meal for 15 minutes on Saute mode.

Nutrition value/serving: calories 240, fat 20.3, fiber 0, carbs 0.4, protein 15.6

Zucchini Meat Cups
Prep time: 10 minutes | Cooking time: 15 minutes | Servings: 4

Ingredients:
- 1 cup zucchini, grated
- ½ cup ground beef
- 1.4 cup carrot, grated
- 1 teaspoon onion powder
- ½ teaspoon salt
- ¼ cup Cheddar cheese, shredded
- 1 tablespoon sesame oil
- ½ teaspoon ground black pepper
- 1 cup water, for cooking

Directions:
Squeeze the grated zucchini, if needed and place it in the big mixing bowl. Add ground beef, carrot, onion powder, salt, cheese, and ground black pepper. Then brush the muffin molds (cups) with sesame oil. Place the zucchini-meat mixture in the muffin molds. Pour water in the instant pot. Insert the steamer rack. Place the muffin molds with the meat-zucchini mixture in the instant pot. Cook the meal for 15 minutes on Manual (High pressure). Then allow the natural pressure release for 10 minutes.

Nutrition value/serving: calories 121, fat 7.1, fiber 1.4, carbs 5.5, protein 9

Green Hash
Prep time: 10 minutes | Cooking time: 10 minutes | Servings: 2

Ingredients:
- ½ cup fresh spinach, chopped
- ½ cup fresh parsley, chopped
- ¼ cup cauliflower, shredded
- 2 eggs, beaten
- 1 teaspoon avocado oil
- ½ teaspoon ground black pepper
- ½ teaspoon salt
- ½ cup Cheddar cheese, shredded

Directions:
Brush the instant pot bowl with avocado oil. After this, in the mixing bowl mix up together eggs, parsley, spinach, cauliflower, ground black pepper, salt, and cheese. Stir the mixture until homogenous and transfer in the instant pot bowl. Flatten the mixture with the help of the wooden spatula and close the lid. Cook the green hash for 10 minutes on High pressure (Manual mode). Then make a quick pressure release and open the lid. Cool the green hash to the room temperature and cut into servings.

Nutrition value/serving: calories 191, fat 14.2, fiber 1.2, carbs 3.1, protein 13.6

Breakfast Avocado Bombs

Prep time: 20 minutes | *Cooking time:* 8 minutes | *Servings:* 2

Ingredients:
- 1 avocado, peeled, halved, pitted
- 5 bacon slices
- 1 oz Cheddar cheese, shredded
- ½ teaspoon avocado oil
- ¼ teaspoon white pepper
- 1 cup water, for cooking

Directions:
Mix up together cheese with white pepper. Then fill every avocado half with cheese mixture and stick them together. Wrap the avocado in the bacon slices and brush with avocado oil. Wrap the avocado in foil. Pour water in the instant pot and insert the steamer rack. Place the wrapped avocado in the instant pot and cook for 8 minutes on Manual mode (high pressure). Then allow natural pressure release for 10 minutes. Remove the cooked avocado from the foil, cut it into halves and transfer in the serving plates.

Nutrition value/serving: calories 540, fat 46.5, fiber 6.8, carbs 9.7, protein 23.1

Spiced Hard-Boiled Eggs

Prep time: 15 minutes | *Cooking time:* 10 minutes | *Servings:* 4

Ingredients:
- 4 eggs
- ½ teaspoon dried sage
- ¼ teaspoon chili flakes
- 1 teaspoon butter, softened
- ¼ teaspoon dried parsley
- ¼ teaspoon dried thyme
- 1 cup water, for cooking

Directions:
Pour water in the instant pot and insert the steamer rack. Place the eggs on the rack and close the lid. Cook the eggs on Manual (high pressure) for 5 minutes. Then make a quick pressure release. Cool the eggs in ice water for 10 minutes. Meanwhile, churn together sage, butter, chili flakes, parsley, and thyme. Then peel the eggs and cut them into halves. Spread every egg half with a spiced butter mixture.

Nutrition value/serving: calories 72 fat 5.3, fiber 0.1, carbs 0.5, protein 5.6

Minced Beef Pancakes

Prep time: 10 minutes | *Cooking time:* 14 minutes | *Servings:* 2

Ingredients:
- 7 oz minced beef
- 1 egg, beaten
- 1 tablespoon coconut flour
- 1 teaspoon ground black pepper
- ½ teaspoon ground turmeric
- 1 teaspoon garlic powder
- 1 teaspoon coconut oil
- 1 teaspoon dried parsley

Directions:
Mix up together minced beef and egg. Add ground black pepper, coconut flour, and turmeric. After this, add garlic powder and dried parsley. Grease the instant pot bowl with coconut oil. After this, transfer the meat mixture in the instant pot and flatten it well in the shape of a pancake. Cook the meat pancake on Saute mode for 7 minutes from each side. Transfer the cooked beef pancake on the paper towel to get rid of extra oil. Cut the cooked meal into halves.

Nutrition value/serving: calories 260, fat 11.1, fiber 2.1, carbs 4.8, protein 33.8

Ham Roll

Prep time: 15 minutes | Cooking time: 3 hours | Servings: 4

Ingredients:
- 1-pound spiral ham, raw, sliced
- ½ cup Mozzarella, shredded
- 1 teaspoon salt
- 1 teaspoon ground paprika
- ½ teaspoon dried thyme
- ½ teaspoon dried rosemary
- 1 teaspoon avocado oil
- 1 tablespoon mustard
- 1 cup water, for cooking

Directions:
Sprinkle the sliced ham with salt, ground paprika, thyme, and rosemary. Then place the ham on the chopping board in one layer. Sprinkle the surface of the ham with shredded Mozzarella and roll it. Brush the ham roll with mustard and wrap in the foil. Pour water in the instant pot and insert the steamer rack. Place the wrapped ham roll in the instant pot and cook it on Manual mode (Low pressure) for 3 hours.

Nutrition value/serving: calories 148, fat 4.6, fiber 0.8, carbs 2.5, protein 23.2

Fluffy Eggs

Prep time: 10 minutes | Cooking time: 5 minutes | Servings: 1

Ingredients:
- 2 eggs
- ¼ teaspoon chives
- ½ teaspoon chili flakes
- 1 teaspoon sesame oil

Directions:
Brush the instant pot bowl with sesame oil. Then crack eggs in the bowl and separate the egg whites and egg yolks. Whisk the egg whites until you get soft peaks. Preheat the instant pot on Saute mode for 3 minutes. With the help of the spoon make 2 rounds from the egg whites in the instant pot and cook them on Saute mode for 2 minutes. After this, place the egg yolks in the center of every egg white round. Sprinkle them with chives and chili flakes. Close the lid and cook the eggs on Saute mode for 3 minutes more or until the egg yolks are solid.

Nutrition value/serving: calories 166, fat 13.3, fiber 0, carbs 0.7, protein 11.1

Bacon Eggs with Chives

Prep time: 7 minutes | Cooking time: 10 minutes | Servings: 2

Ingredients:
- 2 eggs
- 1 tablespoon chives
- 2 bacon slices, chopped
- ¼ teaspoon almond butter
- ¼ teaspoon salt
- ¼ teaspoon ground black pepper

Directions:
Preheat the instant pot on Saute mode for 4 minutes. Then place the chopped bacon inside and cook it for 3 minutes. Stir the bacon and crack the eggs over it. Add almond butter. Sprinkle the eggs with salt and ground black pepper. Close the lid. Cook the eggs for 2 minutes on Saute mode. Then open the lid and sprinkle the eggs with chives. Cook them for 1 minute more.

Nutrition value/serving: calories 179, fat 13.5, fiber 0.3, carbs 1.2, protein 13.1

Avocado Boats with Omelet

Prep time: 15 minutes | *Cooking time:* 10 minutes | *Servings:* 2

Ingredients:
- 1 avocado, halved, pitted
- 2 eggs, beaten
- 1 tablespoon cream
- 1 teaspoon fresh dill
- 1 oz Parmesan, grated
- 1 cup water, for cooking

Directions:
Remove ½ part of avocado meat with the help of the scooper. You will get avocado boats. In the mixing bowl combine together eggs, cream, dill, and Parmesan. Pour the egg mixture in the prepared avocado boats. Pour water and insert the steamer rack in the instant pot. Carefully arrange the avocado boats in the instant pot. You can cover the surface of every avocado boat with foil if desired. Cook the meal for 10 minutes on Steam mode.

Nutrition value/serving: calories 319, fat 27.4, fiber 6.8, carbs 10, protein 10

Breakfast Egg Hash

Prep time: 10 minutes | *Cooking time:* 20 minutes | *Servings:* 4

Ingredients:
- 4 eggs, beaten
- 6 oz celery stalk, chopped
- 1 cup bok choy, chopped
- ¼ white onion, diced
- 1 teaspoon ground paprika
- ½ teaspoon salt
- 1 tablespoon butter
- ½ teaspoon dried basil

Directions:
Preheat the instant pot on Saute mode for 3 minutes. Then add butter and melt it on the same cooking mode. Add chopped bok choy and celery stalk. Then add onion and mix up the vegetable mixture well. After this, close the lid and sauté the ingredients for 5 minutes. Open the lid and mix up the mixture one more time. In the mixing bowl combine together eggs with salt and ground paprika. Pour the egg mixture over the vegetables and stir gently. Close the lid and cook the hash brown for 10 minutes pr until eggs are firm.

Nutrition value/serving: calories 102, fat 7.4, fiber 1.2, carbs 2.9, protein 6.3

Bacon Tacos

Prep time: 15 minutes | *Cooking time:* 5 minutes | *Servings:* 4

Ingredients:
- 10 bacon slices
- ½ cup Cheddar cheese, shredded
- ½ cup white cabbage, shredded
- 1 tablespoon taco seasonings
- 1 teaspoon coconut oil
- 8 oz chicken breast, skinless, boneless
- 1 tomato, chopped

Directions:
Rub the chicken breast with Taco seasonings well and place it in the instant pot. Add coconut oil and cook the chicken for 20 minutes on Saute mode. Flip the chicken breast after 10 minutes of cooking. Then remove the cooked chicken from the instant pot and chop it. Line the table with paper foil. Put the bacon crosswise on it to get the shape of the net. Then with the help of the round cutter make 4 rounds (tortillas). Preheat the instant pot on Saute mode well. Then place the first bacon round. Cook it for 3 minutes from each side. Repeat the same steps with all bacon rounds. After this, place the cooked bacon "net" on the plate. Top every bacon "net" with chopped chicken, cheese, and tomato. Fold it in the shape of tacos.

Nutrition value/serving: calories 401, fat 27.1, fiber 0.4, carbs 3.5, protein 33.4

Mason Jar Omelet

Prep time: 10 minutes | Cooking time: 8 minutes | Servings: 2

Ingredients:
- 2 eggs, beaten
- ¼ cup heavy cream
- ¼ cup Mozzarella, shredded
- ½ teaspoon salt
- 1 teaspoon ground black pepper
- 1 tablespoon fresh dill, chopped
- 1 teaspoon coconut oil, melted
- 1 cup water, for cooking

Directions:
Mix up together eggs with heavy cream, salt, cheese, ground black pepper, and dill. Then brush every mason jar with coconut oil gently. Pour the egg mixture in every mason jar Pour water in the instant pot and insert the steamer rack. Arrange the mason jars on the rack and close the lid. Cook the omelet for 8 minutes on Manual mode (High pressure). Then make quick pressure release and remove the mason jars from the instant pot.

Nutrition value/serving: calories 151, fat 12.9, fiber 0.5, carbs 2.4, protein 7.3

Cauliflower Bake

Prep time: 15 minutes | Cooking time: 2 minutes | Servings: 4

Ingredients:
- 1-pound cauliflower, chopped
- ½ teaspoon ground black pepper
- 3 oz Parmesan, grated
- ½ cup cream
- 1 teaspoon dried cilantro
- 1 teaspoon garlic powder
- 1 teaspoon mustard
- 1 cup water, for cooking

Directions:
Pour water in the instant pot and insert the steamer rack. Place the cauliflower in the rack and cook it on Manual mode (High pressure) for 2 minutes. Make a quick pressure release. After this, place the hot cauliflower in the big bowl. Add cheese, ground black pepper, cilantro, cream, garlic powder, and mustard. Mix up the cauliflower well until cheese is melted.

Nutrition value/serving: calories 123, fat 6.6, fiber 3.1, carbs 8.7, protein 9.7

Cauliflower Toast

Prep time: 15 minutes | Cooking time: 8 minutes | Servings: 2

Ingredients:
- ½ cup cauliflower, shredded
- ½ cup ground chicken
- 1 teaspoon butter
- 1 tablespoon coconut flour, ground
- ½ teaspoon salt
- ¼ cup Cheddar cheese

Directions:
Mix up together shredded cauliflower and ground chicken. Add coconut flour and salt. Make balls from the mixture. After this, press them gently to get the shape of toasts. Place butter in the instant pot and melt it on Saute mode. Then arrange the prepared cauliflower toast in the instant pot. Cook the toasts for 4 minutes from each side or until they are light brown Place the cooked toasts in the plate and top with Cheddar cheese.

Nutrition value/serving: calories 156, fat 9.4, fiber 0.9, carbs 3.2, protein 14.5

Sausage Casserole

Prep time: 10 minutes | *Cooking time:* 50 minutes | *Servings:* 5

Ingredients:
- 10 ground Italian sausages
- 1 teaspoon Italian seasonings
- 4 eggs, beaten
- ½ teaspoon salt
- 1 teaspoon sesame oil
- ¼ cup Cheddar cheese, shredded
- 1 cup water, for cooking

Directions:

Preheat the instant pot on Sauté mode for 5 minutes. Then pour sesame oil inside, add Italian sausages. Cook them for 10 minutes on sauté mode. Stir the sausages every 2 minutes. Meanwhile, mix up together eggs, salt, Italian seasonings, and Cheddar cheese. When the ground sausages are cooked, add them in the egg mixture and stir. Transfer the mixture in the baking pan and flatten it. Then clean the instant pot bowl and pour water inside. Insert the steamer rack. Place the baking pan with casserole in the instant pot. Cook it for 35 minutes on Sauté mode.

Nutrition value/serving: calories 424, fat 32.6, fiber 0, carbs 2.4, protein 25.8

Frittata with Greens

Prep time: 10 minutes | *Cooking time:* 10 minutes | *Servings:* 2

Ingredients:
- 2 eggs, beaten
- 2 tablespoons heavy cream
- 1/3 cup fresh spinach, chopped
- ¼ cup fresh arugula, chopped
- 1 teaspoon coconut oil, melted
- ½ teaspoon ground paprika
- ¼ teaspoon salt
- 1 cup water, for cooking

Directions:

In the mixing bowl mix up together eggs, heavy cream, arugula, spinach, salt, and ground paprika Then brush the baking pan with melted coconut oil Pour the egg mixture in the baking pan. Pour water and insert the steamer rack in the instant pot. Place the baking pan with frittata on the rack and close the lid. Cook the frittata for 10 minutes on Manual mode (high pressure).

Nutrition value/serving: calories 138, fat 12.3, fiber 0.4, carbs 1.3, protein 6.1

Cheese Egg Balls

Prep time: 10 minutes | *Cooking time:* 14 minutes | *Servings:* 4

Ingredients:
- 4 eggs, beaten
- ½ cup Mozzarella, shredded
- 1 teaspoon dried basil
- 1 tablespoon heavy cream
- 1 cup water, for cooking

Directions:

Mix up together eggs, dried basil, and heavy cream. Then pour the liquid in the silicone egg molds. Top every mold with Mozzarella. Then pour water in the instant pot and insert the trivet. Place the silicone egg molds on the trivet. Cook the egg balls for 7 minutes on Manual mode (High pressure). Then allow the natural pressure release for 7 minutes more. Cool the egg balls to the room temperature and remove from the silicone molds.

Nutrition value/serving: calories 86, fat 6.4, fiber 0, carbs 0.6, protein 6.6

Breakfast Crustless Quiche

Prep time: 10 minutes | *Cooking time:* 25 minutes | *Servings:* 8

Ingredients:
- 7 eggs, beaten
- 3 oz Gouda cheese, shredded
- 6 oz Feta cheese, crumbled
- ½ teaspoon white pepper
- 1 tablespoon fresh dill, chopped
- ¼ cup dried tomatoes, chopped
- ¼ cup heavy cream
- 1 cup fresh spinach, chopped
- 1 teaspoon sesame oil
- ½ teaspoon salt
- 1 cup water, for cooking

Directions:
Pour water in the instant pot and insert the trivet. After this, in the mixing bowl combine together eggs, Gouda and Feta cheese, white pepper, fresh dill, dried tomatoes, heavy cream, spinach, and salt. Brush the round baking pan with sesame oil from inside and pour egg mixture inside. Insert the baking pan on the trivet and close the lid. Cook the quiche for 25 minutes on manual mode (High pressure). Allow the natural pressure release. Cool the cooked quiche for 5-10 minutes and then cut into the servings.

Nutrition value/serving: calories 170, fat 13.3, fiber 0.2, carbs 2.2, protein 10.8

Breakfast Taco Omelet

Prep time: 10 minutes | *Cooking time:* 35 minutes | *Servings:* 2

Ingredients:
- 1 cup ground beef
- 1 teaspoon taco seasonings
- 3 eggs, beaten
- ¼ cup heavy cream
- 1 teaspoon dried basil
- ¼ teaspoon dried oregano
- 1 teaspoon butter

Directions:
Preheat the instant pot on sauté mode for 2 minutes. Then place the butter in the hot instant pot and melt it. Add ground beef and taco seasonings. Mix up well. Sauté the meat mixture for 10 minutes. Stir it every 2 minutes. Meanwhile, in the mixing bowl mix up together eggs, cream, dried basil, and dried oregano. Pour the egg mixture over the cooked meat and cook on sauté mode for 25 minutes or until the omelet is firm.

Nutrition value/serving: calories 298, fat 22.2, fiber 0.1, carbs 2.1, protein 21.7

Keto Shakshuka

Prep time: 5 minutes | *Cooking time:* 20 minutes | *Servings:* 2

Ingredients:
- 2 eggs
- 1 bell pepper, chopped
- 1 garlic clove, diced
- ½ white onion, diced
- ¼ teaspoon salt
- 1 tablespoon marinara sauce
- 1 teaspoon tomato paste
- ¼ cup of water
- 1 tablespoon coconut oil
- ½ cup kale, chopped
- ½ teaspoon ground cumin

Directions:
Preheat the instant pot on sauté mode. Then add coconut oil and melt it. When the oil starts shimmering, add diced onion and garlic. Saute the vegetables for 3 minutes. Then add salt, marinara sauce, tomato paste, water, and kale. Sprinkle the mixture with ground cumin and bell pepper. Mix up well. Saute the vegetables for 5 minutes or until they are soft. After this, crack the eggs over the vegetables and close the lid. Saute the meal for 10 minutes more.

Nutrition value/serving: calories 173, fat 11.7, fiber 2, carbs 11.5, protein 7.4

Morning Bacon Bombs
Prep time: 15 minutes | Cooking time: 1 minute | Servings: 4

Ingredients:
- 8 oz cauliflower
- 2 tablespoons cream cheese
- 4 bacon slices, cooked, chopped
- 1 teaspoon fresh parsley, chopped
- ½ teaspoon ground black pepper
- ¼ teaspoon garlic powder
- ½ teaspoon chili flakes
- 1 cup water, for cooking

Directions:
Pour water in the instant pot and insert trivet. Then place cauliflower on the trivet and cook for 1 minute on Manual (high pressure). Then make a quick pressure release. Remove the cauliflower from the instant pot and chop it into the tiny pieces or just mash with the help of the fork. Place the prepared cauliflower in the bowl. Add cream cheese, parsley, ground black pepper, garlic powder, and chili flakes. Mix up the mixture with the help of the spoon until you get a smooth mixture. After this, with the help of the scooper, make cauliflower balls. Coat every ball in the bacon mixture. Store the bacon balls in the fridge for up to 1 day.

Nutrition value/serving: calories 136, fat 9.8, fiber 1.5, carbs 3.7, protein 8.6

Egg Muffins
Prep time: 10 minutes | Cooking time: 5 minutes | Servings: 4

Ingredients:
- 4 eggs, beaten
- 1 bell pepper, chopped
- ¼ cup fresh parsley, chopped
- ¼ teaspoon ground paprika
- ¼ teaspoon salt
- ¼ cup cream cheese
- 1 cup water, for cooking

Directions:
In the mixing bowl combine together eggs, bell pepper, parsley, ground paprika, salt, and cream cheese. When the mixture is homogenous, pour it in the silicone muffin molds. Pour water in the instant pot and insert trivet. Place the muffin molds on the trivet and close the lid. Cook the egg muffins on Manual mode (high pressure) for 5 minutes. Then make a quick pressure release and remove the muffins from the instant pot.

Nutrition value/serving: calories 125, fat 9.6, fiber 0.6, carbs 3.3, protein 7.1

Egg Sandwich
Prep time: 15 minutes | Cooking time: 15 minutes | Servings: 4

Ingredients:
- 4 bacon slices
- 4 eggs
- 1 cup water, for cooking

Directions:
Pour water in the instant pot and insert trivet. Place the eggs on the trivet and cook them for 5 minutes on Manual mode (High pressure). Then make a quick pressure release and transfer the eggs in the ice water. Leave them there for 10 minutes. Meanwhile, clean the instant pot and discard the trivet. Preheat the instant pot on sauté mode for 3 minutes. Then place the bacon slices inside and cook them on sauté mode for 2 minutes from each side. Meanwhile, peel the eggs and cut into halves. Place the cooked bacon on the egg halves and cover with the remaining egg halves to make the sandwiches. Pierce the egg sandwiches with toothpicks for convenience.

Nutrition value/serving: calories 166, fat 12.3, fiber 0, carbs 0.6, protein 12.6

Keto Oatmeal

Prep time: 5 minutes | Cooking time: 1.5 hours | Servings: 2

Ingredients:
- 2 tablespoons coconut flakes
- 1 tablespoon flax seeds
- 2 tablespoons hemp seeds
- ½ cup of coconut milk
- 1 tablespoon almond meal
- 1 teaspoon Erythritol
- 1 teaspoon vanilla extract
- ¼ cup of water

Directions:
Combine together all ingredients in the instant pot and stir well with the spoon. Close the lid and cook Keto oatmeal for 1.5 hours on Low pressure (Manual mode). Stir the cooked meal well before serving.

Nutrition value/serving: calories 239, fat 22, fiber 3.3, carbs 9, protein 5.3

Oregano Egg en Cocotte

Prep time: 8 minutes | Cooking time: 2 minutes | Servings: 1

Ingredients:
- 1 egg
- 1 teaspoon cream
- ½ teaspoon butter, softened
- ¼ teaspoon chives, chopped
- ¼ teaspoon salt
- 1 teaspoon dried oregano
- 1 cup water, for cooking

Directions:
Grease the ramekin with butter. Add cream in the ramekin. Then crack the egg. After this, top the cracked egg with salt, oregano, ground black pepper, and chives. Pour water in the instant pot and insert trivet. Place the ramekin with egg on the trivet and close the lid. Cook the meal on Manual mode (Low pressure) for 2 minutes. When the meal is cooked, remove it from the instant pot. Remove the cooked egg from the ramekin.

Nutrition value/serving: calories 84, fat 6.5, fiber 0.2, carbs 0.8, protein 5.7

Hot Jalapeno Poppers Mix

Prep time: 10 minutes | Cooking time: 11 minutes | Servings: 2

Ingredients:
- 5 oz chicken fillet
- 2 jalapeno peppers, sliced
- ½ teaspoon ranch seasonings
- 2 teaspoons cream cheese
- ½ teaspoon sesame oil
- ¼ cup heavy cream
- 1 oz Parmesan, grated

Directions:
Chop the chicken fillet and sprinkle it with ranch seasonings. Then preheat the instant pot on sauté mode for 2 minutes and add sesame oil. Then add chicken and sauté it for 3 minutes from each side. After this, place the cooked chicken in the bowl and shred it with the help of the fork. Return the chicken back in the instant pot and add cream cheese, heavy cream, sliced jalapeno, and Parmesan. Mix up well. Sauté the meal for 3 minutes more or until the cheese is melted.

Nutrition value/serving: calories 262, fat 16.3, fiber 0.6, carbs 2.1, protein 25.8

Morning Pudding

Prep time: 10 minutes | *Cooking time:* 15 minutes | *Servings:* 2

Ingredients:
- 2 eggs, beaten
- 1 tablespoon almond flour
- 1 teaspoon coconut flour
- ½ teaspoon of cocoa powder
- 4 tablespoons coconut milk
- 1 tablespoon butter, melted
- 1 teaspoon Erythritol
- ¼ teaspoon vanilla extract
- ¼ teaspoon ground cinnamon
- 1 cup water, for cooking

Directions:
In the mixing bowl mix up together eggs, melted butter, and coconut milk. After this, add almond flour, coconut flour, cocoa powder, Erythritol, vanilla extract, and ground cinnamon. Whisk the batter until it is smooth. Pour water in the instant pot bowl and insert the trivet. Pour pudding batter in the baking pan and insert it on the trivet. Cover the pudding surface with foil. Pierce the foil with the help of the toothpick. Cook the breakfast on Manual (High pressure) for 15 minutes. Then allow the natural pressure release. Remove the cooked pudding from the instant pot. Remove the foil and cut the breakfast into halves.

Nutrition value/serving: calories 212, fat 19.1, fiber 1.8, carbs 6.6, protein 7.3

Breakfast Stuffed Avocado

Prep time: 10 minutes | *Cooking time:* 3 minutes | *Servings:* 2

Ingredients:
- 1 avocado, halved, pitted
- 1 egg, beaten
- 1 teaspoon cream cheese
- 1 oz bacon, crumbled
- 2 oz Parmesan, grated
- 1 cup water, for cooking

Directions:
Pour water in the instant pot and insert the steamer rack. Mix up together cream cheese, egg, bacon, and cheese. The fill the avocado holes with egg mixture. Place the avocado in the instant pot. Close the lid and cook the meal for 3 minutes on Manual mode (high pressure). Then make a quick pressure release.

Nutrition value/serving: calories 410, fat 34.4, fiber 6.7, carbs 10.1, protein 19.2

Layered Casserole

Prep time: 10 minutes | *Cooking time:* 15 minutes | *Servings:* 4

Ingredients:
- 1 cup ground chicken
- 1 cup Cheddar cheese, shredded
- 2 tablespoons cream cheese
- 1 teaspoon butter, melted
- ½ teaspoon taco seasonings
- ½ teaspoon salt
- 1 cup leek, chopped
- ¼ cup of water

Directions:
Grease the instant pot bowl with butter. In the mixing bowl combine together ground chicken and taco seasonings. Then place the ground chicken in the instant pot and flatten it to make the chicken layer. After this, top the chicken with leek and salt. Then top the leek with cheese. Mix up together cream cheese and water. Pour the liquid over the casserole and close the lid. Cook the casserole on Saute mode for 15 minutes.

Nutrition value/serving: calories 222, fat 14.7, fiber 0.4, carbs 4.1, protein 17.9

Chili Casserole
Prep time: 10 minutes | Cooking time: 20 minutes | Servings: 2

Ingredients:
- ½ cup ground beef
- 1 teaspoon tomato paste
- ½ white onion, diced
- ½ teaspoon ground cumin
- ½ teaspoon ground thyme
- ¼ teaspoon salt
- 1/3 cup Cheddar cheese, shredded
- 1 chili pepper, chopped
- 1 teaspoon coconut oil, melted
- 1 cup water, for cooking

Directions:
In the mixing bowl combine together ground beef, tomato paste, white onion, ground cumin, thyme, salt, and chili pepper. Then brush the baking pan with coconut oil. Place the ground beef mixture in the baking pan. Flatten the surface of the mixture. After this, top the meat mixture with Cheddar cheese. Pour water in the instant pot and insert the trivet. Cover the baking pan with foil and place it on the trivet. Cook the chili casserole for 20 minutes on Manual mode (High pressure). Then make a quick pressure release.

Nutrition value/serving: calories 177, fat 12.8, fiber 0.9, carbs 3.9, protein 11.8

Breakfast Hot Cacao
Prep time: 5 minutes | Cooking time: 15 minutes | Servings: 2

Ingredients:
- 1 cup heavy cream
- ½ cup of water
- 1 tablespoon cocoa powder
- 1 teaspoon butter
- 1 tablespoon Erythritol

Directions:
In the mixing bowl mix up together cocoa powder and heavy cream. When the liquid is smooth, pour it in the instant pot bowl. Add water and sauté the liquid for 5 minutes. After this, add butter and Erythritol. Stir well. Saute the hot cacao for 10 minutes more.

Nutrition value/serving: calories 153, fat 16.3, fiber 0.5, carbs 7.1, protein 1.2

Zucchini Cheese Fritters
Prep time: 10 minutes | Cooking time: 10 minutes | Servings: 4

Ingredients:
- 2 zucchini, grated
- 1/3 cup Mozzarella, shredded
- 1 egg, beaten
- 2 tablespoons almond flour
- 1 teaspoon butter, melted
- ½ teaspoon salt
- ½ teaspoon ground turmeric
- ¼ teaspoon dried sage

Directions:
Mix up together grated zucchini and egg. When the mixture is homogenous, add shredded Mozzarella and almond flour. After this, add salt, ground turmeric, and dried sage. Mix up the mixture. Preheat the instant pot on sauté mode for 2 minutes. Then toss butter inside and melt it. With the help of the spoon make the fritters and place them in the hot butter. Saute the fritters for 3 minutes from each side.

Nutrition value/serving: calories 69, fat 4.4, fiber 1.5, carbs 4.4, protein 4

Cauliflower Fritters

Prep time: 10 minutes | *Cooking time:* 7 minutes | *Servings:* 4

Ingredients:
- 2 cups cauliflower, shredded
- ½ cup Cheddar cheese, shredded
- 2 eggs, beaten
- 1 teaspoon olive oil
- ½ teaspoon chili powder

Directions:
In the mixing bowl combine together shredded cauliflower and Cheddar cheese. Add eggs and chili powder. With the help of the fork stir the mixture until homogenous. Preheat the instant pot on sauté mode for 2 minutes. Add olive oil and heat it for 1 minute. With the help of 2 spoons make the medium size fritters and arrange them in the instant pot. Cook the cauliflower fritters for 2 minutes from each side. If you want a golden-brown crust, cook the fritters for 2 additional minutes from each side.

Nutrition value/serving: calories 112, fat 8.2, fiber 1.4, carbs 3.2, protein 7.3

Breakfast Spaghetti Squash Casserole

Prep time: 15 minutes | *Cooking time:* 25 minutes | *Servings:* 4

Ingredients:
- 10 oz spaghetti squash, trimmed
- ½ cup ground beef
- 1 teaspoon onion powder
- ½ teaspoon garlic powder
- 1 teaspoon dried dill
- 1 teaspoon dried parsley
- ½ teaspoon salt
- 1 teaspoon dried oregano
- ½ cup mozzarella, shredded
- 1 tablespoon marinara sauce
- 1 cup water, for cooking

Directions:
Cut the spaghetti squash into the halves and clean it. Then pour water and insert the trivet in the instant pot. Place the spaghetti squash on the trivet and cook it on Manual mode (high pressure) for 10 minutes. Then make a quick pressure release. After this, remove the squash from the instant pot. Clean the instant pot and remove the trivet. Place ground beef in the instant pot. Add garlic powder, dried dill, dried parsley, salt, dried oregano, and marinara sauce. Mix up the mixture well and sauté it for 10 minutes. Stir it with the help of the spatula from time to time to avoid burning. Meanwhile, shred the spaghetti squash with the help of the forks. Top the cooked ground beef with shredded spaghetti squash. Then top the squash with mozzarella. Close the lid and sauté the casserole for 5 minutes or until the cheese is melted.

Nutrition value/serving: calories 73, fat 3.2, fiber 0.4, carbs 6.7, protein 5

Sweet Porridge

Prep time: 10 minutes | *Cooking time:* 10 minutes | *Servings:* 2

Ingredients:
- ¾ cup of coconut milk
- ¼ cup of organic almond milk
- ¾ cup of water
- 1 tablespoon almond butter
- 2 teaspoons chia seeds
- 1 teaspoon hemp seeds
- 1 tablespoon toasted coconut
- 2 tablespoons walnuts, chopped
- 1 teaspoon vanilla extract
- 1 teaspoon liquid stevia

Directions:
Preheat the instant pot on sauté mode for 5 minutes. Then pour coconut milk, organic almond milk, and water inside. On sauté mode bring the liquid to boil and switch off the instant pot. Stirring constantly add chia seeds, hemp seeds, toasted coconut, and walnuts. Then add almond butter, vanilla extract, and liquid stevia. Stir the mixture for 1 minute or until it will be thick. Then transfer it in the serving bowls. The porridge is recommended to serve warm/hot.

Nutrition value/serving: calories 380, fat 35.3, fiber 6.1, carbs 11.4, protein 8.3

Bacon Salad with Eggs
Prep time: 10 minutes | Cooking time: 15 minutes | Servings: 4

Ingredients:
- 4 eggs
- 6 bacon slices
- 1 tablespoon lemon juice
- 1 pecan, chopped
- ½ teaspoon ground paprika
- ¼ teaspoon cayenne pepper
- ¼ teaspoon salt
- 1 cup arugula, chopped
- ½ cup lettuce, chopped
- 1 cup water, for cooking

Directions:
Pour water and insert the trivet in the instant pot. Place the eggs on the trivet and cook on manual mode (high pressure) for 5 minutes. Then make a quick pressure release. Remove the eggs from the instant pot and cool them in the ice/cold water for 10 minutes. Meanwhile, clean the instant pot and remove the trivet. Preheat it on manual mode for 1 minute. Then place the bacon in the instant pot in one layer. Cook it for 3 minutes from each side or until crunchy. Meanwhile, peel the eggs and chop them. Place the chopped eggs in the salad bowl. Add arugula and lettuce. When the bacon is cooked, cool it to the room temperature and chop roughly. Add bacon in the salad mixture. Then sprinkle it with lemon juice, ground paprika, salt, and cayenne pepper. Add pecans. Shake the salad gently.

Nutrition value/serving: calories 246, fat 18.9, fiber 0.6, carbs 1.9, protein 16.7

Classic Breakfast Casserole
Prep time: 10 minutes | Cooking time: 20 minutes | Servings: 4

Ingredients:
- 7 oz breakfast sausages, chopped
- 4 oz Monterey Jack cheese, shredded
- ½ red onion, sliced
- 1 bell pepper, diced
- 2 oz avocado, chopped
- 4 eggs, beaten
- ¼ cup heavy cream
- ½ teaspoon salt
- ½ teaspoon cayenne pepper
- 1 teaspoon coconut oil

Directions:
Toss the coconut oil in the instant pot and melt it on sauté mode. Then add onion and chopped breakfast sausages. Cook them on sauté mode for 5 minutes. Stir them from time to time. Then add bell pepper and cook the ingredients for 3 minutes more. Meanwhile, mix up together cheese, eggs, avocado, cayenne pepper, salt, and heavy cream. Pour the liquid over the breakfast sausages and close the lid. Cook the casserole on sauté mode for 10 minutes or until the egg mixture is solid.

Nutrition value/serving: calories 417, fat 33.8, fiber 1.7, carbs 5.6, protein 23

Low-Carb Flaxseed Brule
Prep time: 15 minutes | Cooking time: 20 minutes | Servings: 2

Ingredients:
- 2 egg yolks
- ½ cup heavy whipped cream
- 1 teaspoon vanilla extract
- 1 teaspoon Erythritol
- 1 teaspoon flaxseeds
- ½ teaspoon chia seeds
- 1 cup water, for cooking

Directions:
Pour water and insert the steamer rack in the instant pot. After this, in the mixing bowl whisk together egg yolks, heavy whipped cream, vanilla extract, Erythritol, flaxseeds, and chia seeds. When you get a smooth batter, pour it in the ramekin and cover with foil. Arrange the ramekin in the instant pot. Cook it on Manual mode (Low pressure) for 20 minutes. Then allow natural pressure release for 10 minutes and remove the cooked meal from the instant pot.

Nutrition value/serving: calories 187, fat 17.1, fiber 1.5, carbs 6, protein 4.1

Mini Frittatas

Prep time: 15 minutes | Cooking time: 15 minutes | Servings: 4

Ingredients:
- 6 oz ground sausages
- 1 cup broccoli, shredded
- 2 oz Parmesan, grated
- 4 eggs, beaten
- 1 tablespoon coconut milk
- ½ teaspoon ghee
- 1 cup water, for cooking

Directions:
In the mixing bowl combine together broccoli, ground sausages, grated cheese, and coconut milk. Then add eggs and stir the frittata mixture gently. Grease the silicone egg molds with ghee. Pour the egg mixture in every silicone mold. After this, pour water in the instant pot and insert the steamer rack. Place the silicone molds with frittatas on the rack and close the lid. Cook the breakfast on Manual (High pressure) for 15 minutes. Then allow the natural pressure release for 10 minutes. Cool the frittatas little and remove them from the molds.

Nutrition value/serving: calories 274, fat 21, fiber 0.7, carbs 2.6, protein 19.1

Egg Benedict Sandwich

Prep time: 15 minutes | Cooking time: 2 minutes | Servings: 1

Ingredients:
- 2 egg whites
- 1 egg
- 1 tablespoon almond meal
- ¼ teaspoon salt
- 1 teaspoon butter, melted
- 1/3 teaspoon baking powder
- 1 spinach leaf
- 1 cup water, for cooking

Directions:
Put the melted butter in the ramekin. Add salt, almond meal, and baking powder. Whisk the mixture. Then add egg whites and whisk the mixture. Pour the water in the instant pot and insert trivet. Place the ramekin with egg white mixture on the trivet and cook it for 1 minute on High pressure (Manual mode). Then make a quick pressure release. Crack the egg in the silicone egg mold. Remove the ramekin with cooked egg whites from the instant pot. Insert the silicone mold with egg on the trivet and cook it for 1 minute –High pressure – Quick pressure release. Remove the cooked egg white from the ramekin and cut it into halves (crosswise). When the egg is cooked, remove it from the instant pot. Place the cooked egg on one half of the baked egg white. Top with spinach leaf and remaining baked egg white half.

Nutrition value/serving: calories 261, fat 20, fiber 1, carbs 3.4, protein 18.2

Nutritious Taco Skillet

Prep time: 10 minutes | Cooking time: 35 minutes | Servings: 2

Ingredients:
- 1 ½ cup ground beef
- 1 teaspoon taco seasonings
- ½ cup Mexican cheese, shredded
- 1 teaspoon chili powder
- ½ teaspoon onion powder
- ½ white onion, diced
- ¼ teaspoon ground cumin
- 1 egg, beaten
- 1 teaspoon tomato paste
- ¼ cup of water
- 1 teaspoon coconut oil

Directions:
Toss coconut oil in the instant pot and preheat it on sauté mode until it is melted. Add ground beef. Sprinkle the meat with Taco seasonings, chili powder, onion powder, ground cumin, and diced onion. Stir the mixture with the help of a spatula. Saute the ground beef mixture for 10 minutes. Stir it from time to time. After this, add shredded Mexican cheese, tomato paste, and water. Mix up well. Saute the taco mixture for 5 minutes more. Then pour the beaten egg over the ground beef. Stir the meal well and cook on sauté mode for 5 minutes more.

Nutrition value/serving: calories 298, fat 19.3, fiber 1.2, carbs 6.1, protein 24.5

Wontons

Prep time: 20 minutes | *Cooking time:* 12 minutes | *Servings:* 2

Ingredients:
- 5 oz ground pork
- 1 tablespoon chives, chopped
- 1 tablespoon dried cilantro
- ¼ teaspoon oyster sauce
- ½ teaspoon soy sauce
- ½ teaspoon garlic powder
- 1 egg, beaten
- 1 cup water, for cooking

Directions:
In the mixing bowl combine together ground pork, chives, cilantro, oyster sauce, soy sauce, and garlic powder. Then add egg and mix up the mixture until homogenous. Pour water in the instant pot and insert the steamer rack. Then transfer the ground pork mixture in the silicone egg molds and transfer the mold in the instant pot. Cook the wontons on Manual mode (high pressure) for 12 minutes. Then allow the natural pressure release for 10 minutes more.

Nutrition value/serving: calories 136, fat 4.7, fiber 0.1, carbs 0.9, protein 21.6

Breakfast Kale Bread

Prep time: 25 minutes | *Cooking time:* 60 minutes | *Servings:* 6

Ingredients:
- 1 egg, beaten
- 1 teaspoon baking powder
- 1 teaspoon lemon juice
- 1 cup kale, grinded
- 1 tablespoon flaxseeds meal
- ½ cup coconut flour
- ¼ cup almond meal
- ¼ teaspoon salt
- 2 tablespoons sesame oil
- ½ teaspoon dried sage
- 1/3 cup water
- 1 teaspoon pumpkin seeds, chopped
- 1 cup water, for cooking

Directions:
Mix up together beaten egg, baking powder, lemon juice, 1/3 cup of water, dried sage, sesame oil, salt, almond meal, and coconut flour. Then add flaxseeds meal and grinded kale. Knead the soft and non-sticky dough. After this, line the round baking pan with paper foil and put the kneaded dough inside. Press it little. Sprinkle the surface of dough with pumpkin seeds. Pour water in the instant pot and insert the trivet. Arrange the baking pan with dough on the trivet and close the lid. Cook the kale bread 45 minutes on manual (high pressure). Then allow the natural pressure release for 15 minutes more. Open the instant pot lid and remove the baking pan with bread from it. Cool the bread for 10-15 minutes.

Nutrition value/serving: calories 129, fat 8.9, fiber 5.1, carbs 9.7, protein 3.8

Egg Scramble

Prep time: 5 minutes | *Cooking time:* 5 minutes | *Servings:* 2

Ingredients:
- ¼ teaspoon ground paprika
- ¼ teaspoon ground turmeric
- ¼ teaspoon chili flakes
- 1 tablespoon butter
- 1 tablespoon heavy cream
- 2 eggs, beaten
- ¼ teaspoon salt

Directions:
Set sauté mode and place butter in the instant pot. Melt the butter and add beaten eggs and heavy cream. Cook it for 1 minute and add chili flakes. Scramble the eggs with the help of the fork well. Then cook the scrambled eggs for 2 minutes more. Transfer the cooked egg scramble in the plates and sprinkle with ground paprika and ground turmeric.

Nutrition value/serving: calories 142, fat 13, fiber 0.2, carbs 0.9, protein 5.8

Parmesan Chicken Balls

Prep time: 15 minutes | *Cooking time:* 20 minutes | *Servings:* 6

Ingredients:
- 2 cups ground chicken
- ½ cup Parmesan, grated
- 1 teaspoon onion powder
- ¼ teaspoon ground cumin
- ½ teaspoon ground thyme
- 1 teaspoon dried parsley
- 2 tablespoons almond meal
- 1 cup water, for cooking

Directions:
Mix up together ground chicken, Parmesan, onion powder, ground cumin, thyme, dried parsley, and almond meal. With the help of the scooper make the balls or use the fingertips for this step. Pour water in the instant pot and insert the steamer rack. Place the chicken balls on the steamer rack and close the lid. Cook the meal on Steam mode for 20 minutes.

Nutrition value/serving: calories 103, fat 4.5, fiber 0.3, carbs 0.9, protein 14.1

Blueberry Muffins

Prep time: 10 minutes | *Cooking time:* 18 minutes | *Servings:* 7

Ingredients:
- 1 cup almond flour
- ¼ cup coconut flour
- ½ teaspoon baking powder
- 2 tablespoons coconut oil, melted
- 2 tablespoons Erythritol
- ¼ cup blueberries
- 2 eggs, beaten
- ½ teaspoon vanilla extract
- 1 cup water, for cooking

Directions:
In the mixing bowl combine together almond flour and coconut flour. Add Erythritol and baking powder. After this, add coconut oil, eggs, and vanilla extract. Stir the mixture until homogenous with the help of the spatula. Then add blueberries and mix up the mixture until homogenous. Transfer the muffin mixture in the muffin molds and arrange them on the steamer rack. Cover the muffins with foil. Pour water in the instant pot and arrange the steamer rack inside. Cook the muffins on Manual mode – high pressure (more) for 18 minutes. Then make a quick pressure release. Cool the muffins well and then remove them from the molds.

Nutrition value/serving: calories 169, fat 13.2, fiber 3.6, carbs 11.6, protein 5.6

Chicken Fritters

Prep time: 10 minutes | *Cooking time:* 10 minutes | *Servings:* 2

Ingredients:
- ½ cup broccoli, shredded
- 1 cup ground chicken
- ¼ cup fresh cilantro, blended
- 1 egg, beaten
- ½ teaspoon ground black pepper
- 1 tablespoon flaxseed meal
- 1 cup water, for cooking

Directions:
Mix up together shredded broccoli and blended cilantro. Add ground chicken, egg, ground black pepper, and flaxseed meal. Stir it will. With the help of the fingertips make the medium fritters. Pour water in the instant pot. Line the steamer rack with foil. Place the fritters on the rack and insert them in the instant pot. Cook the chicken fritters for 10 minutes on manual mode (high pressure). Then make a quick pressure release and remove the fritters from the instant pot.

Nutrition value/serving: calories 193, fat 8.6, fiber 1.7, carbs 3.1, protein 24.4

Crustless Egg Pie

Prep time: 15 minutes | Cooking time: 25 minutes | Servings: 6

Ingredients:
- 4 eggs, beaten
- 7 oz chicken fillet, shredded, cooked
- ¼ cup heavy cream
- ¼ cup coconut flour
- 1 cup green beans, chopped
- ½ teaspoon salt
- ½ teaspoon ground nutmeg
- ½ teaspoon butter, softened
- 1 cup water, for cooking

Directions:
Grease the baking pan with butter. Then place the green beans in the pan in one layer. Top the green beans with shredded chicken. After this, in the mixing bowl combine together beaten eggs, heavy cream, coconut flour, salt, and ground nutmeg. Pour the egg mixture over the shredded chicken. Cover the baking pan with foil. Pour water and insert the rack in the instant pot. Place the baking pan with pie in the instant pot and close the lid. Cook the pie on High pressure (manual mode) for 25 minutes. Then make a quick pressure release. Cool the cooked pie to the room temperature and cut it into the servings.

Nutrition value/serving: calories 151, fat 8.1, fiber 2.7, carbs 5.1, protein 14.4

Mini Casserole in Jars

Prep time: 20 minutes | Cooking time: 15 minutes | Servings: 4

Ingredients:
- 1 cup ground pork
- ¼ onion, diced
- 1 garlic clove, diced
- ½ cup Cheddar cheese, shredded
- ½ cup kale, chopped
- 1 teaspoon coconut oil, melted
- ½ teaspoon salt
- 1 cup water, for cooking

Directions:
Mix up together ground pork, diced onion, garlic, and salt. Then brush the mason jars with coconut oil. After this, fill every jar with ground pork mixture. Top the ground pork with kale and Cheddar cheese and place the jars on the trivet. Cover every jar with foil. Pour water in the instant pot and insert the trivet. Cook the casseroles on Manual (High pressure) for 15 minutes. Then allow the natural pressure release for 10 minutes and remove the casserole from the instant pot.

Nutrition value/serving: calories 307, fat 22.1, fiber 0.3, carbs 0.2, protein 24

Salmon Balls

Prep time: 10 minutes | Cooking time: 4 minutes | Servings: 2

Ingredients:
- 7 oz salmon fillet
- ½ teaspoon ground coriander
- 1 tablespoon flax meal
- 1 teaspoon dried oregano
- 1 tablespoon pork rinds
- 1 teaspoon almond butter
- ¼ teaspoon salt

Directions:
Chop the salmon fillet roughly and place it in the blender. Blend the fish until smooth. After this, transfer the blended salmon in the bowl. Add the ground coriander, flax meal, dried oregano, pork rinds, and salt. After this, make the balls from the fish mixture. Toss almond butter in the instant pot and melt it on sauté mode. Place the salmon balls in the instant pot and cook on sauté mode for 2 minutes from each side.

Nutrition value/serving: calories 238, fat 14.5, fiber 2.1, carbs 3, protein 26.3

Spinach Casserole

Prep time: 10 minutes | *Cooking time:* 3 hours 10 minutes | *Servings:* 4

Ingredients:

- 10 oz breakfast sausages, chopped
- 1 bell pepper, chopped
- 1 teaspoon coconut oil
- ½ teaspoon salt
- ½ teaspoon chili flakes
- 1 tomato, chopped
- 4 eggs, beaten
- ¼ cup heavy cream
- 1 teaspoon ground black pepper
- 2 cups spinach, chopped

Directions:

Toss the coconut oil in the instant pot and melt it on sauté mode. Then add breakfast sausages and cook them on sauté mode for 10 minutes. Stir them from time to time to avoid burning. Meanwhile, in the mixing bowl mix up together chopped bell pepper, salt, chili flakes, tomato, eggs, heavy cream, ground black pepper, and spinach. Pour the mixture over the breakfast sausages and mix up gently. Close the lid and cook the casserole on Manual mode (low pressure) for 3 hours.

Nutrition value/serving: calories 356, fat 28.6, fiber 1.1, carbs 4.3, protein 20.4

Chicken Salad

Prep time: 15 minutes | *Cooking time:* 6 minutes | *Servings:* 2

Ingredients:

- ½ red onion, diced
- 2 eggs, hard-boiled, peeled
- 3 oz celery stalk, chopped
- 1 tablespoon cream
- ½ teaspoon salt
- ½ teaspoon ground black pepper
- 1 teaspoon olive oil
- 8 oz chicken fillet
- ¼ teaspoon dried oregano

Directions:

Cut the chicken fillet into the strips and sprinkle with dried oregano. After this, preheat the instant pot on sauté mode for 2 minutes. Add olive oil and chicken strips. Cook the chicken on sauté mode for 3 minutes from each side. Meanwhile, in the salad bowl mix up together diced onion, celery stalk, salt, cream, and ground black pepper. Then chop the eggs and add them in the salad too. Add the chickens trip and mix up the salad well.

Nutrition value/serving: calories 322, fat 15.6, fiber 1.5, carbs 4.8, protein 39.

Broccoli Toast Spread

Prep time: 15 minutes | *Cooking time:* 5 minutes | *Servings:* 4

Ingredients:

- 1 cup broccoli, chopped
- 1 tablespoon butter
- ½ teaspoon garlic powder
- 1 tablespoon fresh parsley, chopped
- 1 oz pork rinds
- ½ teaspoon salt
- 1 cup water, for cooking

Directions:

Pour water and insert the steamer rack in the instant pot. Place the broccoli in the instant pot and cook it on Steam mode for 5 minutes. Then transfer the cooked broccoli in the blender. Add butter, garlic powder, parsley, pork rinds, and salt. Blend the mixture until it is smooth. Place the cooked spread in the bowl and refrigerate it for at least 30 minutes.

Nutrition value/serving: calories 75, fat 5.5, fiber 0.7, carbs 1.8, protein 5.3

Green Egg Bites
Prep time: 10 minutes | Cooking time: 4 minutes | Servings: 2

Ingredients:
- 2 eggs, beaten
- 1 tablespoon cream cheese
- 1 tablespoon fresh spinach, chopped
- 1 oz collard greens, chopped
- ¼ teaspoon salt
- ¼ teaspoon coconut oil, melted
- 1 cup water, for cooking

Directions:
Place the collard greens and fresh spinach in the blender. Blend the greens until smooth and transfer them in the mixing bowl. Add eggs, cream cheese, salt, and stir well. After this, brush the silicone egg molds with coconut oil. Pour the egg mixture inside the molds. Pour water in the instant pot and insert the trivet. Place the mold with eggs in the instant pot and cook them for 4 minutes on Manual mode (high pressure). Then make a quick pressure release. Cool the egg bites for 3-5 minutes and then remove from the molds.

Nutrition value/serving: calories 89, fat 6.8, fiber 0.5, carbs 1.3, protein 6.3

Breakfast Sausages
Prep time: 5 minutes | Cooking time: 11 minutes | Servings: 4

Ingredients:
- 12 oz breakfast turkey sausage links, chopped
- 1 teaspoon ground paprika
- 1 teaspoon dried basil
- 1 teaspoon avocado oil
- ¼ teaspoon ground coriander

Directions:
Pour the avocado oil in the instant pot. Press sauté mode and preheat the oil. Then place sausages in the hot oil. Sprinkle them with ground paprika, dried basil, and ground coriander. Stir the sausages with the help of the spatula every 3 minutes. Cook the sausages for 11 minutes.

Nutrition value/serving: calories 145, fat 8.7, fiber 0.3, carbs 1.8, protein 18.5

Lunch
Provolone Chicken Soup
Prep time: 10 minutes | Cooking time: 18 minutes | Servings: 4

Ingredients:
- 3 oz bacon, chopped
- 10 oz chicken fillet, chopped
- 3 oz Provolone cheese, grated
- 1 tablespoon cream cheese
- 1 white onion, diced
- ½ teaspoon salt
- ½ teaspoon ground black pepper
- 1 teaspoon dried parsley
- 1 garlic clove, diced
- 4 cups of water

Directions:
Place the chopped bacon in the instant pot and cook it for 5 minutes on sauté mode. Stir it from time to time to avoid burning. After this, transfer the cooked bacon in the plate and dry little with the paper towel. Then add onion and diced garlic in the instant pot. Sauté the vegetables for 2 minutes and add chicken and cream cheese. Stir well and sauté the ingredients for 5 minutes. After this, add salt, ground black pepper, dried parsley, water, and Provolone cheese. Stir the soup mixture well. Close the lid and cook the soup for 5 minutes on manual mode (high pressure) Then make a quick pressure release. Add the cooked bacon in the soup. Stir the cooked soup well before serving.

Nutrition value/serving: calories 346, fat 20.7, fiber 0.7, carbs 3.8, protein 34.4

Jalapeno Soup
Prep time: 10 minutes | Cooking time: 20 minutes | Servings: 4

Ingredients:
- ½ cup ground pork
- 1 teaspoon garlic powder
- 1 bell pepper, diced
- 1 jalapeno pepper, sliced
- 1 teaspoon coconut oil
- 1 tomato, chopped
- ½ teaspoon salt
- 1 teaspoon thyme
- 4 cups of water

Directions:
Put the coconut oil in the instant pot and preheat it on Saute mode. When the coconut oil starts shimmering, add bell pepper and jalapeno pepper. Cook the vegetables for 1 minute and stir them. Add ground pork, garlic powder, tomato, salt, and thyme. Stir well and sauté the ingredients for 2 minutes. Then add water and close the lid. Cook the jalapeno soup for 5 minutes on Manual mode (high pressure). Then allow the natural pressure release for 5 minutes.

Nutrition value/serving: calories 142, fat 9.4, fiber 0.9, carbs 3.7, protein 10.7

Aromatic Lasagna with Basil
Prep time: 15 minutes | Cooking time: 10 minutes | Servings: 6

Ingredients:
- 2 eggplants, peeled, sliced
- 1 cup ground pork
- 3 tablespoons marinara sauce
- 1 white onion, diced
- 1 oz fresh basil, chopped
- ½ cup Ricotta cheese
- ½ cup Mozzarella, shredded
- ½ teaspoon dried oregano
- ¼ teaspoon salt
- 1 cup water, for cooking

Directions:
In the mixing bowl combine together ground pork, diced onion, basil, and dried oregano. Add salt and stir the meat mixture well with the help of the spoon. Line the baking pan with paper foil. Then place the sliced eggplants in the baking pan to make the layer. Sprinkle the eggplants with marinara sauce. Top the marinara sauce with ground pork mixture. Then spread the mixture with Ricotta cheese and shredded Mozzarella. Cover the lasagna with foil. Pour water in the instant pot and insert the trivet. Place the lasagna on the trivet and close the lid. Cook the lasagna for 10 minutes on manual mode (high pressure). Then make a quick pressure release. Cool the cooked lasagna little before serving.

Nutrition value/serving: calories 251, fat 13.5, fiber 7.2, carbs 14.9, protein 18.7

Keto "Potato" Soup

Prep time: 15 minutes | Cooking time: 4 minutes | Servings: 2

Ingredients:
- 1 cup cauliflower, chopped
- 1 oz bacon, chopped, cooked
- 2 oz Cheddar cheese, shredded
- 2 tablespoons cream cheese
- 1 oz leek, chopped
- 1 cup of water
- ½ teaspoon salt
- ½ teaspoon cayenne pepper

Directions:
Pour water in the instant pot. Add cauliflower, cream cheese, leek, salt, and cayenne pepper. Close the lid and cook soup mixture for 4 minutes on Manual mode (high pressure). Allow the natural pressure release for 10 minutes. Then add cheese and stir the soup until it is melted. With the help of the immersion blender, blend the soup until you get the creamy texture. Then ladle the soup in the serving bowls and top with bacon.

Nutrition value/serving: calories 248, fat 19, fiber 1.6, carbs 5.7, protein 14.3

Egg Soup

Prep time: 5 minutes | Cooking time: 15 minutes | Servings: 2

Ingredients:
- 2 eggs, beaten
- 2 cups chicken broth
- 1 tablespoon chives, chopped
- ½ teaspoon salt
- ½ teaspoon chili flakes

Directions:
Pour chicken broth in the instant pot. Add chives, salt, and chili flakes. Saute the liquid for 10 minutes. Then add beaten eggs and stir the soup well. Cook the soup for 5 minutes more.

Nutrition value/serving: calories 102, fat 5.8, fiber 0.1, carbs 1.3, protein 10.5

Beef Cabbage Soup

Prep time: 10 minutes | Cooking time: 15 minutes | Servings: 6

Ingredients:
- 1 cup white cabbage, shredded
- ½ cup kale, chopped
- 11 oz beef sirloin, chopped
- ½ teaspoon salt
- 1 teaspoon dried basil
- ½ teaspoon fennel seeds
- ½ teaspoon ground black pepper
- 1 garlic clove, diced
- 1 teaspoon almond butter
- 5 cups of water

Directions:
Put almond butter in the instant pot and melt it on sauté mode. Add white cabbage and diced garlic. Cook the vegetables for 5 minutes. Stir them occasionally. Then add chopped beef sirloin, fennel seeds, ground black pepper, salt, and stir well. Add basil and water. Then add kale and close the lid. Cook the soup on Manual mode (high pressure) for 5 minutes. Then make a quick pressure release.

Nutrition value/serving: calories 120, fat 4.8, fiber 0.8, carbs 2.1, protein 16.7

Bacon Chowder

Prep time: 10 minutes | Cooking time: 20 minutes | Servings: 4

Ingredients:
- 1 cup fresh spinach, chopped
- ½ cup heavy cream
- 4 oz bacon, chopped, cooked
- 1 teaspoon dried dill
- ½ teaspoon salt
- 4 chicken thighs, skinless, boneless, chopped
- ½ teaspoon cayenne pepper
- ½ teaspoon ground thyme
- 1 teaspoon coconut oil
- 1 teaspoon minced garlic
- 4 cups of water
- ½ cup mushrooms, chopped

Directions:
Put coconut oil in the instant pot and melt it on sauté mode. Then add chopped chicken thighs, salt, dill, cayenne pepper, and ground thyme. Stir the chicken well and sauté for 5 minutes. After this, add minced garlic and chopped mushrooms. Stir well and cook for 5 minutes more. Then add heavy cream and water. Then add chopped spinach and bacon. Close the lid and cook the chowder on Manual mode (high pressure) for 10 minutes. Then make a quick pressure release and open the lid. Cool the chowder for 10-15 minutes before serving.

Nutrition value/serving: calories 249, fat 19.4, fiber 0.4, carbs 2, protein 16.4

Butternut Squash Soup

Prep time: 10 minutes | Cooking time: 25 minutes | Servings: 6

Ingredients:
- 2 cups butternut squash, chopped
- 2 garlic cloves, peeled, diced
- 1 teaspoon curry powder
- ½ teaspoon ginger, minced
- 1 white onion, diced
- 1 teaspoon salt
- 1 teaspoon ground paprika
- 1 tablespoon butter
- 5 cups chicken broth
- 2 tablespoons Ricotta cheese

Directions:
Melt butter in sauté mode. Then add garlic and onion. Saute the vegetables until they are golden brown. Then add butternut squash, ginger, salt, ground paprika, and ricotta cheese. Then add curry powder and chicken broth. Close the lid and cook the soup on manual mode (high pressure) for 15 minutes. Then make a quick pressure release. Blend the soup with the help of the immersion blender.

Nutrition value/serving: calories 87, fat 3.6, fiber 1.4, carbs 8.7, protein 5.5

Tortilla Soup

Prep time: 10 minutes | Cooking time: 30 minutes | Servings: 2

Ingredients:
- ½ Poblano pepper, chopped
- ¼ teaspoon minced garlic
- ¼ teaspoon ground coriander
- ½ cup tomatoes, canned
- 1 tablespoon dried cilantro
- ¼ teaspoon salt
- 2 cups chicken broth
- 8 oz chicken breast, skinless, boneless
- 1 tablespoon lemon juice
- 1 teaspoon butter
- ¼ cup Cheddar cheese, shredded
- 2 low carb tortillas, chopped

Directions:
Melt butter in sauté mode. When the butter is melted, add chopped Poblano pepper, minced garlic, ground coriander, and dried cilantro. Add chicken breast and cook the ingredients for 10 minutes. Stir them from time to time. After this, add canned tomatoes, salt, and chicken broth. Close the lid and cook the soup on manual mode (high pressure) for 15 minutes. Then make a quick pressure release and open the lid. Add lemon juice and sauté the soup for 5 minutes more. Ladle the soup into the bowls and top with Cheddar cheese and chopped low carb tortillas.

Nutrition value/serving: calories 336, fat 13, fiber 8.3, carbs 16.1, protein 36.2

Asian Style Zucchini Soup

Prep time: 10 minutes | *Cooking time:* 25 minutes | *Servings:* 4

Ingredients:
- ½ teaspoon minced ginger
- ¼ teaspoon minced garlic
- 1 teaspoon coconut oil
- 10 oz beef sirloin steak, chopped
- ½ cup cremini mushrooms, sliced
- 4 cups chicken broth
- ½ teaspoon salt
- 1 zucchini, trimmed
- 1 teaspoon chives, chopped

Directions:

Heat up instant pot on sauté mode. Toss coconut oil and melt it. Then add minced ginger and minced garlic. Stir well and add chopped steak. Sauté the mixture for 5 minutes. Meanwhile, with the help of the spiralizer make the zucchini noodles. Add mushrooms in the beef mixture. Then sprinkle it with salt. Add chicken broth and cook the soup on Manual mode (high pressure) for 12 minutes. Then make a quick pressure release and open the lid. Add spiralized noodles and stir the soup. Let it rest for 5 minutes. Top the cooked soup with chives.

Nutrition value/serving: calories 191, fat 7, fiber 0.6, carbs 3.2, protein 27.2

Chili Verde

Prep time: 10 minutes | *Cooking time:* 3 hours 5 minutes | *Servings:* 2

Ingredients:
- 9 oz pork shoulder, chopped
- ½ cup salsa Verde
- 1 teaspoon sesame oil
- ½ cup chicken broth
- ¼ teaspoon cayenne pepper
- ¼ teaspoon salt

Directions:

Pour sesame oil in the instant pot and preheat it on sauté mode for 3 minutes. Meanwhile, mix up together pork shoulder, cayenne pepper, and salt. Add the pork shoulder in the hot oil and sauté the meat for 2 minutes. Then stir it with the help of the spatula and add chicken broth and salsa Verde. Close the lid. Cook the meal on manual (low pressure) for 3 hours. When the time is over, shred the meat.

Nutrition value/serving: calories 418, fat 30.1, fiber 0.3, carbs 2.9, protein 31.7

Keto Taco Soup

Prep time: 10 minutes | *Cooking time:* 25 minutes | *Servings:* 5

Ingredients:
- 2 cups ground beef
- 1 teaspoon onion powder
- 1 teaspoon taco seasonings
- 1 garlic clove, diced
- 1 teaspoon chili flakes
- 1 teaspoon ground cumin
- 1 tablespoon tomato paste
- ½ cup heavy cream
- 5 cups of water
- 1 teaspoon coconut oil
- 1 tablespoon cream cheese
- 1 jalapeno pepper, sliced

Directions:

Toss the coconut oil in the instant pot and melt it on sauté mode. Add ground beef and onion powder. After this, add taco seasonings and diced garlic. Mix up the ingredients well. Then sprinkle the meat mixture with chili flakes and ground cumin. Saute the ground beef for 10 minutes. Mix it up with the help of the spatula every 3 minutes. Then add tomato paste, heavy cream, and water. Add sliced jalapeno pepper and close the lid. Cook the soup on Manual (high pressure) for 10 minutes. Then allow the natural pressure release for 10 minutes and ladle the soup into the bowls.

Nutrition value/serving: calories 170, fat 12.7, fiber 0.3, carbs 2.4, protein 11.2

Chicken Enchilada Soup
Prep time: 10 minutes | *Cooking time:* 32 minutes | *Servings:* 4

Ingredients:
- 1-pound chicken fillet
- ½ white onion, chopped
- 1 bell pepper, chopped
- 1 jalapeno pepper, chopped
- 1 tablespoon avocado oil
- 1 tablespoon tomato paste
- 1 teaspoon apple cider vinegar
- 1 teaspoon chipotle pepper
- ½ teaspoon garlic powder
- ½ teaspoon ground cumin
- ½ teaspoon ground coriander
- ½ teaspoon ground paprika
- 1/3 teaspoon salt
- 1 teaspoon dried oregano
- 4 cups of water

Directions:
Pour avocado oil in the instant pot. Add white onion, bell pepper, and jalapeno pepper. Saute the vegetables on sauté mode for 5 minutes. Meanwhile, in the shallow bowl combine together garlic powder, cumin, coriander, paprika, salt, and dried oregano. Add the spices in the vegetables. Then add tomato paste, chipotle pepper, and apple cider vinegar. Add water and chicken fillet. Close the lid and cook enchilada soup on Manual mode (high pressure) for 25 minutes. Then make a quick pressure release and open the lid. With the help of 2 forks shred the chicken fillet and stir the soup.

Nutrition value/serving: calories 244, fat 9.1, fiber 1.4, carbs 5.5, protein 33.7

Creamy Cauliflower Soup
Prep time: 10 minutes | *Cooking time:* 15 minutes | *Servings:* 2

Ingredients:
- 1 tablespoon cream cheese
- 1 oz bacon, chopped, cooked
- 2 oz Cheddar cheese, shredded
- 2 cups cauliflower, chopped
- ½ teaspoon salt
- 1 teaspoon dried oregano
- 2 cups chicken broth
- ½ teaspoon ground nutmeg
- ½ medium white onion, diced

Directions:
Place onion and cream cheese in the instant pot. Cook the ingredients on sauté mode until onion is light brown. Then add chopped cauliflower, salt, dried oregano, and ground nutmeg. Cook the vegetables for 3 minutes. Then stir them well and add chicken broth. Cook the soup on Manual (High pressure) for 4 minutes. Then make a quick pressure release and open the lid. With the help of immersion blender, blend the soup until smooth. Ladle the soup in the bowls and top with Cheddar cheese and cook bacon.

Nutrition value/serving: calories 286, fat 18.8, fiber 3.2, carbs 9.7, protein 19.9

Kale Soup
Prep time: 10 minutes | *Cooking time:* 17 minutes | *Servings:* 4

Ingredients:
- 3 cups of water
- 9 oz sausages, chopped
- 2 oz Parmesan
- ½ cup heavy cream
- 2 cups kale, chopped
- ½ teaspoon ground black pepper
- ¼ onion, diced
- 1 teaspoon dried basil
- 1 tablespoon olive oil

Directions:
Pour olive oil in the instant pot and add the onion. Saute the onion for 3 minutes. Then stir well and add sausages. Mix up well and cook them for 3 minutes. After this, add water, kale, basil, and ground black pepper. Saute the mixture for 8 minutes. Then add heavy cream and Parmesan. Close the lid and cook the soup on manual mode (high pressure) for 3 minutes. Then make a quick pressure release. Let the cooked kale soup cool for 10-15 minutes before serving.

Nutrition value/serving: calories 364, fat 30.2, fiber 0.7, carbs 5.3, protein 18.4

Bone Broth Soup

Prep time: 7 minutes | Cooking time: 10 minutes | Servings: 2

Ingredients:
- 1 eggplant, trimmed, chopped
- 2 cups bone broth
- ¼ cup carrot, grated
- 1 tablespoon butter
- ½ teaspoon salt
- 1 teaspoon dried dill

Directions:
In the mixing bowl combine together eggplants and salt. Leave the vegetables for 5 minutes. Meanwhile, toss the butter in the instant pot and melt it on sauté mode. Add grated carrot and cook it for 2 minutes. Meanwhile, dry the eggplants. Add them in the carrot and stir. Sprinkle the vegetables with dried dill. Then add bone broth and close the lid. Cook the soup for 5 minutes on Manual mode (high pressure). Then make a quick pressure release.

Nutrition value/serving: calories 200, fat 6.2, fiber 8.5, carbs 15.1, protein 22.5

Buffalo Chicken Soup

Prep time: 10 minutes | Cooking time: 15 minutes | Servings: 5

Ingredients:
- 1 white onion, diced
- ½ cup celery stalk, chopped
- ½ teaspoon minced garlic
- 1 teaspoon olive oil
- 1-pound chicken breast, cooked, shredded
- 4 cups chicken broth
- 1 tablespoon buffalo sauce

Directions:
In the instant pot bowl mix up together onion, minced garlic, and olive oil. Cook the ingredients on sauté mode for 4 minutes. Then stir them well and add shredded chicken breast. Add chicken broth and buffalo sauce. Mix up well. Cook the soup on soup mode for 10 minutes.

Nutrition value/serving: calories 154, fat 4.3, fiber 0.7, carbs 3.4, protein 23.4

Sausages & Vegetable Stew

Prep time: 10 minutes | Cooking time: 25 minutes | Servings: 2

Ingredients:
- 4 oz sausages, chopped
- ½ cup savoy cabbage, chopped
- 2 oz turnip, chopped
- ¼ cup bok choy, chopped
- 1 teaspoon ground cumin
- ¼ teaspoon fennel seeds
- ½ cup heavy cream
- ½ teaspoon salt
- 1 teaspoon butter

Directions:
Preheat the instant pot on sauté mode for 2 minutes. Toss the butter inside and melt it. After this, add sausages and cook them for 5 minutes on sauté mode. Stir them from time to time. Then add salt, fennel seeds, ground cumin, and heavy cream. Add savoy cabbage, turnip, and bok choy. Stir the stew well. Cook the stew on stew mode for 15 minutes.

Nutrition value/serving: calories 331, fat 29.4, fiber 1.3, carbs 4.5, protein 12.5

Keto Lunch Bowl

Prep time: 10 minutes | *Cooking time:* 25 minutes | *Servings:* 2

Ingredients:
- ½ cup broccoli, chopped
- 8 oz chicken fillet, chopped
- 1 green bell pepper, chopped
- 1 teaspoon ground black pepper
- ½ teaspoon dried cilantro
- 1 cup chicken broth
- ½ teaspoon salt
- ½ teaspoon almond butter

Directions:
Place almond butter, bell pepper, and broccoli in the instant pot. Cook the ingredients on sauté mode for 5 minutes. Stir them with the help of the spatula from time to time. After this, add chopped chicken fillet, ground black pepper, salt, and cilantro. Add chicken broth and mix up the meal well. Close the lid and cook it on stew mode for 20 minutes. When the meal is cooked, let it rest for 10 minutes before serving.

Nutrition value/serving: calories 289, fat 11.6, fiber 2.1, carbs 7.9, protein 37.4

Cobb Salad

Prep time: 10 minutes | *Cooking time:* 21 minutes | *Servings:* 4

Ingredients:
- 1-pound chicken breast, skinless, boneless
- 1 avocado, pitted, peeled
- 4 eggs
- 1 cup lettuce, chopped
- 1 tablespoon lemon juice
- ¼ teaspoon salt
- ½ teaspoon white pepper
- ½ cup white cabbage, shredded
- 4 oz Feta cheese, crumbled
- 1 tablespoon coconut oil
- ½ teaspoon chili flakes
- 1 tablespoon heavy cream
- 1 tablespoon apple cider vinegar
- ½ teaspoon garlic powder
- 1 cup water, for cooking

Directions:
Pour water and insert the trivet in the instant pot. Place the eggs on the trivet and close the lid. Cook them in manual mode (high pressure) for 5 minutes. Then make a quick pressure release. Cool the eggs in ice water. Then peel the eggs. Cut the eggs and avocado into the wedges. After this, rub the chicken breast with lemon juice, salt, and coconut oil. Place the chicken breast in the instant pot and cook it on sauté mode for 7 minutes from each side. The cooked chicken should be light brown. Make the sauce: whisk together chili flakes, olive oil, heavy cream, apple cider vinegar, and garlic powder. In the big salad bowl combine together lettuce, eggs, avocado, white pepper, white cabbage, and crumbled feta. Chop the cooked chicken roughly and add in the salad. Shake the salad well. Then sprinkle the cooked cobb salad with sauce.

Nutrition value/serving: calories 417, fat 27.9, fiber 3.8, carbs 7.4, protein 34.9

Lobster Salad

Prep time: 10 minutes | *Cooking time:* 4 minutes | *Servings:* 4

Ingredients:
- 4 lobster tails, peeled
- 1 teaspoon avocado oil
- ¼ teaspoon salt
- 2 cucumbers, chopped
- ¼ cup whipped cream
- 1 tablespoon apple cider vinegar
- 1 teaspoon dried dill
- ½ cup celery stalk, chopped
- 1 cup water, for cooking

Directions:
Pour water and insert the trivet in the instant pot. Arrange the lobster tails on the trivet and cook them on Manual mode (high pressure) for 4 minutes. Then make a quick pressure release. Cool the cooked lobster tails little and chop them roughly. Place the chopped lobster tails in the salad bowl. Add cucumbers, dried ill, and celery stalk. After this, make the salad sauce: in the shallow bowl combine together salt, avocado oil, whipped cream, dill, and apple cider vinegar. Sprinkle the salad with sauce and mix up it well with the help of 2 spoons.

Nutrition value/serving: calories 139, fat 3.7, fiber 1, carbs 6.3, protein 1.3

Italian Style Salad

Prep time: 5 minutes | *Cooking time:* 5 minutes | *Servings:* 2

Ingredients:
- 8 oz shrimps, peeled
- 1 teaspoon Italian seasonings
- 1 teaspoon olive oil
- ½ cup cherry tomatoes, halved
- ¼ teaspoon chili flakes
- ½ teaspoon coconut oil

Directions:
Toss coconut oil in the instant pot. Melt it on sauté mode and add peeled shrimps. Cook the shrimps for 1 minute from each side. Then place the shrimps in the bowl. Add chili flakes, Italian seasonings, halved cherry tomatoes, and olive oil. Shake the salad before serving.

Nutrition value/serving: calories 173, fat 5.5, fiber 0.5, carbs 3.5, protein 26.2

Egg & Cheese Salad with Dill

Prep time: 15 minutes | *Cooking time:* 4 minutes | *Servings:* 3

Ingredients:
- 3 eggs
- 2 tablespoons cream cheese
- 1 tablespoon dried dill
- ½ cup Cheddar cheese, shredded
- ¼ teaspoon minced garlic
- 1 cup water, for cooking

Directions:
Pour water and insert rack in the instant pot. Place the eggs in the instant pot, close the lid and cook them for 4 minutes on Manual mode (high pressure). Then make a quick pressure release. Cool the eggs in cold water for 10 minutes. After this, peel the eggs and grate them. In the mixing bowl combine together grated eggs, shredded cheese, minced garlic, dill, and cream cheese. Mix up the salad well.

Nutrition value/serving: calories 165, fat 13, fiber 0.1, carbs 1.4, protein 11

Crab Salad

Prep time: 10 minutes | *Cooking time:* 2 minutes | *Servings:* 2

Ingredients:
- 10 oz crab meat
- 1 tablespoon sour cream
- 1 tablespoon cream
- ¼ teaspoon minced garlic
- 1 tablespoon cream cheese
- ½ teaspoon lime juice
- ½ red onion, diced
- ¼ cup fresh cilantro, chopped
- ¼ cup fresh spinach, chopped
- ¼ teaspoon salt
- ¼ teaspoon ground cumin
- 1 cup water, for cooking

Directions:
Pour water in the instant pot. Line the trivet with the paper foil and insert the instant pot. Place the crab meat on the trivet and cook it on Manual mode (high pressure) for 2 minutes. Then make a quick pressure release and remove the crab meat from the instant pot. Chop it and place it in the salad bowl. Add diced onion, spinach, and cilantro. In the shallow bowl make the salad dressing: whisk together sour cream, cream, minced garlic, cream cheese, and lime juice. Then add salt and ground cumin. Add the dressing in the salad and stir it well.

Nutrition value/serving: calories 175, fat 6, fiber 0.8, carbs 6.4, protein 18.9

Chicken Paprika

Prep time: 10 minutes | *Cooking time:* 25 minutes | *Servings:* 2

Ingredients:
- 2 chicken thighs, skinless, boneless
- 2 tablespoons ground paprika
- 1 tablespoon almond meal
- 1 teaspoon tomato paste
- ½ teaspoon dried celery root
- ½ cup heavy cream
- 1 tablespoon butter
- ½ teaspoon salt
- ½ teaspoon white pepper
- ¼ teaspoon ground nutmeg
- 1 tablespoon lemon juice

Directions:

Melt butter in sauté mode. Meanwhile, rub the chicken thighs with salt and white pepper. Cook the chicken thighs on sauté mode for 4 minutes from each side. Meanwhile, in the mixing bowl combine together almond meal, dried celery root, and ground nutmeg. In the separated bowl combine together heavy cream, tomato paste, and lemon juice. Pour the heavy cream liquid in the chicken. Then add almond meal mixture and stir gently. Cook the meal on meat mode for 15 minutes.

Nutrition value/serving: calories 476, fat 30.3, fiber 3.3, carbs 6.5, protein 44.8

Sour Cauliflower Salad

Prep time: 10 minutes | *Cooking time:* 9 minutes | *Servings:* 2

Ingredients:
- 1 cup cauliflower, chopped
- 2 eggs
- 1/3 teaspoon salt
- ½ cup purple cabbage, shredded
- 1 tablespoon lemon juice
- 1 tablespoon cream cheese
- 4 oz bacon, chopped, cooked
- 1 cup water, for cooking

Directions:

Pour water and insert the trivet in the instant pot. Place the eggs on the trivet and cook them on manual mode (high pressure) for 5 minutes. Then make a quick pressure release. Cool the eggs. Place the cauliflower on the trivet and cook on steam mode for 4 minutes. Make a quick pressure release. Peel and chop the eggs. Place the eggs in the mixing bowl. Add cooked cauliflower, salt, shredded purple cabbage, lemon juice, cream cheese, and bacon. Mix up the salad.

Nutrition value/serving: calories 406, fat 29.9, fiber 1.7, carbs 5.1, protein 28.2

Warm Radish Salad

Prep time: 10 minutes | *Cooking time:* 11 minutes | *Servings:* 4

Ingredients:
- 3 cups radish, sliced
- 7 oz chicken fillet, chopped
- 1 tablespoon lemon juice
- 1 teaspoon olive oil
- ¼ teaspoon salt
- 1 teaspoon butter
- 1 tablespoon dried parsley
- ½ teaspoon sesame oil

Directions:

Mix up together chopped chicken fillet with lemon juice, olive oil, and salt. Place the chicken in the instant pot and cook it on sauté mode for 3 minutes from each side. Then add radish and butter, and sauté the ingredients for 5 minutes. Transfer the cooked salad in the bowl. Add dried parsley and sesame oil. Mix up the salad.

Nutrition value/serving: calories 133, fat 6.5, fiber 1.4, carbs 3.1, protein 15

Crack Chicken

Prep time: 10 minutes | *Cooking time:* 10 minutes | *Servings:* 4

Ingredients:
- 1-pound chicken breast
- 1 teaspoon salt
- 1 teaspoon garlic powder
- ½ teaspoon ground black pepper
- 1 teaspoon sesame oil
- ½ cup chicken broth
- 2 tablespoons cream cheese
- ½ teaspoon ground cumin
- ½ teaspoon ground coriander
- ½ teaspoon onion powder
- ½ teaspoon chives

Directions:

Cut the chicken breast into 4 servings. Then sprinkle the chicken with salt, garlic powder, sesame oil, and ground black pepper. Place the chicken in the instant pot and cook it on sauté mode for 2 minutes from each side. Then add chicken broth and cream cheese. Sprinkle the ingredients with ground cumin, coriander, onion powder, and chives. Stir the chicken with the help of the spatula and close the lid. Cook the crack chicken on poultry mode for 5 minutes.

Nutrition value/serving: calories 167, fat 6, fiber 0.2, carbs 1.3, protein 25.3

Salsa Chicken

Prep time: 15 minutes | *Cooking time:* 17 minutes | *Servings:* 2

Ingredients:
- ¼ cup hot salsa
- 10 oz chicken breast, skinless, boneless
- 1 teaspoon taco seasoning
- ¼ teaspoon salt
- ¼ teaspoon chili flakes
- 1 tablespoon cream cheese
- ¼ cup chicken broth

Directions:

Place the chicken breast in the instant pot. Sprinkle the poultry with taco seasoning, salt, and chili flakes. Then add cream cheese, salsa, and chicken broth. Close and seal the lid. Cook the meal on manual mode (high pressure) for 17 minutes. Then allow the natural pressure release for 10 minutes and shred the chicken. Serve the shredded chicken with hot sauce from the instant pot.

Nutrition value/serving: calories 198, fat 5.5, fiber 0.5, carbs 3.3, protein 31.5

Lemon Carnitas

Prep time: 10 minutes | *Cooking time:* 30 minutes | *Servings:* 4

Ingredients:
- 13 oz pork butt, chopped
- ¼ cup white onion, diced
- 1 teaspoon ghee
- ½ teaspoon garlic powder
- 1 tablespoon lemon juice
- ¼ teaspoon grated lemon zest
- ½ teaspoon chipotle powder
- 1 cup of water
- ½ teaspoon salt
- 1 cup lettuce leaves

Directions:

Put pork butt, white onion, ghee, garlic powder, lemon juice, grated lemon zest, and chipotle powder in the instant pot. Saute the ingredients for 5 minutes. Then mix up the meat mixture with the help of the spatula and add salt and water. Close and seal the lid and cook ingredients on manual mode (high pressure) for 25 minutes. When the time is over, make a quick pressure release and open the lid. Shred the cooked pork with the help of the fork. Then fill the lettuce leaves with shredded pork.

Nutrition value/serving: calories 194 fat 7.3, fiber 0.3, carbs 1.4, protein 28.9

Smoky Pulled Pork

Prep time: 10 minutes | *Cooking time:* 20 minutes | *Servings:* 4

Ingredients:
- 1-pound pork loin
- 1 teaspoon smoked paprika
- ½ teaspoon liquid smoke
- ½ teaspoon ground coriander
- ½ teaspoon salt
- 1 teaspoon onion powder
- 1 teaspoon tomato paste
- 1 cup chicken broth

Directions:
Put the pork loin in the instant pot. Add smoked paprika, liquid smoke, ground coriander, salt, onion powder, tomato paste, and chicken broth. Close the lid and cook the pork on manual mode (high pressure) for 20 minutes. When the time is over, make a quick pressure release and open the lid. Remove the pork loin from the instant pot and shred it. Place the cooked pulled pork in the bowl and sprinkle it with ½ part of liquid from the instant pot.

Nutrition value/serving: calories 233, fat 8, fiber 0.3, carbs 1.3, protein 36.7

Chicken & Dumplings Soup

Prep time: 10 minutes | *Cooking time:* 25 minutes | *Servings:* 4

Ingredients:
- 4 cups chicken broth
- 4 chicken wings
- ½ onion, diced
- 1 tablespoon dried dill
- ½ teaspoon salt
- ¼ cup coconut flour
- 2 tablespoons water
- 1 teaspoon ghee

Directions:
In the mixing bowl combine together water and coconut flour. Knead the non-sticky dough. Add more coconut flour if the dough is sticky. Then make the log from the dough and cut it into pieces. After this, place the ghee in the instant pot and preheat it on sauté mode. When the ghee is melted, add diced onion and cook it until light brown. After this, add chicken wings, dried ill, and salt. Add chicken broth and close the lid. Cook the soup on manual mode (high pressure) for 10 minutes. Then make a quick pressure release. Open the lid and add prepared dough pieces (dumplings). Sauté the soup for 5 minutes more.

Nutrition value/serving: calories 179, fat 9.5, fiber 3.5, carbs 10.8, protein 11.9

Zoodle Soup

Prep time: 10 minutes | *Cooking time:* 25 minutes | *Servings:* 2

Ingredients:
- 2 cups chicken broth
- ½ teaspoon salt
- ½ teaspoon chili flakes
- 1 teaspoon dried oregano
- 1 teaspoon butter
- 8 oz chicken tenderloins
- 1 zucchini, spiralized

Directions:
Melt the butter in sauté mode. Then add chicken tenderloins. Sprinkle them with chili flakes, dried oregano, and salt. Cook the chicken for 3 minutes. Then add chicken broth and close the lid. Cook the soup on manual mode (high pressure) for 10 minutes. When the time is over, make a quick pressure release and open the lid. Add spiralized zucchini and stir the soup. Leave it to rest for 10 minutes.

Nutrition value/serving: calories 170, fat 4.1, fiber 1.4, carbs 4.7, protein 29.1

Hot Sausages Soup
Prep time: 10 minutes | *Cooking time:* 23 minutes | *Servings:* 3

Ingredients:
- 2 cups spinach, chopped
- 2 cups beef broth
- 7 oz sausages, chopped
- 1 teaspoon ghee
- ½ teaspoon salt
- ½ teaspoon ground cumin
- ½ teaspoon ground coriander
- ½ teaspoon dried celery
- ½ teaspoon onion powder
- 2 bell peppers, chopped

Directions:
Preheat the instant pot on sauté mode and place ghee inside. Melt it and add sausages. Cook the sausages for 10 minutes. Stir them from time to time with the help of the spatula. After this, sprinkle the sausages with salt, ground cumin, coriander, dried celery, and onion powder. Add beef broth and bell peppers. Close and seal the lid. Cook the soup on manual mode (high pressure) for 5 minutes. Then make a quick pressure release and open the lid. Stir the soup and add spinach. Cook the soup for 5 minutes more on sauté mode.

Nutrition value/serving: calories 295, fat 21.4, fiber 1.6, carbs 7.8, protein 17.6

Fajita Soup
Prep time: 10 minutes | *Cooking time:* 20 minutes | *Servings:* 4

Ingredients:
- ¼ cup cream cheese
- 12 oz chicken fillet
- ½ teaspoon taco seasonings
- 2 bell peppers, chopped
- ½ cup canned tomatoes
- 3 cups beef broth
- ½ teaspoon salt
- ¼ cup heavy cream
- 1 jalapeno pepper, sliced
- 1 chili pepper, sliced
- 1 tablespoon butter
- ½ teaspoon minced garlic

Directions:
Melt the butter in sauté mode and add chicken fillet. Sprinkle it with taco seasonings, salt, and minced garlic. Cook it for 4 minutes from each side. After this, add cream cheese, canned tomatoes, cream, and bell peppers. Close the lid and cook the soup on manual mode (high pressure) for 10 minutes. Then make a quick pressure release and open the lid. Shred the chicken with the help of the fork. Add sliced chili pepper and jalapeno pepper in the soup and cook it on sauté mode for 5 minutes more.

Nutrition value/serving: calories 320, fat 18.3, fiber 1.2, carbs 7.6, protein 30.4

Kalua Chicken
Prep time: 15 minutes | *Cooking time:* 15 minutes | *Servings:* 3

Ingredients:
- 3 bacon slices
- ¼ teaspoon salt
- ¼ teaspoon of liquid smoked
- 6 chicken thighs, skinless, boneless
- 1/3 cup water

Directions:
Place the bacon at the bottom of the instant pot bowl. Sprinkle the chicken thighs with salt and liquid smoker and place over the bacon. Then add water, close and seal the lid. Cook the chicken on manual mode (high pressure) for 15 minutes. When the time is over, allow the natural pressure release and transfer the chicken tights on the chopping board. Shred the chicken and transfer it in the serving plates. Chop the cooked bacon. Sprinkle the cooked chicken with instant pot liquid and cooked bacon.

Nutrition value/serving: calories 363, fat 21.9, fiber 0, carbs 0.3, protein 45

Southwestern Chili

Prep time: 5 minutes | *Cooking time:* 25 minutes | *Servings:* 2

Ingredients:
- 1 cup ground beef
- ¼ cup celery stalk, chopped
- ¼ onion, chopped
- 1 teaspoon chili powder
- ¼ teaspoon salt
- 1 tablespoon tomato paste
- 1 cup chicken stock
- 1 teaspoon butter
- ½ teaspoon smoked paprika
- 1 tablespoon salsa

Directions:
Put the butter in the instant pot bowl. Add ground beef and cook it on sauté mode for 5 minutes. Then stir the ground beef and sprinkle it with chili powder, salt, smoked paprika, and salsa. Add tomato paste, onion, and celery stalk. Add chicken stock. Close the lid and cook chili on stew mode for 20 minutes.

Nutrition value/serving: calories 173, fat 10.7, fiber 1.6, carbs 5.1, protein 14.3

Clam Chowder

Prep time: 10 minutes | *Cooking time:* 22 minutes | *Servings:* 5

Ingredients:
- 8 oz clams, canned
- ¼ cup clam juice
- ½ cup celery stalk, chopped
- 2 cups cauliflower, chopped
- 2 oz bacon, chopped
- ½ white onion, diced
- ½ teaspoon ground coriander
- ½ teaspoon ground thyme
- ¼ teaspoon salt
- ¼ teaspoon ground black pepper
- ½ teaspoon coconut oil
- 3 cups of water
- ½ cup heavy cream

Directions:
Set sauté mode and put the bacon in the instant pot. Cook it for 5 minutes. Stir it from time to time. After this, transfer the cooked bacon on the plate. Put coconut oil in the instant pot and add the onion. Cook it for 4 minutes or until it is light brown. Then add cauliflower, celery stalk, water, ad clam juice. Close and seal the lid and cook the chowder for 5 minutes on Manual mode (high pressure). When the time is over, make a quick pressure release and open the lid. Blend the mixture with the help of the immersion blender. Then add canned clams, ground coriander, thyme, salt, ground black pepper, and heavy cream. Cook the chowder on sauté mode for 5 minutes more. Ladle the cooked chowder in the bowls and sprinkle with bacon.

Nutrition value/serving: calories 145, fat 9.8, fiber 1.7, carbs 9, protein 5.8

Parsley Meatloaf

Prep time: 15 minutes | *Cooking time:* 30 minutes | *Servings:* 7

Ingredients:
- 2 cups ground beef
- 1 tablespoon parsley, chopped
- 1 teaspoon minced garlic
- 1 egg, beaten
- 1 teaspoon chili powder
- 2 oz Parmesan, grated
- 1 teaspoon butter, melted
- 1 tablespoon pork rinds
- 1 cup water, for cooking

Directions:
In the big bowl combine together ground beef, parsley, minced garlic, egg, chili powder Parmesan, and pork rinds. Mix up the mixture until smooth. After this, pour water and insert the rack in the instant pot. Line the rack with foil and place the ground beef mixture on it. Make the shape of the meatloaf with the help of the fingertips. Then brush the surface of meatloaf with butter and close the lid. Cook the meatloaf for 30 minutes on Manual mode (high pressure). Then make a quick pressure release. Cool the meatloaf well.

Nutrition value/serving: calories 127, fat 8.4, fiber 0.2, carbs 0.7, protein 12.2

Pepper Pork Chops

Prep time: 10 minutes | Cooking time: 25 minutes | Servings: 4

Ingredients:
- 16 oz pork chops
- ½ teaspoon ground black pepper
- ½ teaspoon salt
- ½ teaspoon chili flakes
- ¼ teaspoon cayenne pepper
- 1 tablespoon sesame oil
- 1 teaspoon lemon juice
- ½ teaspoon dried rosemary
- 1 cup water, for cooking

Directions:
In the bowl combine together salt, ground black pepper, chili flakes, cayenne pepper, sesame oil, lemon juice, and dried rosemary. Rub the pork chops with oily mixture and wrap in the foil. Pour water and insert the trivet in the instant pot. Place the wrapped pork chops in the instant pot and cook on manual mode (high pressure) for 25 minutes. When the time is over, make a quick pressure release.

Nutrition value/serving: calories 395, fat 31.6, fiber 0.2, carbs 0.4, protein 25.5

Meat & Collard Greens Bowl

Prep time: 10 minutes | Cooking time: 18 minutes | Servings: 4

Ingredients:
- 1 cup ground pork
- 2 cups collard greens, chopped
- 1 tablespoon butter
- ½ teaspoon salt
- 1 teaspoon minced garlic
- 1 teaspoon ground paprika
- 1 teaspoon ground turmeric
- ¼ cup chicken broth

Directions:
Melt the butter in sauté mode and add ground pork. Sprinkle it with salt, minced garlic, ground paprika, and ground turmeric. Cook the ground pork on sauté mode for 10 minutes. Stir it from time to time to avoid burning. After this, add collard greens and chicken broth. Cook the meal on manual mode (high pressure) for 5 minutes. When the time is finished, make a quick pressure release. Mix up the cooked meal well before serving.

Nutrition value/serving: calories 271, fat 19.5, fiber 1.1, carbs 2.2, protein 21.1

Spinach Saag

Prep time: 5 minutes | Cooking time: 10 minutes | Servings: 4

Ingredients:
- 1-pound spinach, chopped
- 2 tablespoons ghee
- 1 teaspoon garam masala
- ½ teaspoon ground coriander
- 1 teaspoon salt
- ½ teaspoon ground thyme
- ½ teaspoon cayenne pepper
- ½ teaspoon ground turmeric
- 1 teaspoon minced garlic
- ¼ cup of water

Directions:
Place ghee in the instant pot and melt it on sauté mode. After this, add garam masala, ground coriander, salt, thyme, cayenne pepper, turmeric, and minced garlic. Stir the mixture and cook it for 1 minute. Then add spinach and water. Mix up the greens well with the help of the spatula. Close the lid and cook the meal on sauté mode for 5 minutes. Switch off the instant pot. Open the lid and blend the spinach until you get a smooth puree. Place the spinach saag in the serving plates.

Nutrition value/serving: calories 114, fat 9.2, fiber 3.6, carbs 6.3, protein 4.5

Chicken & Mushroom Bowl

Prep time: 10 minutes | *Cooking time:* 20 minutes | *Servings:* 2

Ingredients:
- 1 cup cremini mushrooms, sliced
- 10 oz chicken breast, skinless, boneless, chopped
- ½ cup heavy cream
- 1 teaspoon salt
- ½ teaspoon ground paprika
- ½ teaspoon cayenne pepper
- 1 tablespoon coconut oil

Directions:
Melt coconut oil in the instant pot on sauté mode. Add cremini mushrooms and sauté them for 5 minutes. After this, add chopped chicken breast. Sprinkle the ingredients with salt, ground paprika, and cayenne pepper. Cook them for 5 minutes more. Then add heavy cream and close the lid. Cook the meal on poultry mode for 10 minutes.

Nutrition value/serving: calories 336, fat 21.6, fiber 0.5, carbs 2.9, protein 31.7

Cheddar Soup

Prep time: 20 minutes | *Cooking time:* 5 minutes | *Servings:* 3

Ingredients:
- 1 cup chicken broth
- 1 cup heavy cream
- 1 teaspoon xanthan gum
- 2 cups broccoli, chopped
- ½ cup cheddar cheese, shredded
- ½ teaspoon salt
- 1 teaspoon ground black pepper
- ½ teaspoon chili flakes
- 1 teaspoon ground cumin

Directions:
Pour chicken broth and heavy cream in the instant pot. Add broccoli, salt, ground black pepper, chili flakes, and ground cumin. Close and seal the lid. Cook the mixture on manual mode (high pressure) for 5 minutes. Then allow the natural pressure release for 10 minutes and open the lid. Add xanthan gum and blend the soup with the help of the immersion blender. Ladle the soup in the bowls and top with cheddar cheese.

Nutrition value/serving: calories 252, fat 21.9, fiber 1.8, carbs 6.5, protein 9

Lunch Pot Roast

Prep time: 10 minutes | *Cooking time:* 60 minutes | *Servings:* 4

Ingredients:
- 1-pound beef chuck pot roast, chopped
- 1 cup turnip, chopped
- 1 cup zucchini, chopped
- 1 garlic clove, diced
- 1 teaspoon salt
- 1 teaspoon coconut aminos
- 1 teaspoon ground black pepper
- 1 teaspoon butter
- 2 cups of water

Directions:
Put all ingredients in the instant pot and close the lid. Set meat mode and cook the meal for 60 minutes. When the time is over, open the lid and stir the ingredients carefully with the help of the spoon.

Nutrition value/serving: calories 269, fat 10.5, fiber 1.1, carbs 3.6, protein 38.2

Green Beans with Ham

Prep time: 10 minutes | Cooking time: 6 minutes | Servings: 3

Ingredients:
- 2 cups green beans, chopped
- 7 oz ham, chopped
- ½ white onion, chopped
- 1 teaspoon olive oil
- ½ teaspoon salt
- ½ teaspoon ground nutmeg
- 1 cup water, for cooking

Directions:

Pour water and insert the steamer rack in the instant pot. Place the green bean, ham, and onion in the rack and close the lid. Cook the ingredients on steam mode for 6 minutes. Then make a quick pressure release and transfer the ingredients in the big bowl. Sprinkle them with ground nutmeg, salt, and olive oil. Stir well.

Nutrition value/serving: calories 153, fat 7.5, fiber 3.8, carbs 9.7, protein 12.5

Spiral Ham

Prep time: 10 minutes | Cooking time: 12 minutes | Servings: 5

Ingredients:
- 1-pound spiral ham, sliced
- 1 tablespoon Erythritol
- 2 tablespoons butter, melted
- ½ teaspoon minced ginger
- 1 teaspoon mustard
- 1 cup water, for cooking

Directions:

In the shallow bowl combine together Erythritol, butter, minced ginger, and mustard. Then pour water and insert the trivet in the instant pot. Line the trivet with foil. Brush the spiral ham with butter mixture generously and transfer the ham in the instant pot. Cook the ham on manual mode (high pressure) for 12 minutes. When the time is over, make a quick pressure release and open the lid. Place the cooked spiral ham in the serving plate.

Nutrition value/serving: calories 237, fat 16.6, fiber 0.1, carbs 7.6, protein 17.3

Coconut Soup

Prep time: 10 minutes | Cooking time: 13 minutes | Servings: 4

Ingredients:
- 2 cups of coconut milk
- 2 cups of water
- 1 teaspoon dried lemongrass
- 1 tablespoon lemon juice
- 1 teaspoon curry paste
- ½ cup white mushrooms, chopped
- 1 teaspoon butter

Directions:

Melt the butter in sauté mode. Add mushrooms and sauté them for 3 minutes. Then stir the vegetables and add lemongrass, lemon juice, and curry paste. Add water and coconut milk. Stir the mixture until the curry paste is dissolved. Close the lid and cook the soup on soup mode for 10 minutes.

Nutrition value/serving: calories 296, fat 30.4, fiber 2.8, carbs 7.5, protein 3.1

Corned Beef with Cabbage

Prep time: 10 minutes | *Cooking time:* 43 minutes | *Servings:* 2

Ingredients:
- 10 oz corned beef
- ½ teaspoon ground nutmeg
- ¼ teaspoon ground black pepper
- ¼ teaspoon ground paprika
- ¾ teaspoon salt
- 1 teaspoon dried cilantro
- 1 cup chicken broth
- 1 cup cabbage, chopped
- 1 teaspoon butter

Directions:
Rub the corned beef with ground nutmeg, ground black pepper, ground paprika, salt, and dried cilantro. Place the meat in the instant pot. Add chicken broth and cook it on manual mode (high pressure) for 40 minutes. When the time is over, make a quick pressure release and open the lid. Shred the corned beef with the help of the fork and add chopped cabbage and butter. Cook the meal on manual (high pressure) for 3 minutes more. When the time is over, make a quick pressure release. Stir the cooked meal well.

Nutrition value/serving: calories 290, fat 20.6, fiber 1.2, carbs 3.1, protein 22

Lazy Meat Mix

Prep time: 10 minutes | *Cooking time:* 45 minutes | *Servings:* 2

Ingredients:
- 3 oz chicken fillet, chopped
- 4 oz pork chops, chopped
- 4 oz beef sirloin, chopped
- 1 onion, chopped
- 1 teaspoon tomato paste
- 1 teaspoon dried rosemary
- 1 cup of water
- ½ teaspoon salt
- 1 teaspoon olive oil

Directions:
Preheat the olive oil on sauté mode. Then add chicken, pork chops, and beef sirloin. Add onion and cook the ingredients for 3 minutes. Then stir them well and add tomato paste, dried rosemary, water, and salt. Stir it well until tomato paste is dissolved. Then close the lid and cook the meat mix on meat mode for 40 minutes.

Nutrition value/serving: calories 414, fat 23.3, fiber 1.6, carbs 6, protein 43

Shredded Chicken Salad

Prep time: 10 minutes | *Cooking time:* 12 minutes | *Servings:* 4

Ingredients:
- 9 oz Chinese cabbage, shredded
- 10 oz chicken fillet
- ½ teaspoon lemon juice
- ¼ cup heavy cream
- 1 teaspoon white pepper
- ½ cup of water
- ½ teaspoon salt
- ½ teaspoon ground turmeric
- ¼ teaspoon dried sage
- 1 tablespoon cream cheese
- 1 tablespoon sour cream
- ½ teaspoon dried dill

Directions:
Rub the chicken fillet with white pepper, salt, ground turmeric, and dried sage. Place it in the instant pot. Add water and heavy cream. Close and seal the lid. Cook the chicken on manual mode (high pressure) for 12 minutes. Then make a quick pressure release. Remove the chicken fillet from the instant pot and shred it. Put the shredded chicken in the salad bowl. Add sour cream and cream cheese in the instant pot (to the cream mixture). Then add dill and stir it. Sprinkle the salad with lemon juice and ½ of the cream mixture from the instant pot. Mix up the salad well.

Nutrition value/serving: calories 187, fat 9.7, fiber 0.9, carbs 2.4, protein 22

Beef Curry Soup

Prep time: 10 minutes | *Cooking time:* 30 minutes | *Servings:* 4

Ingredients:
- 1-pound beef sirloin, chopped
- 1 teaspoon curry powder
- 1 cup of coconut milk
- 3 cups of water
- 1 cup snap beans
- ½ teaspoon salt
- ½ teaspoon paprika
- 1 chili pepper, chopped
- 1 tablespoon coconut oil
- 1 white onion, diced

Directions:
Mix up together beef sirloin with curry powder, salt, and paprika. Then put coconut oil in the instant pot and heat it up on sauté mode for 2 minutes. Add beef sirloin and cook it on sauté mode for 10 minutes. Stir it from time to time. After this, add water and coconut milk. Add chili pepper and close the lid. Cook the soup on manual mode (high pressure) for 15 minutes. Then make a quick pressure release and open the lid. Add snap beans and onion. Cook the soup for 2 minutes more on manual mode (high pressure). Then make a quick pressure release.

Nutrition value/serving: calories 403, fat 25, fiber 3.2, carbs 8.9, protein 36.8

Pork Roast with Sauerkraut

Prep time: 15 minutes | *Cooking time:* 35 minutes | *Servings:* 3

Ingredients:
- 2 bacon slices, chopped
- 10 oz pork roast, chopped
- 1 cup sauerkraut
- 1 teaspoon avocado oil
- ½ teaspoon ground turmeric
- ½ teaspoon ground thyme
- ½ teaspoon ground coriander
- 1 cup of water
- 1 bay leaf

Directions:
Heat up avocado oil on sauté mode. Add pork roast and sprinkle it with ground turmeric, thyme, and coriander. Cook the meat for 5 minutes. Stir it from time to time. After this, add bacon, bay leaf, water, and sauerkraut. Close and seal the lid. Cook the meal on manual mode (high pressure) for 30 minutes. Then allow the natural pressure release for 10 minutes.

Nutrition value/serving: calories 277, fat 14.5, fiber 1.6, carbs 2.7, protein 32.1

Cheesy Pork Rinds

Prep time: 5 minutes | *Cooking time:* 8 minutes | *Servings:* 3

Ingredients:
- 4 oz pork rinds
- 1 teaspoon olive oil
- 2 tablespoons cream cheese
- ¾ cup heavy cream
- 1 oz Parmesan, grated
- 1 teaspoon ground paprika

Directions:
Pour olive oil in the instant pot. Add pork rinds and cook them for 2-3 minutes on sauté mode. Then stir the pork rinds and add cream cheese and heavy cream. Sprinkle the ingredients with ground paprika and cook for 3 minutes. After this, add Parmesan. Close the lid and cook the meal for 2 minutes more on sauté mode or until the cheese is melted.

Nutrition value/serving: calories 389, fat 30.6, fiber 0.3, carbs 1.8, protein 28.6

Manhattan Chowder

Prep time: 10 minutes | *Cooking time:* 11 minutes | *Servings:* 2

Ingredients:
- ½ onion, diced
- 2 oz celery stalk, chopped
- 2 oz turnip, chopped
- 1 can clams
- 1 teaspoon butter
- 2 oz pancetta, chopped
- ¼ cup tomatoes, canned
- 2 cups chicken broth
- 1 teaspoon cayenne pepper
- ½ teaspoon ground turmeric
- ½ teaspoon salt

Directions:
Melt butter in sauté mode and add celery stalk and onion. Cook the vegetables for 5 minutes. Stir them constantly. After this, add pancetta, cayenne pepper, salt, and ground turmeric. Cook the ingredients on sauté mode for 2 minutes more. Add turnip, clams with juice, canned tomatoes, and chicken broth. Close the lid and cook the chowder for 4 minutes on manual mode (high pressure). When the time is over, make a quick pressure release.

Nutrition value/serving: calories 187, fat 10.4, fiber 1.7, carbs 11.6, protein 11.3

Ancho Chili

Prep time: 10 minutes | *Cooking time:* 5 minutes | *Servings:* 2

Ingredients:
- 7 oz anchovies, canned
- 1 teaspoon coconut oil
- 1 jalapeno pepper, chopped
- 1 tomato, chopped
- 1 teaspoon dried oregano
- ¼ teaspoon salt
- ¼ cup of water

Directions:
Melt butter in sauté mode and add tomato and chopped jalapeno pepper. After this, sprinkle the ingredients with dried oregano and salt. Cook them on sauté mode for 2 minutes. Then add anchovies and water. Stir well. Cook the chili on manual mode (high pressure) for 3 minutes. Then allow the natural pressure release for 10 minutes.

Nutrition value/serving: calories 238, fat 12.1, fiber 0.9, carbs 2.1, protein 29.1

Seafood Soup

Prep time: 5 minutes | *Cooking time:* 5 minutes | *Servings:* 2

Ingredients:
- 3 oz shrimps, peeled
- 4 oz salmon fillet, chopped
- 1 teaspoon ground thyme
- ½ teaspoon dried rosemary
- 1 teaspoon olive oil
- 1 teaspoon chives, chopped
- 1 banana pepper, chopped
- ½ cup of coconut milk
- ¼ teaspoon salt
- 1 tablespoon cream cheese
- 1 cup of water

Directions:
Put the salmon fillet in the instant pot. Add olive oil and cook the fish on sauté mode for 1 minute from each side. Then add shrimps, ground thyme, dried rosemary, banana pepper, coconut milk, salt, cream cheese, and water. Close the seal the lid. Cook the soup on manual mode (high pressure) for 3 minutes. Then make a quick pressure release. Top the cooked soup with chives.

Nutrition value/serving: calories 322, fat 22.8, fiber 2.5, carbs 9.1, protein 23.1

Tuscan Soup

Prep time: 10 minutes | *Cooking time:* 15 minutes | *Servings:* 4

Ingredients:
- 1 oz bacon, chopped
- 5 oz sausages, chopped
- ½ carrot, chopped
- ½ onion, chopped
- 1 bell pepper, chopped
- ½ cup cauliflower, chopped
- ½ teaspoon dried basil
- ½ teaspoon salt
- ½ teaspoon dried thyme
- 1 cup kale, chopped
- ½ cup heavy cream
- 2 cups chicken broth

Directions:
Put bacon and sausages in the instant pot. Cook the ingredients on sauté mode for 6 minutes. Stir them from time to time. Then add carrot, onion, bell pepper, cauliflower, dried basil, salt, dried thyme, and heavy cream. Add chicken broth and close the lid. Cook the soup on manual (high pressure) for 4 minutes When the time is over, make a quick pressure release and open the lid. Add kale and stir the soup. Cook it on sauté mode for 5 minutes more.

Nutrition value/serving: calories 259, fat 19.4, fiber 1.5, carbs 7.8, 13.5

Winter Soup

Prep time: 7 minutes | *Cooking time:* 35 minutes | *Servings:* 2

Ingredients:
- 1 cup white mushrooms, chopped
- 3 oz turnip, chopped
- ½ cup cabbage, shredded
- 8 oz pork sirloin, chopped
- ½ teaspoon salt
- ½ teaspoon cayenne pepper
- ½ teaspoon dried sage
- 2 cup of water
- ½ cup heavy cream

Directions:
Put mushrooms and cream in the instant pot. Add dried sage, cayenne pepper, and salt. Cook the ingredients for 5 minutes on sauté mode. Add chopped pork sirloin, cabbage, turnip, and water. Close the lid and cook the meal on soup mode for 30 minutes.

Nutrition value/serving: calories 348, fat 18.9, fiber 1.8, carbs 6.1, protein 37.7

Reuben Soup

Prep time: 10 minutes | *Cooking time:* 35 minutes | *Servings:* 6

Ingredients:
- 6 cups chicken broth
- ½ white onion, diced
- 1 teaspoon garlic, diced
- 1 tablespoon ghee
- 1 1/2-pound corned beef, chopped
- 2 cups sauerkraut
- ½ teaspoon fennel seeds
- ½ teaspoon dried thyme
- ½ teaspoon mustard seeds
- ¼ cup heavy cream
- ½ cup Cheddar cheese

Directions:
Put the ghee in the instant pot and melt it on sauté mode. Then add diced onion and brown it for 3-4 minutes. Then add diced garlic, fennel seeds, dried thyme, and mustard seeds. Add heavy cream and stir it. Then add corned beef, sauerkraut, and chicken broth. Close the lid and cook the soup on manual mode (high pressure) for 30 minutes. Then make a quick pressure release and open the lid. Add cheddar cheese and stir it until the cheese is melted. Ladle the hot soup in the serving bowls.

Nutrition value/serving: calories 320, fat 22.8, fiber1.7, carbs 4.5, protein 23.2

Avocado Chicken Salad

Prep time: 15 minutes | *Cooking time:* 10 minutes | *Servings:* 4

Ingredients:
- 2 cups Lettuce Iceberg, chopped
- 1 avocado, pitted, peeled
- 9 oz chicken fillet
- ½ teaspoon salt
- ½ teaspoon ground nutmeg
- 1 teaspoon lemon juice
- ¼ teaspoon lemon zest
- 1 teaspoon sesame oil
- ¼ teaspoon dried dill
- ¼ cup cream, whipped
- 1 teaspoon dried oregano
- ¼ teaspoon Pink salt
- 1 cup water, for cooking

Directions:
Rub the chicken fillet with salt, ground nutmeg, lemon juice, lemon zest, and sesame oil. After this, pour the water in the instant pot and insert the steamer rack Place the chicken fillet on the rack and close the lid. Cook the chicken on Manual mode (high pressure) for 12 minutes. When the time is over, allow the natural pressure release for 10 minutes. After this, remove the chicken fillet from the instant pot and cool it till the room temperature. Meanwhile, chop the avocado into the cubes and put it in the big bowl. Add chopped lettuce. Then make salad dressing: in the shallow bowl mix up together Pink salt, dried oregano, whipped cream, and dried dill. Shred the chicken with the help of 2 forks and transfer it in the avocado bowl. Then sprinkle the salad with whipped cream dressing. With the help of the spoon mix up the salad.

Nutrition value/serving: calories 250, fat 16.7, fiber 3.8, carbs 6.1, protein 19.7

Lettuce Chicken Salad

Prep time: 10 minutes | *Cooking time:* 10 minutes | *Servings:* 2

Ingredients:
- ½ cup radish, sliced
- 7 oz chicken thighs, skinless, boneless
- ¼ cup fresh cilantro, chopped
- 1 cup lettuce, torn
- 1 tablespoon olive oil
- ½ teaspoon salt
- ¼ teaspoon chili flakes
- ½ teaspoon ground black pepper
- 1 tablespoon ghee

Directions:
Sprinkle the chicken thighs with ground black pepper. Then heat up the instant pot on sauté mode for 3 minutes. Add ghee and melt it. Add chicken thighs and sauté them for 5 minutes from each side. Meanwhile, in the salad bowl combine together cilantro, lettuce, and radish. When the chicken thighs are cooked, cool them to the room temperature and chop roughly. Add the chopped chicken in the salad bowl. Shake the salad. Then sprinkle it with salt, chili flakes, and olive oil. Mix up the salad before serving.

Nutrition value/serving: calories 315, fat 20.8, fiber 0.8, carbs 2.2, protein 29.2

Zuppa Toscana

Prep time: 10 minutes | *Cooking time:* 20 minutes | *Servings:* 4

Ingredients:
- ½ cup ground beef
- 3 oz beef sausages, chopped
- 1/3 white onion, diced
- 1 garlic clove, diced
- 4 cups chicken broth
- ½ cup cauliflower, chopped
- ¼ cup of organic almond milk
- 1/3 teaspoon chili flakes
- ½ teaspoon salt
- 1 teaspoon butter

Directions:
Put ground beef, beef sausages, and butter in the instant pot. Set sauté mode and cook the ingredients for 10 minutes. Stir them from time to time with the help of the spatula. Then add diced onion and garlic clove. Mix up the mixture and sauté it for 5 minutes more. After this, add chicken broth, cauliflower, almond milk, chili flakes, and salt. Mix up the soup and close the lid. Cook Zuppa Toscana for 5 minutes on Manual mode (high pressure). Then make a quick pressure release. Let the cooked soup cool for 5-10 minutes before serving.

Nutrition value/serving: calories 175, fat 12.3, fiber 0.5, carbs 3.8, protein 11.5

Broccoli Soup

Prep time: 10 minutes | Cooking time: 25 minutes | Servings: 3

Ingredients:
- 1 ½ cup broccoli florets
- 2 cups chicken broth
- 1 white onion, diced
- ½ teaspoon ground black pepper
- 1/3 cup heavy cream
- ¼ teaspoon salt
- 1 cup Cheddar cheese, shredded
- ½ teaspoon butter

Directions:
Set sauté mode for 10 minutes. Place butter in the instant pot and melt it. Then add white onion and cook it until light brown. Stir it from time to time. After this, add broccoli florets, chicken broth, salt, ground black pepper, and Cheddar cheese. Close the lid and cook soup on manual mode (high pressure) for 8 minutes. When the time is over, make a quick pressure release and open the lid. Put the ½ cup of cooked broccoli in the food processor. Add heavy cream. Blend the broccoli until smooth. Add the cream-broccoli liquid in the soup. Cook the soup on sauté mode for 5 minutes more.

Nutrition value/serving: calories 260, fat 19.2, fiber 2.1, carbs 8.1, protein 14.6

Low Carb Zucchini and Eggplant Soup

Prep time: 10 minutes | Cooking time: 16 minutes | Servings: 3

Ingredients:
- 1 zucchini, chopped
- 1 eggplant, chopped
- ¼ teaspoon dried rosemary
- ¼ teaspoon salt
- ½ cup coconut cream
- 1 cup beef broth
- 1 teaspoon coconut oil
- ½ teaspoon ground paprika

Directions:
Place the zucchini and eggplant in the mixing bowl. Sprinkle the vegetables with dried rosemary and salt. Shake well and leave to rest for 10 minutes. After this, remove the vegetables from the bowl (leave the eggplant juice in the bowl) and transfer it in the instant pot. Add coconut oil. Cook the vegetables on sauté mode for 6 minutes. Stir them well after 3 minutes of cooking. Then add beef broth, coconut cream, and ground paprika. Close the lid. Cook the soup on soup mode for 10 minutes.

Nutrition value/serving: calories 168, fat 12, fiber 7.2 carbs 14, protein 4.9

Side Dishes

Cauliflower Mac&Cheese
Prep time: 15 minutes | Cooking time: 5 minutes | Servings: 4

Ingredients:
- 2 cups cauliflower, shredded
- ½ cup Provolone cheese, grated
- 1 tablespoon cream cheese
- ¼ cup of coconut milk
- ¼ teaspoon salt
- ½ teaspoon white pepper

Directions:
Put shredded cauliflower in the instant pot bowl. Top it with Provolone cheese. After this, in the mixing bowl combine together cream cheese, coconut milk, salt, and white pepper. Pour the liquid over the cheese and close the lid. Cook the side dish on manual mode (high pressure) for 5 minutes. When the time is over, allow the natural pressure release for 5 minutes more. Broil the surface of the cooked meal with the help of the kitchen torch.

Nutrition value/serving: calories 114, fat 8.9, fiber 1.7, carbs 4.1, protein 5.8

Brussels Sprouts Casserole
Prep time: 10 minutes | Cooking time: 4 hours

Ingredients:
- 1 cup Brussels sprouts, halved
- ½ cup heavy cream
- ½ teaspoon ground black pepper
- ½ cup mushrooms, sliced
- 1 teaspoon salt
- 1 oz Monterey Jack cheese, shredded

Directions:
In the mixing bowl combine together cheese with heavy cream, salt, and ground black pepper. Place the Brussel sprouts in the instant pot in one layer. Then top it with sliced mushrooms. Pour the heavy cream mixture over the mushrooms and close the lid. Cook the casserole on manual mode (low pressure) for 4 hours.

Nutrition value/serving: calories 120, fat 10.4, fiber 1.3, carbs 3.9, protein 4.1

Rosemary&Butter Mushrooms
Prep time: 5 minutes | Cooking time: 7 minutes | Servings: 2

Ingredients:
- 8 oz white mushrooms, chopped
- 1 teaspoon dried rosemary
- 2 tablespoons butter
- ½ teaspoon salt
- 1 cup chicken broth
- ¼ cup of coconut milk
- ½ teaspoon dried oregano

Directions:
Put mushrooms and butter in the instant pot and cook them on sauté mode for 4 minutes. Then add chicken broth, dried oregano, salt, and coconut milk Close the lid and cook the side dish on manual mode (high pressure) for 3 minutes. When the time is over, make a quick pressure release. Serve the mushrooms with coconut-butter gravy.

Nutrition value/serving: calories 182, fat 13, fiber 3.4, carbs 9.8, protein 10.2

Bacon Brussels Sprouts

Prep time: 10 minutes | *Cooking time:* 10 minutes | *Servings:* 6

Ingredients:
- 12 oz Brussels sprouts
- 3oz leek, chopped
- 2 oz bacon, chopped
- 1 teaspoon avocado oil
- ½ teaspoon salt
- 1 cup water, for cooking

Directions:
Pour water and insert the steamer rack in the instant pot. Then trim Brussel sprouts and cut them into halves. Arrange the vegetables in the steamer rack and cook on high pressure for 3 minutes Then make a quick pressure release. Remove the Brussel sprouts from the instant pot. Clean the instant pot and rid of the steamer rack. Put bacon in the instant pot. Add avocado oil and cook the ingredients on sauté mode for 4 minutes. Stir them halfway of cooking. Then add leek and cook the mixture for 2 minutes more. Add the Brussel sprouts, mix up well and sauté the meal for 1 minute.

Nutrition value/serving: calories 85, fat 4.3, fiber 2.4, carbs 7.3, protein 5.7

Spinach Mash with Bacon

Prep time: 10 minutes | *Cooking time:* 8 minutes | *Servings:* 3

Ingredients:
- 1 oz bacon, chopped, cooked
- 1 cup spinach, chopped
- 1 tablespoon cream cheese
- ¼ teaspoon minced garlic
- ¼ cup Provolone cheese, grated
- ¼ cup heavy cream
- ¼ cup onion, diced
- ½ teaspoon white pepper
- 1 teaspoon cayenne pepper
- ½ teaspoon salt
- 1 cup water, for cooking

Directions:
Put all ingredients in the instant pot baking pan. Pour water and insert the trivet in the instant pot. Place the baking pan with spinach mixture in the instant pot. Cook the dip on manual (high pressure) 8 minutes. When the time is over, allow the natural pressure release for 10 minutes and open the lid. Mix up the spinach mash carefully with the help of the spoon.

Nutrition value/serving: calories 145, fat 11.9, fiber 0.7, carbs 2.7, protein 7.3

Mashed Cauliflower

Prep time: 10 minutes | *Cooking time:* 4 minutes | *Servings:* 1

Ingredients:
- 1 cup cauliflower, chopped
- ¼ teaspoon salt
- 1 tablespoon butter
- 1 cup water, for cooking

Directions:
Pour water and insert the steamer rack in the instant pot. Place the chopped cauliflower on the rack and close the lid. Cook the vegetables for 4 minutes on Steam mode. When the time is over, make a quick pressure release. Transfer the cooked cauliflower in the bowl. Add butter and salt. With the help of the potato masher mash the vegetables until smooth. Add ¼ cup of water from the instant pot. If the mash is not soft enough – add more water. Mix up the mashed cauliflower well.

Nutrition value/serving: calories 127, fat 11.6, fiber 2.5, carbs 5.3, protein 2.1

Fried Cauliflower Slices

Prep time: 10 minutes | Cooking time: 5 minutes | Servings: 3

Ingredients:
- 9 oz cauliflower head, trimmed
- 1 teaspoon ground nutmeg
- ½ teaspoon ground paprika
- ½ teaspoon ground turmeric
- ½ teaspoon dried oregano
- 1 tablespoon lemon juice
- 1 tablespoon avocado oil
- ¼ teaspoon minced garlic
- 1 tablespoon heavy cream
- 1 cup water, for cooking

Directions:
Slice the cauliflower into the steaks. Then pour water in the instant pot. Insert the steamer rack. Place the cauliflower steaks on the rack and close the lid. Cook the vegetables on manual mode (high pressure) for 2 minutes. Then make a quick pressure release. Remove the cauliflower steaks and clean the instant pot. In the shallow bowl combine together ground nutmeg, paprika, turmeric, oregano, lemon juice, avocado oil, minced garlic, and heavy cream. Carefully brush the cauliflower slices with spice mixture from both side and place in the instant pot in one layer. Cook the cauliflower on sauté mode for 1 minute from each side or until it light brown. Repeat the same steps with remaining cauliflower slices.

Nutrition value/serving: calories 53, fat 3, fiber 2.8, carbs 6.1, protein 2

Mashed Brussel Sprouts

Prep time: 10 minutes | Cooking time: 5 minutes | Servings: 4

Ingredients:
- 2 cups Brussel sprouts
- ½ teaspoon onion powder
- ¼ cup heavy cream, hot
- ¼ teaspoon salt
- 1 cup water, for cooking

Directions:
Pour water and insert the steamer rack in the instant pot. Place the Brussel sprouts in the rack and cook it on manual mode (high pressure) for 5 minutes. When the time is over, make a quick pressure release. Transfer the cooked vegetables in the food processor. Add cream, salt, and onion powder. Blend the mixture until is smooth. Put the cooked mashed Brussel sprouts in the bowls. It is recommended to serve the side dish warm or hot.

Nutrition value/serving: calories 46, fat 2.9, fiber 1.7, carbs 4.5, protein 1.7

Cauliflower Rice

Prep time: 2 minutes | Cooking time: 1 minute | Servings: 2

Ingredients:
- 1 cup cauliflower, shredded
- 5 oz chicken broth

Directions:
Put cauliflower and chicken broth in the instant pot. Set manual mode (high pressure) and cook cauliflower for 1 minute. Then make a quick pressure release. Add salt and ground black pepper if desired.

Nutrition value/serving: calories 24, fat 0.5, fiber 1.3, carbs 2.9, protein 2.4

Soft Spinach with Dill

Prep time: 5 minutes | Cooking time: 10 minutes | Servings: 2

Ingredients:
- 2 cup fresh spinach, chopped
- 1 teaspoon avocado oil
- 1 tablespoon fresh dill, chopped
- 1 teaspoon lemon juice
- ¼ teaspoon salt
- 1 teaspoon butter
- ¼ teaspoon onion powder

Directions:
Set instant pot on sauté mode and adjust 10 minutes. Pour avocado oil and add chopped spinach. Sprinkle the greens with dill, lemon juice, salt, and onion powder. Add butter. Stir the spinach every 2 minutes.

Nutrition value/serving: calories 32, fat 2.4, fiber 1, carbs 2.4, protein 1.3

Mexican Style Keto Rice

Prep time: 5 minutes | Cooking time: 4 minutes | Servings: 5

Ingredients:
- 3 cups cauliflower, shredded
- ½ teaspoon taco seasonings
- ⅕ teaspoon garlic powder
- 1 teaspoon lime juice
- 1 teaspoon dried cilantro
- 1 bell pepper, diced
- 2 cups chicken broth
- ½ teaspoon salt

Directions:
In the shallow bowl combine together taco seasonings, garlic powder, salt, and dried cilantro. Then put shredded cauliflower in the instant pot bowl. Add spice mixture. After this, add lime juice, bell pepper, and chicken broth. Gently mix up the vegetables with the help of the spoon. Close the lid of the instant pot and cook the meal on manual (high pressure) for 4 minutes. When the time is over, make a quick pressure release. Stir the side dish well.

Nutrition value/serving: calories 42, fat 0.7, fiber 1.9, carbs 6.2, protein 3.4

Kale&Parmesan Bowl

Prep time: 5 minutes | Cooking time: 10 minutes | Servings: 3

Ingredients:
- 3 pecans
- 7 oz curly kale, chopped
- 2 oz Parmesan, grated
- 2 tablespoon cream cheese

Directions:
Put the pecans in the grinder and grind until you get smooth mass. Then mix up together grinded pecans with cream cheese. Heat up the instant pot on sauté mode for 2 minutes. Add cream cheese mixture and kale. Cook the ingredients for 4 minutes. Stir them halfway of cooking. Then add cheese. Cook the meal for 4 minutes more or until the kale is tender.

Nutrition value/serving: calories 214, fat 17, fiber 3.9, carbs 8.7, protein 10.9

White Cabbage in Cream

Prep time: 5 minutes | Cooking time: 7 hours | Servings: 4

Ingredients:
- 12 oz white cabbage, roughly chopped
- 1 cup cream
- 1 tablespoon cream cheese
- 1 teaspoon salt
- 1 teaspoon chili powder

Directions:
Put all ingredients in the instant pot bowl and close the lid. Cook the vegetables for 7 minutes on manual mode (high pressure). When the time is over, make a quick pressure release. Open the instant pot lid and stir the cooked side dish well.

Nutrition value/serving: calories 71, fat 4.4, fiber 2.4, carbs 7.2, protein 1.8

Cauliflower Cheese

Prep time: 5 minutes | *Cooking time:* 15 minutes | *Servings:* 2

Ingredients:
- ½ cup cauliflower, cut into florets
- ½ teaspoon dried dill
- ¼ teaspoon dried cilantro
- ¼ teaspoon dried sage
- 3 oz Parmesan, grated
- ¼ cup of organic almond milk

Directions:
Put cauliflower in the instant pot bowl. Sprinkle it with dried dill, cilantro, and sage. In the separated bowl mix up together almond milk and Parmesan. Pour the liquid over the cauliflower and close the lid. Cook the meal on sauté mode for 15 minutes. Stir the cauliflower every 5 minutes to avoid burning.

Nutrition value/serving: calories 164, fat 10.7, fiber 1.2, carbs 4, protein 14.7

Cauli-Tatoes

Prep time: 10 minutes | *Cooking time:* 5 minutes | *Servings:* 2

Ingredients:
- 1 teaspoon cream cheese
- ½ teaspoon salt
- ½ teaspoon ground turmeric
- ½ teaspoon white pepper
- 2 cups cauliflower
- ½ teaspoon garlic powder
- 1 cup water, for cooking

Directions:
Pour water and insert the trivet in the instant pot. Put the cauliflower on the trivet and cook it for 5 minutes on steam mode. Then make a quick pressure release. Open the lid and transfer cooked cauliflower in the food processor. Add salt, ground turmeric, cream cheese, white pepper, and garlic powder. Then add ¾ cup of the remaining water from the instant pot. Blend the mixture until it is smooth (appx for 3-5 minutes).

Nutrition value/serving: calories 36, fat 0.8, fiber 2.8, carbs 6.6, protein 2.3

Butter Spaghetti Squash

Prep time: 10 minutes | *Cooking time:* 6 minutes | *Servings:* 3

Ingredients:
- 2 cups spaghetti squash, cubed
- 2 tablespoons butter
- ½ teaspoon salt
- 1 cup water, for cooking

Directions:
Pour water and insert the steamer rack in the instant pot. Arrange the spaghetti squash cubes in the instant pot and cook them on manual mode (high pressure) for 6 minutes. Then make a quick pressure release and open the lid. Transfer the cooked squash cube sin the serving plates and top them with butter and salt. Wait till butter and salt dissolve.

Nutrition value/serving: calories 89, fat 2, fiber 8.1, carbs 4.7, protein 0.5

Sliced Zucchini Casserole

Prep time: 10 minutes | Cooking time: 5 minutes | Servings: 4

Ingredients:
- 2 zucchini, sliced
- 1 tomato, sliced
- ½ cup kohlrabi, chopped
- ½ cup chicken broth
- 1 teaspoon salt
- 1 teaspoon ground paprika
- 1 tablespoon nuts, chopped
- ½ cup Mozzarella, chopped
- ½ teaspoon sesame oil

Directions:

Brush the instant pot bowl with sesame oil. Place the zucchini slices in the instant pot. Then top them with sliced tomato and chopped kohlrabi. After this, mix up together chicken broth, salt, and ground paprika. Pour the liquid over the ingredients. Then sprinkle the casserole mixture with nuts and Mozzarella. Close the lid and cook the casserole on High pressure (manual mode) for 5 minutes. When the time is over, make a quick pressure release. Cool the cooked casserole to the room temperature.

Nutrition value/serving: calories 57, fat 2.8, fiber 2.3, carbs 6, protein 3.7

Green Beans Casserole

Prep time: 10 minutes | Cooking time: 20 minutes | Servings: 6

Ingredients:
- 1-pound green beans, chopped
- 1 cup button mushrooms, chopped
- 1 garlic clove, diced
- ½ white onion, diced
- 1 teaspoon butter
- 1/3 cup heavy cream
- ½ teaspoon salt
- 2 tablespoons almond meal
- 1 teaspoon Italian seasonings
- 1 teaspoon coconut oil, melted

Directions:

Toss butter in the instant pot and melt it on sauté mode. Add onion and cook it for 2 minutes. Then stir it and add mushrooms. Cook the mixture for 2 minutes more. Stir the ingredients again and add garlic clove, green beans, and salt. Mix up well. In the mixing bowl combine together coconut oil, Italian seasonings, almond meal, and cream. Pour the liquid over the casserole mixture and close the lid. Cook it on sauté mode for 16 minutes.

Nutrition value/serving: calories 79, fat 5.2, fiber 3.2, carbs 7.5, protein 2.5\

Squash Casserole

Prep time: 10 minutes | Cooking time: 5 minutes | Servings: 3

Ingredients:
- 7 oz spaghetti squash, chopped
- 1 zucchini, grated
- ½ cup Cheddar cheese
- 1 tablespoon cream cheese
- ½ teaspoon salt
- 1 teaspoon ground black pepper
- 1 cup water, for cooking

Directions:

Make the layer of spaghetti squash in the baking pan and top it with grated zucchini. After this, sprinkle the zucchini with Cheddar cheese. In the mixing bowl combine together cream cheese, salt, and ground black pepper. Spread the mixture over the Cheddar cheese. Pour water and insert the trivet in the instant pot. Place the baking pan with casserole in the instant pot and cook it on manual mode (high pressure) for 6 minutes. Then make a quick pressure release. Let the cooked casserole rest for 10 minutes before serving.

Nutrition value/serving: calories 120, fat 7.9, fiber 0.9, carbs 7.5, protein 6.2

Cheesy Zucchini Strips

Prep time: 10 minutes | *Cooking time:* 8 minutes | *Servings:* 2

Ingredients:
- 1 zucchini, trimmed
- 1/3 cup Mozzarella, shredded
- 1 teaspoon avocado oil
- 1 tablespoon almond meal
- ¼ teaspoon salt

Directions:
Cut the zucchini into the strips and sprinkle them with salt and almond meal. Then heat up the instant pot on sauté mode for 2-3 minutes. Add avocado oil. Arrange the zucchini strips in one layer in the instant pot and cook them for 2 minutes from each side or until they are light brown. Repeat the same steps with remaining zucchini strips (if you use small instant and can't arrange all vegetables per one time of cooking). Then top the cooked zucchini strips with Mozzarella and close the lid. Cook the side dish on sauté mode for 3 minutes or until the cheese is melted.

Nutrition value/serving: calories 49, fat 2.8, fiber 1.6, carbs 4.2, protein 3.2

Turmeric Cabbage Rice

Prep time: 10 minutes | *Cooking time:* 35 minutes | *Servings:* 5

Ingredients:
- 1 ½ cup white cabbage, shredded
- 1 teaspoon salt
- 1 cup of coconut milk
- 1 teaspoon ground turmeric
- 1 white onion, diced
- 1 tablespoon coconut oil

Directions:
In the mixing bowl combine together salt and shredded cabbage. Leave the vegetables for 5 minutes. Meanwhile, heat up the instant pot bowl on sauté mode for 2 minutes. Add coconut oil and diced onion. Cook the onion for 3 minutes. Then stir it with the help of the spatula and add cabbage. After this, in the bowl combine together ground turmeric and coconut milk. When the liquid starts to be yellow, pour it over the cabbage. Stir the cabbage and close the lid. Cook the cabbage rice on sauté mode for 30 minutes. Stir ti from time to time to avoid burning.

Nutrition value/serving: calories 149, fat 14.2, fiber 2.2, carbs 6.2, protein 1.6

Turnip Creamy Gratin

Prep time: 5 minutes | *Cooking time:* 7 minutes | *Servings:* 2

Ingredients:
- 1 cup turnip, sliced
- 1/3 cup heavy cream
- ¼ teaspoon salt
- ¼ teaspoon dried sage
- 1 teaspoon butter
- 1/3 teaspoon garlic powder
- ½ cup Cheddar cheese, shredded

Directions:
Toss butter in the instant pot and melt it on sauté mode (approx.2-3 minutes). Then add sliced turnip and cook it on sauté mode for 1 minute from each side. Sprinkle the vegetables with salt, dried sage, and garlic powder. Then add heavy cream. Top the turnip with Cheddar cheese and close the lid. Cook the meal on manual mode (high pressure) for 3 minutes. Then make a quick pressure release.

Nutrition value/serving: calories 220, fat 18.8, fiber 1.3, carbs 5.5, protein 8.1

Parmesan Onion Rings

Prep time: 10 minutes | Cooking time: 5 minutes | Servings: 4

Ingredients:
- 1 big white onion
- 1 eggs, beaten
- 1 teaspoon cream cheese
- 2 oz Parmesan, grated
- 2 tablespoons almond meal
- 1 tablespoon butter

Directions:
Trim and peel the onion. Then slice it roughly and separate every onion slice into the rings. In the mixing bowl combine together Parmesan and almond meal. Then take a separated bowl and mix up cream cheese and egg in it. Dip the onion rings in the egg mixture and then coat well in cheese mixture. Toss butter in the instant pot and melt it on sauté mode. Then arrange the onion rings in the melted butter in one layer. Cook the onion rings for 2 minutes from each side on sauté mode.

Nutrition value/serving: calories 122, fat 8.8, fiber 1.2, carbs 4.8, protein 7.1

Rosemary Radish Halves

Prep time: 10 minutes | Cooking time: 10 minutes | Servings: 4

Ingredients:
- 3 cups radish, trimmed
- 1 tablespoon olive oil
- 1 teaspoon dried rosemary
- ½ teaspoon salt

Directions:
Cut the radishes into the halves and sprinkle with salt. In the shallow bowl whisk together olive oil and dried rosemary. After this, sprinkle the radish halves with fragrant oil and shake the vegetables well. Transfer the radishes in the instant pot and cook the on sauté mode for 10 minutes. Stir the vegetables every 2 minutes.

Nutrition value/serving: calories 45, fat 3.6, fiber 1.5, carbs 3.2, protein 0.6

Sweet Baby Carrot

Prep time: 10 minutes | Cooking time: 4 minutes | Servings: 4

Ingredients:
- 1 cup baby carrot
- 1 tablespoon Erythritol
- ½ teaspoon dried thyme
- 2 tablespoons butter, melted
- 1 cup water, for cooking

Directions:
Wash the baby carrot carefully and trim if needed. Then pour water in the instant pot and insert the trivet, Put the prepared baby carrots in the baking pan. Add dried thyme, Erythritol, and butter. Mix up the vegetables well and place over the trivet. Close the lid. Cook the carrot for 4 minutes on manual mode (high pressure). When the time is over make a quick pressure release.

Nutrition value/serving: calories 69, fat 5.8, fiber 1.1, carbs 7.8, protein 0.6

Feta and Zucchini Bowl

Prep time: 5 minutes | Cooking time: 3 minutes | Servings: 4

Ingredients:
- 2 zucchini, chopped
- 1 teaspoon olive oil
- ½ teaspoon chili flakes
- ½ teaspoon paprika
- 2 oz Feta, crumbled

Directions:
Place olive oil, zucchini, chili flakes, and paprika in the instant pot. Stir the ingredients gently and close the lid. Cook zucchini on sauté mode for 2 minutes. Then open the lid and mix up them well with the help of the spatula. Keep cooking zucchini for 1 minute more. Transfer the cooked zucchini into the serving bowls and top with feta cheese.

Nutrition value/serving: calories 64, fat 4.4, fiber 1.2, carbs 4, protein 3.2

Herbed Asparagus

Prep time: 5 minutes | Cooking time: 5 minute | Servings: 2

Ingredients:
- 6 oz asparagus, trimmed
- ¼ teaspoon dried thyme
- ¼ teaspoon salt
- ¼ teaspoon ground black pepper
- ¼ teaspoon dried oregano
- ¼ teaspoon ground nutmeg
- 2 tablespoons butter
- ¼ cup chicken broth

Directions:

In the mixing bowl combine together dried thyme, salt, ground black pepper, oregano, and nutmeg. Then put the asparagus in the instant pot. Sprinkle the vegetables with spice mixture. Stir them gently. Then add butter and chicken broth. Close the lid and cook asparagus on manual mode (high pressure) for 5 minutes. Then make the quick pressure release, open the lid, and shake the asparagus gently.

Nutrition value/serving: calories 127, fat 11.9, fiber 2.1, carbs 3.9, protein 2.7

Cheesy Radish

Prep time: 8 minutes | Cooking time: 3 minutes | Servings: 3

Ingredients:
- 1 ½ cup radish, sliced
- ½ teaspoon minced garlic
- 1 teaspoon sesame oil
- ¼ cup Monterey Jack cheese, shredded
- ¼ cup heavy cream
- 1 tablespoon cream cheese

Directions:

Put radish minced garlic, sesame oil, heavy cream, and cream cheese in the instant pot. Mix up the radish mixture well. Then top it with shredded cheese and close the lid. Cook the radish for 3 minutes on Manual mode (high pressure). Then make a quick pressure release.

Nutrition value/serving: calories 105, fat 9.3, fiber 0.9, carbs 2.6, protein 3.2

Turnip Cubes

Prep time: 10 minutes | Cooking time: 3 minutes | Servings: 6

Ingredients:
- 1-pound turnip, cubed
- 1 teaspoon salt
- ½ teaspoon ground black pepper
- 1 teaspoon avocado oil
- 1 cup water, for cooking

Directions:

Pour water and insert the steamer rack in the instant pot. In the mixing bowl mix up together turnip cubes, salt, and ground black pepper. Sprinkle the vegetables with avocado oil and place them in the steamer rack. Close and seal the lid. Cook the turnip on Manual mode (high pressure) for 3 minutes. Then allow the natural pressure release for 5 minutes.

Nutrition value/serving: calories 23, fat 0.2, fiber 1.4, carbs 5, protein 0.7

Cilantro-Kale Salad

Prep time: 10 minutes | Cooking time: 2 minutes | Servings: 2

Ingredients:
- 2 cups kale, chopped
- ½ cup fresh cilantro, chopped
- 1 pecan, chopped
- ½ teaspoon ground paprika
- ¼ teaspoon salt
- 1 tablespoon avocado oil
- 1 cucumber, chopped
- 1 cup water, for cooking

Directions:

Pour water and insert the steamer rack in the instant pot. Place the kale in the steamer. Close and seal the lid. Cook the greens for 2 minutes on Manual mode (high pressure). Then make a quick pressure release and transfer the kale in the salad bowl. Add chopped cilantro, pecan, and cucumber. After this, sprinkle the salad with ground paprika, salt, and avocado oil. Mix up the salad well.

Nutrition value/serving: calories 98, fat 6.2, fiber 3.1, carbs 9.2, protein 3

Cauliflower Gnocchi

Prep time: 15 minutes | Cooking time: 8 minutes | Servings: 6

Ingredients:
- 2 cups cauliflower, boiled
- 1 egg yolk
- ¼ cup coconut flour
- ½ cup almond meal
- 1 tablespoon cream cheese
- 2 oz Parmesan, grated
- 1 teaspoon dried basil
- 2 tablespoons butter

Directions:
Place the boiled cauliflower in the food processor and blend it until smooth. Then add egg yolk, coconut flour, almond meal, cream cheese, and grated Parmesan. Blend the cauliflower mixture for 15 seconds more. Then transfer the mixture on the chopping board and knead it into the ball. Then cut the dough ball into 3 parts. After this, make 3 logs from the dough. Cut the logs into the small gnocchi with the help of the cutter. Toss the butter in the instant pot and melt it for 2 minutes on sauté mode. Add dried basil and bring the butter to boil (it will take around 1 minute). After this, add prepared gnocchi and cook them for 5 minutes. Stir the gnocchi from time to time.

Nutrition value/serving: calories 155, fat 11.7, fiber 3.8, carbs 7.3, protein 7.1

Thyme Purple Cabbage Steaks

Prep time: 10 minutes | Cooking time: 4 minutes | Servings: 4

Ingredients:
- 10 oz purple cabbage
- 1 teaspoon apple cider vinegar
- 1 teaspoon olive oil
- ½ teaspoon salt
- ½ teaspoon lemon juice
- 1 cup water, for cooking

Directions:
Cut the purple cabbage into 4 cabbage steaks. Pour water and insert the steamer rack in the instant pot. Place the cabbage steaks on the rack and close the lid. Cook the vegetables for 4 minutes on Manual mode (high pressure). Then allow the natural pressure release for 5 minutes. Place the cabbage steaks in the serving plates. In the shallow bowl whisk together apple cider vinegar, olive oil, salt, and lemon juice. Sprinkle every cabbage steak with apple cider vinegar mixture.

Nutrition value/serving: calories 28, fat 1.3, fiber 1.8, carbs 4.1, protein 0.9

Smashed Cauliflower with Goat Cheese

Prep time: 15 minutes | Cooking time: 5 minutes | Servings: 3

Ingredients:
- 1 ½ cup cauliflower, chopped
- ½ teaspoon salt
- 2 oz Goat cheese, crumbled
- 1 tablespoon cream cheese
- 1 cup water, for cooking

Directions:
Pour water and insert the steamer rack in the instant pot. Place the cauliflower in the steamer rack and close the lid. Cook the vegetables on manul mode (high pressure) for 5 minutes. Make a quick pressure release. Place the cooked cauliflower in the food processor and blend it until smooth. Transfer the cauliflower into the bowl. Add salt and cream cheese. Mix up the cauliflower mass well. Place the cooked meal on the plate and top with goat cheese.

Nutrition value/serving: calories 110, fat 7.9, fiber 1.3, carbs 3.2, protein 7

Low Carb Fall Vegetables

Prep time: 10 minutes | *Cooking time:* 8 minutes | *Servings:* 5

Ingredients:
- 1 cup mushrooms, chopped
- 1 cup zucchini, chopped
- 1/2 cup bell pepper, chopped
- 1 eggplant, chopped
- 3 tablespoons butter
- ½ teaspoon salt
- 1 teaspoon dried basil
- 1 teaspoon dried thyme
- ½ teaspoon ground black pepper
- ½ teaspoon cayenne pepper
- 1 cup water, for cooking

Directions:
Pour water and insert the trivet in the instant pot. Put all vegetables in the instant pot baking pan. Sprinkle them with salt, dried basil, thyme, ground black pepper, and cayenne pepper. Mix up the vegetables and top with butter. Arrange the baking pan with vegetables in the instant pot. Close the lid and cook the side dish for 8 minutes on Manual mode (high pressure). Make a quick pressure release.

Nutrition value/serving: calories 96, fat 7.2, fiber 4, carbs 7.9, protein 1.9

Steamed Broccoli

Prep time: 10 minutes | *Cooking time:* 1 minute | *Servings:* 2

Ingredients:
- 1 cup broccoli florets
- ½ teaspoon garlic, diced
- ¼ teaspoon salt
- 1 teaspoon sesame oil
- 1 cup water, for cooking

Directions:
Pour water and insert the steamer rack in the instant pot. Place the broccoli florets in the steamer rack and close the lid. Cook the vegetables on Manual mode (high pressure) for 1 minute. Then make a quick pressure release and transfer the cooked broccoli florets in the serving plates. Sprinkle vegetables with garlic, salt, and sesame oil.

Nutrition value/serving: calories 37, fat 2.4, fiber 1.2, carbs 3.3, protein 1.3

Cheddar Tots with Broccoli

Prep time: 10 minutes | *Cooking time:* 5 minutes | *Servings:* 4

Ingredients:
- 1 cup broccoli, shredded
- ¼ cup Cheddar cheese, shredded
- ¼ teaspoon garlic powder
- ¼ teaspoon salt
- 2 tablespoon almond meal
- ¼ teaspoon ground black pepper
- 1 teaspoon coconut oil
- 1 teaspoon dried dill

Directions:
In the mixing bowl combine together shredded broccoli, cheese, garlic powder, salt, almond meal, ground black pepper, and dried dill. Mix up the mixture with the help of the spoon until homogenous. After this, make the small tots from the mixture. Heat up instant pot bowl on sauté mode for 3 minutes. Then toss coconut oil and melt it (appx.1 minute). Then arrange the tots in the instant pot in one layer and cook tots for 1 minute from each side.

Nutrition value/serving: calories 65, fat 5.1, fiber 1, carbs 2.6, protein 3.1

Vegetable Fritters

Prep time: 10 minutes | *Cooking time:* 6 minutes | *Servings:* 4

Ingredients:
- ½ cup turnip, boiled
- ½ cup cauliflower, boiled
- 1 egg, beaten
- 1 teaspoon dried parsley
- 3 tablespoons coconut flour
- 1 teaspoon avocado oil
- 1/3 teaspoon salt
- 1 teaspoon ground turmeric

Directions:
Mash turnip and cauliflower with the help of the potato masher. Then add egg, dried parsley, coconut flour, salt, and ground turmeric in the mashed mixture and stir well. Make the medium side fritters and place them in the instant pot. Add avocado oil. Cook the fritters on sauté mode for 3 minutes from each side.

Nutrition value/serving: calories 50, fat 1.9, fiber 3, carbs 6, protein 2.6

Steamed Asparagus

Prep time: 5 minutes | *Cooking time:* 1 minute | *Servings:* 2

Ingredients:
- 6 oz asparagus, chopped
- ¼ teaspoon salt
- 1 cup water, for cooking

Directions:
Pour water and insert the steamer rack in the instant pot. Place the chopped asparagus in the steamer rack and close the lid. Cook the vegetables on Manual (high pressure) for 1 minute. Then make a quick pressure release and open the lid. Sprinkle the asparagus with salt.

Nutrition value/serving: calories 17, fat 0.1, fiber 1.8, carbs 3.3, protein 1.9

Roasted Cauliflower Steak

Prep time: 10 minutes | *Cooking time:* 4 minutes | *Servings:* 2

Ingredients:
- 8 oz cauliflower
- 1 teaspoon olive oil
- ½ teaspoon apple cider vinegar
- ¼ teaspoon chili flakes
- ¼ teaspoon salt
- ¼ teaspoon onion powder
- ¼ teaspoon ground turmeric
- 1 cup water, for cooking

Directions:
Cut the cauliflower into medium steaks. In the shallow bowl combine together olive oil, apple cider vinegar, chili flakes, salt, onion powder, and ground turmeric. Then brush the cauliflower steaks with oily mixture form both sides. Pour water and insert the trivet in the instant pot. Arrange the cauliflower steaks in the instant pot in one layer. Cook the vegetables for 4 minutes on manual mode (high pressure). Then make a quick pressure release. Cool the cauliflower steaks for 2-5 minutes before serving.

Nutrition value/serving: calories 51, fat 2.5, fiber 2.9, carbs 6.5, protein 2.3

Cayenne Pepper Green Beans

Prep time: 10 minutes | *Cooking time:* 3 minutes | *Servings:* 4

Ingredients:
- 2 cups green beans, chopped
- 1 teaspoon cayenne pepper
- 1 tablespoon nut oil
- ¼ teaspoon salt
- 1 cup water, for coking

Directions:
Pour water and insert the steamer rack in the instant pot. Place the green beans in the steamer rack. Cook the vegetables for 3 minutes on Manual mode (high pressure). Make a quick pressure release and cool the green beans in ice water for 4 minutes. Transfer the green beans in the mixing bowl and sprinkle with nut oil and salt. Mix up the beans well.

Nutrition value/serving: calories 48, fat 3.5, fiber 2, carbs 4.2, protein 1.1

Marinated Red Bell Peppers

Prep time: 15 minutes | Cooking time: 3 minutes | Servings: 4

Ingredients:
- 4 red bell peppers
- 1 tablespoon apple cider vinegar
- 1 teaspoon olive oil
- 1 teaspoon Italian seasonings
- ¼ teaspoon minced garlic
- 1 cup of water

Directions:
Cut the bell peppers into the strips and put them in the instant pot. Add water and close the lid. Cook the bell peppers on manual (high pressure) for 3 minutes. Then make a quick pressure release and remove the bell peppers from water. Transfer the vegetables in the bowl and sprinkle with olive oil, Italian seasonings, minced garlic, and apple cider vinegar. Mix up the peppers. Leave the cooked meal for 10 minutes to marinate.

Nutrition value/serving: calories 40, fat 1.5, fiber 2, carbs 6.2, protein 1

Broccoli Nuggets

Prep time: 10 minutes | Cooking time: 10 minutes | Servings: 4

Ingredients:
- 1 cup broccoli, chopped
- 1 egg, beaten
- ¼ teaspoon salt
- 3 tablespoons almond meal
- ¼ cup Provolone cheese, grated
- 1 teaspoon butter

Directions:
Put broccoli in the blender and blend until smooth. Then transfer the smooth mixture in the bowl. Add egg and 2 tablespoons of almond meal. Then add cheese and salt. Stir the mixture with the help of the spoon until homogenous. Toss butter in the instant pot and melt it on sauté mode for 1 minute. Make the medium size nuggets and place them in the instant pot. Cook the broccoli nuggets for 3 minutes from each side.

Nutrition value/serving: calories 87, fat 6.6, fiber 1.2, carbs 2.7, protein 5.1

Yellow Squash Noodles

Prep time: 15 minutes | Cooking time: 1 minute | Servings: 4

Ingredients:
- 1-pound yellow squash, peeled
- 1 teaspoon sesame oil
- ½ teaspoon ground cinnamon
- ¼ teaspoon salt
- 1 cup water, for cooking

Directions:
With the help of the spiralizer make the spirals from the squash. Then pour water and insert the steamer rack in the instant pot. Place the squash spirals in the steamer rack and close the lid. Cook the vegetables for 1 minute on Manual mode (high pressure). Transfer the cooked squash spirals (noodles) in the serving plates and sprinkle withs alt, ground nutmeg, and sesame oil.

Nutrition value/serving: calories 29, fat 1.3, fiber 1.4, carbs 4, protein 1.4

Oregano Fennel Steaks

Prep time: 10 minutes | *Cooking time:* 15 minutes | *Servings:* 4

Ingredients:
- 1-pound fennel bulb
- ½ teaspoon ground black pepper
- ¼ teaspoon salt
- 1 teaspoon coconut oil
- 2 tablespoons almond meal
- 1 cup organic almond milk

Directions:
Slice the fennel bulb into the steaks and rub with salt and ground black pepper. Heat up the instant pot on sauté mode. Put coconut oil inside and melt it for 1 minute. Place the fennel slices in the instant pot and cook them for 1 minute. Then flip the fennel steaks on another side and sprinkle with almond meal. After this, pour the almond milk over the fennel steaks and close the lid. Cook the fennel steaks for 10 minutes on Manual mode (low pressure). Serve the fennel steaks with a small amount of almond milk sauce from the instant pot.

Nutrition value/serving: calories 70, fat 3.5, fiber 4.1, carbs 9.2, protein 2.3

Butter Shirataki Noodles

Prep time: 10 minutes | *Cooking time:* 3 minutes | *Servings:* 2

Ingredients:
- 7 oz shirataki noodles
- 1 cup chicken broth
- ½ teaspoon salt
- 1 tablespoon butter

Directions:
Pour chicken broth in the instant pot. Add shirataki noodles and salt. Close the lid and cook the side dish for 3 minutes in Manual mode (high pressure). Then make a quick pressure release and open the lid. Drain the chicken broth. Add butter in the noodles and carefully mix them up.

Nutrition value/serving: calories 91, fat 6.4, fiber 10.5, carbs 0.5, protein 3.2

Asiago Cauliflower Rice

Prep time: 10 minutes | *Cooking time:* 10 minutes | *Servings:* 4

Ingredients:
- 2 cups cauliflower, shredded
- 1 tablespoon almond butter
- ½ white onion, diced
- 1 teaspoon apple cider vinegar
- 2 oz Asiago cheese, shredded
- 1 cup chicken broth
- ¼ teaspoon dried tarragon

Directions:
Heat up the instant pot on sauté mode for 3 minutes. Add almond butter and melt it. Then add shredded cauliflower and diced onion. Cook the vegetables on sauté mode for 2 minutes. Then sprinkle the mixture with apple cider vinegar and dried tarragon. Add chicken broth and close the lid. Cook the meal on manual mode (high pressure) for 4 minutes. Then make a quick pressure release and open the lid. Add Asiago cheese and mix up the meal well.

Nutrition value/serving: calories 102, fat 6.7, fiber 1.9, carbs 4.9, protein 6.7

Spaghetti Squash Mac&Cheese

Prep time: 10 minutes | Cooking time: 15 minutes | Servings: 4

Ingredients:
- 9 oz spaghetti squash, cleaned, seeded
- 3 teaspoons butter
- ¼ teaspoon ground black pepper
- ¼ teaspoon onion power
- 2 oz Parmesan, grated
- ½ cup Edam cheese, grated
- 1 cup water, for cooking

Directions:
Pour water and insert the steamer rack in the instant pot. Place the spaghetti squash in the instant pot and close the lid. Cook the vegetables on manual mode (high pressure) for 10 minutes. Then make a quick pressure release and open the lid. Cool the spaghetti squash till the room temperature. With the help of the fork shred the spaghetti squash. Put the shredded squash in the instant pot. Add butter, ground black pepper, and onion powder. Stir it well. Set sauté mode. Top the shredded squash with Edam cheese and Parmesan and close the lid. Saute the meal for 5 minutes or until the cheese is melted.

Nutrition value/serving: calories 179, fat 13.1, fiber 0, carbs 5.4, protein 11.2

Sichuan Style Green Beans

Prep time: 15 minutes | Cooking time: 7 minutes | Servings: 4

Ingredients:
- 1 tablespoon apple cider vinegar
- ½ teaspoon chili flakes
- ½ teaspoon minced garlic
- 1 tablespoon sesame oil
- ½ teaspoon minced ginger
- 12 oz green beans, trimmed
- 1 cup water, for cooking

Directions:
Pour water and insert the steamer rack in the instant pot. Put the green beans in the rack and close the lid. Cook the vegetables for 7 minutes on steam mode. Then make a quick pressure release. Put the cooked green beans in the bowl. Sprinkle them with chili flakes, minced garlic, minced ginger, sesame oil, and apple cider vinegar. Mix up the green beans and leave for 10 minutes to marinate.

Nutrition value/serving: calories 59, fat 3.5, fiber 2.9, carbs 6.4, protein 1.6

Cauliflower Tortillas

Prep time: 15 minutes | Cooking time: 5 minutes | Servings: 4

Ingredients:
- 1 cup cauliflower, shredded
- 1 egg, beaten
- ½ teaspoon dried cilantro
- 1 teaspoon lemon juice
- ½ teaspoon lemon zest, grated
- ¼ teaspoon ground black pepper
- ¼ teaspoon salt
- 1 tablespoon coconut flour
- 1 teaspoon olive oil

Directions:
Place the shredded cauliflower in the cheesecloth and squeeze well. Then transfer the squeezed cauliflower in the bowl. Add egg, dried cilantro, lemon juice, lemon zest, ground black pepper, salt, and coconut flour. Mix up the cauliflower mixture until smooth. After this, make the small balls from the cauliflower mixture. With the help of the rolling pin roll up the cauliflower balls into the tortillas. Brush the instant pot with olive oil from inside. Place the cauliflower tortillas in the instant pot (cook 2 tortillas per one cooking) and cook them on sauté mode for 2 minutes from each side.

Nutrition value/serving: calories 30, fat 1.3, fiber 1.4, carbs 2.8, protein 2.2

Gouda Vegetable Casserole
Prep time: 15 minutes | Cooking time: 5 minutes | Servings: 4

Ingredients:
- 1 cup collard greens, chopped
- ½ cup white mushrooms, chopped
- 1 cup celery stalk, chopped
- ½ white onion, sliced
- 2 bacon slices, chopped
- 1 teaspoon olive oil
- 1 teaspoon ground black pepper
- 1 teaspoon fresh basil, chopped
- ½ teaspoon salt
- 3 oz Gouda cheese, grated
- 1 tablespoon cream cheese

Directions:
Put chopped bacon in the instant pot and cook it on sauté mode for 3 minutes. Stir the bacon. Add sliced onion and white mushrooms. Cook the vegetables for 2 minutes more. After this, add celery stalk. Sprinkle the mixture with ground black pepper, olive oil, basil, salt, and cream cheese. Close the lid and cook the meal on manual mode (high pressure) for 3 minutes. Then allow the natural pressure release for 10 minutes. After this, open the lid and transfer the casserole in the serving plates. Top the casserole with Gouda cheese.

Nutrition value/serving: calories 162, fat 12.1, fiber 1.3, carbs 3.8, protein 9.9

Warm Antipasto Salad
Prep time: 10 minutes | Cooking time: 5 minutes | Servings: 4

Ingredients:
- 2 cups lettuce, chopped
- 3 mozzarella balls, sliced
- 4 oz ham, chopped
- 2 oz artichoke hearts, chopped, canned
- 1 tomato, chopped
- 1 teaspoon fresh basil, chopped
- ¼ chili pepper, chopped
- 1 tablespoon olive oil
- ¼ teaspoon salt
- 1 kalamata olive, chopped

Directions:
Pour ½ tablespoon of olive oil in the instant pot. Add chopped ham and cook it on sauté mode for 5 minutes. Stir it from time to time. Meanwhile, in the mixing bowl combine together sliced mozzarella, lettuce, chopped artichoke hearts, tomato, basil, chili pepper, and kalamata olive. Add remaining olive oil and salt. Then add hot ham and mix up the salad well.

Nutrition value/serving: calories 181, fat 12.9, fiber 1.6, carbs 4.1, protein 13

Eggplant Gratin
Prep time: 15 minutes | Cooking time: 10 minutes | Servings: 3

Ingredients:
- 1 eggplant, sliced
- ¼ cup heavy cream
- ¼ cup Cheddar cheese, shredded
- 1 teaspoon coconut oil
- ¼ teaspoon salt
- ¼ teaspoon chili powder
- ½ teaspoon garlic powder
- 1 teaspoon fresh parsley, chopped
- 3 oz kohlrabi, chopped

Directions:
Melt coconut oil on sauté mode. Add eggplants and kohlrabi. Sprinkle the vegetables with salt, chili powder, and garlic powder. Mix up well and sauté them for 5 minutes. After this, mix up the vegetables one more time. In the mixing bowl combine together heavy cream, Cheddar cheese, garlic powder, and fresh parsley. Pour the liquid over the sauteed vegetables and close the lid. Cook the gratin for 5 minutes on manual mode (high pressure). Then allow the natural pressure release for 10 minutes.

Nutrition value/serving: calories 134, fat 8.7, fiber 6.6, carbs 11.6, protein 4.7

Beet Cubes with Pecans

Prep time: 15 minutes | *Cooking time:* 15 minutes | *Servings:* 4

Ingredients:
- 7 oz beet, peeled
- 2 pecans, chopped
- ½ teaspoon olive oil
- ¼ teaspoon salt
- 1 cup water, for cooking

Directions:
Cut the beet into the cubes. Pour water and insert the steamer rack in the instant pot. Put the beet cubes in the instant pot and close the lid. Cook the vegetables for 15 minutes on high-pressure mode. Then allow the natural pressure release for 10 minutes. Open the lid and transfer the cooked beet cubes in the serving plates. Sprinkle the vegetables with pecans, salt, and olive oil.

Nutrition value/serving: calories 76, fat 5.7, fiber 1.7, carbs 5.9, protein 1.6

Jalapeno Popper Bread

Prep time: 10 minutes | *Cooking time:* 8 minutes | *Servings:* 4

Ingredients:
- 5 eggs, beaten
- 1 oz bacon, chopped, cooked
- 1 jalapeno pepper, chopped
- ½ teaspoon avocado oil
- ½ cup Cheddar cheese, shredded
- 1 cup water, for cooking

Directions:
In the mixing bowl whisk together eggs, bacon, jalapeno pepper, and cheese. Then brush the instant pot baking pan with avocado oil. Pour the egg mixture in the baking pan. Pour water and insert the trivet in the instant pot. Place the baking pan on the trivet and close the lid. Cook the bread on manual (high pressure) for 8 minutes. Then allow the natural pressure release for 5 minutes. Cool the cooked bread well and then remove it from the baking pan. Slice the bread.

Nutrition value/serving: calories 176, fat 13.2, fiber 0.1, carbs 0.9, protein 13.1

Baked Green Beans

Prep time: 5 minutes | *Cooking time:* 6 minutes | *Servings:* 1

Ingredients:
- 4 oz green beans, chopped
- ½ teaspoon butter
- 1 tablespoon almond meal
- 1 oz Provolone cheese, grated
- 1 cup water, for cooking

Directions:
Pour water and insert the steamer rack in the instant pot. Place the green beans on the rack and cook them on manual mode (high pressure) for 1 minute. After this, make a quick pressure release and open the lid. Place the cooked green beans in the bowl. Add almond meal and grated Provolone cheese. Then clean the instant pot and remove the rack. Put the green beans mixture in the instant pot bowl. Add butter and close the lid. Cook the baked green beans for 5 minutes.

Nutrition value/serving: calories 186, fat 12.6, fiber 4.6, carbs 10, protein 10.6

Garlic Bread

Prep time: 15 minutes | Cooking time: 6 minutes | Servings: 6

Ingredients:
- 5 oz Parmesan, grated
- ½ cup almond meal
- 1 tablespoon cream cheese
- 1 egg, beaten
- 1 teaspoon chives
- 1 tablespoon sesame oil
- 1 teaspoon minced garlic

Directions:
In the mixing bowl mix up together Parmesan, almond meal, and cream cheese. Microwave the mixture for 10 seconds. Then mix it well until smooth and add an egg. Stir it until homogenous. Brush the instant pot bowl with ½ tablespoon of sesame oil. Then place the cheese dough in the instant pot and flatten it in the shape of the pancake. Brush the bread with remaining sesame oil and sprinkle with minced garlic and chives. Cook the bread on sauté mode for 6 minutes. Flip the bread on another side after 5 minutes of cooking.

Nutrition value/serving: calories 159, fat 12.6, fiber 1, carbs 2.8, protein 10.4

Parmesan Broccoli Head

Prep time: 10 minutes | Cooking time: 4 minutes | Servings: 4

Ingredients:
- 9 broccoli head
- 2 oz Parmesan, grated
- 1 teaspoon sesame oil
- ½ teaspoon chili flakes
- 1 cup water, for cooking

Directions:
Pour water and insert the trivet in the instant pot. Sprinkle the broccoli head with sesame oil and chili flakes. Then top it with parmesan and wrap in the foil. Place the wrapped broccoli in the instant pot and close the lid. Cook the vegetable for 4 minutes on Manual mode (high pressure). Make a quick pressure release and open the lid. Remove the broccoli from the foil.

Nutrition value/serving: calories 56, fat 4.2, fiber 0, carbs 0.5, protein 4.6

Side Dish Cauliflower Ziti

Prep time: 10 minutes | Cooking time: 5 minutes | Servings: 4

Ingredients:
- 1 cup cauliflower, chopped
- ¼ teaspoon garlic, diced
- 1/3 onion, diced
- ½ teaspoon chili pepper
- ½ teaspoon salt
- 1 teaspoon tomato paste
- ½ cup cream
- 1 teaspoon olive oil
- 1 tablespoon ricotta cheese
- ½ cup Mozzarella cheese, shredded

Directions:
Mix up together cauliflower and onion. Add garlic, chili pepper, salt, and ricotta cheese. Mix up the vegetables well. Then in the separated bowl mix up together tomato paste and cream. Brush the instant pot bowl with olive oil and put the vegetable mixture inside. Pour the cream mixture over the vegetables. Then top the meal with Mozzarella and close the lid. Cook the cauliflower ziti for 5 minutes on Manual mode (high pressure). When the time is over, allow the natural pressure release for 5 minutes.

Nutrition value/serving: calories 114, fat 8.4, fiber 0.9, carbs 4.2, protein 6

Cauliflower Salad with Provolone Cheese
Prep time: 10 minutes | *Cooking time:* 3 minutes | *Servings:* 2

Ingredients:
- 4 oz cauliflower florets
- ½ teaspoon apple cider vinegar
- ¼ teaspoon chili flakes
- ¼ teaspoon chives
- 1 oz Provolone cheese, chopped
- 1 teaspoon olive oil
- 1 cup water, for cooking

Directions:
Pour water and insert the steamer rack in the instant pot. Place the cauliflower florets in the rack and close the lid. Cook the vegetables for 3 minutes on Manual mode (high pressure). Then make a quick pressure release and open the lid. Place the cauliflower florets in the salad bowl. Sprinkle them with apple cider vinegar, chili flakes, chives, and olive oil. Add chopped Provolone cheese and mix up well.

Nutrition value/serving: calories 84, fat 6.2, fiber 1.4, carbs 3.3, protein 4.7

Spiced Asparagus
Prep time: 10 minutes | *Cooking time:* 4 minutes | *Servings:* 6

Ingredients:
- 1-pound asparagus, trimmed
- 1 teaspoon olive oil
- 1 teaspoon lemon juice
- ½ teaspoon chili powder
- 1 teaspoon chili flakes
- 1 teaspoon ground black pepper
- ½ teaspoon ground coriander
- 1 teaspoon butter, melted
- 1 cup water, for cooking

Directions:
Insert trivet in the instant pot. Add water. Put the asparagus on the trivet, add chili powder, chili flakes, ground black pepper, and butter. Close the lid. Cook the asparagus for 4 minutes on manual mode (high pressure). Then make a quick pressure release and open the lid. Transfer the cooked asparagus in the serving plates and sprinkle with lemon juice, olive oil, and butter. Gently mix the cooked vegetables.

Nutrition value/serving: calories 29, fat 1.6, fiber 1.8, carbs 3.3, protein 1.8

Snacks and Appetizers

Zucchini Fries in Bacon
Prep time: 10 minutes | Cooking time: 10 minutes | Servings:6

Ingredients:
- 2 zucchini, trimmed
- 2 oz Parmesan, grated
- 2 tablespoons almond meal
- 1 teaspoon olive oil
- 1 egg, beaten

Directions:
Cut the zucchini into fries shape and place it in the bowl. Then add egg and shake the vegetables well. In the separated bowl combine together Parmesan and almond meal. Coat the zucchini fries in the cheese mixture. Then heat up the instant pot on sauté mode for 3 minutes. Sprinkle the instant pot bowl with olive oil and arrange the zucchini in one layer. Cook the fries for 1 minute from each side or until they are light brown. Then place the cooked fries on the paper towel and dry little to get rid of oil. Repeat the same steps with the remaining zucchini.

Nutrition value/serving: calories 69, fat 4.6, fiber 1, carbs 3, protein 5.2

Bacon Bites with Asparagus
Prep time: 10 minutes | Cooking time: 4 minutes | Servings:5

Ingredients:
- 4 oz asparagus, trimmed
- 3 oz bacon, sliced
- ½ teaspoon salt
- ¼ teaspoon chili powder
- 1 cup water, for cooking

Directions:
Wrap every asparagus in the bacon and sprinkle with salt and chili powder. After this, pour water in the instant pot and insert the steamer rack. Place the wrapped asparagus in the rack and close the lid. Cook the snack on manual mode (high pressure) for 4 minutes. When the time is over, make a quick pressure release.

Nutrition value/serving: calories 97, fat 7.2, fiber 0.5, carbs 1.2, protein 6.8

Bacon Onion Rings
Prep time: 10 minutes | Cooking time: 7 minutes | Servings:4

Ingredients:
- 1 large white onion, peeled
- 4 bacon slices
- 1 teaspoon olive oil
- ¼ teaspoon dried thyme
- ¼ teaspoon salt
- 1 cup water, for cooking

Directions:
Slice the onion into thick rings. Then wrap every onion ring in the bacon. Pour water and insert the steamer rack in the instant pot. Place the onion rings on the rack and close the lid. Cook the snack for 3 minutes on manual mode (high pressure). Make a quick pressure release and open the lid. Transfer the onion rings on the plate and clean the instant pot. Sprinkle the snack with salt and dried thyme. Then brush with olive oil. Place the onion rings back in the instant pot and cook for 2 minutes from each side on sauté mode.

Nutrition value/serving: calories 128, fat 9.2, fiber 0.8, carbs 3.8, protein 7.5

Oregano Keto Bread Rounds

Prep time: 10 minutes | *Cooking time:* 35 minutes | *Servings:* 6

Ingredients:
- ½ cup Cheddar cheese, shredded
- 4 tablespoons almond meal
- ½ teaspoon baking powder
- 2 eggs, beaten
- 1 teaspoon coconut oil
- 1 teaspoon dried oregano

Directions:
In the mixing bowl combine together shredded cheese with almond meal. Add baking powder and dried oregano. Stir the ingredients with the help of the fork. Then add beaten eggs and knead the non-sticky dough. Add more almond meal if needed. Make 6 balls from the cheese mixture and roll them up with the help of the rolling pin. Preheat the instant pot on sauté mode for 2 minutes. Then add coconut oil and melt it. After this, place the first keto bread round in the instant pot and cook it for 3 minutes. Then flip it on another side and cook for 2 minutes more. Remove the cooked keto bread from the instant pot and cool little. Repeat the same steps with remaining keto bread rounds.

Nutrition value/serving: calories 90, fat 7.4, fiber 0.6, carbs 1.4, protein 5.1

Cabbage Chips

Prep time: 10 minutes | *Cooking time:* 20 minutes | *Servings:* 10

Ingredients:
- 1-pound cabbage
- 1 oz Parmesan, grated
- 1 teaspoon ground paprika
- 1 teaspoon sesame oil

Directions:
Separate the cabbage leaves into the petals. Tear the petals and sprinkle with ground paprika and grated Parmesan. Shake the torn leaves. Heat up the instant pot on sauté mode for 3 minutes. Then place the cabbage petals in one layer in the instant pot. Cook the chips for 2 minutes from each side. Then cook the cabbage chips for 2 minutes more from each side or until they are light crunchy. Repeat the same steps with remaining torn cabbage petals.

Nutrition value/serving: calories 25, fat 1.1, fiber 1.2, carbs 2.9, protein 1.5

Soul Bread

Prep time: 15 minutes | *Cooking time:* 35 minutes | *Servings:* 10

Ingredients:
- 1 cup of protein powder
- ¼ teaspoon salt
- ½ teaspoon baking powder
- ½ teaspoon xanthan gum
- 2 tablespoons cream cheese
- 2 eggs, beaten
- 2 tablespoons sesame oil
- 4 tablespoons whipped cream
- 1 tablespoon butter, melted
- 3 tablespoons coconut flour
- 1 cup water, for cooking

Directions:
In the big mixing bowl combine together protein powder, salt, baking powder, xanthan gum, and coconut flour. Then add cream cheese, eggs, sesame oil, whipped cream, and melted butter. With the help of the hand blender whisk the mixture until you get a smooth batter. Then pour water and insert the rack in the instant pot. Pour the bread batter in the instant pot baking pan and transfer it in the instant pot. Close the lid and cook the soul bread on manual (high pressure) for 35 minutes. When the time is over, make a quick pressure release and open the lid. Cook the cooked bread to the room temperature and remove it from the baking pan. Slice the soul bread into the servings.

Nutrition value/serving: calories 117, fat 7.7, fiber 3.5, carbs 6.8, protein 7

Tender Jicama Fritters

Prep time: 10 minutes | *Cooking time:* 18 minutes | *Servings:* 4

Ingredients:
- 4 oz jicama, peeled, grated
- 1 egg, beaten
- 2 tablespoons Cheddar cheese, shredded
- ½ teaspoon ground coriander
- 1 teaspoon almond butter
- 2 tablespoons coconut flakes
- 1 tablespoon almond flour
- ½ teaspoon baking powder
- ½ teaspoon apple cider vinegar

Directions:
Mix up together jicama, egg, cheese, ground coriander, coconut flakes, baking powder, apple cider vinegar, and almond flour. Stir the mixture with the help of the spoon until homogenous. Then heat up the instant pot on sauté mode for 4 minutes or until it is hot. Add almond butter and melt it. Separate the jicama mixture into 4 parts. With the help of the spoon arrange the fritters in the instant pot (2 fritters per one cooking). Cook them for 3 minutes from each side. The cooked fritters should be golden brown. Dry the fritters with the help of the paper towel if needed.

Nutrition value/serving: calories 85, fat 6.2, fiber 2.2, carbs 4.5, protein 3.8

Spiced Chicken Carnitas

Prep time: 20 minutes | *Cooking time:* 10 minute | *Servings:* 8

Ingredients:
- 1-pound chicken fillet
- ½ teaspoon ground coriander
- ½ teaspoon ground paprika
- ½ teaspoon ground turmeric
- ½ teaspoon salt
- ½ teaspoon dried cilantro
- ½ teaspoon dried oregano
- ½ teaspoon dried thyme
- 1 teaspoon butter
- 1 teaspoon minced garlic
- 1 tablespoon lemon juice
- 1 jalapeno pepper, chopped
- 1 cup chicken broth

Directions:
Put the chicken fillet in the instant pot. Sprinkle it with ground coriander, paprika, turmeric, salt, dried cilantro, oregano, thyme, butter, and minced garlic. Add jalapeno pepper and chicken broth. Close the lid and cook the chicken for 10 minutes on steam mode. When the time is over, allow the natural pressure release for 10 minutes. Open the lid and shred the chicken with the help of the fork. Sprinkle the cooked chicken with lemon juice and stir gently.

Nutrition value/serving: calories 120, fat 4.9, fiber 0.2, carbs 0.6, protein 17.1

Cheese Almond Meal Bites

Prep time: 10 minutes | *Cooking time:* 2 minutes | *Servings:* 4

Ingredients:
- ½ cup Cheddar cheese
- 1 egg, beaten
- ½ teaspoon salt
- 1 cup almond meal
- 1 teaspoon coconut oil

Directions:
Grate the cheese and combine it with egg and salt. When you get a homogenous mixture, make the small balls with the help of the medium scooper. After this, coat the balls in the almond meal. Toss the coconut oil in the instant pot and melt it on sauté mode. Then place the balls in the instant pot and cook for 30 seconds from each side. The almond meal bites have to be served warm.

Nutrition value/serving: calories 220, fat 18.8, fiber 3, carbs 5.4, protein 9.9

Zucchini Parsley Tots

Prep time: 10 minutes | Cooking time: 10 minutes | Servings:6

Ingredients:
- 1 zucchini, grated
- ½ teaspoon ground black pepper
- ¼ teaspoon salt
- 1 oz pumpkin, grated
- 3 tablespoons coconut flour
- 2 oz Provolone cheese, grated
- 1 teaspoon dried parsley
- 1 tablespoon butter

Directions:
Squeeze the grated zucchini to get rid of zucchini juice and place it in the big bowl. Add ground black pepper, salt, grated cheese, and dried parsley. With the help of the fork mix up the mixture. Then add grated pumpkin and coconut flour Stir the mixture. If the zucchini mixture is dry, add a small amount of zucchini liquid. With the help of the fingertips make the zucchini tots (small-sized tots). Toss butter in the instant pot and heat it up on sauté mode. Then arrange the zucchini tots in the instant pot in one layer and cook them for 2 minutes. Then flip the zucchini tots with the help of the spatula and cook for 1 minute more.

Nutrition value/serving: calories 73, fat 4.9, fiber 2.1, carbs 4.3, protein 3.4

Paprika Deviled Eggs

Prep time: 10 minutes | Cooking time: 5 minutes | Servings:2

Ingredients:
- 2 eggs
- 1 teaspoon ground paprika
- ½ teaspoon cream cheese
- ¼ teaspoon salt
- 1 cup water, for cooking

Directions:
Pour water and insert the steamer rack in the instant pot. Place the eggs on the rack and cook them on steamer mode for 5 minutes. Then make a quick pressure release and open the lid. Cool the eggs in the cold water for 5 minutes. Peel the eggs and cut them into halves. Remove the egg yolks and place them in the bowl. Smash the egg yolks with the help of the fork. Add cream cheese and ½ teaspoon of ground paprika. Stir well and fill the egg whites with egg yolk mixture. Top the deviled eggs with remaining paprika.

Nutrition value/serving: calories 69, fat 4.8, fiber 0.4, carbs 1, protein 5.8

Parmesan Tomatoes Slices

Prep time: 10 minutes | Cooking time: 10 minutes | Servings:8

Ingredients:
- 2 tomatoes
- 1 teaspoon basil, chopped
- 2 oz Parmesan, grated
- 1 teaspoon sesame oil

Directions:
Slice the tomatoes into 8 thick slices. Then brush the instant pot bowl with sesame oil and preheat it on sauté mode for 3 minutes or until it is hot. Then put the sliced tomatoes in one layer in instant pot and cook for 1 minute. Then flip the tomatoes on another side and top with ½ teaspoon of fresh basil and half of grated Parmesan. Close the lid and sauté the tomatoes for 4 minutes. Carefully transfer the tomatoes on the plate. Repeat the same steps with remaining tomatoes.

Nutrition value/serving: calories 33, fat 2.2, fiber 0.4, carbs 1.5, protein 2.6

Mini Cheese Pepperoni Pizza

Prep time: 10 minutes | Cooking time: 6 minutes | Servings:4

Ingredients:
- 8 pepperoni slices
- ¼ cup Mozzarella, shredded
- 1 tablespoon low-carb marinara sauce
- 1 kalamata olive, sliced
- 1 cup water, for cooking

Directions:
Pour water in the instant pot and insert the steamer rack. Then arrange 2 pepperoni slices in one muffin mold to get the "pepperoni cups". Repeat the same step with the remaining pepperoni. After this, put Marinara sauce inside the pepperoni cups. Top them with Mozzarella cheese and sliced olive. Place the muffin molds with mini pizzas in the instant pot and close the lid. Cook the meal on manual mode (high pressure) for 6 minutes. When the time is over, make a quick pressure release and remove the mold from the instant pot. Cool the cooked pizzas little before serving.

Nutrition value/serving: calories 62, fat 5.3, fiber 0.1, carbs 0.4, protein 3

Keto Queso Dip

Prep time: 10 minutes | Cooking time: 3 hours | Servings:6

Ingredients:
- 1 teaspoon garlic powder
- 1 tablespoon almond butter
- 1 tablespoon chili, chopped
- 2 cups Mexican cheese, shredded
- 2 tablespoons cream cheese
- ¼ cup heavy cream
- 1 cup water, for cooking

Directions:
Put shredded Mexican cheese in the baking pan. Add garlic powder, almond butter, chili, cream cheese, and heavy cream. Stir the mixture well. Then pour water and insert the steamer rack in the instant pot. Place the baking pan with cheese mixture in the instant pot and close the lid. Close the lid and cook the queso dip for 3 hours on manual mode (low pressure). When the dip is cooked, mix it up well and transfer it in the serving bowl.

Nutrition value/serving: calories 76, fat 6.7, fiber 0.4, carbs 1.7, protein 3.8

Keto Jalapeno Bread

Prep time: 20 minutes | Cooking time: 35 minutes | Servings:8

Ingredients:
- ½ cup coconut flour
- ½ cup almond flour
- ½ teaspoon baking powder
- 4 eggs, beaten
- ½ teaspoon lemon juice
- 2 jalapeno peppers, sliced
- 1 teaspoon butter
- ½ teaspoon salt
- 1 oz Jarlsberg cheese, shredded
- 1 cup water, for cooking

Directions:
In the mixing bowl mix up together coconut flour and almond flour. Add baking powder and lemon juice. Then add eggs and salt. Stir the mixture until smooth. Brush the instant pot baking pan with butter and place the prepared bread dough inside. Then add sliced jalapeno and stir it. Top the bread with shredded cheese. Cover the bread with paper foil. Pour the water in the instant pot and insert the steamer rack. Place the baking pan in the rack and close the lid. Cook the jalapeno bread for 35 minutes on manual mode (high pressure). When the time is over, make a quick pressure release and open the lid. Remove the paper foil from the bread and cool meal well.

Nutrition value/serving: calories 119, fat 7.6, fiber 3.9, carbs 7.1, protein 6

Turnip Fries

Prep time: 10 minutes | *Cooking time:* 12 minutes | *Servings:*4

Ingredients:
- 7 oz turnip, peeled
- ½ teaspoon salt
- ¼ teaspoon ground turmeric
- 1 tablespoon avocado oil

Directions:
Cut the turnip into the French fries shape and sprinkle with avocado oil. Mix up the turnip fries well and place them in the instant pot in one layer. Cook the turnip fries on sauté mode for 3 minutes from each side. Then transfer the cooked turnip fries in the plate and sprinkle with ground turmeric.

Nutrition value/serving: calories 19, fat 0.5, fiber 1.1, carbs 3.5, protein 0.5

Butternut Squash Fries

Prep time: 10 minutes | *Cooking time:* 10 minutes | *Servings:*10

Ingredients:
- 1-pound butternut squash, peeled
- ½ teaspoon dried thyme
- ½ teaspoon salt
- 1 teaspoon sesame oil
- 1 cup water, for cooking

Directions:
Cut the peeled butternut squash into French fries shape. Sprinkle the vegetables with dried thyme, salt, and sesame oil. After this, pour water and insert the steamer rack in the instant pot. Place the butternut squash in the rack and close the lid. Cook the fries for 6 minutes on Manual mode (high pressure). When the time is over, make a quick pressure release and transfer the cooked butternut squash fries in the tray in one layer. Broil the fries for 4 minutes at 400F in the oven.

Nutrition value/serving: calories 25, fat 0.5, fiber 0.9. carbs 5.3, protein 0.5

Popcorn Chicken

Prep time: 10 minutes | *Cooking time:* 12 minutes | *Servings:*4

Ingredients:
- 9 oz chicken fillet
- 1 teaspoon chili powder
- 1 teaspoon ground paprika
- ½ teaspoon salt
- 1 tablespoon sesame oil
- 1 teaspoon coconut oil
- 1 teaspoon lemon juice
- 1 tablespoon almond meal

Directions:
Chop the chicken fillet into the small cubes (popcorn cubes). Then place it in the zip lock bag and add chili powder, ground paprika, salt, sesame oil, and lemon juice. Shake the chicken mixture well and transfer it in the bowl. Sprinkle the chicken with almond meal and shake well. After this, toss the coconut oil in the instant pot and melt it on sauté mode for 2-3 minutes. Then place the chicken popcorn in the instant pot and cook it for 10 minutes. Stir the chicken popcorn every 2 minutes.

Nutrition value/serving: calories 173, fat 10.2, fiber 0.6, carbs 1, protein 18.9

Crunchy Green Beans
Prep time: 10 minutes | Cooking time: 10 minutes | Servings:10

Ingredients:
- 1-pound green beans
- 2 eggs, beaten
- 1/3 cup coconut flakes
- ½ teaspoon salt
- ½ teaspoon ground black pepper
- 1 tablespoon coconut oil
- 1 cup water, for cooking

Directions:
Pour water and insert the steamer rack in the instant pot. Place the green beans in the rack and close the lid. Cook the vegetables on Manual mode (high pressure) for 4 minutes. Then make a quick pressure release and cool the green beans in ice water. After this, clean the instant pot and remove the steamer rack. Mix up together eggs with salt and ground black pepper. Then dip green beans in the egg mixture. After this, coat them in coconut flakes. Put the coconut oil in the instant pot and melt it on sauté mode. Place the green beans in one layer and cook for 1 minute from each side or until the green beans are light brown. Repeat the same steps with remaining green beans.

Nutrition value/serving: calories 48, fat 3.2, fiber 1.8, carbs 3.8, protein 2

Keto Breadsticks
Prep time: 15 minutes | Cooking time: 13 minutes | Servings:8

Ingredients:
- ½ cup Mozzarella cheese, shredded
- 3 tablespoons cream cheese
- 1 egg, beaten
- 1 cup almond flour

Directions:
Mix up together shredded Mozzarella and almond flour. Then add egg and cream cheese. Mix up the cheese mixture well and then knead it in the dough ball. Preheat the instant pot on saute mode for 3 minutes. Meanwhile, place the dough ball on the baking paper and cover it with the second baking paper sheet. Roll up the dough into the flatbread shape. Remove the baking paper that covers the dough and transfer the dough in the instant pot. Close the lid and cook the meal for 10 minutes. Then open the lid and remove the meal with the baking paper from the instant pot. Let it cool well and then cut it into the sticks.

Nutrition value/serving: calories 110, fat 8.8, fiber 1.5, carbs 3.2, protein 4.5

Mini Chicken Skewers
Prep time: 15 minutes | Cooking time: 8 minutes | Servings:4

Ingredients:
- 10 oz chicken fillet
- 1 teaspoon apple cider vinegar
- ¼ teaspoon lemon zest, grated
- ¼ teaspoon ground paprika
- ¼ teaspoon tomato paste
- ¼ tablespoon olive oil
- ¼ teaspoon salt
- 1 cup water, for cooking

Directions:
Chop the chicken into the medium cubes. In the shallow bowl combine together apple cider vinegar, lemon zest, ground paprika, tomato paste, salt, and olive oil. Then mix up together chicken cubes and tomato mixture. After this, string chicken into the wooden skewers. Pour water in the instant pot and insert the trivet. Arrange the chicken skewers in the trivet and close the lid. Cook the meal for 8 minutes on manual mode (high pressure). When the time is over, make a quick pressure release. It is recommended to serve the chicken skewers immediately.

Nutrition value/serving: calories 143, fat 6.2, fiber 0.1, carbs 0.2, protein 20.5

Parmesan Cauliflower Tots

Prep time: 15 minutes | *Cooking time:* 5 minutes | *Servings:* 2

Ingredients:
- 1 oz Parmesan, grated
- ¼ cup cauliflower, shredded
- 1 egg white
- ¼ teaspoon ground paprika
- 1 tablespoon almond flour
- 1 teaspoon butter
- ¼ teaspoon ground black pepper

Directions:
Whisk the egg white little and combine it with Parmesan and shredded cauliflower. Then add ground paprika and ground black pepper. Stir the mixture. Add almond flour and stir the mixture until it is homogenous and non-sticky. Make the small tots with the help of the fingertips. Melt butter in the instant pot on sauté mode. Place the cauliflower tots in the instant pot and cook them for 2 minutes from each side. If you prefer crunchy crust – increase the time of cooking to 3 minutes per one side.

Nutrition value/serving: calories 97, fat 6.7, fiber 0.9, carbs 2.4, protein 7.4

Aromatic Swedish Meatballs

Prep time: 15 minutes | *Cooking time:* 11 minutes | *Servings:* 6

Ingredients:
- ½ cup ground beef
- ½ cup ground pork
- ¼ cup of water
- ½ teaspoon ground black pepper
- ½ white onion, diced
- ½ teaspoon all spices
- 3 tablespoons almond meal
- ½ cup heavy cream
- 1 teaspoon dried dill
- ½ teaspoon minced garlic
- 1 egg yolk
- ½ teaspoon cilantro, chopped
- 1/3 cup chicken broth
- 1 teaspoon avocado oil
- ½ teaspoon salt

Directions:
In the mixing bowl, mix up together ground beef, ground pork, water, ground black pepper, diced onion, all spices, almond meal, dried dill, minced garlic, and egg yolk. Stir the ground meat mixture well. Then make the small meatballs. Place them in the instant pot and add avocado oil. Cook them on sauté mode for 3 minutes from each side. Then add chicken broth, salt, cilantro, and heavy cream. Close the lid and cook the meatballs for 5 minutes on manual mode (high pressure). Then make a quick pressure release. Cool the meatballs to the room temperature.

Nutrition value/serving: calories 168, fat 12.9, fiber 0.7, carbs 2.3, protein 10.6

Kale Wraps

Prep time: 10 minutes | *Cooking time:* 15 minutes | *Servings:* 4

Ingredients:
- 4 kale leaves
- ½ cup ground chicken
- ¼ teaspoon chili flakes
- ¼ teaspoon salt
- ¼ teaspoon onion powder
- ¼ teaspoon garlic powder
- 1 teaspoon butter
- 1 teaspoon chives, chopped

Directions:
Toss butter in the instant pot. Set instant pot on sauté mode for 15 minutes. Add ground chicken. Sprinkle it with chili flakes, salt, onion powder, and garlic powder. Stir well and sauté the mixture for 5 minutes. Then stir it well and cook for 10 minutes more. When the ground chicken is cooked, switch off the instant pot. Fill the kale leaves with chicken and wrap.

Nutrition value/serving: calories 53, fat 2.3, fiber 0.4, carbs 2.5, protein 5.8

Bread Twists

Prep time: 15 minutes | Cooking time: 20 minutes | Servings: 7

Ingredients:
- 4 tablespoons almond flour
- 4 tablespoons coconut flour
- ¼ teaspoon salt
- ½ teaspoon baking powder
- 1 teaspoon apple cider vinegar
- 1 tablespoon butter
- ¾ cup Cheddar cheese, shredded
- 1 egg, beaten
- 1 tablespoon water
- 1 cup water, for cooking

Directions:
In the mixing bowl combine together butter and Cheddar cheese. Place the mixture in the microwave and heat it up for 30 seconds. Stir the mixture until smooth. In the separated bowl combine together almond flour, coconut flour, salt, baking powder, apple cider vinegar, and egg. When the mixture is smooth, add cheese mixture and knead the dough. After this, roll up the dough and cut it into the triangles. Twist every triangle. Pour water and insert the steamer rack in the instant pot. Line the rack with baking paper. Arrange the twists in the rack in one layer and brush with 1 tablespoon of water. Then close the lid and cook the meal for 20 minutes on manual mode (high pressure). Then make a quick pressure release and remove the twists from the instant pot.

Nutrition value/serving: calories 114, fat 8.6, fiber 2.2, carbs 4.1, protein 5.3

Cheese Chips

Prep time: 5 minutes | Cooking time: 30 minutes | Servings: 5

Ingredients:
- 5 Cheddar cheese slices

Directions:
Line the instant pot with baking paper. Then place Cheddar cheese slices inside in one layer (put 2 Cheddar slices). The close the lid and cook cheese chips for 15 minutes on sauté mode or until the chips are dry (it depends on your instant pot type). When the time is over, open the lid and remove the cheese chips with baking paper. Cool the chips and then remove them from the baking paper with the help of the metal spatula. Repeat the same steps with remaining cheese slices.

Nutrition value/serving: calories 113, fat 9.3, fiber 0, carbs 0.4, protein 7

Butter Coffee

Prep time: 10 minutes | Cooking time: 10 minutes | Servings: 2

Ingredients:
- 2 teaspoons instant coffee
- 2 tablespoons butter
- 1 cup of water
- ¼ cup heavy cream

Directions:
Pour water in the instant pot and bring it to boil on sauté mode. Then add instant coffee and stir it until coffee is dissolved. Then add butter and switch off the instant pot. Let the butter melts. Then pour the cooked butter coffee in the serving cups.

Nutrition value/serving: calories 154, fat 17.1, fiber 0, carbs 0.4, protein 0.4

Pumpkin Spices Latte

Prep time: 10 minutes | Cooking time: 10 minutes | Servings: 2

Ingredients:
- ½ cup of coconut milk
- ¼ cup of water
- 2 teaspoons instant coffee
- 1 teaspoon pumpkin spices
- 1 teaspoon pumpkin puree

Directions:
Pour water in the instant pot. Add instant coffee and stir the liquid until it is dissolved. Then set sauté mode and bring the liquid to boil (it will take appx.3-5 minutes). Add pumpkin spices and pumpkin puree. Saute the liquid for 2 minutes more. Meanwhile, whisk the coconut milk with the help of the hand whisker until you get big foam. Pour hot coffee in the serving cups. Add coconut milk with foam.

Nutrition value/serving: calories 142, fat 14.4, fiber 1.5, carbs 4.1, protein 1.5

Salty Nuts Mix

Prep time: 10 minutes | Cooking time: 7 minutes | Servings: 5

Ingredients:
- 1 teaspoon coconut aminos
- 1 teaspoon coconut oil
- ½ teaspoon sesame oil
- ¼ teaspoon chili powder
- 1 teaspoon salt
- 2 tablespoons walnuts
- 5 pecans
- 1 tablespoon pistachios
- 1 tablespoon cashew

Directions:
Place coconut oil and sesame oil in the instant pot. Heat up the oils on sauté mode for 1 minute. Then add coconut aminos, chili powder, walnuts, pecans, pistachios, and cashew. Mix up the nuts and cook them for 5 minutes. Stir the nuts every 1 minute. Add salt and mix up the mixture. Transfer the nut mix in the paper bag.

Nutrition value/serving: calories 144, fat 14.4, fiber 1.9, carbs 3.3, protein 2.7

Heart of Palm Dip

Prep time: 10 minutes | Cooking time: 8 minutes | Servings: 8

Ingredients:
- 1-pound heart of palm, chopped
- 1 garlic clove, diced
- 1 tablespoon avocado oil
- 1 teaspoon lemon juice
- ½ teaspoon salt
- ¼ teaspoon ground black pepper
- ¼ teaspoon fennel seeds
- ¼ cup heavy cream
- 1 oz Provolone cheese, grated

Directions:
Pour avocado oil in the instant pot and heat it up. Add diced garlic, ground black pepper, and fennel seeds. Cook the ingredients for 2 minutes or until they become aromatic. Meanwhile, put the heart of palms in the blender. Add lemon juice. Blend the mixture until smooth. Add heavy cream and cheese in the hot oil mixture and bring it to boil. Remove the liquid from the heat and add it in the blender heart of palm. Stir well. Store the dip in the fridge for up to 8 hours.

Nutrition value/serving: calories 45, fat 2.9, fiber 1.5, carbs 3.1, protein 2.5

Taco Shells

Prep time: 15 minutes | Cooking time: 50 minutes | Servings:4

Ingredients:
- 4 lettuce leaves
- ¼ cup radish, chopped
- 10 oz beef sirloin
- ½ teaspoon dried cilantro
- ½ teaspoon salt
- ½ teaspoon dried oregano
- 1 teaspoon taco seasoning
- 1 teaspoon green chile
- ½ cup chicken broth
- 1 teaspoon ground paprika
- 1 teaspoon cream cheese

Directions:
Put beef sirloin, dried cilantro, salt, oregano, taco seasonings, green chile, ground paprika, and chicken broth in the instant pot. Close the lid and cook meat on stew/meat mode for 50 minutes. When the time is over, remove the meat from the instant pot and shred it. Then mix up together 3 tablespoons chicken broth from instant pot and cream cheese. Stir the liquid in the shredded meat and stir well. Then fill the lettuce leaves with shredded beef.

Nutrition value/serving: calories 146, fat 5, fiber 0.4, carbs 1.5, protein 22.4

Mini Margharita Pizzas in Mushroom Caps

Prep time: 15 minutes | Cooking time: 10 minutes | Servings:4

Ingredients:
- 4 Portobello mushroom caps
- 1/3 cup Mozzarella, shredded
- 1 teaspoon fresh basil, chopped
- 1 teaspoon cream cheese
- ¼ teaspoon dried oregano
- 1 teaspoon tomato sauce
- 1 cup water, for cooking

Directions:
Pour water and insert the trivet in the instant pot. Then mix up together shredded Mozzarella, basil, cream cheese, and dried oregano. Fill the mushroom caps with the Mozzarella mixture. Top every Portobello cap with tomato sauce and transfer in the trivet. Close the lid and cook pizzas for 10 minutes on manual mode (high pressure). When the time is over, make a quick pressure release and transfer the cooked Margharita pizzas on the plate.

Nutrition value/serving: calories 10, fat 0.7, fiber 0.1, carbs 0.3, protein 0.8

Keto Guacamole Deviled Eggs

Prep time: 20 minutes | Cooking time: 5 minutes | Servings:6

Ingredients:
- 6 eggs
- 1 avocado, pitted, peeled
- 2 tablespoons lemon juice
- ¼ teaspoon salt
- 1 tablespoon cream cheese
- 1 teaspoon chives, chopped
- 1 cup water, for cooking

Directions:
Pour water and insert the steamer rack in the instant pot. Place the eggs in the trivet and close the lid. Cook them on Manual (high pressure) for 5 minutes. Then allow the natural pressure release for 5 minutes. Cool the eggs in ice water and peel. Then cut them into halves and remove the egg yolks. Place the egg yolks in the bowl. Chop the avocado and add it in the egg yolks. Smash the mixture with the fork until smooth. Then add cream cheese, salt, and lemon juice. Mix up well and add chives. Stir the guacamole mixture little. Fill the egg whites with guacamole mass.

Nutrition value/serving: calories 138, fat 11.5, fiber 2.3, carbs 3.4, protein 6.4

Hot Tempeh

Prep time: 10 minutes | Cooking time: 9 minutes | Servings:4

Ingredients:
- 8 oz tempeh
- 1 teaspoon chili powder
- ¼ teaspoon ground paprika
- ¼ teaspoon ground turmeric
- 1 teaspoon avocado oil

Directions:
Cut the tempeh into 4 servings. After this, in the shallow bowl mix up together chili powder, ground paprika, turmeric, and avocado oil. Rub the tempeh with chili powder mixture from each side. Preheat the instant pot on sauté mode for 3 minutes. Then add tempeh and cook it for 3 minutes from each side.

Nutrition value/serving: calories 114, fat 6.4, fiber 0.4, carbs 5.9, protein 10.6

Garlic Aioli

Prep time: 15 minutes | Cooking time: 4 minutes | Servings:4

Ingredients:
- 4 garlic cloves, peeled
- 1 teaspoon lime juice
- 1 teaspoon mustard
- ½ cup heavy cream
- ¼ teaspoon ground black pepper
- ¼ teaspoon salt
- 1 cup water, for cooking

Directions:
Wrap the garlic in the foil. Then pour water and insert the steamer rack in the instant pot. Place the wrapped garlic in the rack and close the lid. Cook it on manual (high pressure) for 4 minutes Then allow the natural pressure release for 5 minutes and open the lid. Remove the garlic from the foil and transfer it in the bowl. Smash it with the help of the fork until you get puree texture. After this, add lime juice, mustard, ground black pepper, salt. Stir the mixture. Whip the heavy cream. Then combine together whipped cream and garlic mixture. Store the meal in the fridge for up to 4 days.

Nutrition value/serving: calories 61, fat 5.8, fiber 0.2, carbs 2, protein 0.7

Pesto Wings

Prep time: 10 minutes | Cooking time: 15 minutes | Servings:6

Ingredients:
- 6 chicken wings
- 1 teaspoon ground paprika
- 1 teaspoon butter
- 4 teaspoons pesto sauce
- 2 tablespoons cream cheese

Directions:
Rub the chicken wings with ground paprika. Toss butter in the instant pot and heat it up on sauté mode. When the butter is melted, place the chicken wings inside (in one layer) and cook them for 3 minutes from each side or until you get light brown color. Then add pesto sauce and cream cheese. Coat the chicken wings in the mixture well, bring to boil, and close the lid. Saute the wings for 4 minutes.

Nutrition value/serving: calories 127, fat 9.6, fiber 0.3, carbs 3.7, protein 6.4

Bacon Avocado Bombs

Prep time: 20 minutes | Cooking time: 10 minutes | Servings: 8

Ingredients:
- 1 avocado, pitted, peeled
- 3 eggs
- 2 bacon slices, chopped
- 4 tablespoons cream cheese
- ½ teaspoon green onion, minced
- 1 cup water, for cooking

Directions:
Pour water and insert the steamer rack in the instant pot. Place the egg on the rack and close the lid. Cook them for 5 minutes on steam mode. When the time is over, allow the natural pressure release for 5 minutes more. Then cool the eggs in ice water and peel. Clean the instant pot and remove the steamer rack. Put the chopped bacon slices in the instant pot and cook them on sauté mode for 5 minutes or until crunchy. Stir the bacon every minute. Meanwhile, chop the avocado and eggs into tiny pieces and place the ingredients in the big bowl. Add minced green onion and cream cheese. With the help of the fork mix up the mixture and smash it gently (we don't need smooth texture). Then add cooked bacon and stir until homogenous. With the help of the scopper make the balls and refrigerate them for 10-15 minutes. Store the bacon avocado bombs in the fridge in the closed vessel for up to 8 days.

Nutrition value/serving: calories 118, fat 10.3, fiber 1.7, carbs 2.5, protein 4.7

Bacon Sushi

Prep time: 15 minutes | Cooking time: 4 minutes | Servings: 6

Ingredients:
- 6 bacon slices
- 1 cucumber
- 3 teaspoons cream cheese
- ¼ teaspoon ground black pepper
- ¼ teaspoon salt
- ¼ teaspoon dried thyme
- ½ teaspoon coconut oil

Directions:
Sprinkle the bacon slices with dried thyme, salt, and ground black pepper. Put coconut oil in the instant pot. Melt it on sauté mode. Then arrange the bacon in one layer. Cook it for 1 minute and flip on another side. Cook the bacon for 1 minute more. Then transfer the bacon on the paper towel and dry well. Place the dried bacon on the sushi mat in the shape of the net. Then spread the bacon net with cream cheese. Cut the cucumber into the sticks. Place the cucumber sticks over the cream cheese. Roll the bacon in the shape of sushi and cut into 6 servings.

Nutrition value/serving: calories 120, fat 9, fiber 0.3, carbs 2.2, protein 7.5

Ranch Poppers

Prep time: 15 minutes | Cooking time: 4 minute | Servings: 8

Ingredients:
- ½ cup ground chicken
- ¼ cup zucchini, grated
- 1 teaspoon dried cilantro
- ¼ teaspoon garlic powder
- 1 teaspoon almond flour
- 1 teaspoon olive oil
- ½ teaspoon salt

Directions:
Mix up together ground chicken, grated zucchini, cilantro, garlic powder, and almond flour. Add salt and stir the mas until homogenous. Make the small balls (poppers) with the help of the fingertips. Pour olive oil in the instant pot. Arrange the ranch poppers in the instant pot and cook them for 1.5 minutes from each side.

Nutrition value/serving: calories 43, fat 3, fiber 0.4, carbs 0.9, protein 3.3

Keto Taquitos

Prep time: 15 minutes | Cooking time: 20 minutes | Servings:6

Ingredients:
- 3 low carb tortillas
- ¼ teaspoon onion powder
- ¼ cup Cheddar cheese, shredded
- 5 oz chicken breast, skinless, boneless
- ½ teaspoon ground black pepper
- ¼ teaspoon salt
- ½ teaspoon cayenne pepper
- 1 teaspoon butter
- 1 cup water, for cooking

Directions:
Rub the chicken breast with salt, cayenne pepper, and ground black pepper. Pour water and insert the steamer rack in the instant pot. Arrange the chicken in the steamer rack and close the lid. Cook it on manual mode (high pressure) for 15 minutes. Then make a quick pressure release and transfer the chicken on the chopping board. Shred the chicken. Place the shredded chicken in the mixing bowl. Add onion powder and shredded Cheddar cheese. Mix up the mixture well. Then spread tortillas with chicken mixture and roll. Clean the instant pot and remove the rack. Toss the butter in the instant pot, melt it on sauté mode. Arrange the rolled tortillas in the instant pot in one layer. Cook them for 2 minutes from each side. When taquitos are cooked, remove them from the instant pot and cut into 6 servings.

Nutrition value/serving: calories 93, fat 3.8, fiber 3.6, carbs 6.3, protein 7.7

Chicken Celery Boats

Prep time: 10 minutes | Cooking time: 10 minutes | Servings:2

Ingredients:
- 2 celery stalks
- 3 oz chicken fillet
- ¼ teaspoon minced garlic
- ¼ teaspoon salt
- 1 teaspoon cream cheese
- 1 cup water, for cooking

Directions:
Pour water and insert the steamer rack in the instant pot. Put the chicken on the rack and close the lid. Cook it on manual mode (high pressure) for 10 minutes. Then make a quick pressure release and remove the chicken from the instant pot. Shred the chicken and mix it up with minced garlic, salt, and cream cheese. Fill the celery stalks with chicken mixture.

Nutrition value/serving: calories 90, fat 3.8, fiber 0.3, carbs 0.7, protein 12.6

Keto Nachos

Prep time: 10 minutes | Cooking time: 27 minutes | Servings:2

Ingredients:
- ½ cup mini bell peppers
- ½ cup ground beef
- ¼ teaspoon chili powder
- ¼ teaspoon ground cumin
- ¼ teaspoon dried thyme
- ¼ teaspoon onion powder
- ¼ teaspoon garlic powder
- 2 oz Provolone cheese, grated
- 1 teaspoon coconut oil

Directions:
Put coconut oil in the instant pot and preheat it on sauté mode until it is melted. Then add ground beef, chili powder, ground cumin, thyme, onion powder, and garlic powder. Mix up the mixture well with the help of a spatula and cook on sauté mode for 15 minutes. Stir it from time to time. When the time is over, cut the mini bell peppers into halves and place them in the instant pot. Cook the keto nachos for 10 minutes more. The cooked bell peppers shouldn't be soft.

Nutrition value/serving: calories 213, fat 14, fiber 1.2, carbs 6.5, protein 15

Edamame Hummus

Prep time: 15 minutes | *Cooking time:* 5 minutes | *Servings:* 8

Ingredients:
- 1 ½ cup edamame beans, shelled
- 1 teaspoon salt
- ½ teaspoon harissa
- 1 garlic clove, peeled
- 4 tablespoons olive oil
- 1 tablespoon lemon juice
- 1 avocado, pitted, peeled, chopped
- 1 cup water, for cooking

Directions:

Pour water in the instant pot. Add edamame beans and garlic, and close the lid. Cook the beans on manual mode (high pressure) for 2 minutes. Then make a quick pressure release and open the lid. Transfer the edamame beans and garlic in the blender. Add 1/3 cup of water from the instant pot. Then add harissa, salt, lemon juice, and avocado. Blend the mixture until it is smooth and soft. Add more water if the texture of the hummus is very thick. Then add olive oil and pulse the hummus for 10 seconds. Transfer the cooked edamame hummus in the serving bowl.

Nutrition value/serving: calories 99, fat 9, fiber 2.2, carbs 3.5, protein 2.5

Crab Spread

Prep time: 10 minutes | *Cooking time:* 4 minutes | *Servings:* 6

Ingredients:
- ½ cup cauliflower, chopped
- 10 oz crab meat
- 1 teaspoon minced garlic
- ½ cup cream cheese
- 1 tablespoon fresh cilantro, chopped
- 1 cup water, for cooking

Directions:

Place crab meat and cauliflower in the instant pot. Add water and close the lid. Cook the ingredients for 4 minutes on manual mode (high pressure). Then remove the cooked cauliflower and crab meat from the instant pot. Chop the crab meat into small pieces. Then smash the cauliflower with the help of the fork. The smashed mixture shouldn't be smooth. Mix up together cauliflower, crab meat, minced garlic, cream cheese, and cilantro. Mix up the spread well and store it in the fridge for up to 3 days.

Nutrition value/serving: calories 112, fat 7.6, fiber 0.2, carbs 2, protein 7.6

Bacon-Wrapped Shrimps

Prep time: 15 minutes | *Cooking time:* 8 minutes | *Servings:* 4

Ingredients:
- 4 king shrimps, peeled
- 4 bacon slices
- ¼ teaspoon chili flakes
- ¼ teaspoon ground black pepper
- ¼ teaspoon salt
- ½ teaspoon avocado oil
- 1 cup water, for cooking

Directions:

Brush the instant pot bowl with avocado oil and heat it up for 2 minutes on sauté mode. Arrange the bacon slices in one layer and cook for 2 minutes from each side. Cool the cooked bacon. Clean the instant pot. Place the steamer rack and pour water in the instant pot. Place the shrimps in the mixing bowl. Add chili flakes, ground black pepper, and salt. Mix up the spices and shrimps. Then wrap every shrimp in cooked bacon. Secure them with toothpicks. Place the shrimps on the rack and close the lid. Cook the seafood for 2 minutes on manual mode (high pressure). When the time is over, make a quick pressure release.

Nutrition value/serving: calories 127, fat 8.3, fiber 0.1, carbs 0.4, protein 12.4

Tuna Steak Skewers

Prep time: 15 minutes | Cooking time: 5 minutes | Servings: 4

Ingredients:
- 2 tuna steaks
- ¼ teaspoon salt
- 1 teaspoon ground paprika
- ¾ teaspoon dried sage
- 1 cup water, for cooking

Directions:
Chop the tuna steaks into medium cubes and sprinkle with salt, ground paprika, and dried sage. Then string the meat on the skewers. Pour water and insert the steamer rack in the instant pot. Arrange the tuna steak skewers on the rack and close the lid. Cook the snack for 5 minutes on manual mode (high pressure). Then allow the natural pressure release for 10 minutes.

Nutrition value/serving: calories 158, fat 5.4, fiber 0.3, carbs 0.4, protein 25.5

Marinated Olives

Prep time: 10 minutes | Cooking time: 4 minutes | Servings: 7

Ingredients:
- 7 kalamata olives
- 2 tablespoons lemon juice
- ¼ teaspoon peppercorns
- ¼ teaspoon minced garlic
- ¼ teaspoon fennel seeds
- ¼ teaspoon thyme
- 1 bay leaf
- 4 tablespoons avocado oil

Directions:
Pour avocado oil in the instant pot. Add bay leaf, thyme, fennel seeds, minced garlic, peppercorns, and lemon juice. Cook the ingredients on sauté mode for 4 minutes or until it is brought to boil. Then add olives and coat them in the oil mixture well. Switch off the instant pot. Transfer the cooked olives in the glass can and let them cool to room temperature. Marinate the olives for 2-3 days in the fridge.

Nutrition value/serving: calories 18, fat 1.5, fiber 0.6, carbs 1, protein 0.2

Chicharrones

Prep time: 15 minutes | Cooking time: 35 minutes | Servings: 4

Ingredients:
- 8 oz pork skin
- ¼ teaspoon salt
- ½ teaspoon avocado oil
- 1 cup water, for cooking

Directions:
Pour water in the instant pot. Add pork skin and close the lid. Cook it on manual mode (high pressure) for 25 minutes. Then allow the natural pressure release for 10 minutes. Remove the pork skin from the instant pot. Clean the instant pot. Chop the pork skin into small pieces and return back in the instant pot. Add oil and salt. Mix up well. Cook the meal on sauté mode for 10 minutes. Stir it from time to time to avoid burning.

Nutrition value/serving: calories 309, fat 17.8, fiber 0, carbs 0, protein 34.8

Keto Spanakopita Pie Slices

Prep time: 20 minutes | *Cooking time:* 50 minutes | *Servings:* 6

Ingredients:
- 4 tablespoons butter, softened
- 4 tablespoons coconut flour
- 4 tablespoons almond flour
- ¼ teaspoon baking powder
- ¼ teaspoon ground nutmeg
- ¼ teaspoon salt
- 3 eggs
- 1 cups fresh spinach, chopped
- 1 cup cheddar cheese, shredded
- 2 tablespoons cream cheese
- 1 cup water, for cooking

Directions:
Make the spanakopita crust: mix up together butter, coconut flour, almond flour, baking powder, ground nutmeg, and salt. Crack 1 egg inside the mixture and knead the non-sticky dough. Then line the instant pot baking pan with baking paper and place the dough inside. Flatten it in the shape of the pie crust. In the mixing bowl combine together cream cheese, shredded Cheddar cheese, spinach, and cracked remaining eggs. Stir it well. Place the mixture over the pie crust and flatten it. Cover the surface of spanakopita with baking paper. Pour water and insert the rack in the instant pot. Place the pan with spanakopita in the instant pot and close the lid. Cook the spanakopita for 50 minutes on manual (high pressure). Then make a quick pressure release. Cool the cooked meal to room temperature and slice.

Nutrition value/serving: calories 319, fat 27.5, fiber 4.1, carbs 7.8, protein 12.9

Dog Nuggets

Prep time: 10 minutes | *Cooking time:* 20 minutes | *Servings:* 6

Ingredients:
- 5 oz Piza keto dough
- 3 pork sausages
- 1 cup water, for cooking

Directions:
Roll up the dough and cut it into 6 strips. Then cut every pork sausage into halves. Roll every sausage half in the doughs trip. Pour water in the instant pot and insert the steamer rack. Line the rack with baking paper. Place the dog nuggets on the baking paper and close the lid. Cook the snack for 20 minutes on manual mode (high pressure). Then make a quick pressure release and transfer the meal in the serving plate.

Nutrition value/serving: calories 199, fat 10.2, fiber 3.2, carbs 6.7, protein 20.1

Keto Cheetos

Prep time: 25 minutes | *Cooking time:* 5 minutes | *Servings:* 6

Ingredients:
- 1 cup Cheddar cheese, shredded
- 2 egg whites, whisked
- ¾ teaspoon cream of tartar
- 1 tablespoon coconut flour
- 1 tablespoon coconut oil

Directions:
Place the cheese in one layer on the plate and freeze it. Then transfer the frozen cheese in the blender and blend until you get crumbs. Add cream of tartar, egg whites, and coconut flour. Blend the mixture until smooth and transfer it in the pastry bag. Place the coconut oil in the instant pot and melt it on sauté mode. Make the small sticks from the cheese mixture (using the pastry bag) and cook them for 2 minutes from each side or until they are light brown. Dry the cooked Cheetos with the help of the paper towel if needed.

Nutrition value/serving: calories 112, fat 8.9, fiber 0.8, carbs 1.9, protein 6.2

Cauliflower PopCorn

Prep time: 15 minutes | *Cooking time:* 20 minutes | *Servings:* 6

Ingredients:
- 1 cup cauliflower florets
- ½ teaspoon ground nutmeg
- ¼ teaspoon salt
- ½ teaspoon ground paprika
- 1 tablespoon avocado oil
- 1 egg, beaten
- 1 tablespoon coconut flakes
- 1 teaspoon lemon juice
- 1 cup water, for cooking

Directions:
Pour water and place the cauliflower florets in the instant pot. Cook them in manual mode (high pressure) for 3 minutes. Then make a quick pressure release and transfer cauliflower in the mixing bowl. Clean the instant pot. Sprinkle the cauliflower with salt, ground nutmeg, paprika, and lemon juice. Gently shake the mixture. Pour avocado oil in the instant pot. Add beaten egg in the cauliflower and stir well. Then sprinkle the vegetables with coconut flakes and shake well to coat. Place the cauliflower in the instant pot and cook for 15 minutes or until light brown. Stir it from time to time. Transfer the cooked cauliflower popcorn in the big bowl.

Nutrition value/serving: calories 22, fat 1.4, fiber 0.7, carbs 1.4, protein 1.4

Cheese Pops

Prep time: 10 minutes | *Cooking time:* 5 minutes | *Servings:* 4

Ingredients:
- 4 oz Provolone cheese
- 1 egg, beaten
- ¼ cup coconut flakes
- ¼ teaspoon salt
- ¼ teaspoon cayenne pepper
- 1 teaspoon sesame oil

Directions:
Cut the cheese into 4 cubes. Then mix up together coconut flakes, salt, and cayenne pepper. Then dip every cheese cube in the egg and coat in the coconut flakes. Brush the instant pot with sesame oil. Place the cheese cubes in the instant pot in one layer and cook on sauté mode for 1 minute from each side or until they are light brown.

Nutrition value/serving: calories 143, fat 11.5, fiber 0.5, carbs 1.5, protein 8.8

Chocolate Bacon

Prep time: 20 minutes | *Cooking time:* 3 minutes | *Servings:* 4

Ingredients:
- 1 oz black chocolate
- 4 bacon slices

Directions:
Cut every bacon slice into halves and place them in the instant pot in one layer. Cook them for 1 minute from each side on sauté mode or until bacon is crunchy. Then cool the bacon and place it in the freezer for 10 minutes. Melt the dark chocolate in a microwave oven until liquid (appx 40 seconds). Then remove the bacon from the freezer. Dip every bacon piece in the melted chocolate (dip ½ part of every bacon piece).

Nutrition value/serving: calories 145, fat 11.1, fiber 0.7, carbs 3.5, protein 7.8

Chocolate Shake

Prep time: 15 minutes | Cooking time: 20 minutes | Servings:6

Ingredients:
- 2 cups heavy cream
- 4 tablespoons cocoa powder
- 4 teaspoons Erythritol
- 1 teaspoon vanilla extract
- ½ cup of organic almond milk
- 1 tablespoon coconut flakes

Directions:
Pour almond milk, vanilla extract, and Erythritol in the instant pot. Bring the liquid to boil on sauté mode. Then add cocoa powder and switch off the instant pot. With the help of the immersion blender, blend the liquid until you get strong foam. Keep blending and start to add heavy cream. Blend the mixture for 2 minutes more. Then add coconut flakes and blend the shake for 1 minute. Pour the cooked shake in the serving glasses.

Nutrition value/serving: calories 156, fat 15.8, fiber 1.1, carbs 7.3, protein 1.6

Egg Yolk Spread

Prep time: 10 minutes | Cooking time: 5 minutes | Servings:4

Ingredients:
- 4 eggs
- 1 tablespoon cream cheese
- 1 tablespoon fresh parsley, chopped
- ¼ teaspoon chili flakes
- 1 teaspoon mustard
- 1 cup water, for cooking

Directions:
Pour water and insert the steamer rack in the instant pot. Place the eggs on the rack and close the lid. Cook the eggs on manual mode (high pressure) for 5 minutes. Then allow natural pressur release for 5 minutes more and transfer the eggs in ice water. Peel the eggs and cut into halves. Remove the eggs yolks and transfer them in the bowl. Add parsley, cream cheese, chili flakes, and mustard. Mash the mixture with the help of the fork. Transfer the cooked egg yolk mixture in the bowl.

Nutrition value/serving: calories 67, fat 5.6, fiber 0.2, carbs 1, protein 3.1

Chili Pumpkin Seeds

Prep time: 10 minutes | Cooking time: 5 minutes | Servings:6

Ingredients:
- 1 cup pumpkin seeds
- 1 teaspoon olive oil
- 1 teaspoon chili powder
- ½ teaspoon salt

Directions:
Mix up together pumpkin seeds with olive oil and place in the instant pot. Cook the seeds on sauté mode for 5 minutes. Stir them every minute with the help of the spatula to avoid burning. Then transfer the cooked pumpkin seeds in the bowl, add chili powder, and salt. Shake the seeds. Store the cooked snack in the paper bag.

Nutrition value/serving: calories 132, fat 11.4, fiber 1.1, carbs 4.3, protein 5.7

Cheese Meatballs with Greens
Prep time: 10 minutes | Cooking time: 12 minutes | Servings:4

Ingredients:
- 1 cup ground beef
- 1 oz goat cheese, crumbled
- 1 teaspoon chives, chopped
- 1 oz scallion, chopped
- 1 tablespoon almond flour
- ½ teaspoon salt
- 1 teaspoon olive oil
- ¼ teaspoon ground black pepper
- 1 cup water, for cooking

Directions:
In the mixing bowl mix up together ground beef, chives, goat cheese, scallions, almond flour, salt, and ground black pepper. With the help of the scooper make the small meatballs. Pour olive oil in the skillet and heat it up (or use instant pot (sauté mode) for this step). Place the meatballs in the hot oil and cook for 1 minute from each side. Then pour water in the instant pot and insert the steamer rack. Put the meatballs in the instant pot and close the lid. Cook the appetizer for 8 minutes on manual mode (high pressure). Then make a quick pressure release and transfer the meatballs in the serving plate.

Nutrition value/serving: calories 96, fat 6.7, fiber 0.4, carbs 1, protein 7.6

Wrapped Chicken Cubes
Prep time: 10 minutes | Cooking time: 15 minutes | Servings:2

Ingredients:
- 4 oz chicken fillet
- 2 bacon slices
- ¼ teaspoon salt
- ¼ teaspoon dried basil
- 1 tablespoon heavy cream
- 1 teaspoon butter

Directions:
Cut the chicken fillet into cubes and sprinkle with salt and dried basil. Then cut the bacon slices into the 4 pieces. Wrap the chicken cubes in the bacon and secure with toothpicks. Place them in the instant pot. Add heavy cream and butter. Cook the chicken cubes on sauté mode for 15 minutes. Stir the meal every 5 minutes.

Nutrition value/serving: calories 253, fat 16.8, fiber 0, carbs 0.5, protein 23.6

Keto Crackers
Prep time: 7 minutes | Cooking time: 5 minutes | Servings:10

Ingredients:
- 1 cup Mozzarella, shredded
- 3 tablespoons cream cheese
- ½ cup almond flour
- 1 egg, beaten
- ½ teaspoon sesame oil

Directions:
Make the dough: mix up together Mozzarella cheese, cream cheese, almond flour, and egg. Knead the mixture until you get a soft dough. Then roll it up and cut into cracker squares. Use the cutter for this step or do it with the help of a knife. Then brush the instant pot bowl with sesame oil. Arrange the crackers in instant pot in one layer (5-6 cracker squares) and cook them on sauté mode for 3 minutes from each side. The cooked crackers should be golden brown. Repeat the same steps with remaining uncooked crackers.

Nutrition value/serving: calories 60, fat 4.9, fiber 1.1, carbs 7.3, protein 0.9

Fish and Seafood

Fish Saag

Prep time: 10 minutes | *Cooking time:* 5 minutes | *Servings:* 4

Ingredients:
- 1 teaspoon tomato paste
- ½ white onion, diced
- 4 tablespoons coconut milk
- ½ teaspoon ginger, minced
- ¼ teaspoon garlic powder
- ½ teaspoon garam masala
- ½ teaspoon ground turmeric
- 1 cup spinach, chopped
- ¼ teaspoon salt
- ½ cup of water
- 12 oz haddock fillet
- 1 teaspoon olive oil
- ¼ teaspoon ground black pepper

Directions:
Put in the blender: tomato paste, diced onion, ginger, garlic powder, garam masala, ground turmeric, and chopped spinach. Blend the mixture until is smooth (appx.2 minutes). Then add water and pulse it for 10 seconds. Pour the liquid in the instant pot. Insert the steamer rack over it. Brush the haddock fillet with olive oil and sprinkle with salt and ground black pepper. Place the fish on the foil. Fold the foil to get the fish package and transfer it on the steamer rack. Close and seal the lid. Cook the fish saag for 5 minutes on steam mode (high pressure). When the time is over, make a quick pressure release and remove the fish. Cut the haddock fillet into the servings and place it on the plate. Top every fish serving with spinach sauce (from the instant pot).

Nutrition value/serving: calories 151, fat 5.6, fiber 1, carbs 3.2, protein 21.5

Brazilian Fish Stew

Prep time: 10 minutes | *Cooking time:* 14 minutes | *Servings:* 6

Ingredients:
- 6 halibut fillet, chopped (6 oz each fish fillet)
- 1 tablespoon almond butter
- 1 tablespoon lemon juice
- 1 teaspoon fresh parsley, chopped
- 1 white onion, diced
- 1 green bell pepper, chopped
- 2 garlic cloves, diced
- 1 teaspoon tomato paste
- 1 cup chicken broth
- 3 tablespoons coconut milk
- 1 teaspoon ground coriander
- 1 teaspoon paprika
- ½ teaspoon white pepper
- ¼ teaspoon chili powder

Directions:
Make the stew sauce: combine together almond butter, lemon juice, parsley, onion, bell pepper, diced garlic, tomato paste, chicken broth, coconut milk, ground coriander, paprika, white pepper, and chili powder. Then transfer the mixture in the instant pot and close the lid. Cook the ingredients for 8 minutes on manual mode (high pressure). Then allow the natural pressure release and open the lid. Stir the stew sauce well and set sauté mode for 6 minutes. Cook the stew on sauté mode for 1 minute and then add chopped halibut fillets. Close the lid and sauté the stew for the remaining 5 minutes.

Nutrition value/serving: calories 247, fat 7.7, fiber 1.2, carbs 4.8, protein 38.1

Fish Casserole

Prep time: 5 minutes | *Cooking time:* 15 minutes | *Servings:* 6

Ingredients:
- 1 cup white mushrooms, chopped
- 1 tablespoon coconut oil
- 1 teaspoon ground black pepper
- 1 tablespoon fresh cilantro, chopped
- 1 cup whipped cream
- 1-pound cod, chopped
- 2 oz Parmesan, grated
- 1 teaspoon dried oregano

Directions:

Toss coconut oil in the instant pot and melt it on sauté mode. Then add chopped white mushrooms and cook for 5 minutes. Stir them from time to time. After this, add ground black pepper, dried oregano, and chopped cod. Stir the ingredients with the help of the spatula and cook for 2 minutes. Then add fresh cilantro and whipped cream. Mix up the casserole and cook it for 3 minutes. Then top the meal with Parmesan and close the lid. Cook the casserole for 5 minutes.

Nutrition value/serving: calories 192, fat 11.2, fiber 0.3, carbs 1.7, protein 21.2

Salmon Pie

Prep time: 15 minutes | *Cooking time:* 20 minutes | *Servings:* 4

Ingredients:
- 10 oz salmon fillet, chopped
- ½ teaspoon ground coriander
- ½ teaspoon salt
- ½ cup green peas
- ½ cup heavy cream
- 1 teaspoon coconut oil
- 1 teaspoon sesame oil
- ½ cup almond meal
- 2 tablespoons butter, softened
- 1 cup water, for cooking

Directions:

Toss the coconut oil in the instant pot bowl and melt it on sauté mode. When the oil is melted, add chopped salmon fillet. Sprinkle it with coriander and cook for 1 minute from each side. After this, add salt, green peas, and heavy cream. Close the lid and sauté the fish for 3 minutes. Meanwhile, make the pie dough: mix up together almond meal and butter. Knead the dough. Brush the instant pot baking pan with sesame oil. Then place the dough inside and flatten it in the shape of the pie crust. Put the salmon fillet mixture (stuffing) inside the pie crust and flatten it. Cover the pie with foil and secure the edges. Then clean the instant pot and pour water inside. Arrange the steamer rack and put the pie on it. Cook the salmon pie for 15 minutes on Manual mode (high pressure). When the time is over, make a quick pressure release and open the lid. Remove the foil and let the pie cool for 10-15 minutes. Cut it into the servings. Transfer the serving in the table with the help of the spatula.

Nutrition value/serving: calories 300, fat 24, fiber 2.4, carbs 5.6, protein 17.6

Pesto Salmon

Prep time: 10 minutes | *Cooking time:* 10 minutes | *Servings:* 3

Ingredients:
- 9 oz salmon fillet (3 oz every salmon fillet)
- 3 teaspoons pesto sauce
- 1 teaspoon butter
- 2 tablespoons organic almond milk

Directions:

Melt butter in sauté mode. Meanwhile, mix up together almond milk and pesto sauce. Brush the salmon fillets with pesto mixture from both sides and put in the melted butter. Cook the fish for 3 minutes from each side on sauté mode.

Nutrition value/serving: calories 166, fat 9.9, fiber 0.1, carbs 3, protein 17.3

Tuna Salad

Prep time: 15 minutes | Cooking time: 5 minutes | Servings: 5

Ingredients:
- 3 eggs
- ½ red onion, diced
- ½ teaspoon minced garlic
- 1 avocado, pitted, peeled, chopped
- 1 celery stalk, chopped
- 3 tablespoons ricotta cheese
- 1 teaspoon lemon juice
- ½ teaspoon ground paprika
- 8 oz tuna, canned
- 1 cup water, for cooking

Directions:
Pour water and insert the steamer rack in the instant pot. Put eggs on the rack and close the lid. Cook the eggs on steam mode for 5 minutes. Allow the natural pressure release for 5 minutes. The cool the eggs in cold water. Peel the eggs. Meanwhile, make the salad sauce: mix up together ricotta cheese, lemon juice, minced garlic, and ground paprika. In the salad bowl combine together, onion, avocado, and celery stalk. Shred the canned tuna and add it in the salad bowl too. After this, add salad sauce. Chop the eggs and add in the salad too. Mix up the cooked meal.

Nutrition value/serving: calories 223, fat 14.9, fiber 3.1, carbs 5.5, protein 17.4

Tandoori Salmon

Prep time: 15 minutes | Cooking time: 3 minutes | Servings: 2

Ingredients:
- ½ teaspoon garam masala
- ½ teaspoon ground paprika
- 1 teaspoon minced ginger
- ½ teaspoon ground turmeric
- ½ teaspoon salt
- ½ teaspoon chili powder
- ½ teaspoon minced garlic
- 1 tablespoon lemon juice
- 1 tablespoon olive oil
- 10 oz salmon fillet
- 1 cup water, for cooking

Directions:
Cut the salmon fillet into 2 servings. After this, in the mixing bowl combine together garam masala, paprika, minced ginger, ground turmeric, salt, chili powder, minced garlic, lemon juice, and olive oil. Stir the mixture until smooth. Rub the salmon fillets with the spice mixture and arrange it in the steamer rack. Pour water in the instant pot and insert the steamer rack with salmon inside. Close the lid and cook the meal for 3 minutes on steam mode (high pressure). When the time is over, make a quick pressure release and open the lid.

Nutrition value/serving: calories 259, fat 16.1, fiber 0.7, carbs 2.1, protein 27.9

Cheese Melt

Prep time: 10 minutes | Cooking time: 6 minutes | Servings: 2

Ingredients:
- 2 low carb tortillas
- ¼ cup Cheddar cheese, shredded
- 4 oz tuna, canned
- 1 teaspoon cream cheese
- ½ teaspoon Italian seasonings
- 1 teaspoon sesame oil

Directions:
Shred the tuna and mix it with Italian seasonings and cream cheese. Then spread the mixture over the tortillas. Top the mixture with Cheddar cheese and fold into the shape of pockets. Pour sesame oil in the instant pot and heat it up on sauté mode for 2 minutes. Then arrange the cheese pockets in the instant pot and cook them for 2 minutes from each side. Transfer the cooked meal in the serving plates. It is recommended to eat the cheese melts immediately after cooking.

Nutrition value/serving: calories 272, fat 14.5, fiber 7, carbs 12.4, protein 21.7

Prosciutto Shrimp Skewers

Prep time: 15 minutes | *Cooking time:* 4 minutes | *Servings:* 7

Ingredients:
- 1-pound shrimps, peeled
- 4 oz prosciutto, sliced
- ½ teaspoon olive oil
- ¼ teaspoon chili powder
- 1 cup water, for cooking

Directions:
Wrap every shrimp in prosciutto and string on the skewers. Then sprinkle the shrimps with olive oil and chili powder. Pour water in the instant pot and arrange the steamer rack. Place the shrimp skewers in the steamer and close the lid. Cook the meal for 4 minutes on manual mode (high pressure). When the time is over, make a quick pressure release and open the lid. Transfer the cooked shrimp skewers on the plate.

Nutrition value/serving: calories 104, fat 2.4, fiber 0, carbs 1.3, protein 18.2

Lime Salmon Burger

Prep time: 10 minutes | *Cooking time:* 8 minutes | *Servings:* 6

Ingredients:
- 14 oz salmon fillet
- 1 teaspoon mustard
- ½ teaspoon lime zest, grated
- 1 tablespoon lime juice
- ½ teaspoon chives, chopped
- ½ teaspoon ground black pepper
- ½ teaspoon cayenne pepper
- 1 teaspoon olive oil
- ¼ teaspoon ground coriander
- 12 Cheddar cheese slices

Directions:
Chop the salmon fillet and put it in the blender. Blend the fish until smooth and transfer it in the mixing bowl. Add mustard, lime zest, lime juice, chives, ground black pepper, cayenne pepper, and ground coriander. Stir the mixture with the help of the spoon and make 6 burgers, Brush the instant pot with olive oil. Place the salmon burgers in the instant pot in one layer. Set sauté mode and cook them for 5 minutes. Then flip the burgers on another side and cook for 3 minutes more. When the fish burgers are cooked, transfer them on the plate and cool for 5 minutes. Then place every salmon burger on the cheese slice and top with the remaining cheese slice. Pierce every burger with a toothpick.

Nutrition value/serving: calories 324, fat 23.6, fiber 0.2, carbs 1.2, protein 27

Curry Fish

Prep time: 15 minutes | *Cooking time:* 4 minutes | *Servings:* 4

Ingredients:
- 1-pound cod fillet
- 1 teaspoon curry paste
- 2 tablespoons coconut milk
- ½ teaspoon sesame oil
- 1 cup water, for cooking

Directions:
In the shallow bowl whisk together coconut milk and curry paste. Add sesame oil and stir the liquid. After this, chop the cod fillet into the big cubes. Pour the curry mixture over the fish and mix up. Then pour water and insert the steamer rack. Put the fish cubes in the steamer rack and close the lid. Cook the meal on steam mode for 4 minutes. When the time is over, allow the natural pressure release for 5 minutes.

Nutrition value/serving: calories 122, fat 4.1, fiber 0.2, carbs 0.8, protein 20.5

Fried Salmon

Prep time: 10 minutes | *Cooking time:* 7 minutes | *Servings:* 4

Ingredients:
- 1 teaspoon Erythritol
- ¼ teaspoon lemongrass
- ¼ teaspoon ground nutmeg
- ½ teaspoon cayenne pepper
- ¼ teaspoon salt
- 1-pound salmon fillet
- 1 tablespoon coconut oil

Directions:
Cut the salmon fillet into 4 fillets. In the shallow bowl combine together spices: lemongrass, ground nutmeg, cayenne pepper, and salt. Rub every salmon fillet with spices. Then toss coconut oil in the instant pot and melt it on sauté mode (approximately 2-3 minutes). Place the salmon fillets in one layer and cook them for 2 minutes from each side. Then sprinkle the salmon fillets with Erythritol and flip on another side. Cook the fish for 1 minute more and transfer in the plate.

Nutrition value/serving: calories 181, fat 10.5, fiber 0.1, carbs 1.5, protein 22

Spicy Mackerel

Prep time: 15 minutes | *Cooking time:* 8 minutes | *Servings:* 4

Ingredients:
- 1-pound fresh mackerel, trimmed
- 1 teaspoon dried oregano
- ½ teaspoon chili powder
- ¼ teaspoon ground black pepper
- ½ teaspoon salt
- ¼ teaspoon chili flakes
- ½ teaspoon dried sage
- 1 teaspoon dried basil
- 1 tablespoon olive oil
- 1 cup water, for cooking

Directions:
In the mixing bowl mix up together dried oregano, chili powder, ground black pepper, salt, chili flakes, dried sage, and dried basil. Then rub the fish with spicy mixture generously. After this, brush it with olive oil and place in the steamer rack, Pour water and insert the steamer rack in the instant pot Close the lid and cook the fish for 8 minutes on Manual mode (high pressure). When the time is over, make a quick pressure release.

Nutrition value/serving: calories 330, fat 23.8, fiber 0.3, carbs 0.6, protein 27.2

Salmon in Fragrant Sauce

Prep time: 10 minutes | *Cooking time:* 5 minutes | *Servings:* 2

Ingredients:
- 10 oz salmon fillet
- 1 teaspoon fresh parsley, chopped
- ½ teaspoon lime zest, grated
- 1 teaspoon minced garlic
- 1 jalapeno pepper, diced
- 1 teaspoon Erythritol
- 2 tablespoons avocado oil
- 1 teaspoon ground paprika
- ½ teaspoon ground coriander
- 2 tablespoons lemon juice
- 1 cup water, for cooking

Directions:
Cut the salmon fillet into 2 servings. Pour water and insert the steamer rack in the instant pot. Place the salmon fillets on the rack and close the lid. Steam the fish for 5 minutes on Steam mode. When the time is over make a quick pressure release and transfer the fish on the plates. While the fish is cooking, make the fragrant sauce: in the bowl combine together parsley, lime zest, minced garlic, diced jalapeno pepper, Erythritol, avocado oil, paprika, ground coriander, and lemon juice. Pour the sauce over the cooked salmon.

Nutrition value/serving: calories 218, fat 10.8, fiber 1.4, carbs 5.2, protein 28.2

Shrimp Salad with Avocado

Prep time: 10 minutes | Cooking time: 7 minutes | Servings: 4

Ingredients:
- ½ avocado, chopped
- 7 oz shrimps, peeled
- 1 cup lettuce, chopped
- 2 bacon slices, chopped
- 2 tablespoons heavy cream
- 1 teaspoon peanuts, chopped
- ½ teaspoon ground black pepper
- ¼ teaspoon Pink salt
- 1 cup water, for cooking

Directions:
Pour water and insert the steamer rack in the instant pot. Place the shrimps in the rack and close the lid. Cook them on manual mode (high pressure) for 1 minute. Then make quick pressure release and transfer the shrimps in the salad bowl. Remove the steamer rack and clean the instant pot bowl. Place the bacon in the instant pot and cook it on sauté mode for 6 minutes. Stir it every minute to avoid burning. Then transfer the cooked bacon to the shrimps. Add chopped bacon, lettuce, and peanuts. Then in the shallow bowl mix up together heavy cream, peanuts, ground black pepper, and Pink salt. Pour the liquid over the salad and shake it gently.

Nutrition value/serving: calories 194, fat 12.9, fiber 1.9, carbs 4, protein 15.7

Seafood Omelet

Prep time: 15 minutes | Cooking time: 10 minutes | Servings:4

Ingredients:
- 4 eggs, beaten
- 2 tablespoons cream cheese
- ½ teaspoon chili flakes
- 1 oz Parmesan, grated
- 5 oz crab meat, canned, chopped
- ½ teaspoon butter, melted
- 1 teaspoon chives, chopped
- 1 cup water, for cooking

Directions:
In the mixing bowl combine together eggs, cream cheese, chili flakes, and chives. Brush the instant pot baking pan with butter and pour the egg mixture inside. Top the egg mixture with chopped crab meat and grated Parmesan. Whisk the mixture gently with the help of the fork. Pour water and insert the steamer rack in the instant pot. Place the instant pot baking pan in the rack and close the lid. Cook the omelet on steam mode for 10 minutes. When the time is over, allow the natural pressure release for 5 minutes.

Nutrition value/serving: calories 139, fat 8.7, fiber 0, carbs 1.4, protein 12.7

Shrimp Tacos

Prep time: 10 minutes | Cooking time: 1 minute | Servings:5

Ingredients:
- 5 low carb tortillas
- ½ cup white cabbage, shredded
- 2 oz Cotija cheese, crumbled
- 1 tablespoon lemon juice
- ½ teaspoon ground cumin
- ½ teaspoon cayenne pepper
- ¼ teaspoon garlic powder
- ¼ teaspoon onion powder
- ½ teaspoon chili powder
- 1 tablespoon green onions, chopped
- 1 tablespoon fresh cilantro, chopped
- 2 tablespoons avocado oil
- 3 tablespoons heavy cream
- 1-pound shrimps, peeled
- 1 cup water, for cooking

Directions:
Pour water and insert the steamer rack in the instant pot. In the mixing bowl combine together lemon juice, ground cumin, cayenne pepper, garlic powder, onion powder, and chili powder. Coat the shrimps in the mixture and transfer in the steamer rack. Close the lid and cook them for 1 minute on Manual mode (high pressure). Make a quick pressure release and open the lid. Make the taco sauce: mix up together heavy cream, avocado oil, cilantro, and green onions. Then mix up together shredded white cabbage and sauce. Place the cooked shrimps on the tortillas. Add shredded cabbage mixture and Cotija cheese. Fold the tortillas into the tacos.

Nutrition value/serving: calories 272, fat 10.9, fiber 7.7, carbs 15, protein 27

Shrimp Cocktail

Prep time: 10 minutes | *Cooking time:* 1 minute | *Servings:* 6

Ingredients:
- 16 oz shrimps, peeled
- 1 cup low carb ketchup
- ½ tablespoon lemon juice
- 1 teaspoon horseradish, grated
- ¼ teaspoon white pepper
- ½ teaspoon salt
- 1 cup water, for cooking

Directions:

Pour water and insert the steamer rack in the instant pot. Sprinkle the shrimps with salt and place in the steamer rack. Cook the seafood for 0 minutes on manual mode (high pressure). Make a quick pressure release and transfer the shrimps in the serving plate. Then make shrimp cocktail sauce: in the sauce bowl, mix up together low carb ketchup, lemon juice, horseradish, and white pepper. Dip the shrimps in the sauce.

Nutrition value/serving: calories 99, fat 1.3, fiber 0.1, carbs 1.3, protein 17.3

Mussels Casserole

Prep time: 10 minutes | *Cooking time:* 13 minutes | *Servings:* 4

Ingredients:
- 9 oz mussels, canned
- 1 cup cauliflower, chopped
- ½ cup Cheddar cheese, shredded
- ½ cup heavy cream
- 1 teaspoon Italian seasonings
- 1 teaspoon olive oil
- 1 teaspoon salt
- 1 tablespoon fresh dill, chopped
- 1 cup water, for cooking

Directions:

Pour water and insert the trivet in the instant pot. Place the cauliflower on the trivet and cook it on manual mode (high pressure) for 3 minutes. Then make a quick pressure release. Transfer the cauliflower in the instant pot casserole mold. Add canned mussels, cheese, heavy cream, Italian seasonings, olive oil, salt, and dill. Mix up the casserole and cover it with foil. Place the casserole mold on the trivet and close the lid. Cook the casserole for 10 minutes on manual mode (high pressure). When the time is over, make a quick pressure release. Mix up the casserole with the help of the spoon before serving.

Nutrition value/serving: calories 185, fat 13.2, fiber 0.7, carbs 4.9, protein 12.1

Skagenrora

Prep time: 10 minutes | *Cooking time:* 1 minute | *Servings:* 4

Ingredients:
- 11 oz shrimps, peeled
- ½ cup of coconut milk
- 1 tablespoon ricotta cheese
- 2 tablespoons fresh parsley, chopped
- 1 teaspoon lime juice
- ¼ teaspoon chili powder
- ¼ teaspoon ground black pepper
- 1 red onion, chopped
- 1 cup water, for cooking

Directions:

Pour water and insert the steamer rack in the instant pot. Put the shrimps in the rack and close the lid. Cook them on manual mode (high pressure) for 1 minute. When the time is over, make a quick pressure release and transfer the shrimps in the salad bowl. In the separated bowl mix up together coconut milk, ricotta cheese, fresh parsley, lime juice, chili powder, and ground black pepper. The sauce is cooked. Combine together shrimps with chopped red onion. Add sauce and mix it up.

Nutrition value/serving: calories 180, fat 8.9, fiber 1.4, carbs 6, protein 19.3

Butter Scallops

Prep time: 10 minutes | *Cooking time:* 7 minutes | *Servings:* 4

Ingredients:
- 1-pound scallops
- 3 tablespoons butter
- ½ teaspoon dried rosemary
- ¼ teaspoon salt

Directions:
Put butter in the instant pot. Set sauté mode and melt butter (it will take approximately 3 minutes. Add dried rosemary and salt. Stir the butter. Then place the scallops in the hot butter in one layer. Cook them on sauté mode for 2 minutes. Then flip the scallops on another side and cook for 2 minutes more. Serve the scallops with hot butter.

Nutrition value/serving: calories 177, fat 9.5, fiber 0.1, carbs 2.8, protein 19.1

Cajun Crab Casserole

Prep time: 10 minutes | *Cooking time:* 15 minutes | *Servings:* 6

Ingredients:
- ½ cup celery stalks, chopped
- ½ white onion, diced
- 3 eggs, beaten
- 1 tablespoon dried parsley
- 10 oz crab meat, chopped, canned
- 1 teaspoon Cajun seasonings
- ½ cup white Cheddar cheese, shredded
- ½ teaspoon salt
- ½ teaspoon ground black pepper
- ½ teaspoon cayenne pepper
- ½ cup heavy cream
- 1 teaspoon sesame oil

Directions:
Heat up the instant pot on sauté mode for 3 minutes and add sesame oil. Add diced onion and cook it for 2 minutes. Stir it well. Switch off the instant pot. Add celery stalk in the onion and mix up. Then add beaten eggs, dried parsley, crab meat, Cajun seasonings, cheese, salt, ground black pepper, cayenne pepper, and heavy cream. Stir the casserole carefully with the help of a spatula and close the lid. Cook the meal on stew mode for 10 minutes.

Nutrition value/serving: calories 159, fat 9.7, fiber 0.4, carbs 2.8, protein 11.5

Crab Melt with Zucchini

Prep time: 15 minutes | *Cooking time:* 8 minutes | *Servings:* 4

Ingredients:
- 1 large zucchini
- 1 teaspoon avocado oil
- ½ cup Monterey Jack cheese, shredded
- 1 green bell pepper, finely chopped
- 9 oz crab meat, chopped
- 2 tablespoons ricotta cheese
- 1 cup water, for cooking

Directions:
Trim the ends of zucchini and slice it lengthwise into 4 slices. Then pour water in the instant pot and insert the trivet. Place the zucchini slices in the baking mold. Brush them with avocado oil gently. After this, in the mixing bowl combine together Monterey Jack cheese, bell pepper, crab meat, and ricotta cheese. Spread the mixture over the zucchini and transfer it on the trivet. Close the instant pot lid and cook the meal on manual mode (high pressure) for 8 minutes. When the time is over, make a quick pressure release.

Nutrition value/serving: calories 144, fat 6.4, fiber 1.3, carbs 6.7, protein 13.6

Baked Snapper

Prep time: 10 minutes | Cooking time: 10 minutes | Servings: 4

Ingredients:
- 1-pound snapper, trimmed, cleaned
- 1 tablespoon lemongrass
- 1 tablespoon sage
- 1 teaspoon avocado oil
- 1 teaspoon salt
- 1 teaspoon red pepper
- 1 cup water, for cooking

Directions:
Pour water and insert trivet in the instant pot. Rub the fish with salt and red pepper. Then fill it with sage and lemongrass. Brush the fish with avocado oil and transfer on the trivet. Close the lid and cook the snapper for 10 minutes on manual mode (high pressure). When the time is over, make a quick pressure release and open the lid. Remove the sage and lemongrass from the fish.

Nutrition value/serving: calories 151, fat 2.2, fiber 0.7, carbs 2.9, protein 27.9

Salmon Salad

Prep time: 10 minutes | Cooking time: 8 minutes | Servings: 2

Ingredients:
- ½ cup curly kale, chopped
- 7 oz salmon fillet, chopped
- 1 teaspoon onion flakes
- ½ teaspoon salt
- 1 teaspoon coconut oil
- 1 teaspoon olive oil
- ½ teaspoon chili flakes
- ¼ cup cherry tomatoes, halved

Directions:
Place coconut oil in the instant pot and heat it up on sauté mode. When the coconut oil is melted, add salmon fillet. Sprinkle the fish with salt and chili flakes. Cook it for 2 minutes from each side on sauté mode. Then transfer the cooked salmon in the salad bowl. Add curly kale, onion flakes, salt, olive oil, and halved cherry tomatoes, Shake the salad.

Nutrition value/serving: calories 202, fat 11.2, fiber 2.2, carbs 6, protein 21.7

Butter Cod Loin

Prep time: 10 minutes | Cooking time: 15 minutes | Servings: 2

Ingredients:
- 8 oz cod loin
- 1 tablespoon oregano
- ¼ teaspoon chili flakes
- 3 tablespoons butter
- ½ teaspoon salt
- ¼ teaspoon minced ginger

Directions:
Put butter and chili flakes in the instant pot bowl. Set sauté mode and melt the mixture. Add minced ginger, salt, oregano, and stir it. Then arrange the cod loin inside. Cook it on sauté mode for 6 minutes from each side. Serve the fish topped with hot butter mixture from the instant pot.

Nutrition value/serving: calories 251, fat 18.5, fiber 1, carbs 1.6, protein 20.5

Cod in Cream Sauce

Prep time: 5 minutes | *Cooking time:* 15 minutes | *Servings:* 4

Ingredients:
- 16 oz salmon fillet
- 1 cup heavy cream
- 1 teaspoon minced garlic
- 1 tablespoon fresh parsley, chopped
- 1 teaspoon chives, chopped
- 1 oz Parmesan, grated
- 1 cup water, for cooking

Directions:

Mix up together water and minced garlic and pour the liquid in the instant pot. Insert trivet and place a salmon fillet in it. Close the lid and cook the fish on steam mode for 5 minutes. Then allow the natural pressure release for 5 minutes and transfer the fish on the plate. Cut it into servings After this, remove the liquid from the instant pot. Discard the trivet. Pour heavy cream in the instant pot. Add parsley and chives. Bring the liquid to boil on sauté mode. Then add cheese and switch off the instant pot. Stir the liquid carefully until the cheese is melted. Pour the cooked cream sauce over the salmon.

Nutrition value/serving: calories 278, fat 19.6, fiber 0.1, carbs 1.4, protein 25

Salmon and Kohlrabi Gratin

Prep time: 10 minutes | *Cooking time:* 14 minutes | *Servings:* 3

Ingredients:
- 8 oz salmon fillet, chopped
- ¼ teaspoon ground black pepper
- ½ teaspoon salt
- 4 oz kohlrabi, chopped
- ½ cup heavy cream
- 1 tablespoon almond meal
- 1 teaspoon lemon juice
- 1 teaspoon sesame oil
- 3 oz Provolone cheese, grated
- 1 cup water, for cooking

Directions:

Pour water and insert the steamer rack in the instant pot. Place kohlrabi in the steamer and cook it on steam mode for 4 minutes. Then make a quick pressure release. Brush the instant pot pan mold with sesame oil. Place the salmon in it. Then sprinkle the fish with salt and ground black pepper. Top the fish with kohlrabi. After this, sprinkle the mixture with lemon juice, almond meal, heavy cream, and Provolone cheese. Place the mold in the steamer rack and close the lid. Cook the gratin on manual mode (high pressure) for 10 minutes. Then make quick pressure realize.

Nutrition value/serving: calories 304, fat 22.2, fiber 1.7, carbs 4.1, protein 23.4

Mussel Chowder

Prep time: 10 minutes | *Cooking time:* 30 minutes | *Servings:* 4

Ingredients:
- 1 cup heavy cream
- 1 cup chicken broth
- 6 oz mussels, canned
- 1 zucchini, chopped
- 1 teaspoon paprika
- ½ teaspoon salt
- 1 onion, diced
- 1 teaspoon coconut oil

Directions:

Toss coconut oil in the instant pot. Add onion and cook the ingredients on sauté mode for 5 minutes. Then stir well and cook for 3 minutes more. After this, add zucchini and salt. Saute the ingredients for 2 minutes more. Add paprika, salt, chicken stock, and heavy cream. Close the lid and cook the chowder on soup mode for 20 minutes. Then open the lid and with the help of the immersion blender, blend the chowder until it gets the creamy texture. Add mussels and cook the chowder for 5 minutes more on sauté mode.

Nutrition value/serving: calories 180, fat 13.7, fiber 1.3, carbs 7.2, protein 7.9

Paprika Salmon Skewers

Prep time: 15 minutes | Cooking time: 5 minutes | Servings: 4

Ingredients:
- 1-pound salmon fillet, fresh, cubed
- 1 tablespoon paprika
- ½ teaspoon salt
- ½ teaspoon ground turmeric
- 1 teaspoon avocado oil
- ½ teaspoon lemon juice
- 1 cup water, for cooking

Directions:
Make the sauce: mix up together paprika, salt, ground turmeric, avocado oil, and lemon juice. Then coat the salmon cubes in the sauce well and string on the wooden skewers. Pour water and insert trivet in the instant pot. Arrange the salmon skewers on the trivet and close the lid. Cook the meal on manual mode (high pressure) for 5 minutes. Then make a quick pressure release and remove the fish from the instant pot.

Nutrition value/serving: calories 158, fat 7.4, fiber 0.8, carbs 1.2, protein 22.3

Tuscan Shrimps

Prep time: 10 minutes | Cooking time: 25 minutes | Servings: 4

Ingredients:
- 1-pound shrimps, peeled
- ¼ teaspoon minced garlic
- 1 teaspoon butter
- 1 teaspoon coconut oil
- ½ white onion, diced
- 1 teaspoon apple cider vinegar
- 1 cup heavy cream
- ¼ teaspoon salt
- ½ teaspoon ground black pepper
- 2 cups spinach, chopped
- 3 oz Provolone cheese, grated
- 1 tablespoon almond flour
- 1 teaspoon Italian seasonings
- 1 teaspoon dried cilantro
- ¼ cup of water

Directions:
Heat up instant pot on sauté mode for 3 minutes. Then place butter and coconut oil inside. Heat up the ingredients for 2 minutes and add minced garlic and diced onion. Add apple cider vinegar and stir the ingredients. Sauté them for 5 minutes. Stir the mixture from time to time. Then add salt, ground black pepper, cilantro, Italian seasonings, and stir well. Add water and bring the mixture to boil on sauté mode. Add spinach and almond flour. Stir it well and cook for 3 minutes. Then add heavy cream and shrimps. Cook the meal on sauté mode for 10 minutes.

Nutrition value/serving: calories 385, fat 24.7, fiber 1.4, carbs 6.7, protein 34

Parmesan Scallops

Prep time: 8 minutes | Cooking time: 11 minutes | Servings: 4

Ingredients:
- 11 oz scallops
- 4 oz Parmesan, grated
- 1 tablespoon butter, melted
- ½ teaspoon avocado oil
- 1 teaspoon garlic powder

Directions:
Brush scallops with butter and sprinkle with garlic powder. Brush the instant pot bowl with avocado oil and heat it up for 3 minutes on sauté mode. Then place the scallops in the instant pot in one layer and cook them for 3 minutes. Flip the scallops and top with grated Parmesan. Close the lid and sauté the meal for 5 minutes more.

Nutrition value/serving: calories 188, fat 6.9, fiber 0.1, carbs 3.4, protein 22.4

Seafood Bisque

Prep time: 5 minutes | Cooking time: 10 minutes | Servings: 3

Ingredients:
- 1 tablespoon coconut oil
- 1 oz leek, chopped
- ½ red onion, diced
- 1 teaspoon celery, chopped
- ½ teaspoon ground thyme
- ½ teaspoon lemon zest, grated
- 3 tablespoons cream cheese
- 1 cup chicken broth
- 1 tablespoon scallions, chopped
- 1 oz bacon, chopped, cooked
- ½ teaspoon salt
- 9 oz shrimps, peeled

Directions:
Put coconut oil in the instant pot and melt it on sauté mode for 2 minutes. Then add leek, red onion, and celery. Sprinkle the ingredients with ground thyme, lemon zest, and salt. Mix up well and cook on sauté mode for 4 minutes. Then add cream cheese and stir well until homogenous. Then and chicken stock and shrimps. Mix up the meal well and close the lid. Cook it on manual mode (high pressure) for 2 minutes. When the time is over, make a quick pressure release. Top the cooked meal with bacon and scallions.

Nutrition value/serving: calories 253, fat 13.9, fiber 0.7, carbs 5.4, protein 25.7

Lobster Bisque

Prep time: 10 minutes | Cooking time: 15 minutes | Servings: 4

Ingredients:
- 1 teaspoon tomato paste
- 1 tablespoon celery, grated
- 1 white onion, diced
- ¼ teaspoon minced garlic
- 1 tablespoon butter
- 3 cups chicken broth
- 1 tablespoon ground paprika
- ½ teaspoon ground black pepper
- ½ cup heavy cream
- 4 lobster tails
- ½ teaspoon salt
- 1 tablespoon chives, chopped

Directions:
Melt the butter in the instant pot on sauté mode for 3 minutes. Then add celery and onion. Cook the vegetables for 2 minutes. After this, stir them well and add minced garlic. Mix up well. Add lobster tails and cook them for 1 minute from each side. After this, mix up together tomato paste and heavy cream. Add the liquid in the instant pot. Then add chicken broth, ground black pepper, ground paprika, and salt. Close the lid. Cook the bisque for 3 minutes on manual mode (high pressure). When the time is over, make a quick pressure release. Top the meal with chopped chives.

Nutrition value/serving: calories 170, fat 9.7, fiber 1.4, carbs 5.2, protein 4.7

Tarragon Lobster

Prep time: 10 minutes | Cooking time: 8 minutes | Servings: 3

Ingredients:
- 12 oz lobster tails
- 1 tablespoon tarragon
- 1 tablespoon lemon juice
- 2 tablespoons butter, melted
- ¼ teaspoon salt
- 1 cup water, for cooking

Directions:
With the help of the scissors and knife trim and clean the lobster tails from shells. Then pour water and insert the steamer rack in the instant pot. Arrange the lobster tails on the rack and close the lid. Cook the seafood for 3 minutes on manual mode (high pressure). When the time is over, make a quick pressure release and open the lid. Transfer the lobsters on the plate and clean the instant pot. Remove the steamer rack from the instant pot. Put the melted butter, tarragon, lemon juice, and salt in the instant pot and cook it for 3 minutes on sauté mode. Top every lobster tail with fragrant butter liquid.

Nutrition value/serving: calories 172, fat 8.7, fiber 0.1, carbs 0.4, protein 21.8

Mussels Mariniere

Prep time: 10 minutes | Cooking time: 8 minutes | Servings: 5

Ingredients:
- 2 garlic cloves, diced
- 1 white onion, diced
- 1 tablespoon fresh parsley, chopped
- 1 cup chicken broth
- ¼ cup of coconut milk
- 1 tablespoon avocado oil
- 1 tablespoon lemon juice
- 1-pound fresh mussels

Directions:

Pour avocado oil in the instant pot. Add diced garlic and onion. Cook the vegetables on sauté mode for 4 minutes. Stir them after 2 minutes of cooking. Then add parsley, lemon juice, and coconut milk. Mix up the mixture and cook it for 1 minute. Add mussels and chicken broth, Close the lid and cook the meal on manual mode (high pressure) for 3 minutes. When the time is over, make a quick pressure release.

Nutrition value/serving: calories 129, fat 5.6, fiber 0.9, carbs 6.9, protein 12.4

Tuna Cakes

Prep time: 15 minutes | Cooking time: 4 minutes | Servings: 4

Ingredients:
- 10 oz tuna, canned
- 1 egg, beaten
- 1 teaspoon dried oregano
- ½ teaspoon salt
- 1 teaspoon ground coriander
- 3 tablespoons coconut flour
- ½ teaspoon chili flakes
- 1 cup water, for cooking

Directions:

Place the canned tuna in the bowl and smash it with the help of the fork. When the tuna is smooth, add egg, dried oregano, salt, ground coriander, coconut flour, and chili flakes. Stir the tuna cakes mixture well. After this, pour water and insert the steamer rack in the instant pot. With the help of the scooper make the medium size tuna cakes and place them on the trivet on one layer. Close the lid and cook the meal on manual mode (high pressure) for 5 minutes. Then allow the natural pressure release for 5 minutes more and transfer the tuna cakes on the plate.

Nutrition value/serving: calories 175, fat 7.8, fiber 2.4, carbs 3.7, protein 21.4

Salmon under Parmesan Blanket

Prep time: 10 minutes | Cooking time: 11 minutes | Servings: 4

Ingredients:
- 1-pound salmon fillet
- 1 teaspoon chili flakes
- ¼ teaspoon cayenne pepper
- 1 teaspoon olive oil
- ½ teaspoon ground paprika
- ½ teaspoon dried thyme
- 4 oz Parmesan, grated
- 1 cup water, for cooking

Directions:

In the shallow bowl combine together chili flakes, cayenne pepper, ground paprika, and dried thyme. Then rub the salmon fillet with spices. After this, brush the fish fillet with olive oil. Heat up the instant pot on sauté mode for 3 minutes. Then place the salmon fillet in the hot instant pot and cook for 2 minutes from each side. Then remove the fish from the instant pot. Clean the instant pot and pour water inside. Insert the steamer rack and line it with foil. Place the salmon fillet in the instant pot and top with grated Parmesan. Close the lid and cook the meal on manual (high pressure) for 5 minutes. Then make a quick pressure release. Transfer the cooked fish on the plate and cut it into servings.

Nutrition value/serving: calories 253, fat 14.3, fiber 0.2, carbs 1.3, protein 31.2

Salmon Poppers

Prep time: 15 minutes | *Cooking time:* 10 minutes | *Servings:* 6

Ingredients:
- 10 oz salmon fillet, chopped
- 3 eggs, beaten
- 1 tablespoon pork rinds
- 1 jalapeno pepper, chopped
- 1 tablespoon cream cheese
- ¼ teaspoon garlic powder
- 1 teaspoon dried oregano
- ½ teaspoon salt
- 1 tablespoon coconut oil
- ½ teaspoon onion powder

Directions:
Put the salmon fillet in the food processor. Add egg, pork rinds, jalapeno pepper, cream cheese, garlic powder, dried oregano, salt, and onion powder. Blend the mixture until smooth. Then with the help of the scooper make the small poppers. Toss the coconut oil in the instant pot and melt it on sauté mode. Then place the salmon poppers in the instant pot in one layer. Cook the meal for 3 minutes from each side or until it is light brown. Dry the cooked salmon poppers with the help of the paper towels if needed.

Nutrition value/serving: calories 135, fat 8.8, fiber 0.2, carbs 0.8, protein 13.7

Tuna Rolls

Prep time: 20 minutes | *Cooking time:* 20 minutes | *Servings:* 4

Ingredients:
- 4 kale leaves
- 10 oz tuna, canned
- ½ white onion, minced
- 1 teaspoon ground coriander
- ½ teaspoon salt
- ½ teaspoon ground paprika
- ¼ teaspoon ground nutmeg
- 2 oz leek, chopped
- 1 teaspoon avocado oil
- 1 cup water, for cooking

Directions:
Pour avocado oil in the instant pot. Add chopped leek and minced white onion. Cook the vegetables on sauté mode for 5 minutes. Stir the mixture from time to time with the help of the spatula. Then add tuba, salt, ground coriander, ground paprika, ground nutmeg, and mix up well. Then transfer the mixture in the bowl and clean the instant pot. Pour water and insert the steamer rack in the instant pot. Then fill every kale leaf with tuna mix tuna mixture and roll. Arrange the tuna rolls on the rack and close the lid. Cook the tuna rolls on manual mode (high pressure) for 15 minutes. Then allow the natural pressure release for 10 minutes.

Nutrition value/serving: calories 157, fat 6, fiber 1, carbs 5.3, protein 19.7

Fish Sticks

Prep time: 15 minutes | *Cooking time:* 7 minutes | *Servings:* 2

Ingredients:
- 8 oz tilapia fillet
- ¼ cup coconut flakes
- 1 egg, beaten
- ¼ teaspoon chili flakes
- ¼ teaspoon ground nutmeg
- 1 tablespoon sesame oil
- 1 cup water, for cooking

Directions:
Cut the tilapia fillet into 2 sticks. Then pour water and insert the steamer rack in the instant pot. Line the rack with foil and place the tilapia sticks on it. Close the lid and cook them for 3 minutes on manual mode (high pressure). When the time is over, make a quick pressure release and open the lid. Dip the cooked fish sticks in the egg and then coat in the coconut flakes. Clean the instant pot and remove the steamer rack. Pour sesame oil in the instant pot and place the tilapia sticks. Cook them for 1 minute from each side on sauté mode or until the fish sticks are light brown.

Nutrition value/serving: calories 222, fat 13.5, fiber 1, carbs 1.8, protein 24.2

Crab Rangoon Dip

Prep time: 10 minutes | *Cooking time:* 1.5 hours | *Servings:* 4

Ingredients:
- 1 teaspoon Erythritol
- 3 tablespoons cream cheese
- 1 tablespoon chives, chopped
- ½ cup whipped cream
- 6 oz crab meat, chopped
- ¼ teaspoon garlic powder

Directions:
Place all ingredients in the instant pot and stir well. Close the lid and cook the dip on manual (low pressure) for 1.5 hours.

Nutrition value/serving: calories 109, fat 8, fiber 0, carbs 2.8, protein 6.3

Coriander Seabass

Prep time: 7 minutes | *Cooking time:* 5 minutes | *Servings:* 4

Ingredients:
- 1 teaspoon ground coriander
- ½ teaspoon salt
- ½ teaspoon ground black pepper
- 12 oz Seabass fillet
- 1 cup water, for cooking

Directions:
In the shallow bowl combine together salt, ground coriander, and ground black pepper. Cut the fish fillet into 4 servings. Pour water and insert the steamer rack in the instant pot. Line the steamer rack with baking paper and place the Seabass on it. Sprinkle the fish with coriander mixture and close the lid. Cook the Seabass on manual mode (high pressure) for 5 minutes. When the time is over, make a quick pressure release.

Nutrition value/serving: calories 106, fat 6.3, fiber 0.7, carbs 5.2, protein 8

Dill Halibut

Prep time: 15 minutes | *Cooking time:* 8 minutes | *Servings:* 2

Ingredients:
- 1 tablespoon dried dill
- 2 tablespoons butter, softened
- 10 oz halibut steaks (5 oz each steak)
- ¼ teaspoon salt
- ¼ teaspoon ground paprika
- ¼ cup heavy cream

Directions:
Place butter and dill in the instant pot. Add salt and ground paprika. Melt the mixture on sauté mode. Then add heavy cream and halibut steaks. Close and seal the lid. Cook the fish on manual mode (high pressure) for 2 minutes. When the time is over, allow the natural pressure release for 10 minutes. Serve the fish with hot dill-butter sauce.

Nutrition value/serving: calories 348, fat 21.2, fiber 0.3, carbs 1.4, protein 36.8

Bacon-Wrapped Cod

Prep time: 15 minutes | *Cooking time:* 10 minutes | *Servings:* 4

Ingredients:
- 1-pound cod fillet
- 5 bacon slices
- ½ teaspoon lime zest, grated
- ¼ teaspoon chili flakes
- 1/3 teaspoon salt
- ¼ teaspoon cayenne pepper
- 1 teaspoon olive oil
- ½ teaspoon fresh thyme
- 1 cup water, for cooking

Directions:
Pour olive oil in the instant pot and heat it up on sauté mode for 2 minutes. Meanwhile, rub the cod fillet with lime zest, chili flakes, salt, cayenne pepper, and fresh thyme. When the oil is hot, place the bacon inside in one layer and cook it for 1 minute from each side. Then remove the bacon from the instant pot and cool it to the room temperature. Wrap the fish in the cooked bacon and secure the fish fillet with toothpicks if needed. Clean the instant pot and pour water inside. Insert the steamer rack and line it with baking paper. Place the wrapped cod on the rack and close the lid. Cook the meal on manual mode (high pressure) for 5 minutes. When the time is over, make a quick pressure release and transfer the fish on the plate. Cut it into servings.

Nutrition value/serving: calories 230, fat 12.1, fiber 0.1, carbs 0.5, protein 29.1

Spinach and Tilapia Casserole

Prep time: 20 minutes | *Cooking time:* 8 minutes | *Servings:* 6

Ingredients:
- 1-pound tilapia fillet
- 2 cups fresh spinach, chopped
- 4 teaspoons butter
- ¼ cup cream cheese
- 1 cup Cheddar cheese, shredded
- ½ cup heavy cream
- 1 teaspoon salt
- 1 teaspoon ground black pepper
- ½ teaspoon cayenne pepper
- 1 teaspoon dried oregano

Directions:
Chop the tilapia fillet roughly. In the mixing bowl combine together dried oregano, cayenne pepper, ground black pepper, and salt. Then grease the instant pot bowl with butter and place fresh spinach inside. After this, add cream cheese and chopped tilapia. Sprinkle the fish with Cheddar cheese and heavy cream. Close the lid and cook casserole on manual mode (high pressure) for 8 minutes. When the time is over, allow the natural pressure release for 10 minutes.

Nutrition value/serving: calories 233, fat 16.6, fiber 0.5, carbs 1.6, protein 20.1

Fish Pie

Prep time: 15 minutes | *Cooking time:* 21 minutes | *Servings:* 5

Ingredients:
- 12 oz Pollock, chopped
- ½ cup heavy cream
- ½ white onion, diced
- 3 celery stalks, chopped
- 1 bay leaf
- ½ cup broccoli, chopped
- ¼ cup green peas
- ½ teaspoon salt
- ½ teaspoon ground black pepper
- 1 tablespoon dried parsley
- 1 teaspoon butter
- ½ cup almond meal
- 1 egg, beaten
- 1 tablespoon coconut oil, melted

Directions:
In the mixing bowl combine together egg, almond meal, and coconut oil. Knead the dough. Place it in the freezer. After this, place all remaining ingredients in the instant pot and stir well. Close the lid and cook the mixture on sauté mode for 15 minutes. Then stir it well. Grate the frozen almond dough with the help of the grated. Then top the fish mixture with the grated dough and close the lid. Cook the fish pie on manual (high pressure) for 6 minutes. When the time is over, make a quick pressure release and open the lid. Cool the fish pie little and only after this cut it into the servings.

Nutrition value/serving: calories 236, fat 14.5, fiber 2.3, carbs 5.8, protein 21.2

Mackerel Pate

Prep time: 10 minutes | Cooking time: 5 minutes | Servings: 5

Ingredients:
- 12 oz mackerel fillet
- 1 teaspoon mustard
- 1 teaspoon lemon juice
- 2 tablespoons cream cheese
- 1 teaspoon butter, softened
- 1 cup water, for cooking

Directions:
Pour water and insert the steamer rack in the instant pot. Place the mackerel fillet on the rack and close the lid. Cook the fish on manual mode (high pressure) for 5 minutes. Then make a quick pressure release and open the lid. Transfer the cooked mackerel in the food processor. Add mustard, lemon juice, cream cheese, and butter. Blend the mixture until smooth. Transfer the cooked pate in the bowl and store it in the fridge for up to 4 days.

Nutrition value/serving: calories 202, fat 14.5, fiber 0.1, carbs 0.4, protein 16.7

Crab Rangoon Fat Bombs

Prep time: 10 minutes | Cooking time: 7 minutes | Servings: 2

Ingredients:
- 2 bacon slices, chopped
- 5 oz crab meat, canned, chopped
- ¼ cup Cheddar cheese, shredded
- ½ teaspoon garlic powder
- ¼ teaspoon onion powder
- ¼ teaspoon ground black pepper

Directions:
Put the chopped bacon in the instant pot and cook it on sauté mode until golden brown (appx. 5-7 minutes). Stir the bacon from time to time. Meanwhile, in the mixing bowl combine together crab meat, Cheddar cheese, garlic powder, onion powder, and ground black pepper. Stir the mixture with the help of the spoon until homogenous. Cool the cooked bacon to the room temperature. With the help of the scooper make the small balls from the crab meat mixture. Coat every crab ball in the chopped bacon.

Nutrition value/serving: calories 227, fat 13.9, fiber 0.2, carbs 2.6, protein 19.6

Crab&Broccoli Casserole

Prep time: 20 minutes | Cooking time: 10 minutes | Servings: 3

Ingredients:
- ½ cup broccoli florets
- 6 oz crab meat, chopped
- 1 cup Cheddar cheese
- 2 tablespoons ricotta cheese
- ½ teaspoon dried dill
- ½ teaspoon dried parsley
- ½ teaspoon dried oregano
- ½ teaspoon ground black pepper
- ¼ cup of coconut milk
- ½ teaspoon salt
- 1 cup water, for cooking

Directions:
Mix up together crab meat with ricotta cheese. Then place the mixture in the instant pot casserole mold in one layer. Top it with broccoli florets and sprinkle with dill, parsley, oregano, ground black pepper, and salt. Then top the vegetables with Cheddar cheese and coconut milk. Pour water and insert the steamer rack in the instant pot. Place the casserole mold over the rack and close the lid. Cook the meal on manual mode (high pressure) for 10 minutes. Then allow the natural pressure release for 10 minutes and remove it from the instant pot.

Nutrition value/serving: calories 270, fat 19.2, fiber 1.1, carbs 4.6, protein 18.6

Tuna and Bacon Cups

Prep time: 15 minutes | Cooking time: 7 minutes | Servings: 4

Ingredients:
- 4 bacon slices
- 10 oz tuna, chopped
- 1 egg, beaten
- 1 teaspoon cream cheese
- ½ teaspoon ground nutmeg
- 2 oz Mozzarella, shredded
- 1 cup water, for cooking

Directions:
In the mixing bowl combine together tuna, egg, cream cheese, ground nutmeg, and Mozzarella Stir the mixture until homogenous. Arrange the bacon in the shape of the cups in the muffin molds. Then fill every bacon cup with tuna mixture. Pour water and insert the steamer rack in the instant pot. Place the muffin molds with bacon cups in the instant pot and close the lid. Cook the meal on manual mode (high pressure) for 7 minutes. When the time is over, make a quick pressure release and open the lid. Cool the meal little and remove it from the molds.

Nutrition value/serving: calories 295, fat 17.7, fiber 0.1, carbs 1, protein 31.3

Halibut Ceviche

Prep time: 20 minutes | Cooking time: 1 minute | Servings: 2

Ingredients:
- 6 oz halibut fillet
- 1 tomato, chopped
- ¼ red onion, diced
- 1 tablespoon fresh cilantro, chopped
- ½ jalapeno pepper, chopped
- ¼ teaspoon minced garlic
- 2 tablespoons lemon juice
- ¼ teaspoon salt
- ¼ teaspoon ground black pepper
- 1 teaspoon avocado oil
- 1 cup water, for cooking

Directions:
Pour water and insert the steamer rack in the instant pot. Line it with the baking paper and place the halibut fillet on it. Close the lid and cook fish for 1 minute on manual mode (high pressure). When the time is over, make a quick pressure release and open the lid. Cool the fish well. Meanwhile, in the mixing bowl combine together tomato, onion, cilantro, jalapeno pepper, and minced garlic. Then sprinkle the halibut with lemon juice, avocado oil, and ground black pepper. Massage the fish gently and leave for 10 minutes to marinate. Then chop the halibut roughly and add in the mixing bowl. Shake the cooked meal gently and transfer in the serving glasses.

Nutrition value/serving: calories 115, fat 2.5, fiber 1, carbs 3.5, protein 18.7

Parchment Fish

Prep time: 15 minutes | Cooking time: 10 minutes | Servings: 4

Ingredients:
- 1-pound salmon fillet
- 4 lemon slices
- ½ teaspoon salt
- 1 teaspoon dried thyme
- ½ teaspoon dried rosemary
- ½ white onion, sliced
- 1 tablespoon avocado oil
- 1 teaspoon butter
- ½ teaspoon cayenne pepper
- 1 cup water, for cooking

Directions:
Pour water and insert the steamer rack in the instant pot. Then place the sliced onion on the parchment. Top it with a salmon fillet. Sprinkle the fish with dried thyme, rosemary, and salt. Then top the fish with lemon slices, cayenne pepper, and butter. Sprinkle the ingredients with avocado oil and wrap in the shape of the packet. Place the fish packet on the rack and close the lid. Cook the meal on manual (high pressure) for 10 minutes. When the time is over, allow the natural pressure release for 10 minutes. Remove the cooked meal from the instant pot.

Nutrition value/serving: calories 173, fat 8.5, fiber 0.9, carbs 2.5, protein 22.3

Poached Cod

Prep time: 15 minutes | Cooking time: 10 minutes | Servings: 4

Ingredients:
- 1-pound cod fillet
- 1 tablespoon avocado oil
- ¾ teaspoon salt
- 1 teaspoon Italian seasonings
- 1 teaspoon ground black pepper
- 1 cup of water

Directions:
In the shallow bowl combine together avocado oil, salt, Italian seasonings, and ground black pepper. Then rub the cod fillet with a spice mixture from both sides and leave for 10 minutes to marinate. Meanwhile, pour water and insert the steamer rack in the instant pot. Line the rack with baking paper. Then place the cod on the rack and close the lid. Cook the fish on steam mode for 10 minutes. Then make a quick pressure release.

Nutrition value/serving: calories 101, fat 1.8, fiber 0.3, carbs 0.7, protein 20.4

Light Shrimp Pad Thai

Prep time: 10 minutes | Cooking time: 12 minutes | Servings: 4

Ingredients:
- ½ white onion, diced
- 1 egg, beaten
- 1 teaspoon coconut oil
- 1-pound shrimps, peeled
- 1 teaspoon dried cilantro
- 1 tablespoon walnuts, chopped
- 1 teaspoon minced garlic
- 1 teaspoon apple cider vinegar
- 1 teaspoon stevia

Directions:
Toss coconut oil in the instant pot and melt it for 2 minutes on sauté mode. Then add onion and cook it on sauté mode for 4 minutes or until onion is light brown. Then add shrimps and mix up well. Cook the ingredients for 2 minutes more. Stir well and sprinkle with cilantro, minced garlic, and stevia. Stir well and cook for 2 minutes more. After this, add the apple cider vinegar. Stir well. Then add walnuts and beaten egg. Whisk the mixture and cook for 3 minutes.

Nutrition value/serving: calories 179, fat 5.3, fiber 0.4, carbs 3.5, protein 27.9

Coated Coconut Shrimps

Prep time: 10 minutes | Cooking time: 10 minutes | Servings: 4

Ingredients:
- 4 king shrimps, peeled
- 1 egg, beaten
- 1 teaspoon cream cheese
- ¼ teaspoon cayenne pepper
- ½ cup coconut flakes
- ½ teaspoon salt
- 2 tablespoons coconut oil

Directions:
Mix up together coconut flakes with cayenne pepper and salt. In the separated bowl mix up together the egg with cream cheese. Then dip the shrimps in the egg mixture and coat in the coconut mixture. Repeat the same step one more time. Toss the coconut oil in the instant pot and melt it for minutes on sauté mode. Then arrange the prepared shrimps and cook them on sauté mode for 3 minutes from each side or until they are light brown.

Nutrition value/serving: calories 134, fat 11.5, fiber 0.9, carbs 1.7, protein 6.2

Steamed Crab Legs

Prep time: 12 minutes | Cooking time: 5 minutes | Servings: 3

Ingredients:
- 10 oz crab legs
- 1 cup water, for cooking

Directions:
Pour water and insert the trivet in the instant pot. Arrange the crab legs on the trivet and close the lid. Cook the meal on steam mode for 5 minutes. When the time is over, allow the natural pressure release for 10 minutes. Remove the cooked crab legs from the instant pot.

Nutrition value/serving: calories 95, fat 1.4, fiber 0, carbs 0, protein 18.1

Salmon with Lemon

Prep time: 15 minutes | Cooking time: 10 minutes | Servings: 2

Ingredients:
- 10 oz salmon fillet
- 4 lemon slices
- 1 teaspoon salt
- 1 teaspoon butter, softened
- 1 cup water, for cooking

Directions:
Rub the salmon fillet with salt and softened butter. Then pour water and insert the trivet in the instant pot. Line the trivet with baking paper and place the salmon fillet on it. Top the salmon with the lemon slices and close the lid. Cook the meal for 10 minutes on Steam mode. When the time is over, allow the natural pressure release and open the lid. Cut the cooked salmon into the servings.

Nutrition value/serving: calories 208, fat 10.7, fiber 0.4, carbs 1.3, protein 27.7

Zingy Fish

Prep time: 10 minutes | Cooking time: 15 minutes | Servings: 4

Ingredients:
- 1 cup broccoli florets
- 1-pound coley fillet, chopped
- 3 tablespoons apple cider vinegar
- 1 orange slice
- 1 tablespoon olive oil
- 1 cup water, for cooking

Directions:
In the mixing bowl combine together broccoli florets, coley fillet, apple cider vinegar, and olive oil. Chop the orange slice and add it in the fish mixture. Shake the fish mixture well and place it in the instant pot mold. Pour water and insert the steamer rack. Place the mold with the fish mixture in the instant pot and close the lid. Cook the meal on steam mode for 15 minutes. When the time is over, make a quick pressure release

Nutrition value/serving: calories 169, fat 4.7, fiber 0.6, carbs 4, protein 26.7

Thyme Cod

Prep time: 10 minutes | Cooking time: 10 minutes | Servings: 2

Ingredients:
- 8 oz cod fillet
- 1 teaspoon dried thyme
- ½ teaspoon garlic powder
- 1 teaspoon sesame oil
- 1 cup water, for cooking

Directions:
Rub the cod fillet with dried thyme, and garlic powder. Then sprinkle the fish with sesame oil. Wrap it in the foil. Pour water and insert the steamer rack in the instant pot. Place the wrapped fish in the instant pot and close the lid. Cook the meal on manual mode (high pressure) for 10 minutes. When the time is over, make a quick pressure release and remove it from the instant pot.

Nutrition value/serving: calories 115, fat 3.3, fiber 0.3, carbs 0.8, protein 20.4

Poultry
Chicken Tonnato
Prep time: 20 minutes | *Cooking time:* 15 minutes | *Servings:* 4

Ingredients:
- 1 teaspoon capers
- 2 oz tuna, canned
- ½ teaspoon minced garlic
- 1 teaspoon dried oregano
- 1 teaspoon lemon juice
- 1 tablespoon fresh basil, chopped
- 4 tablespoons ricotta cheese
- 2 tablespoons avocado oil
- ¼ teaspoon salt
- ½ teaspoon ground black pepper
- 1-pound chicken breast, skinless, boneless
- 1 cup water, for cooking

Directions:
Pour water in the instant pot and add chicken breast. Close and seal the lid and cook the chicken on manual (high pressure) for 15 minutes. When the time is over, allow the natural pressure release for 10 minutes. Meanwhile, place all remaining ingredients from the list above in the food processor. Blend the mixture until smooth. When the chicken is cooked, remove it from the instant pot and slice into servings. Then arrange the chicken in the plate and top with blended sauce.

Nutrition value/serving: calories 189, fat 6.2, fiber 0.6, carbs 1.8, protein 29.8

Paprika Chicken Wings
Prep time: 10 minutes | *Cooking time:* 17 minutes | *Servings:* 4

Ingredients:
- 11 oz chicken wings
- 1 tablespoon ground paprika
- 1 tablespoon avocado oil
- 1 teaspoon ground nutmeg
- 1 teaspoon sage
- 1 cup water, for cooking

Directions:
Place the chicken wings in the bowl and sprinkle with ground paprika, sage, and ground nutmeg. Then sprinkle the chicken wings with avocado oil and mix up with the help of the fingertips. After this, heat up the instant pot on sauté mode for 3 minutes. Then place the chicken wings in the instant pot in one layer. Cook the chicken wings for 2 minutes from each side or until they are light brown. After this, remove the chicken wings and clean the instant pot. Pour water and insert the steamer rack in instant pot. Line the steamer rack with foil and arrange the chicken wings. Cook the chicken on manual mode (high pressure) for 10 minutes. When the time is over, make a quick pressure release.

Nutrition value/serving: calories 161, fat 6.7, fiber 1, carbs 1.5, protein 22.9

Garlic Chicken Drumsticks
Prep time: 10 minutes | *Cooking time:* 25 minutes | *Servings:* 4

Ingredients:
- 4 chicken drumsticks
- 1 teaspoon minced garlic
- 1 teaspoon garlic powder
- 3 tablespoons butter, melted
- 1 teaspoon dried parsley
- 1 oz Parmesan, grated
- 1 cup water, for cooking

Directions:
Pour water and insert the trivet in the instant pot. Then line it with baking paper. Rub the chicken drumsticks with minced garlic, parsley, and garlic powder. Then brush with butter and place on the trivet. Close the lid and cook the chicken for 15 minutes on manual mode (high pressure. Meanwhile, preheat the instant pot to 365F and line the baking tray with baking paper. When the time is over, make a quick pressure release and transfer the cooked chicken drumsticks in the tray. Top the chicken with Parmesan and place in the preheated oven. Cool the meal for 10 minutes more or until cheese is light brown.

Nutrition value/serving: calories 180, fat 12.8, fiber 0.1, carbs 1, protein 15.2

Chicken Provencal

Prep time: 10 minutes | *Cooking time:* 17 minutes | *Servings:* 4

Ingredients:
- 1 tablespoon coconut oil
- 2 oz pancetta, chopped
- 3 oz leek, chopped
- 1-pound chicken fillet, chopped
- ½ teaspoon ground thyme
- ½ teaspoon salt
- ½ teaspoon ground black pepper
- 2 tablespoons apple cider vinegar
- ½ cup mushrooms, sliced
- 1 cup chicken broth

Directions:
Place the coconut oil in the instant pot and melt it on sauté mode. Add pancetta and cook it for 5 minutes. Stir it from time to time. After this, add leek and mix up well. Cook the ingredients for 3 minutes. Then add chicken. Sprinkle the mixture with ground thyme, salt, and ground black pepper. Mix up the ingredients well and cook for 2 minutes. After this, add mushrooms and apple cider vinegar. Add chicken broth and close the lid. Cook the meal on manual mode (high pressure) for 7 minutes. When the time is over, make a quick pressure release and transfer the meal in the serving bowls.

Nutrition value/serving: calories 348, fat 18.2, fiber 0.6, carbs 4.1, protein 39.9

Chicken with Blue Cheese Sauce

Prep time: 10 minutes | *Cooking time:* 15 minutes | *Servings:* 3

Ingredients:
- 12 oz chicken fillet
- 1 teaspoon butter
- ½ teaspoon salt
- ½ teaspoon ground paprika
- ½ teaspoon cayenne pepper
- ½ cup heavy cream
- 2 oz Blue cheese, crumbled
- 1 teaspoon dried cilantro

Directions:
Cut the chicken fillet into 3 servings. Rub every chicken fillet with salt, ground paprika, and cayenne pepper. Then place butter in the instant pot and add chicken fillets. Cook the chicken on sauté mode for 5 minutes from each side. Then add heavy cream and dried cilantro. Cook the mixture for 3 minutes. After this, add Blue cheese and carefully stir the meal. Cook it for 2 minutes.

Nutrition value/serving: calories 364, fat 22.6, fiber 0.2, carbs 1.4, protein 37.4

Flying Jacob Casserole

Prep time: 15 minutes | *Cooking time:* 25 minutes | *Servings:* 6

Ingredients:
- 1-pound chicken breast, cooked, chopped
- 1 cup heavy cream
- 4 egg whites, whisked
- ½ cup chili pepper, chopped
- 1 teaspoon Italian seasonings
- 1 tablespoon peanuts, chopped
- ½ teaspoon salt
- 1 teaspoon dried parsley
- 1 cup water, for cooking

Directions:
In the mixing bowl combine together heavy cream with Italian seasonings and dried parsley. Add salt and stir gently. Then place the chopped chicken in the instant pot casserole mold. Flatten it to make the layer. Pour whisked egg mixture over the chicken and flatten it with the help of the spatula. After this, top the mixture with heavy cream mixture and chopped peanuts. Top the meal with chili pepper and cover with the foil. Pour water and insert the steamer rack in the instant pot. Place the casserole on the rack and close the lid. Cook it on manual mode (high pressure) for 25 minutes. When the time is over, make a quick pressure release and open the lid. Remove the foil and cool the casserole for 10-15 minutes.

Nutrition value/serving: calories 188, fat 10.5, fiber 1, carbs 3.2, protein 19.6

Chicken Caprese Casserole

Prep time: 15 minutes | *Cooking time:* 10 minutes | *Servings:* 4

Ingredients:
- 11 oz chicken breast, skinless, boneless, chopped
- 1 tablespoon fresh basil, chopped
- 3 teaspoons pesto sauce
- 1 cup Mozzarella cheese, shredded
- 3 tablespoons cream cheese
- ½ cup cherry tomatoes, halved
- ½ teaspoon salt
- ½ teaspoon white pepper
- 1 cup water, for cooking

Directions:
In the mixing bowl combine together chicken breast, basil, salt, white pepper, pesto sauce, and shredded Mozzarella. Add cream cheese and mix up the mixture well. Then place mixture in the casserole mold for instant pot. Then top the mixture with cherry tomatoes and cover with foil. Pour water and insert the steamer rack in the instant pot. Place the casserole on the rack and close the lid. Cook the meal for 10 minutes on steam mode. When the time is over, make a quick pressure release and open the lid. Remove the foil from the casserole. Cool the meal for 10-15 minutes.

Nutrition value/serving: calories 157, fat 7.5, fiber 0.4, carbs 1.8, protein 19.7

Cajun Chicken Salad

Prep time: 10 minutes | *Cooking time:* 25 minutes | *Servings:* 2

Ingredients:
- 8 oz chicken fillet
- 1 teaspoon Cajun seasonings
- 1 teaspoon tomato paste
- ¼ teaspoon salt
- ½ cup chicken broth
- 1 cup radish, chopped
- 1 tablespoon fresh parsley, chopped
- 1 cup lettuce, chopped
- 1 tablespoon olive oil
- ½ teaspoon chili flakes
- 1 teaspoon apple cider vinegar

Directions:
Rub the chicken with Cajun seasonings and place it in the instant pot. Add tomato paste and chicken broth. Stir the mixture gently. Close the lid and cook the chicken on stew mode for 25 minutes. Meanwhile, in the salad bowl combine together chopped radish and lettuce. Sprinkle the vegetables with salt, olive oil, and chili flakes. Add apple cider vinegar and mix up well. When the chicken is cooked, remove it from the instant pot, cool little and chop. Add chopped chicken in the salad bowl. Mix up the salad well with the help of the spoon.

Nutrition value/serving: calories 302, fat 15.9, fiber 1.3, carbs 3.7, protein 34.8

Caesar Salad

Prep time: 10 minutes | *Cooking time:* 15 minutes | *Servings:* 6

Ingredients:
- 1-pound chicken breast, skinless, boneless
- 1 teaspoon sesame oil
- 2 bacon slices, chopped
- 2 cups lettuce, chopped
- 2 oz Parmesan, grated
- 1 tablespoon heavy cream
- 1 teaspoon cream cheese
- ½ teaspoon mustard
- ¼ teaspoon lemon zest, grated
- ½ garlic clove, diced
- 1 cup water, for cooking

Directions:
Pour water and insert the trivet in the instant pot. Place the chicken on the trivet and close the lid. Cook the chicken for 10 minutes and when the time is over, make a quick pressure release. Open the lid and cool the chicken well. Clean the instant pot and remove the trivet. Place the chopped bacon in the instant pot and cook it on sauté mode for 4 minutes or until crunchy. Stir the bacon from time to time to avoid burning. Meanwhile, chop the chicken roughly and place in the salad bowl. Add lettuce, garlic, and sesame oil. Mix up well. Make the dressing: mix up together heavy cream, mustard, and lemon zest. Add cooked bacon and dressing in the salad. Mix up the salad well. Top the cooked meal with grated Parmesan.

Nutrition value/serving: calories 172, fat 8.6, fiber 0.2, carbs 1.3, protein 21.7

Hoagie Bowl

Prep time: 20 minutes | *Cooking time:* 10 minutes | *Servings:* 4

Ingredients:
- 4 oz turkey breast, skinless, boneless
- 2 oz salami, chopped
- 3 oz deli ham, chopped
- 4 oz Cheddar cheese, chopped
- ½ cup lettuce, chopped
- 1 tomato, chopped
- 1 pickled banana pepper, chopped
- ¾ red onion, chopped
- 2 tablespoon heavy cream
- 1 teaspoon apple cider vinegar
- 1 teaspoon avocado oil
- ½ teaspoon dried oregano
- ½ teaspoon salt
- 1 cup water, for cooking

Directions:
Pour water and insert the trivet in the instant pot. Place the turkey on the trivet and close the lid. Cook it on manual (high pressure) for 10 minutes. When the time is over, allow the natural pressure release for 10 minutes. Then remove the turkey from the instant pot and cool it well. After this, chop it and transfer it in the mixing bowl. Add salami, deli ham, Cheddar cheese, lettuce, tomato, chopped pickled banana pepper, and onion. Shake the salad gently. In the shallow bowl make the dressing: whisk together heavy cream, apple cider vinegar, avocado oil, and salt. Then pour the dressing over the salad and mix up well with the help of the spoon.

Nutrition value/serving: calories 257, fat 17.9, fiber 1.5, carbs 6, protein 17.9

BLT Chicken Wrap

Prep time: 10 minutes | *Cooking time:* 10 minutes | *Servings:* 4

Ingredients:
- 4 low carb tortillas
- 4 bacon slices
- 1 cup lettuce, chopped
- 10 oz chicken fillet
- ½ teaspoon salt
- ¼ teaspoon cayenne pepper
- 2 oz Parmesan, grated
- 1 tablespoon heavy cream
- 1 tablespoon lemon juice
- 1 cup water, for cooking

Directions:
Place the bacon in the instant pot and cook it on sauté mode for 3 minutes. Then flip it on another side and cook for 2 minutes more. Place the cooked bacon on the tortillas. Then clean the instant pot and pour water inside. Insert the trivet. Rub the chicken with salt and cayenne pepper and put it in the instant pot. Close the lid. Cook it on steam mode for 10 minutes. Then make a quick pressure release and open the lid. Chop the chicken and put it over the bacon. Add lettuce and Parmesan. In the mixing bowl, mix up together lemon juice and heavy cream. Pour the mixture over Parmesan. Roll the tortillas into the wraps.

Nutrition value/serving: calories 379, fat 19.7, fiber 7.1, carbs 13.4, protein 35.3

Pizza Stuffed Chicken

Prep time: 15 minutes | *Cooking time:* 12 minutes | *Servings:* 5

Ingredients:
- 1-pound chicken breast, skinless, boneless
- 1 teaspoon minced garlic
- 1 teaspoon Italian seasonings
- 1/3 teaspoon onion powder
- ¼ teaspoon ground black pepper
- 1 tablespoon tomato paste
- ½ cup chicken broth
- ½ cup Mozzarella cheese, shredded

Directions:
Cut the chicken into 5 servings and beat them gently with the help of the kitchen hammer. Then rub every piece with Italian seasonings, onion powder, minced garlic, and ground black pepper. Then sprinkle every chicken piece with Mozzarella and roll them to make the pockets. Secure every roll with a toothpick. Pour chicken broth in the instant pot. Add tomato paste and stir well. Place the chicken rolls in the instant pot and close the lid. Cook them on manual mode (high pressure) for 12 minutes. When the time is over, make a quick pressure release and open the lid. If you like the golden-brown crust, broil the rolls in the preheated to 400F oven for 4 minutes.

Nutrition value/serving: calories 122, fat 3.2, fiber 0.2, carbs 1.3, protein 20.7

Chicken Patties

Prep time: 10 minutes | Cooking time: 8 minutes | Servings:3

Ingredients:
- 9 oz chicken fillet, cooked
- 3 tablespoons coconut flour
- 1 teaspoon cream cheese
- 1 egg, beaten
- 1 teaspoon minced onion
- ¼ teaspoon garlic powder
- ¾ teaspoon chili flakes
- ½ teaspoon salt
- 1 tablespoon avocado oil

Directions:
Shred the chicken and put it in the mixing bowl. Add coconut flour, egg, cream cheese, minced onion, garlic powder, chili flakes, and salt. Stir the chicken mixture until homogenous. Then place the avocado oil in the instant pot and heat it up on sauté mode for 2 minutes. With the help of the spoon make the medium size patties and place them in the hot oil. Cook the patties for 3 minutes from each side on sauté mode or until they are light brown.

Nutrition value/serving: calories 224, fat 9.5, fiber 3.3, carbs 5.7, Protein 27.7

Mozzarella Chicken Fillets

Prep time: 10 minutes | Cooking time: 20 minutes | Servings: 4

Ingredients:
- 12 oz chicken fillet
- ½ cup white mushrooms, chopped
- 3 oz leek, chopped
- 1 cup chicken broth
- ½ teaspoon salt
- 2 tablespoons apple cider vinegar
- ½ teaspoon ground paprika
- ½ teaspoon sage
- 1 teaspoon sesame oil
- 5 oz Mozzarella cheese, shredded

Directions:
Pour sesame oil in the instant pot and heat it up on sauté mode for 1 minute. Then add white mushrooms and cook them for 4 minutes. Stir the vegetables well and add leek, salt, ground paprika, and sage, Mix up well and sauté the mixture for 5 minutes more. After this, add chicken broth and apple cider vinegar. Add chicken fillet and close the lid. Cook the chicken on manual (high pressure) for 10 minutes. When the time is over, make a quick pressure release and open the lid. Top the chicken fillet with Mozzarella and close the lid. Leave the meal for 5-10 minutes or until the cheese is melted.

Nutrition value/serving: calories 288, fat 13.5, fiber 0.6, carbs 4.8, protein 35

Bruschetta Chicken

Prep time: 10 minutes | Cooking time: 8 minutes | Servings: 2

Ingredients:
- 8 oz chicken fillet
- ¼ teaspoon ground black pepper
- 1/3 teaspoon salt
- ¼ teaspoon sage
- ¼ teaspoon minced garlic
- 1/3 cup chicken broth
- 3 tablespoons apple cider vinegar
- ½ teaspoon Italian seasonings
- 2 teaspoons coconut oil
- ¼ cup cherry tomatoes, halved
- 1 teaspoon fresh basil, chopped
- ½ teaspoon sesame oil
- 1 oz Provolone cheese grated

Directions:
Toss coconut oil in the instant pot and heat it up for 2 minutes on sauté mode. Then cut the chicken fillet into 2 servings. Place the chicken in the hot coconut oil and sprinkle with salt, sage, and Italian seasonings. Cook the chicken fillets for 3 minutes and then flip on another side. Cook the fillets for 3 minutes more. After this, add minced garlic, chicken broth, and apple cider vinegar. Close the lid and cook the meal on manual mode (high pressure) for 10 minutes. When the time is over, make a quick pressure release and open the lid. Transfer the chicken in the plate In the mixing bowl combine together cherry tomatoes, basil, and sesame oil. Mix up the ingredients. Top the chicken with tomato mixture. Then sprinkle the meal with grated cheese.

Nutrition value/serving: calories 336, fat 19, fiber 0.4, carbs 1.7, protein 53.7

Greek Chicken

Prep time: 10 minutes | *Cooking time:* 10 minutes | *Servings:* 3

Ingredients:

- 10 oz chicken breast, skinless, boneless, chopped
- ½ oz jumbo olives, chopped
- 1 tablespoon olive oil
- ¼ teaspoon cayenne pepper
- 1 teaspoon dried oregano
- 1 teaspoon dried thyme
- ½ teaspoon salt
- ¼ teaspoon chili flakes
- 1/3 cup water
- 1 cucumber, chopped
- 3 tablespoons heavy cream
- ¼ teaspoon garlic powder
- 1 tablespoon lemon juice
- ½ teaspoon dried dill
- 3 oz Feta cheese, crumbled

Directions:

Sprinkle the chopped chicken with cayenne pepper, dried oregano, thyme, salt, and chili flakes. Then sprinkle the chicken with olive oil and place it in the instant pot. Set sauté mode and cook the chicken for 5 minutes. Stir it from time to time. Then add water and close the lid. Cook the chicken for 5 minutes on manual mode (high pressure). Then make a quick pressure release and open the lid. Transfer the cooked chicken in the serving bowls. Add chopped cucumber in every bowl. In the shallow bowl mix up together heavy cream, garlic powder, lemon juice, and dried dill. Pour the liquid over the cucumbers. Top the meal with crumbled Feta cheese.

Nutrition value/serving: calories 299, fat 19.2, fiber 1.1, carbs 6.5, protein 25.3

Chicken Rendang

Prep time: 15 minutes | *Cooking time:* 20 minutes | *Servings:* 4

Ingredients:

- ¾ teaspoon Galang, chopped
- ¼ white onion, chopped
- 1 teaspoon lemongrass, chopped
- ½ teaspoon garlic, diced
- ¾ teaspoon minced ginger
- ¼ teaspoon chili pepper, minced
- 1 tablespoon nut oil
- 1/3 cup coconut milk
- ½ teaspoon cardamom pods
- ¼ teaspoon ground cinnamon
- 1 anise star
- 1 tablespoon coconut flakes
- 4 chicken thighs
- ¼ cup of water

Directions:

Place Galang, white onion, garlic, minced ginger, and chili pepper in the instant pot. Add nut oil and cook the mixture on sauté mode for 4 minutes. Stir the mixture from time to time. Then add coconut milk, cardamom pods, anise star, and coconut flakes. Stir well. Put the chicken thighs in the mixture and coat them well with the help of the spoon. Close the lid and cook the chicken on manual mode (high pressure) for 15 minutes. When the time is over, allow the natural pressure release for 10 minutes.

Nutrition value/serving: calories 343, fat 15.2, fiber 2.7, carbs 7.1, protein 43.3

Chicken Zucchini Enchiladas
Prep time: 15 minutes | Cooking time: 13 minutes | Servings:6

Ingredients:
- 1 tablespoon avocado oil
- ½ white onion, diced
- 1 green bell pepper, chopped
- 1 chili pepper, chopped
- ½ teaspoon ground cumin
- ½ teaspoon ground coriander
- 1 garlic clove, diced
- 1-pound chicken breast, cooked, shredded
- 1 cup Cheddar cheese, shredded
- 2 zucchini, trimmed
- ½ cup heavy cream
- 1 tablespoon Enchilada sauce

Directions:
Put onion and bell pepper in the instant pot. Add avocado oil, ground cumin, coriander, and diced garlic. Cook the ingredients on sauté mode for 5 minutes. Stir them from time to time. Then add shredded chicken and Enchilada sauce. Mix up the mixture well and cook it for 3 minutes more. Transfer the cooked mixture into the mixing bowl. After this, clean the instant pot. Slice the zucchini lengthwise. You should get 18 slices. Place the layer of 3 zucchini slices on the chopping board and spread it with chicken mixture. Roll it and transfer in the instant pot. Repeat the same step with all remaining zucchini and chicken mixture. Then top the zucchini rolls with Cheddar cheese and heavy cream. Close and seal the lid. Cook enchiladas for 5 minutes on manual mode (high pressure). When the time is over, make a quick pressure release.

Nutrition value/serving: calories 225, fat 12.4, fiber 1.6, carbs 6.2, protein 22.2

Chicken Cacciatore
Prep time: 15 minutes | Cooking time: 25 minutes | Servings: 5

Ingredients:
- 5 chicken thighs, boneless
- ½ teaspoon salt
- ½ teaspoon ground black pepper
- 2 garlic cloves, diced
- ¼ onion, diced
- ¼ cup bell pepper, chopped
- ½ cup cremini mushrooms, chopped
- ¼ cup tomatoes, canned
- ½ teaspoon dried rosemary
- ½ teaspoon dried cumin
- ½ teaspoon dried thyme
- ¼ teaspoon ground coriander
- ½ cup kale, chopped
- 1 tablespoon coconut oil
- ½ cup chicken broth

Directions:
Toss the coconut oil in the instant pot and melt it on sauté mode. Then place the chicken thighs in the hot oil and cook them for 3 minutes from each side or until the chicken is light brown. After this, sprinkle the chicken with salt and ground black pepper. Add garlic, onion, and bell pepper. Add mushrooms and stir the ingredients. Then add canned tomatoes, rosemary, cumin, thyme, and ground coriander. Stir the ingredients with the help of the spatula well and add chicken broth. Close and seal the lid. Cook the meal on manual mode (high pressure) for 15 minutes. When the time is over, make a quick pressure release and open the lid. Add kale and close the lid. Cook the meal for 2 minutes more on manual mode (high pressure). Then make a quick pressure release and open the lid. Stir the meal well before serving

Nutrition value/serving: calories 319, fat 13.8, fiber 0.7, carbs 3.2, protein 43.5

Coconut Chicken Tenders

Prep time: 10 minutes | *Cooking time:* 7 minutes | *Servings:* 4

Ingredients:
- 11 oz chicken fillet
- ½ cup coconut flour
- 2 eggs, beaten
- 1 oz Parmesan, grated
- ¼ teaspoon ground black pepper
- 1 tablespoon cream cheese
- 1 cup water, for cooking

Directions:
Cut the chicken fillet into the tenders. Then sprinkle them with ground black pepper. In the mixing bowl combine together Parmesan and coconut flour. After this, in the separated mixing bowl mix up together cream cheese and eggs. Dip every chicken tender in the egg mixture and then coat them well in the coconut flour mixture. Pour water and insert the steamer rack in the instant pot. Line the steamer rack with baking paper. Place the chicken tenders on the rack and close the lid. Cook the meal for 7 minutes on manual mode (high pressure). When the time is over, make a quick pressure release and open the lid. Transfer the cooked chicken tenders on the plate. If you prefer golden-brown crust – broil the cooked chicken tenders in the preheated to 400F oven for 5 minutes.

Nutrition value/serving: calories 219, fat 10.6, fiber 0.7, carbs 1.6, protein 28.1

Balsamic Roast Chicken

Prep time: 15 minutes | *Cooking time:* 16 minutes | *Servings:* 2

Ingredients:
- 2 chicken thighs, skinless, boneless
- 3 tablespoons balsamic vinegar
- 3 tablespoons avocado oil
- ¼ teaspoon salt
- ¼ teaspoon cayenne pepper
- ¼ teaspoon chili flakes
- ¼ teaspoon ground paprika
- ½ cup chicken broth
- 1 teaspoon peppercorns

Directions:
In the mixing bowl mix up together chicken thighs, balsamic vinegar, avocado oil, salt, cayenne pepper, chili flakes, and ground paprika. Leave the chicken or 10 minutes to marinate. Preheat the instant pot on sauté mode for 3 minutes. Then place the chicken thighs and all liquid from them in the instant pot and cook for 3 minutes from each side. Add chicken broth and peppercorns. Close and seal the lid. Cook the chicken for 10 minutes on manual mode (high pressure). When the time is over, make a quick pressure release. Transfer the chicken in the plate and shred it gently. Sprinkle the meal with the chicken broth liquid from the instant pot.

Nutrition value/serving: calories 324, fat 13.9, fiber 1.4, carbs 2.6, protein 43.9

Chicken & Snap Pea Salad

Prep time: 15 minutes | *Cooking time:* 14 minutes | *Servings:* 8

Ingredients:
- 1 teaspoon Erythritol
- 1 teaspoon mustard
- 1 tablespoon sesame oil
- ¼ teaspoon ground black pepper
- ¼ teaspoon ground paprika
- ¼ teaspoon ground turmeric
- ¼ teaspoon garlic powder
- ½ teaspoon onion powder
- 3 tablespoons olive oil
- ½ red onion, sliced
- 1-pound chicken breast, skinless, boneless
- 1 bell pepper, chopped
- 2 cup green peas
- 1 cup water, hot

Directions:
Make the salad dressing: whisk together Erythritol, mustard, sesame oil, and paprika. Then in the shallow bowl combine together ground black pepper, turmeric, garlic powder, and onion powder. Sprinkle the chicken breast with spice mixture and massage well with the help of the fingertips. Brush the chicken with olive oil and place it in the instant pot. Cook the chicken breast for 4 minutes on sauté mode. Then flip it on another side and cook for 5 minutes more. After this, add hot water and insert the trivet. Place the green peas and bell pepper on the trivet and close the lid. Cook the ingredients on manual mode (high pressure) for 4 minutes. When the time is over, allow the natural pressure release for 5 minutes. Transfer the green peas and bell pepper in the salad bowl. Add red onion. Then chop the chicken and add it in the salad bowl too. Shake the salad and sprinkle with dressing.

Nutrition value/serving: calories 165, fat 8.7, fiber 2.3, carbs 8.1, protein 14.4

Spinach Stuffed Chicken

Prep time: 15 minutes | *Cooking time:* 18 minutes | *Servings:* 2

Ingredients:
- 10 oz chicken breast, skinless, boneless
- 3 oz Goat cheese, crumbled
- 1 cup spinach, chopped
- ½ teaspoon salt
- ½ teaspoon onion powder
- ¼ teaspoon ground turmeric
- ¼ teaspoon dried thyme
- 1 teaspoon apple cider vinegar
- 1 tablespoon olive oil
- 1 cup water, for cooking

Directions:
Pour olive oil in the instant pot and heat it up on sauté mode for 2-3 minutes. Add spinach Sprinkle it with salt, onion powder, ground turmeric, and dried thyme. Stir the ingredients well and sauté for 5 minutes. Stir with the help of the spatula from time to time. When the time is over, add crumbled Goat cheese and apple cider vinegar and mix up. Transfer the mixture in the bowl and clean the instant pot. Cut the chicken breast into 2 servings. Cut the chicken breast in the shape of Hasselback. Fill every Hasselback cut with spinach mixture. Wrap the chicken in the foil. Pour water and insert the steamer rack in the instant pot. Place the wrapped chicken on the rack and close the lid. Cook the meal on steam mode (high pressure) for 10 minutes. When the time is over, allow the natural pressure release and open the lid. Remove the chicken from the foil.

Nutrition value/serving: calories 421, fat 25.8, fiber 0.5, carbs 2.2, protein 43.6

Chicken Scarpariello
Prep time: 10 minutes | *Cooking time:* 20 minutes | *Servings:* 2

Ingredients:
- 1 tablespoon olive oil
- ½ teaspoon salt
- 1 Italian sausages link
- 2 chicken thighs, skinless, boneless
- ½ cup bell pepper, chopped
- 1 garlic clove, diced
- ½ cup chicken broth
- 1 chili pepper, chopped
- 1 tablespoon apple cider vinegar
- 1 teaspoon rosemary

Directions:
Pour olive oil in the instant pot. Chop the sausage link and place it in the instant pot. Cook it on sauté mode for 5 minutes. Stir the sausages from time to time with the help of the spatula. After this, remove the sausages from the instant pot. Place chicken thighs in the instant pot and cook them for 3 minutes from each side. After this, add bell pepper, garlic clove, salt, rosemary, and chili pepper. Cook the chicken for 3 minutes more. Then sprinkle it with apple cider vinegar and cook and flip the chicken thighs on another side. Add chicken broth and cooked sausages. Close the lid and cook the meal on manual (high pressure) for 6 minutes. When the time is over, make a quick pressure release and open the lid.

Nutrition value/serving: calories 426, fat 21,9, fiber 0.8, carbs 4,5, protein 50.7

Chicken Divan Casserole
Prep time: 15 minutes | *Cooking time:* 10 minutes | *Servings:* 4

Ingredients:
- 1 ½ cup broccoli florets
- 11 oz chicken breast, boiled
- ½ cup Mozzarella, shredded
- 1 garlic clove, minced
- ½ teaspoon salt
- ½ teaspoon white pepper
- ¼ cup heavy cream
- ¼ cup of coconut milk
- 2 tablespoons almond flour
- ¼ teaspoon avocado oil
- 1 cup water, for cooking

Directions:
Shred the chicken with the help of the fork and put it in the big bowl. Add broccoli florets and shredded Mozzarella. Then add garlic clove, salt, white pepper, and heavy cream. Add coconut milk and mix up the chicken mixture until homogenous. After this, brush the instant pot casserole mold with avocado oil and transfer the chicken mixture inside it. Flatten the surface of the chicken mixture with the help of the spatula. Then sprinkle it with almond flour. Pour water and insert the trivet in the instant pot. Place the casserole mold on the trivet and close the lid. Cook the meal on manual mode (high pressure) for 10 minutes. When the time is over, allow the natural pressure release for 10 minutes more.

Nutrition value/serving: calories 253, fat 16.1, fiber 2.8, carbs 6.9, protein 22.1

Orange Chicken
Prep time: 15 minutes | *Cooking time:* 22 minutes | *Servings:* 4

Ingredients:
- 5 tablespoons orange juice
- 1 teaspoon lemon juice
- 1 teaspoon apple cider vinegar
- 1 tablespoon olive oil
- ¼ teaspoon chili flakes
- ½ teaspoon minced ginger
- ¼ teaspoon garlic powder
- 1 tablespoon coconut flour
- 1 teaspoon orange zest, grated
- ½ cup chicken broth
- ½ teaspoon salt
- 15 oz chicken breast, skinless, boneless, roughly chopped

Directions:
In the mixing bowl combine together orange juice, orange zest, lemon juice, apple cider vinegar, olive oil, chili flakes, minced ginger, salt, and garlic powder. Then pour the orange mixture over the chicken and mix up well. Marinate the chicken in the orange mixture for at least 10 minutes. After this, heat up the instant pot on sauté mode for 2 minutes. Add the chicken mixture and cook it for 5 minutes. After this, stir it well with the help of the spatula and add chicken broth. Close the lid and cook the meal on stew/meat mode for 15 minutes.

Nutrition value/serving: calories 182, fat 6.9, fiber 1.4, carbs 4.6, protein 23.9

Chicken Stroganoff
Prep time: 10 minutes | Cooking time: 15 minutes | Servings: 3

Ingredients:
- ¼ cup baby Bella mushrooms, sliced
- 1 medium white onion, sliced
- 1 garlic clove, diced
- ¼ teaspoon ground black pepper
- ½ teaspoon ground paprika
- ½ cup of coconut milk
- 1 oz Parmesan, grated
- 1 teaspoon butter
- 8 oz chicken fillet
- ¼ cup chicken broth

Directions:
Place butter in the instant pot. Add white onion, mushrooms, and garlic. Cook the ingredients for 5 minutes on sauté mode. Stir the ingredients from time to time. Meanwhile, cut the chicken fillet into the strips and sprinkle with ground paprika and ground black pepper. Put the chicken strips in the instant pot. Add coconut milk and chicken broth. Then add grated cheese and mix up the ingredients with the help of the spoon. Close and seal the lid. Cook the chicken stroganoff on steam mode for 8 minutes. When the time is over, make a quick pressure release and open the lid. Let the cooked meal rest for 5-10 minutes before serving.

Nutrition value/serving: calories 299, fat 18.7, fiber 1.9, carbs 6.8, protein 26.9

Pecan Chicken
Prep time: 10 minutes | Cooking time: 17 minutes | Servings: 2

Ingredients:
- 6 oz chicken fillet
- 3 pecans, grinded
- 1 egg, beaten
- 1 teaspoon coconut cream
- ½ teaspoon cayenne pepper
- ¼ teaspoon salt
- 1 teaspoon butter
- 1 cup water, for cooking

Directions:
Cut the chicken fillet into 2 servings. Pour water and insert the trivet in the instant pot. Line the trivet with the baking paper. Then rub the chicken fillets with salt and cayenne pepper. Put the chicken on the trivet and close the lid. Cook it for 5 minutes on Steam mode. When the time is over, make a quick pressure release. Open the lid and transfer the chicken on the plate. Clean the instant pot and remove the trivet. Then in the mixing bowl whisk together the egg with coconut cream. Dip the chicken pieces in the egg mixture. After this, coat every fillet in the grinded pecans. Toss butter in the instant pot and melt it on sauté mode (appx.2-3minutes). Place the coated pecan chicken in the instant pot and cook it for 5 minutes from each side.

Nutrition value/serving: calories 363, fat 26.1, fiber 2.4, carbs 3.6, protein 29.8

Cayenne Pepper Chicken Meatballs
Prep time: 15 minutes | Cooking time: 6 minutes | Servings: 3

Ingredients:
- 1 cup ground chicken
- ½ teaspoon cayenne pepper
- 3 tablespoons almond flour
- 1 teaspoon dried dill
- 1 egg, beaten
- 1 onion, minced
- ½ teaspoon minced ginger
- 1 oz Mozzarella, shredded
- ½ teaspoon onion powder
- 2 tablespoons water
- 1 cup water, for cooking

Directions:
In the mixing bowl combine together ground chicken, cayenne pepper, almond flour, dried dill, egg, minced onion, ginger, Mozzarella, and onion powder. When the mixture is homogenous, add 2 tablespoons water and mix up the mixture with the help of the spoon. Then make the meatballs using scooper. Pour water and insert the trivet in the instant pot. Line the trivet with baking paper. Place the meatballs on the trivet in one layer. Close and seal the lid. Cook the chicken meatballs for 6 minutes on manual mode (high pressure). When the time is over, make a quick pressure release and transfer the cooked meatballs in the serving plates.

Nutrition value/serving: calories 197, fat 10, fiber 1.7, carbs 6.2, protein 20.1

Chicken Cheese Calzone

Prep time: 15 minutes | *Cooking time:* 20 minutes | *Servings:* 4

Ingredients:
- 4 oz chicken breast, shredded
- ¼ cup Mozzarella, shredded
- 1 bacon, slice, cooked, chopped
- 1 tablespoon cream cheese
- 1 tablespoon coconut cream
- 1 egg, beaten
- ½ cup almond flour
- 2 tablespoons flax seeds, grinded
- 1 teaspoon butter, softened
- 1 cup water, for cooking

Directions:
Make the calzone dough: in the mixing bowl combine together butter, flax seeds, almond flour, and egg. Knead the non-sticky dough. Make the calzone filling: in the mixing bowl combine together chicken breast, shredded Mozzarella, bacon, cream cheese, and coconut cream. Roll up the almond flour dough and make 4 rounds with the help of the cutter. Then place the shredded chicken mixture on the dough rounds and fold them. Secure edges of calzones with the help of the fork. After this, pour water and insert the steamer rack in the instant pot. Line the rack with the baking paper and place the calzones on it. Close the lid and cook the calzones for 20 minutes on steam mode (high pressure). When the time is over, make a quick pressure release and open the lid. Transfer the calzones on the plate and cool little.

Nutrition value/serving: calories 143, fat 9.7, fiber 1.4, carbs 2.2, protein 11.3

Butter Chicken Stew

Prep time: 10 minutes | *Cooking time:* 25 minutes | *Servings:* 4

Ingredients:
- 4 tablespoons butter
- ½ cup asparagus, chopped
- 1 garlic clove, peeled, diced
- ½ teaspoon minced ginger
- 1 teaspoon tomato paste
- ½ teaspoon garam masala
- ½ teaspoon smoked paprika
- ½ teaspoon ground cumin
- ½ cup whipped cream
- 1 teaspoon dried parsley
- 10 oz chicken thighs, skinless, boneless
- ¼ cup chicken broth
- ¼ teaspoon salt
- ¼ teaspoon chili flakes

Directions:
Place butter in the instant pot. Add diced garlic, minced ginger, and garam masala. Cook the ingredients on sauté mode for 4 minutes. Stir the mixture from time to time. Then add ground cumin, parsley, and chicken thighs. Sprinkle the chicken with salt and chili flakes. Cook it for 3 minutes from each side on sauté mode. Add chicken broth and whipped cream. Close the lid. Cook the chicken for 10 minutes on steam mode (high pressure). Then make quick pressure release and open the lid. Add asparagus and close the lid. Cook the stew for 5 minutes more on stew mode.

Nutrition value/serving: calories 291, fat 21.6, fiber 0.6, carbs 2.1, protein 21.9

Chicken Cauliflower Rice

Prep time: 10 minutes | Cooking time: 16 minutes | Servings: 3

Ingredients:
- 8 oz chicken fillet, chopped
- 1 small onion, diced
- 1 tablespoon sesame oil
- 1 tablespoon butter
- 1 oz scallions, chopped
- 1 cup cauliflower, shredded
- 1 cup chicken broth
- ½ teaspoon salt
- 1 teaspoon smoked paprika

Directions:
Sprinkle the chopped chicken fillet with salt and smoked paprika. Place it in the instant pot and add sesame oil and onion; sauté the ingredients for 5 minutes on sauté mode. Then add butter, chicken broth, and close the lid. Cook the chicken on Manual (high pressure) for 5 minutes. When the time is over, make a quick pressure release and open the lid. Add shredded cauliflower and mix up well. Cook the meal in manual mode for 1 minute. When the time is over, allow the natural pressure release for 5 minutes. Mix up the cooked meal well before serving.

Nutrition value/serving: calories 253, fat 14.6, fiber 1.8, carbs 5.3, protein 24.7

Chicken Crust Pizza

Prep time: 10 minutes | Cooking time: 10 minutes | Servings: 6

Ingredients:
- 1 cup ground chicken
- ½ teaspoon ground black pepper
- ¼ teaspoon salt
- 1 teaspoon smoked paprika
- ½ teaspoon onion powder
- 1 tablespoon coconut flour
- 1 egg, beaten
- 1 tablespoon avocado oil
- 1 teaspoon fresh basil, chopped
- ¼ cup Cheddar cheese, shredded
- ½ cup Mozzarella, shredded
- 2 tablespoons coconut cream

Directions:
In the mixing bowl combine together ground chicken, ground black pepper, salt, smoked paprika, onion powder, and coconut flour; add Cheddar cheese. Then add egg and mix up the mass until it is homogenous. After this, brush the instant pot bowl with avocado oil and heat up on sauté mode for 2 minutes. Then place the ground chicken mixture in the instant pot bowl and flatten well to get the shape of the pizza crust. Cook it for 5 minutes. Then flip it on another side with the help of 2 spatulas. Sprinkle the chicken crust with fresh basil, coconut cream, and Mozzarella. Close the lid and cook the meal on sauté mode for 5 minutes.

Nutrition value/serving: calories 107, fat 6.3, fiber 1.2, carbs 2.4, protein 10.1

Asiago Chicken Drumsticks

Prep time: 15 minutes | Cooking time: 5 hours | Servings: 4

Ingredients:
- 4 chicken drumsticks, boneless
- 1/3 teaspoon salt
- ¼ teaspoon white pepper
- ½ teaspoon onion powder
- 1 teaspoon minced onion
- 1 teaspoon dried dill
- 1/3 cup chicken broth
- ¼ cup apple cider vinegar
- 2 tablespoons cream cheese
- 5 oz Asiago cheese, grated
- 1 teaspoon arrowroot powder

Directions:
In the big bowl combine together salt, white pepper, onion powder, minced onion, dried dill, chicken broth, and apple cider vinegar. Add cream cheese and 3 oz of Asiago cheese. Whisk the mixture until salt is dissolved. Then add chicken drumsticks and let the ingredients marinate for 10 minutes. Then transfer the chicken drumsticks and ½ part of chicken broth liquid in the instant pot. Close and seal the lid. Cook the meal on Low pressure (manual mode) for 4 hours. When the time is over, open the lid. Combine together the remaining chicken liquid and remaining Asiago cheese. Add arrowroot and stir it. Pour the liquid over the chicken and close the lid. Cook the meal on Low pressure for 1 hour more.

Nutrition value/serving: calories 233, fat 14.6, fiber 0.1, carbs 1.6, protein 22.4

Chicken Stuffed Avocado

Prep time: 15 minutes | *Cooking time:* 5 minutes | *Servings:* 2

Ingredients:
- 1 avocado, pitted, halved
- 4 oz chicken fillet, boiled
- 1 tablespoon cream cheese
- ¼ teaspoon minced garlic
- ½ teaspoon dried oregano
- ¼ cup Cheddar cheese, shredded
- ¼ teaspoon ground nutmeg
- 1 teaspoon butter, melted
- 1 cup water, for cooking

Directions:
Shred the boiled chicken and combine it with minced garlic and cream cheese. Then add dried oregano, Cheddar cheese, and ground nutmeg. Scoop ½ part of avocado meat in the chicken mixture. Mix up the chicken mixture well until homogenous. Brush the avocado halves with butter. Then fill every avocado half with chicken mixture. Pour water and insert the steamer rack in the instant pot. Arrange the avocado halves on the rack and close the lid. Cook the meal on manual (high pressure) for 5 minutes. When the time is over, make a quick pressure release and open the lid. Transfer the cooked meal on the plates.

Nutrition value/serving: calories 407, fat 32.3, fiber 7, carbs 9.5, protein 22.3

Chicken Cordon Bleu

Prep time: 15 minutes | *Cooking time:* 5 minutes | *Servings:* 2

Ingredients:
- 6 oz chicken fillet
- 2 ham slices
- 2 Swiss cheese slices
- ¼ teaspoon salt
- ¼ teaspoon white pepper
- 1 teaspoon butter, melted
- ½ cup chicken broth

Directions:
Beat the chicken fillets with the help of the kitchen hammer to make 2 chicken pieces in the shape of the pancake. Then brush every chicken piece with melted butter and top with ham and Swiss cheese. Then sprinkle them with white pepper and salt. Roll the chicken. Pour chicken broth in the instant pot. Place the rolled chicken in the chicken broth and close the lid. Cook the meal on manual mode (high pressure) for 5 minutes. When the time is over, make a quick pressure release and remove the meal from the instant pot.

Nutrition value/serving: calories 341, fat 18.8, fiber 0.4, carbs 3, protein 38.1

Herbed Whole Chicken

Prep time: 15 minutes | *Cooking time:* 50 minutes | *Servings:* 8

Ingredients:
- 3-pound whole chicken
- 1 teaspoon ground cumin
- ½ teaspoon ground nutmeg
- 1 teaspoon fresh thyme
- 1 teaspoon fresh rosemary
- 1 teaspoon smoked paprika
- 1 teaspoon sage
- 1 tablespoon fresh basil, chopped
- ½ teaspoon cayenne pepper
- 1 teaspoon ground turmeric
- 1 teaspoon onion powder
- ¼ cup sesame oil
- 1 teaspoon dried oregano
- 1 teaspoon salt
- 3 garlic cloves, peeled
- 1 ½ cup water, for cooking

Directions:
Pour water in the instant pot and add garlic cloves. Then insert the trivet. In the mixing bowl combine together sesame oil with all spices and herbs from the list above. Rub the chicken with oil mixture well and place it in the instant pot (on the trivet). Close the lid and set manual mode (high pressure). Cook the chicken for 50 minutes. When the time is over, allow the natural pressure release for 10 minutes.

Nutrition value/serving: calories 472, fat 35.5, fiber 0.5, carbs 1.5, protein 35.5

Ground Chicken Mix

Prep time: 10 minutes | *Cooking time:* 14 minutes | *Servings:* 3

Ingredients:
- 8 oz ground chicken
- 2 medium celery stalks, chopped
- 2 oz fennel, chopped
- ½ teaspoon ground black pepper
- 1 teaspoon smoked paprika
- 1 tablespoon cream cheese
- 1 teaspoon coconut oil
- 1/3 teaspoon salt

Directions:
Place the coconut oil in the instant pot and melt it. Add celery stalk and fennel. Cook the vegetables for 4 minutes on sauté mode. Stir them after 2 minutes of cooking. Meanwhile, in the mixing bowl combine ground chicken, ground black pepper, smoked paprika, and salt. Add the ground chicken mixture in the instant pot and cook on sauté mode for 3 minutes. After this, add cream cheese, stir well and close the lid. Cook the ground chicken mix for 7 minutes more.

Nutrition value/serving: calories 181, fat 8.5, fiber 1.4, carbs 2.9, protein 22.7

Bacon-Wrapped Chicken Tenders

Prep time: 15 minutes | *Cooking time:* 14 minutes | *Servings:* 6

Ingredients:
- 10 oz chicken breast, skinless, boneless
- 3 bacon slices
- ¼ teaspoon salt
- ¼ teaspoon ground black pepper
- ¼ teaspoon ground turmeric
- 1 cup water, for cooking

Directions:
Rub the chicken breast with ground black pepper, ground turmeric, and salt. Pour water and insert trivet in the instant pot. Arrange the chicken breast on the trivet and close the lid. Cook it on manual mode (high pressure) for 10 minutes. When the time is over, make a quick pressure release and remove the chicken from the instant pot. Shred it with the help of the fork and knife. After this, clean the instant pot and remove the trivet. Cut every bacon slice into halves. Place the bacon halves in the instant pot and cook on sauté mode for 2 minutes from each side. After this, make the small tenders from the shredded chicken mixture with the help of the fingertips. Then wrap every tender in the cooked bacon and secure with the toothpick.

Nutrition value/serving: calories 106, fat 5.2, fiber 0, carbs 0.3, protein 13.6

Chicken and Spinach Bowl

Prep time: 10 minutes | *Cooking time:* 15 minutes | *Servings:* 4

Ingredients:
- 10 oz chicken fillet, chopped
- ½ teaspoon paprika
- ¼ teaspoon salt
- ¼ teaspoon ground black pepper
- ½ teaspoon cayenne pepper
- 1 tablespoon sesame oil
- 1 red onion, sliced
- 1 cup fresh spinach, chopped
- ¼ cup of water

Directions:
Heat up instant pot on sauté mode for 3 minutes. In the mixing bowl combine together paprika, salt, chicken fillet, ground black pepper, ½ tablespoon of sesame oil, and cayenne pepper. Shake the ingredients gently and place them in the instant pot. Close the lid and sauté them for 5 minutes. Then stir the chicken well and add water. Close the lid and sauté it for 10 minutes more. Meanwhile, mix up together spinach and red onion. Add remaining sesame oil. Place the spinach mixture in the serving bowls and top them with cooked chicken.

Nutrition value/serving: calories 179, fat 8.8, fiber 1, carbs 3.2, protein 21.1

Keto Chicken Burger

Prep time: 10 minutes | Cooking time: 10 minutes | Servings: 2

Ingredients:
- ½ cup ground chicken
- 1 tomato, sliced
- 4 lettuce leaves
- ¼ teaspoon cayenne pepper
- 1 teaspoon dried dill
- ½ teaspoon onion powder
- ¼ teaspoon garlic powder
- 1 tablespoon almond meal
- ¼ teaspoon salt
- 1 cup water, for cooking

Directions:
Pour water and insert the trivet in the instant pot. In the mixing bowl combine together ground chicken with cayenne pepper, dried dill, onion powder, garlic powder, salt, and almond meal. Stir the ground mixture until smooth. Then make 2 balls from the ground chicken mixture, press them gently in the shape of a burger and place them in the trivet. Close the lid and cook the chicken balls for 10 minutes on manual mode (high pressure). When the time is over, make the quick pressure release. Place the chicken balls on 2 lettuce leaves. Top them with sliced tomato and remaining lettuce leaves.

Nutrition value/serving: calories 96, fat 4.2, fiber 1, carbs 3.3, protein 11.3

Chicken Liver Pate

Prep time: 15 minutes | Cooking time: 8 minutes | Servings: 8

Ingredients:
- 2-pound chicken liver
- 1/3 cup butter, softened
- ½ white onion, diced
- ½ teaspoon salt
- ½ teaspoon ground black pepper
- ½ teaspoon dried oregano
- 1 cup water, for cooking

Directions:
Put 1 tablespoon of butter in the instant pot and melt it on sauté mode for 3 minutes. After this, add diced onion and cook it for 5 minutes or until it is golden brown. Then transfer the onion in the big bowl and clean the instant pot. Pour water and insert the trivet in the instant pot. Mix up together chicken liver with salt and ground black pepper. Place the liver on the trivet (you can line the trivet with baking paper) and close the lid. Cook the chicken liver on steam mode for 8 minutes. When the time is over, allow the natural pressure release for 10 minutes and open the lid. Transfer the chicken liver in the food processor and blend it until smooth. Then add smooth liver in the onion; add butter and dried oregano. Stir the pate until homogenous. Store it in the fridge for up to 7 days.

Nutrition value/serving: calories 261, fat 15.1 fiber 0.2, carbs 1.8, protein 27.9

Coconut Chicken Cubes

Prep time: 10 minutes | Cooking time: 12 minutes | Servings: 3

Ingredients:
- 10 oz chicken fillet
- 3 tablespoons coconut flakes
- 2 tablespoons coconut flour
- 4 tablespoons butter
- ½ teaspoon salt
- ½ teaspoon turmeric
- ½ teaspoon chili powder
- 2 tablespoons cream cheese

Directions:
Chop the chicken fillet into medium cubes. Then sprinkle them with salt, turmeric, and chili powder. After this, dip every chicken cube in cream cheese. In the bowl mix up together coconut flakes and coconut flour. Coat every chicken cube in the coconut mixture. Melt butter in the instant pot on sauté mode (appx. 3-4 minutes). Then arrange the chicken cubes in the hot butter in one layer. Cook the coconut chicken cubes for 4 minutes and then flip them on another side. Cook the meal for 4 minutes more.

Nutrition value/serving: calories 379, fat 27, fiber 2.7, carbs 4.8, protein 28.9

Chicken Lettuce Rolls

Prep time: 10 minutes | Cooking time: 11 minutes | Servings: 4

Ingredients:
- 4 lettuce leaves
- 8 oz chicken, grinded
- 1 garlic clove, diced
- 1 teaspoon dried parsley
- ¼ teaspoon chili flakes
- ¼ carrot, grated
- 1 teaspoon coconut oil
- 1 teaspoon ricotta cheese
- 1 tablespoon heavy cream
- 1 teaspoon apple cider vinegar

Directions:
In the bowl mix up grinded chicken, garlic, parsley, chili flakes, and carrot. Put the coconut oil in the instant pot. Set sauté mode and heat it up for 1 minute. Then add chicken mixture. Cook it on sauté mode 5 minutes. Stir it from time to time with the help of a spatula. After this, add heavy cream and ricotta cheese. Stir well. Add apple cider vinegar. Stir the chicken one more time and cook it for 5 minutes more. Then fill the lettuce leaves with chicken mixture and roll them in the shape of pockets.

Nutrition value/serving: calories 114, fat 4.4, fiber 0.2, carbs 1, protein 16.8

Turkey Bolognese Sauce

Prep time: 10 minutes | Cooking time: 17 minutes | Servings: 4

Ingredients:
- ¼ cup carrot, grated
- ½ white onion, minced
- 1 garlic clove, diced
- ¼ teaspoon salt
- 10 oz ground turkey
- 1/3 teaspoon chili flakes
- ½ teaspoon dried thyme
- 1 teaspoon tomato paste
- 1 oz Swiss cheese, grated
- ½ scoop stevia powder
- 1 tablespoon coconut oil
- 1/3 cup water

Directions:
Toss coconut oil in the instant pot and melt it on sauté mode. Then add carrot, garlic, and onion. Cook the ingredients for 5 minutes. Stir them with the help of the spatula after 3 minutes of cooking. Then add salt and ground turkey, Sprinkle the ingredients with chili flakes, dried thyme, and stevia powder. Mix up well and sauté for 3 minutes. After this, mix up water with tomato paste. Pour the liquid over the ground turkey. Stir the sauce well and close the lid. Cook it on manual mode (high pressure) for 4 minutes. When the time is over, make the quick pressure release and open the lid. Top the sauce with Swiss cheese and mix up until the cheese is melted. The sauce is cooked.

Nutrition value/serving: calories 205, fat 13.2, fiber 0.6, carbs 2.9, protein 21.6

Turkey Stuffed Mushrooms

Prep time: 20 minutes | Cooking time: 10 minutes | Servings: 4

Ingredients:
- 8 white mushrooms
- 1 cup ground turkey
- 1/3 minced onion
- ¼ teaspoon minced garlic
- 1 teaspoon cream cheese
- 1 egg yolk
- 2 oz Mozzarella, shredded
- 2 teaspoons almond meal
- 1 cup water, for cooking

Directions:
In the mixing bowl mix up ground turkey with minced onion, cream cheese, egg yolk, and almond meal. When the mixture is homogenous, add shredded Mozzarella. Trim and clean the mushrooms. Then fill the mushrooms with ground turkey mixture. Pour water and insert the steamer rack in the instant pot. Place the mushrooms in the steamer rack in one layer and close the lid. Cook the mushrooms for 10 minutes on steam mode (high pressure). When the time is finished, allow the natural pressure release for 10 minutes. Carefully transfer the cooked mushrooms on the plate.

Nutrition value/serving: calories 281, fat 14.3, fiber 1.4, carbs 6, protein 32.6

Cornish Game Hens

Prep time: 15 minutes | *Cooking time:* 25 minutes | *Servings:* 4

Ingredients:
- 1 cornish game hen (8 oz bird)
- ½ teaspoon ground paprika
- ¼ teaspoon ground turmeric
- 1 tablespoon sesame oil
- ½ teaspoon ground black pepper
- ½ teaspoon salt
- 1 cup of water

Directions:
Rub the cornish game hen with ground paprika, turmeric, salt, and ground black pepper. Then brush the bird with sesame oil and transfer in the instant pot. Add water. Close and seal the lid. Cook the bird on manual mode (high pressure) for 25 minutes. When the time is finished, make the quick pressure release and open the lid. Transfer the cooked bird on the serving plate.

Nutrition value/serving: calories 211, fat 11.2, fiber 0.4, carbs 0.8, protein 25.8

Blackened Chicken

Prep time: 20 minutes | *Cooking time:* 60 minutes | *Servings:* 8

Ingredients:
- 3-pound whole chicken
- 2 tablespoons butter, melted
- 1 tablespoon avocado oil
- 2 tablespoons blackening spice seasoning mix
- 1 tablespoon dried cilantro
- 1 tablespoon apple cider vinegar
- 1 cup water, for cooking

Directions:
Mix up together butter, avocado oil, blackening seasoning mix, dried cilantro, and apple cider vinegar. Then rub the chicken with the oil mixture. Preheat the instant pot on sauté mode for 3 minutes. Then place chicken in the instant pot and cook it for 5 minutes. After this, flip the chicken on another side and cook it for 5 minutes more. After this, remove the chicken from the instant pot. Pour water in the instant pot. Add chicken and close the lid. Cook the chicken on poultry mode for 50 minutes. When the time is over, let the chicken stay in liquid for 30 minutes more.

Nutrition value/serving: calories 380, fat 26.5, fiber 0.1, carbs 0.1, protein 35.2

Anniversary Chicken

Prep time: 10 minutes | *Cooking time:* 21 minutes | *Servings:* 2

Ingredients:
- 8 oz chicken breast, skinless, boneless
- ½ teaspoon chili flakes
- ½ teaspoon salt
- ½ teaspoon chili powder
- ¼ teaspoon ground turmeric
- ¼ teaspoon garlic powder
- 1 teaspoon coconut oil
- 1 cup water, for cooking

Directions:
Rub the chicken breast with chili flakes, salt, chili powder, turmeric, and garlic powder. Heat up the coconut oil in the instant pot on sauté mode for 3 minutes. Then place the chicken breast in the coconut oil and cook it for 4 minutes from each side; remove the chicken from the instant pot. Clean the instant pot and pour water inside. Insert the trivet in the instant pot. Then place the chicken breast on the trivet and close the lid. Cook the poultry on manual mode (high pressure) for 10 minutes. When the time is over, make the quick pressure release. Slice the chicken breast into servings.

Nutrition value/serving: calories 153, fat 5.3, fiber 0.3, carbs 0.8, protein 24.2

Ajiaco

Prep time: 10 minutes | Cooking time: 33 minutes | Servings: 5

Ingredients:
- 13 oz chicken breast
- ½ white onion, chopped
- 2 garlic clove, chopped
- 1 teaspoon salt
- ½ teaspoon ground black pepper
- 1 tablespoon sesame oil
- 1 cup green peas, frozen
- 1 tablespoon fresh cilantro, chopped
- 1 teaspoon scallions, chopped
- ½ teaspoon guascas
- 1 ½ cup chicken broth

Directions:
In the bog bowl place white onion, garlic clove, salt, ground black pepper, sesame oil, cilantro green peas, scallions, and guascas. Mix up the ingredients well and leave for 1 hour to marinate. Then preheat the instant pot on sauté mode for 3 minutes. Put the chicken mixture in the instant pot and cook it for 10 minutes. Stir the ingredients from time to time. Then add chicken broth and close the lid. Cook ajiaco for 20 minutes on poultry mode. Then remove the chicken breast from the instant pot and shred it. Transfer the shredded chicken breast in the serving plates and top with chicken broth from the instant pot.

Nutrition value/serving: calories 150, fat 5.1, fiber 1.8, carbs 6.1, protein 18.9

Ground Turkey Chili

Prep time: 10 minutes | Cooking time: 35 minutes | Servings: 4

Ingredients:
- 2 cups ground turkey
- 2 oz leek, chopped
- 1 white onion, chopped
- 1 teaspoon salt
- ½ cup crushed tomatoes
- 1 teaspoon chili powder
- ½ teaspoon cayenne pepper
- 1 chili pepper, chopped
- 1 tablespoon avocado oil
- ½ teaspoon ground cumin
- ½ teaspoon dried oregano
- 1 cup of water

Directions:
On the instant pot set sauté mode. Add avocado oil and onion. Then add leek and ground turkey Stir the ingredients. Add chili powder, cayenne pepper, chili pepper, ground cumin, and dried oregano. Stir it and sauté for 10 minutes. After this, add crushed tomatoes and water. Mix up the chili mixture well and close the lid. Cook the chili for 20 minutes on stew/meat mode.

Nutrition value/serving: calories 167, fat 2.9, fiber 2.4, carbs 8.1, protein 27.9

Ethiopian Spicy Doro Wat Soup

Prep time: 10 minutes | Cooking time: 19 minutes | Servings: 3

Ingredients:
- 3 chicken drumsticks
- 1 teaspoon Berbere spices, divided
- 1/3 teaspoon salt
- 2 tablespoons ghee
- ½ white onion, diced
- 1 teaspoon garlic, diced
- ½ teaspoon fresh ginger, grated
- 1 egg, boiled
- 1 ½ cup chicken broth
- 1 teaspoon tomato paste
- 1 teaspoon lemon juice

Directions:
Set sauté function on your instant pot. Heat up the instant pot for 2 minutes. In the bowl combine together drumsticks and Berbere spices. Add salt. Then put ghee in the instant pot. Add spiced chicken drumsticks and onion. Add garlic and ginger. Cook the chicken for 5 minutes. Stir it well. Add tomato paste and chicken broth. Stir the soup gently. Close and seal the lid and cook it on steam mode (high pressure) for 12 minutes. When the time is over, make the quick pressure release and open the lid. Peel the boiled egg and cut it on 3 servings. Ladle the soup in the bowls and top it with egg and sprinkle with lemon juice.

Nutrition value/serving: calories 204, fat 13.3, fiber 0.5, carbs 3.2, protein 17.3

Turkey Soup
Prep time: 10 minutes | Cooking time: 16 minutes | Servings: 4

Ingredients:
- 3 oz turnip, chopped
- 2 celery stalks, chopped
- ¼ cup Edamame beans
- 1 tablespoon cream cheese
- 3 cups chicken broth
- 8 oz turkey breast, skinless, boneless, chopped
- 1 tablespoon sesame oil
- ½ teaspoon salt
- ½ teaspoon chili flakes
- 1 teaspoon dried oregano

Directions:
Pour sesame oil in the instant pot and preheat it for 1 minute on sauté. Then add celery stalk and chopped turkey breast. Sprinkle the chicken with salt and chili flakes. Add the dried oregano. Then add cream cheese and Edamame beans. Cook the ingredients on sauté mode for 10 minutes Stir them from time to time with the help of a spatula. Then add chicken broth and turnip. Close and seal the lid. Cook the turkey soup for 5 minutes on high-pressure mode (manual mode). When the time is over, make the quick pressure release and open the lid. Ladle the cooked soup in the serving bowls.

Nutrition value/serving: calories 135, fat 6.3, fiber 2, carbs 6.9, protein 15.9

Chicken Fricassee
Prep time: 10 minutes | Cooking time: 28 minutes | Servings: 6

Ingredients:
- 3 bacon slices, chopped
- 6 chicken thighs
- ½ yellow onion, diced
- 1 celery stalk, chopped
- 1 carrot, chopped
- ¼ cup mushrooms, chopped
- 1 teaspoon arrowroot powder
- 3 tablespoons apple cider vinegar
- 2 cups chicken broth
- 1 cup of water
- ½ teaspoon thyme
- 1 bay leaf
- 1 tablespoon lime juice
- 1/3 teaspoon salt
- 1/3 cup heavy cream
- 1 egg yolk

Directions:
Preheat instant pot on sauté mode for 2 minutes and add chopped bacon. Cook it for 4 minutes or until it is crispy. Then remove the bacon in the bowl. Rub the chicken thighs with salt, thyme, and place in the instant pot. Cook it for 3 minutes from each side. Add onion, celery stalk, mushrooms, carrot, arrowroot, and lime juice. Mix up the ingredients and cook them for 6 minutes. Then add bay leaf, apple cider vinegar, chicken broth, and water. Close and seal the lid and cook the meal on manual mode (high pressure) for 10 minutes. When the time is over, make the quick pressure release. Whisk together heavy cream and egg yolk. While stirring the chicken mixture - add the heavy cream liquid. Then sauté the meal for 3 minutes. Place the meal in the bowls. Top the fricassee with cooked bacon.

Nutrition value/serving: calories 264, fat 17.3, fiber 0.6, carbs 3.9, protein 21.6

Chicken Steamed Balls
Prep time: 10 minutes | Cooking time: 15 minutes | Servings: 2

Ingredients:
- 2 tablespoon almond flour
- 6 oz ground chicken
- 1 teaspoon dried dill
- ¼ carrot, boiled, mashed
- ¼ teaspoon salt
- 1/3 teaspoon ground black pepper
- 1 cup water, for cooking

Directions:
In the bowl mix up together almond flour, ground chicken, dill, mashed carrot, salt, and ground black pepper. Then make 2 balls from the chicken mixture. Pour water and insert the steamer in the instant pot. Place the chicken balls inside and cook them for 15 minutes on steam mode (high pressure). When the time is finished, make the quick pressure release and open the lid. The chicken steamed balls are cooked.

Nutrition value/serving: calories 209, fat 9.7, fiber 1.1, carbs 2.8, protein 26.3

South American Garden Chicken

Prep time: 15 minutes | *Cooking time:* 17 minutes | *Servings:* 4

Ingredients:
- 1 cup cauliflower, chopped
- 1 celery stalk, chopped
- 1 tablespoon lemon juice
- 4 chicken thighs, skinless, boneless
- 1 teaspoon pumpkin puree
- ½ teaspoon salt
- 1 teaspoon ground black pepper
- ½ cup chicken broth
- 1 teaspoon ghee
- 1 bay leaf
- ½ onion, diced

Directions:
Sprinkle the chicken thighs with salt and ground black pepper. Place them in the instant pot. Add ghee. Cook the chicken on sauté mode for 4 minutes. Then flip it on another side and cook for 5 minutes more. After this, add celery stalk and cauliflower. Add diced onion. Then add pumpkin puree, lemon juice, and chicken broth. Close and seal the lid. Cook the meal on manual mode (high pressure) for 8 minutes. Then allow the natural pressure release for 5 minutes.

Nutrition value/serving: calories 170, fat 7.4, fiber 1.3, carbs 3.6, protein 23.4

Chicken Moussaka

Prep time: 15 minutes | *Cooking time:* 55 minutes | *Servings:* 6

Ingredients:
- 1 teaspoon avocado oil
- 1 cup ground turkey
- 1 cup eggplants, peeled, chopped
- 1 green bell pepper, chopped
- ¼ cup onion, diced
- ¼ teaspoon garlic, diced
- ½ cup green beans, boiled
- 1 tomato, chopped
- ½ cup heavy cream
- ½ teaspoon salt
- ½ teaspoon white pepper
- 1 cup water, for cooking

Directions:
Brush the instant pot casserole mold with avocado oil. Then add ground turkey inside and sprinkle it with salt and white pepper. Stir the turkey gently with the help of the fork. After this, top the turkey with eggplants, bell pepper, and onion. Sprinkle the ingredients with garlic, green beans, and chopped tomato. After this, pour the heavy cream over the mixture and cover it with foil. Secure the edges of the casserole mold. Pour water and insert the trivet in the instant pot. Place the casserole mold on the trivet and close the lid. Cook moussaka for 55 minutes on stew/meat mode.

Nutrition value/serving: calories 94, fat 4.6, fiber 1.4, carbs 4.3, protein 9.7

Fajita Chicken Casserole

Prep time: 10 minutes | *Cooking time:* 16 minutes | *Servings:* 5

Ingredients:
- 1 cup broccoli, shredded
- 9 oz chicken breast, boneless, skinless, chopped
- ½ teaspoon chili powder
- ½ teaspoon ground black pepper
- ¼ teaspoon salt
- ½ teaspoon chili flakes
- ½ teaspoon ground nutmeg
- 2 bell peppers, roughly chopped
- ½ cup Cheddar cheese, shredded
- ½ cup of coconut milk
- 1 cup chicken broth
- 1 teaspoon ghee

Directions:
Place ghee in the instant pot and melt it on sauté mode. Then add chopped chicken breast. Sprinkle it with chili powder, ground black pepper, salt, chili flakes, and ground nutmeg. Cook the chicken for 8 minutes. Then add bell peppers, broccoli, and coconut milk. Add chicken broth and stir the ingredients with the help of the spoon. After this, top the casserole with Cheddar cheese and close the lid. Cook the meal on manual mode (high pressure) for 6 minutes. Then make the quick pressure release.

Nutrition value/serving: calories 198, fat 12.2, fiber 1.8, carbs 6.9, protein 16.2

Chicken with Black Olives

Prep time: 10 minutes | *Cooking time:* 15 minutes | *Servings:* 2

Ingredients:
- 2 chicken thighs, skinless, boneless, chopped
- ¼ cup black olives, sliced
- ½ cup Mozzarella cheese, shredded
- ½ cup cream
- ½ teaspoon ground black pepper
- 1 teaspoon dried parsley
- ½ teaspoon chili powder

Directions:
Mix up chicken thighs with chili powder, parsley, ground black pepper, and cream. Then put the chicken in the instant pot and cook it on stew mode for 10 minutes. Stir it from time to time with the help of the spatula. Then add black olives and cheese. Stir the ingredients and cook them for 5 minutes more on stew mode.

Nutrition value/serving: calories 359, fat 17.3, fiber 0.9, carbs 3.9, protein 45

Indian Chicken Korma

Prep time: 10 minutes | *Cooking time:* 15 minutes | *Servings:* 3

Ingredients:
- 9 oz chicken fillet, chopped
- ½ teaspoon minced ginger
- ¼ teaspoon minced garlic
- ¼ teaspoon Serrano pepper, chopped
- ½ tomato, chopped
- 1 tablespoon peanuts, chopped
- 1 teaspoon ghee
- 1 cup of water
- ¼ teaspoon fennel seeds
- ¼ teaspoon cumin seeds
- ½ teaspoon ground coriander
- ½ teaspoon ground cumin
- ½ teaspoon smoked paprika
- ½ teaspoon salt
- ½ teaspoon ground turmeric
- ¼ teaspoon ground cinnamon
- ¼ teaspoon ground cardamom
- 1 teaspoon garam masala

Directions:
Blend the minced ginger, garlic, Serrano pepper, and tomato until smooth. Then mix up together the blended mixture with chicken. After this, blend peanuts with ¼ cup of water. Place the chicken mixture and ghee in the instant pot. Add fennel seeds, cumin seeds, ground coriander, cumin, paprika, salt, turmeric, cinnamon, cardamom, and garam masala. Carefully stir the chicken with the help of the spatula. Add remaining water and close the lid. Cook the meal on manual (high pressure) for 10 minutes. Then make the quick pressure release and open the lid. Add the blended peanut mixture and close the lid. Cook the chicken korma for 5 minutes on stew mode.

Nutrition value/serving: calories 199, fat 9.4, fiber 0.9, carbs 2.1, protein 25.7

Meat

Rosemary Barbecue Pork Chops

Prep time: 15 minutes | *Cooking time:* 18 minutes | *Servings:* 2

Ingredients:
- 2 pork chops
- 1 teaspoon dried rosemary
- 1 teaspoon avocado oil
- ½ teaspoon salt
- 1 tablespoon BBQ sauce
- 1 tablespoon cream cheese

Directions:
Mix up together dried rosemary and avocado oil. Rub the pork chops with rosemary mixture and leave for 10 minutes to marinate. After this, place them in the instant pot and cook on sauté mode for 4 minutes from each side. Then add BBQ sauce, cream cheese, and salt. Close the lid and cook the pork chops for 10 minutes on sauté mode.

Nutrition value/serving: calories 290, fat 22, fiber 0.4, carbs 3.5, protein 18.4

Kalua Pork

Prep time: 25 minutes | *Cooking time:* 40 minutes | *Servings:* 4

Ingredients:
- 12 oz pork shoulder, chopped
- ½ teaspoon liquid smoke
- 1 teaspoon salt
- 1 cup water, for cooking

Directions:
In the mixing bowl mix up together chopped pork shoulder with salt and liquid smoke. Leave the meat for 15 minutes to marinate. When the time is over, pour the water and insert the trivet in the instant pot. Line the trivet with baking paper. Place the meat on the trivet in one layer and close the lid. Cook the meal on manual mode (high pressure) for 40 minutes. When the time is over, allow the natural pressure release for 15 minutes. Transfer the cooked meat in the bowls and shred with the help of the fork.

Nutrition value/serving: calories 248, fat 18.2, fiber 0, carbs 0, protein 19.8

Parmesan Pork

Prep time: 10 minutes | *Cooking time:* 35 minutes | *Servings:* 4

Ingredients:
- 4 pork chops
- 1 teaspoon white pepper
- 1 teaspoon sesame oil
- ½ cup heavy cream
- 1 teaspoon dried basil
- 4 oz Parmesan, grated

Directions:
Brush the instant pot bowl with sesame oil from inside. Sprinkle pork chops with white pepper and dried basil and put in the instant pot. Then top the meat with Parmesan and heavy cream. Close the lid and cook it on manual mode (high pressure) for 35 minutes. When the time is over, allow the natural pressure release for 10 minutes.

Nutrition value/serving: calories 410, fat 32.7, fiber 0.1, carbs 1.8, protein 27.5

Garlic Pork Loin

Prep time: 10 minutes | *Cooking time:* 60 minutes | *Servings:* 5

Ingredients:
- 1-pound pork loin, boneless
- 4 garlic cloves, peeled
- 1 white onion, peeled
- 1 teaspoon salt
- 1 teaspoon peppercorns
- 1 bay leaf
- 1 cup chicken broth

Directions:
Put all ingredients in the instant pot and close the lid. Set meat/stew mode and cook the pork loin for 60 minutes. When the time is over, chop the meat into the servings and put in the serving bowls. Add the meat liquid from the instant pot.

Nutrition value/serving: calories 241, fat 13, fiber 0.7, carbs 3.4, protein 26.2

Fragrant Pork Belly

Prep time: 15 minutes | *Cooking time:* 65 minutes | *Servings:* 6

Ingredients:
- 15 oz pork belly
- 1 teaspoon thyme
- 1 teaspoon cumin seeds
- 1 teaspoon fennel seeds
- 1 teaspoon salt
- 1 teaspoon olive oil
- 1 teaspoon garlic, minced
- 1 cup water, for cooking

Directions:
Rub the pork belly with minced garlic, thyme, cumin seeds, fennel seeds, and salt, Then brush it carefully with olive oil. Wrap the pork belly in the foil. Pour water and insert the trivet in the instant pot. Put the wrapped pork belly on the trivet and close the lid. Cook the meal on manual mode (high pressure) for 65 minutes. When the time is over, allow the natural pressure release for 10 minutes. Remove the foil and slice the pork belly into the servings.

Nutrition value/serving: calories 337, fat 20, fiber 0.2, carbs 0.6, protein 32.9

Parmesan Pork Tenderloins

Prep time: 10 minutes | *Cooking time:* 35 minutes | *Servings:* 4

Ingredients:
- 12 oz pork tenderloin
- ½ white onion, diced
- 1 teaspoon ground black pepper
- ½ teaspoon ground nutmeg
- 1 teaspoon sesame oil
- ½ cup heavy cream
- 2 oz Parmesan, grated
- 1/3 cup water

Directions:
Preheat the instant pot on sauté mode for 4 minutes. Meanwhile, rub the pork tenderloin with ground black pepper and nutmeg. Then brush it with sesame oil from each side. Place the meat in the instant pot and cook it on sauté mode for 3 minutes from both sides. After this, add water and bring it to the boil (appx.5 minutes). Then combine together cream with Parmesan. Pour the liquid over the meat and close the lid. Cook the meat on manual mode (high pressure) for 20 minutes. When the time is over, make the quick pressure release and open the lid. Slice the pork tenderloin and sprinkle it with cheese sauce.

Nutrition value/serving: calories 237, fat 12.8, fiber 0.5, carbs 2.7, protein 27.4

Keto Ham

Prep time: 10 minutes | *Cooking time:* 30 minutes | *Servings:* 4

Ingredients:
- 11 oz spiraled ham
- 1 teaspoon Erythritol
- ¼ teaspoon dried rosemary
- ¼ teaspoon salt
- 1 teaspoon ground cinnamon
- 2 tablespoons butter, melted
- 1 cup water, for cooking

Directions:
Slice the spiral ham and sprinkle it with salt. Then wrap it in foil. Pour water and insert the steamer rack in the instant pot. Place the wrapped ham on the rack and close the lid. Cook it on manual mode (high pressure) for 5 minutes. Then allow the natural pressure release for 10 minutes and open the lid. Transfer the ham in the bowl and clean the instant pot. Place the butter in the instant pot. Add Erythritol, salt, dried rosemary, and ground cinnamon. On sauté mode heat up the liquid. Add the ham and coat it well. Cook the meat on sauté mode for 5 minutes and then flip on another side and cook for 5 minutes more.

Nutrition value/serving: calories 218, fat 15.9, fiber 0.3, carbs 4.2, protein 14.8

Jalapeno Pulled Pork

Prep time: 10 minutes | Cooking time: 65 minutes | Servings: 2

Ingredients:
- 8 oz pork shoulder, boneless, chopped
- 1 jalapeno pepper, chopped
- 1 teaspoon minced garlic
- 1 cup of water
- 1 teaspoon salt
- 1 teaspoon peppercorns
- ½ teaspoon chili pepper
- 1 teaspoon tomato paste
- ½ teaspoon ground cumin

Directions:
Place the pork shoulder in the instant pot. Add minced garlic, water, salt, peppercorns, chili pepper, and tomato paste. Then add ground cumin and stir the ingredients gently with the help of the spoon. Close the lid. Cook the meat on meat stew mode for 60 minutes. When the time is over, open the lid and strain the liquid. Then shred the meat with the help of the fork. Add the strained liquid and chopped jalapeno pepper. Close the lid and cook the pulled pork for 5 minutes on sauté mode.

Nutrition value/serving: calories 343, fat 24.5, fiber 0.7, carbs 2.4, protein 26.9

Char Siu

Prep time: 20 minutes | Cooking time: 25 minutes | Servings: 3

Ingredients:
- 7 oz pork butt meat
- 1 teaspoon Erythritol
- 1 tablespoon BBQ sauce (Japanese style)
- 1 teaspoon apple cider vinegar
- ½ teaspoon garlic powder
- 1 tablespoon avocado oil
- ½ teaspoon salt
- 1 cup water, for cooking

Directions:
Make the marinade: in the big bowl mix up together Erythritol, BBQ sauce, apple cider vinegar, garlic powder, avocado oil, and salt. Then brush the meat well and leave to marinate for 20 minutes. After this, wrap the meat in the foil. Pour water and insert the trivet in the instant pot. Place the wrapped meat on the trivet and close the lid. Cook the meat on manual mode (high pressure) for 20 minutes. When the time is over, allow the natural pressure release for 10 minutes. Meanwhile, preheat the oven to 375F. Remove the cooked meat from the foil and slice it. Broil the pork butt in the oven for 5 minutes.

Nutrition value/serving: calorie 189, fat 11.6, fiber 0.3, carbs 2.5, protein 17.5

Chili Spare Ribs

Prep time: 15 minutes | Cooking time: 25 minutes | Servings: 3

Ingredients:
- 9 oz pork spare ribs
- 1 teaspoon tomato paste
- 2 tablespoons avocado oil
- 1 teaspoon chili powder
- ½ teaspoon chili flakes
- 1 teaspoon apple cider vinegar
- ¼ teaspoon salt
- 1 cup water, for cooking

Directions:
In the shallow bowl whisk together tomato paste, avocado oil, chili powder, chili flakes, salt, and apple cider vinegar. Generously brush the spare ribs with tomato paste mixture and leave for 10 minutes to marinate. Meanwhile, pour water and insert the steamer rack in the instant pot. Place the ribs in the instant pot baking pan. Then place the pan on the rack and close the lid. Cook the spare ribs for 25 minutes on Manual mode (high pressure). When the time is finished, make the quick pressure release and transfer the meal on the plate.

Nutrition value/serving: calories 176, fat 12, fiber 0.8, carbs 1.4, protein 15.5

Taiwanese Braised Pork Belly

Prep time: 15 minutes | Cooking time: 32 minutes | Servings: 6

Ingredients:
- 1-pound pork belly, chopped
- 1 oz shallot, chopped, fried
- 1 teaspoon ginger, sliced
- 1 teaspoon minced garlic
- ½ teaspoon anise
- 1 teaspoon salt
- 1 teaspoon ground cinnamon
- 1 tablespoon apple cider vinegar
- 1 tablespoon avocado oil
- 1 teaspoon swerve
- ½ cup of water

Directions:
Place the chopped pork belly in the instant pot and start to cook it on sauté mode. After 6 minutes stir the pork belly well and add ginger and garlic. Then add avocado oil and stir well. Cook the pork belly on sauté mode for 4 minutes more. After this, add swerve, apple cider vinegar, ground cinnamon, salt, and shallot. Add water and close the lid. Cook the meal on manual mode (high pressure) for 22 minutes. When the time is over, make the quick pressure release.

Nutrition value/serving: calories 360, fat 20.7, fiber 0.4, carbs 2, protein 35.2

Korean Style Pork Ribs

Prep time: 15 minutes | Cooking time: 20 minutes | Servings: 5

Ingredients:
- 1-pound beef chuck short ribs, chopped
- 1 tablespoon chives, chopped
- ½ teaspoon salt
- 2 tablespoons avocado oil
- ½ teaspoon minced garlic
- ¼ teaspoon sesame seeds
- 4 tablespoons apple cider vinegar
- 1 tablespoon Monk fruit
- ½ shallot, chopped
- ½ teaspoon white pepper
- 1 tablespoon butter
- 1 jalapeno pepper, chopped

Directions:
Make the marinade: put shallot in the blender. Add salt, avocado oil, minced garlic, apple cider vinegar, Monk fruit, chopped jalapeno pepper, and white pepper. Blend the mixture until smooth. Then combine together chopped ribs with blended mixture. Coat the ribs well and leave for 15 minutes to marinate. After this, toss the butter in the instant pot and melt it on sauté mode. Place the beef ribs in the instant pot bowl in one layer and cook them for 8 minutes from each side. Then add remaining marinade and sesame seeds. Cook the ribs for 2 minutes from each side more.

Nutrition value/serving: calories 282, fat 24, fiber 0.4, carbs 1.3, protein 15.5

Pork and Turnip Cake

Prep time: 15 minutes | Cooking time: 40 minutes | Servings: 6

Ingredients:
- 6 oz turnip, grated
- 1 cup ground pork
- ½ teaspoon ground black pepper
- 1 teaspoon cumin
- 1 white onion, minced
- ½ teaspoon salt
- 3 tablespoons butter, soften
- ½ cup almond flour
- 1 egg, beaten
- ½ teaspoon baking powder
- 1 cup water, for cooking

Directions:
Make the pie crust: in the big bowl combine together egg, baking powder, almond flour, and butter. Knead the soft and non-sticky dough. Line the instant pot baking mold with baking paper. Roll up the dough with the help of the rolling pin and transfer in the baking mold. Flatten it in the shape of the pie crust. After this, mix up ground pork with grated turnip, ground black pepper, cumin, minced onion, salt, and transfer the mixture over the pie crust. Flatten it. Then cover the pie with foil. Pour water and insert the trivet in the instant pot. Place the pie on the trivet and close the lid. Cook it on manual mode (high pressure) for 40 minutes. When the time is finished, make the quick pressure release. Cool the pie to the room temperature and slice into servings.

Nutrition value/serving: calories 247, fat 18.6, fiber 1.3, carbs 4.6, protein 15.4

Kalua Pig

Prep time: 15 minutes | *Cooking time:* 50 minutes | *Servings:* 6

Ingredients:
- 1 ½-pound pork shoulder, chopped
- 1 teaspoon salt
- 1 tablespoon liquid smoke
- 1 cup of water

Directions:
Sprinkle the meat with salt and liquid smoke. Mix up well. After this, pour water in the instant pot. Place the chopped meat in the instant pot in one layer and close the lid. Cook the meal on chili/beans mode for 50 minutes. When the time is over, allow the natural pressure release for 15 minutes. Open the lid and shred the meat with the help of the forks.

Nutrition value/serving: calories 331, fat 24.3, fiber 0, carbs 0, protein 26.4

Greek Style Pork Chops

Prep time: 15 minutes | *Cooking time:* 30 minutes | *Servings:* 3

Ingredients:
- 3 pork chops
- 1 teaspoon lemon juice
- 1 teaspoon dried oregano
- 1 teaspoon dried cilantro
- ¼ teaspoon onion powder
- ¼ teaspoon garlic powder
- 1/3 teaspoon salt
- ½ teaspoon ground black pepper
- 1 cup water, for cooking

Directions:
In the shallow bowl mix up dried oregano, cilantro, onion powder, garlic powder, salt, and ground black pepper. Then rub every pork chops with the spice mixture. Sprinkle the meat with lemon juice and leave for 5-7 minutes to marinate. Meanwhile, pour water and insert the steamer rack in the instant pot. Then arrange the meat on the steamer rack and close the lid. Cook the pork chops on manual mode (high pressure) for 30 minutes. When the time is over, make the quick pressure release and open the lid.

Nutrition value/serving: calories 260, fat 20, fiber 0.3, carbs 0.9, protein 18.2

Curry Pork Sausages

Prep time: 10 minutes | *Cooking time:* 20 minutes | *Servings:* 4

Ingredients:
- 4 pork sausages
- 1 teaspoon curry paste
- ½ cup coconut cream
- 1 tablespoon coconut oil

Directions:
Toss the coconut oil in the instant pot and heat it up on sauté mode until it is melted. Then place the pork sausages in hot coconut oil and cook them on sauté mode for 3 minutes from each side. Meanwhile, in the bowl whisk together curry paste with coconut cream until you get a smooth mixture. When the sausages are cooked from both sides, add curry paste liquid and close the lid. Cook the sausages for 10 minutes on manual mode (high pressure).

Nutrition value/serving: calories 178, fat 16.8, fiber 0.7, carbs 2, protein 6.1

Sage Pork Loin

Prep time: 10 minutes | *Cooking time:* 35 minutes | *Servings:* 12

Ingredients:
- 4-pound pork loin
- 1 tablespoon dried sage
- 1 tablespoon avocado oil
- 1 teaspoon salt
- 1 teaspoon ground black pepper
- 1 teaspoon apple cider vinegar
- 1 teaspoon ground nutmeg
- 1 bay leaf
- 1 cup water, for cooking

Directions:
Pour water in the instant pot. Add bay leaf and insert the steamer rack. Then rub the pork loin with dried sage, salt, ground black pepper, ground nutmeg, and sprinkle the meat with avocado oil and apple cider vinegar. Massage the pork loin with the help of the fingertips and transfer in the steamer rack. Close the lid. Cook the sage pork loin for 35 minutes on manual mode (high pressure). When the time of cooking is finished, make the quick pressure release and open the lid. Slice the cooked meal.

Nutrition value/serving: calories 407, fat 23.5, fiber 0.2, carbs 0.4, protein 45.6

Spinach and Fennel Pork Stew

Prep time: 10 minutes | *Cooking time:* 40 minutes | *Servings:* 4

Ingredients:
- 2 cups fresh spinach, chopped
- 8 oz fennel, chopped
- 10 oz pork tenderloin, chopped
- 1 teaspoon salt
- 1 teaspoon onion powder
- 1 teaspoon cumin seeds
- 1 cup chicken broth
- 1 teaspoon dried rosemary
- 1 teaspoon butter

Directions:
Put butter in the instant pot and melt it on sauté mode. Then add the chopped meat and cook it on sauté mode for 3-4 minutes. Stir it well and sprinkle with salt, onion powder, cumin seeds, and dried rosemary. Add chicken broth and close the lid. Cook the meat on sauté mode for 35 minutes. When the time is finished, stir the meat well and add fennel and fresh spinach. Stir the stew and close the lid. Cook the meal on manual mode (high pressure) for 3 minutes. When the time is finished, make the quick pressure release. Allow the cooked stew cool for 5-10 minutes before serving.

Nutrition value/serving: calories 145, fat 4.1, fiber 2.3, carbs 5.8, protein 21.1

Garlic Smoky Ribs

Prep time: 15 minutes | *Cooking time:* 18 minutes | *Servings:* 4

Ingredients:
- 11 oz pork ribs
- 1 tablespoon onion powder
- ½ teaspoon minced garlic
- ½ teaspoon salt
- ½ teaspoon chili powder
- 1 teaspoon liquid smoke
- 1 cup water, for cooking

Directions:
Sprinkle the pork ribs with onion powder, salt, and chili powder. Shake the pork ribs and add minced garlic and liquid smoke. Shake them one more time and put in the steamer rack. Pour water in the instant pot. Then place the steamer rack with ribs in water and close the lid. Cook the meal on manual mode (high pressure) for 18 minutes. When the cooking time is finished, allow the natural pressure release for 10 minutes.

Nutrition value/serving: calories 220, fat 13.9, fiber 0.2, carbs 1.7, protein 20.9

Ground Meat Stew

Prep time: 15 minutes | Cooking time: 40 minutes | Servings: 4

Ingredients:
- 1 cup ground beef
- ½ cup ground pork
- 2 bacon slices, chopped
- 1 onion, diced
- ½ cup celery stalk, chopped
- 1 cup chicken broth
- ½ teaspoon salt
- 1 teaspoon chili flakes
- 1 teaspoon dried dill
- 1 teaspoon dried cilantro
- 1 teaspoon dried parsley
- 1 teaspoon olive oil
- 1 tablespoon heavy cream
- ½ cup broccoli, chopped

Directions:

Pour olive oil in the instant pot. Add bacon and cook it for 3 minutes or until it is light brown, Add ground pork and ground beef. Stir the ingredients and start to cook them on sauté mode. After 5 minutes of cooking, add salt, chili flakes, dried dill, cilantro, and parsley. Then add chicken broth, broccoli, heavy cream, celery stalk, and diced onion. Close the lid and cook the stew on chili bean mode for 30 minutes.

Nutrition value/serving: calories 283, fat 19.2, fiber 1.1, carbs 4.4, protein 22.2

Pork&Mushrooms Ragout

Prep time: 10 minutes | Cooking time: 28 minutes | Servings: 4

Ingredients:
- 1 cup shiitake mushrooms, sliced
- ½ cup okra, chopped
- 11 oz pork tenderloin
- 1 teaspoon Erythritol
- ½ teaspoon salt
- 1 tablespoon lemon juice
- 1 teaspoon dried rosemary
- 2 tablespoons olive oil
- 1/3 cup water
- 2 tablespoons cream cheese

Directions:

Cut the pork tenderloin into the strips and put in the instant pot. Add olive oil and stir well. Set sauté mode and cook the meat for 3 minutes. After this, stir the meat and sprinkle it with salt, lemon juice, and dried rosemary. Stir again. Add Erythritol, okra, cream cheese, and mushrooms. Mix up ingredients well. Add water and close the lid. Cook the ragout with the closed lid on stew mode for 20 minutes.

Nutrition value/serving: calories 215, fat 11.7, fiber 1.3, carbs 6.3, protein 21.6

Mesquite Ribs

Prep time: 10 minutes | Cooking time: 30 minutes | Servings: 2

Ingredients:
- 8 oz pork baby ribs
- ¼ cup apple cider vinegar
- 1 teaspoon soy sauce
- 1 teaspoon mesquite seasonings
- ½ cup of water

Directions:

Pour water in the big bowl. Add apple cider vinegar, soy sauce, and mesquite seasonings. Then put the pork baby ribs in the apple cider vinegar mixture and leave for 5 minutes to marinate. After this, transfer the mixture in the instant pot and close the lid. Cook the meal on manual mode (high pressure) for 30 minutes. When the time is over, make the quick pressure release and remove the ribs from the instant pot.

Nutrition value/serving: calories 331, fat 27.2, fiber 0, carbs 0.9, protein 18.3

Keto Pork Posole

Prep time: 10 minutes | *Cooking time:* 29 minutes | *Servings:* 6

Ingredients:
- 1-pound pork shoulder, chopped
- 1 shallot, chopped
- 1 garlic clove, peeled
- ½ cup radish, sliced
- 1 chipotle chili, chopped
- ½ teaspoon dried oregano
- 1 teaspoon chili powder
- ½ teaspoon salt
- 1 cup of water
- 3 tablespoons fresh cilantro, chopped

Directions:
Place all ingredients except cilantro and radish in the instant pot. Close and seal the lid. Cook the meal for 25 minutes on manual mode (high pressure). When the cooking time is finished, make the quick pressure release and open the lid. Add cilantro and radish and stir posole. Close the lid and cook the meal for 4 minutes more on Manual mode (high pressure). When the meal is cooked, make the quick pressure release and open the lid. Cook posole for 5-10 minutes before serving.

Nutrition value/serving: calories 231, fat 16.4, fiber 0.7, carbs 1.9, protein 17.9

Hoisin Meatballs

Prep time: 15 minutes | *Cooking time:* 15 minutes | *Servings:* 4

Ingredients:
- 1 cup beef broth
- 1 teaspoon hoisin sauce
- 1 egg, beaten
- 1 tablespoon scallions, chopped
- 1 tablespoon white onion, diced
- ½ teaspoon minced garlic
- ¼ teaspoon salt
- ¼ teaspoon ground black pepper
- 2 cups ground beef

Directions:
Pour beef broth in the instant pot. Add hoisin sauce and stir gently with the help of the spoon. After this, in the mixing bowl mix up egg, scallions, white onion, minced garlic, salt, and ground black pepper. Add ground beef and stir the mass until homogenous. Then make the medium size meatballs and put them in the instant pot. Close and seal the lid. Cook the meatballs on manual mode (high pressure) for 15 minutes. When the time is over, allow the natural pressure release for 5 minutes.

Nutrition value/serving: calories 160, fat 9.7, fiber 0.2, carbs 1.4, protein 15.8

Tender Pork Satay

Prep time: 10 minutes | *Cooking time:* 15 minutes | *Servings:* 4

Ingredients:
- 4 pork loin chops
- ½ white onion, sliced
- 2 tablespoons peanut butter
- 1 teaspoon apple cider vinegar
- ½ teaspoon ground black pepper
- ½ cup chicken broth
- ½ teaspoon onion powder
- 1 teaspoon coconut flour
- 1 teaspoon chili powder

Directions:
Place the peanut butter in the instant pot and heat it up on sauté mode for 3-4 minutes. Meanwhile, chop the loin chops roughly. Add the meat in the instant pot. Then add ground black pepper, onion powder, and chili powder. Stir the meat well and cook it for 2 minutes more. Then add apple cider vinegar and chicken broth. Add sliced onion and coconut flour. Stir the ingredients. Close the instant pot lid and cook satay on manual mode (high pressure) for 9 minutes. When the time of cooking is finished, make a quick pressure release. Serve the pork satay with gravy.

Nutrition value/serving: calories 320, fat 24.3, fiber 1.3, carbs 4.1, protein 21

Ham and Cheese Dinner Casserole

Prep time: 10 minutes | Cooking time: 13 minutes | Servings: 4

Ingredients:
- ½ cup Cheddar cheese, shredded
- 2 oz Jarlsberg cheese, shredded
- 4 eggs, beaten
- 8 oz ham, chopped
- 1 tablespoon butter
- 1 teaspoon ground black pepper
- ½ teaspoon ground paprika
- ½ teaspoon salt
- ½ teaspoon ground turmeric
- 1 teaspoon dried oregano

Directions:
Put butter in the instant pot and melt it. Add chopped ham and sauté it for 4 minutes. Stir it in half the time of cooking. Then sprinkle the ham with ground black pepper, paprika, salt, and dried oregano. Stir well. Add eggs and stir the ingredients until homogenous. After this, add all cheese and close the lid. Cook the meal on manual mode (high pressure) for 4 minutes. Then make the quick pressure release and open the lid. The casserole tastes the best when it is hot.

Nutrition value/serving: calories 293, fat 21, fiber 1.2, carbs 3.6, protein 22.2

Blackberry Pork Chops

Prep time: 10 minutes | Cooking time: 15 minutes | Servings: 2

Ingredients:
- ¼ cup blackberries
- 1 teaspoon Erythritol
- 1 teaspoon butter, melted
- 1 teaspoon cream
- 2 pork chops
- ½ teaspoon ground paprika
- ¼ teaspoon salt
- ½ teaspoon dried cilantro
- 1 cup water, for cooking

Directions:
Pour water and insert the trivet in the instant pot. Then rub the pork chops with cilantro, salt, and ground paprika. Put the pork chops on the trivet and close the lid. Cook the meat on manual mode (high pressure) for 8 minutes. Then make the quick pressure release and open the lid. Place the blackberries, Erythritol, and cream in the blender and blend the mixture until smooth. Clean the instant pot and remove the trivet. Pour the blended blackberry mixture in the instant pot. Add butter and bring the liquid to boil on sauté mode. Then add the cooked pork chops. Coat the meat well in the blackberry sauce and cook for 1 minute from each side on sauté mode. Serve the pork chops with remaining blackberry sauce.

Nutrition value/serving: calories 283, fat 22.1, fiber 1.2, carbs 2.1, protein 18.4

Pork and Celery Curry

Prep time: 10 minutes | Cooking time: 35 minutes | Servings: 4

Ingredients:
- 10 oz pork loin, chopped
- 1 cup celery stalk, chopped
- 1 teaspoon curry paste
- 1 tablespoon fresh cilantro, chopped
- ½ cup coconut cream
- ½ cup of water
- 1 teaspoon avocado oil
- ½ teaspoon fennel seeds

Directions:
Pour avocado oil in the instant pot. Add chopped pork loin and cook it on sauté mode for 6 minutes (for 3 minutes from each side). Then add fennel seeds and water. Cook the ingredients for 4 minutes more. Meanwhile, in the bowl whisk together curry paste with coconut cream. When the mixture is smooth, pour it over the meat. Add celery stalk and close the lid. Cook the meal on meat/stew mode for 20 minutes. Then stir it well and add cilantro. Cook the curry for 5 minutes more.

Nutrition value/serving: calories 146, fat 10.3, fiber 0.7, carbs 1.7, protein 11.6

Beef and Squash Ragu

Prep time: 10 minutes | *Cooking time:* 30 minutes | *Servings:* 4

Ingredients:
- 7 oz beef loin, chopped
- 6 oz Kabocha squash, cubed
- ¼ teaspoon ground cinnamon
- ¼ teaspoon ground nutmeg
- ½ teaspoon salt
- 1 teaspoon ground paprika
- 1 tablespoon cream cheese
- 1 turnip, chopped
- 1 tablespoon almond butter
- ¼ cup chicken broth

Directions:
Melt almond butter in the instant pot on sauté mode. Sprinkle the chopped beef with ground cinnamon, nutmeg, salt, and ground paprika. Put the meat in the hot almond butter and cook it for 3 minutes. Then flip the meat on another side and cook for 2 minutes more. Add turnip and cream cheese. Then add chicken broth and Kabocha squash. Cook the ragu for 20 minutes on sauté mode. Stir it every 3 minutes with the help of the spatula to avoid burning.

Nutrition value/serving: calories 154, fat 6.5, fiber 1.8, carbs 6.8, protein 17.3

Beef Loin with Acorn Squash

Prep time: 15 minutes | *Cooking time:* 40 minutes | *Servings:* 4

Ingredients:
- 8 oz acorn squash, halved, seeded
- 1-pound beef loin
- 1 tablespoon olive oil
- 1 teaspoon salt
- 1 teaspoon ground black pepper
- 2 garlic cloves, peeled
- 1 teaspoon dried rosemary
- 1 cup of water
- ½ teaspoon ground turmeric
- 1 cup water, for cooking

Directions:
Rub the acorn squash with olive oil and dried rosemary. Place the vegetable in the steamer rack. Then pour water in the instant pot and insert the steamer rack inside. Close the lid and cook the squash for 8 minutes. When the time of cooking is finished, allow the natural pressure release for 10 minutes and remove the vegetable from the instant pot. Then cut it into cubes and put it in the serving plate. After this, clean the instant pot and remove the steamer rack. Chop the beef loin into the cubes and put in the instant pot. Add salt, ground black pepper, garlic cloves, water, and ground turmeric. Close the lid and cook the beef on manual mode (high pressure) for 30 minutes. When the time is over, make the quick pressure release. Place the cooked beef over the acorn squash and sprinkle with hot beef gravy.

Nutrition value/serving: calories 265, fat 13.1, fiber 1.2, carbs 7.1, protein 31

Beef Tips

Prep time: 10 minutes | *Cooking time:* 30 minutes | *Servings:* 3

Ingredients:
- 1 cup turnip, peeled, chopped
- 7 oz beef, chopped
- ¼ cup apple cider vinegar
- 1 tablespoon avocado oil
- 1 white onion, diced
- ½ teaspoon salt
- 1 teaspoon ground black pepper
- 1 cup of water
- 1 teaspoon ground coriander
- 1 teaspoon cream cheese
- 1 teaspoon fresh cilantro, chopped

Directions:
Pour avocado oil in the instant pot. Add beef and onion. Sauté the ingredients for 5 minutes. Then sprinkle them with salt, ground black pepper, and coriander. Mix up with the help of the spatula. Then add apple cider vinegar and water. Insert the steamer rack over the meat and place the chopped turnip on it. Close the lid and cook the meal on manual mode (high pressure) for 15 minutes. When the time is over, allow the natural pressure release for 10 minutes. Mash the cooked turnip and mix it up with cream cheese. Place the mashed turnip in the serving plates and top with meat, cilantro, and gravy.

Nutrition value/serving: calories 166, fat 5.2, fiber 2, carbs 7.1, protein 21.1

Onion Baby Back Ribs
Prep time: 10 minutes | Cooking time: 40 minutes | Servings: 6

Ingredients:
- 1-pound pork baby back ribs
- 1 teaspoon onion powder
- 2 white onions, sliced
- 2 tablespoons butter
- ½ cup heavy cream
- 1 teaspoon thyme
- 1 teaspoon dried rosemary
- ½ teaspoon salt

Directions:
Melt butter in the instant pot on sauté mode. Then sprinkle the baby back ribs with onion butter, thyme, and rosemary and put in the hot butter. Cook the meat for 3 minutes and then flip on another side. Add salt, sliced onion, and heavy cream. Close the lid and cook the meal on stew/meat mode for 30 minutes.

Nutrition value/serving: calories 362, fat 30.1, fiber 1, carbs 4.3, protein 17.8

Beef & Cabbage Stew
Prep time: 10 minutes | Cooking time: 15 minutes | Servings: 4

Ingredients:
- 1 cup ground beef
- 2 cups white cabbage, shredded
- 1 tablespoon coconut oil
- 1 teaspoon salt
- 1 teaspoon ground black pepper
- ½ cup of water
- 1 teaspoon tomato paste
- ½ cup of organic almond milk
- 1 teaspoon dried dill

Directions:
Place cabbage in the big bowl. Sprinkle it with ground black pepper and salt. Shake the cabbage. After this, add dill. Put coconut oil in the instant pot. Melt it on sauté mode. Add ground beef and cook it for 5 minutes. Stir the meat from time to time with the help of the spatula. Add organic almond milk, water, and tomato paste. Stir the ingredients until you get a homogenous mixture. Then add shredded cabbage, mix the ingredients up and close the lid. Cook the stew on manual mode (high pressure) for 10 minutes. Then make the quick pressure release and open the lid. Stir the stew well before serving.

Nutrition value/serving: calories 113, fat 7.9, fiber 1.2, carbs 3.8, protein 7.3

Tender Salisbury Steak
Prep time: 10 minutes | Cooking time: 30 minutes | Servings: 4

Ingredients:
- 1 cup ground beef
- 1 egg white
- 1 tablespoon water
- 1 teaspoon chili powder
- ½ teaspoon salt
- 1 teaspoon olive oil
- 1 cup white mushrooms, sliced
- 1 white onion, sliced
- ½ teaspoon tomato paste
- ½ teaspoon dill, chopped
- ½ cup chicken broth

Directions:
Make the steaks: in the mixing bowl mix up ground beef, egg white, 1 tablespoon of water, chili powder, and salt. Make the medium size steaks from the meat mixture. Then pour olive oil in the skillet. Cook the steaks on medium-high heat for 2 minutes from each side. Meanwhile, place the mushrooms in the instant pot. Add onion, tomato paste, dill, and chicken broth. Then put the steaks over the mushrooms and close the lid. Cook the meal on manual mode (high pressure) for 27 minutes. When the time is over, make the quick pressure release.

Nutrition value/serving: calorie 102, fat 5.6, fiber 1, carbs 3.9, protein 9

Cumin Kielbasa

Prep time: 7 minutes | Cooking time: 10 minutes | Servings: 4

Ingredients:
- 8 oz kielbasa, sliced
- 1 teaspoon cumin seeds
- 3 tablespoons butter
- 1 tablespoon cream cheese
- ¼ teaspoon salt
- 1 oz Jarlsberg cheese, grated

Directions:
Place butter in the instant pot. Add cumin seeds and salt. Melt the ingredients on sauté mode. Add kielbasa and cook for 3 minutes. Then flip on another side and cook for 3 minutes more. After this, sprinkle the kielbasa with cheese and cream cheese. Stir well and sauté for 4 minutes more.

Nutrition value/serving: calories 241, fat 21.6, fiber 0.1, carbs 2.5, protein 9.6

Prosciutto and Eggs Salad

Prep time: 10 minutes | Cooking time: 6 minutes | Servings: 4

Ingredients:
- 4 eggs
- 5 oz prosciutto, sliced
- 1 cup lettuce, chopped
- 1 tablespoon lemon juice
- 1 teaspoon flax seeds
- 1 tablespoon avocado oil
- ½ teaspoon ground black pepper
- 1 cup water, for cooking

Directions:
Pour water in the instant pot and insert the steamer rack. Place the eggs in the steamer rack and close the lid. Cook the eggs on manual mode (high pressure) for 6 minutes. When the time is over, make the quick pressure release. Open the lid and place the eggs in the cold water. Cool them well and after this peel. Chop the slices prosciutto roughly and put in the salad bowl. Add lettuce, flax seeds, and avocado oil. Then chop the eggs roughly and add in a salad bowl. Add lemon juice and ground black pepper. Shake the salad gently.

Nutrition value/serving: calories 125, fat 7, fiber 0.5, carbs 1.9, protein 13.2

Mississippi Roast

Prep time: 10 minutes | Cooking time: 40 minutes | Servings: 3

Ingredients:
- 11 oz chuck roast, chopped
- 1 tablespoon sesame oil
- ¼ cup white onion, chopped
- 1 chili pepper, chopped
- ¼ cup chicken broth
- 1 jalapeno pepper, chopped
- ½ teaspoon peppercorns
- 1 tablespoon coconut oil
- ½ teaspoon salt

Directions:
Set sauté mode and pour sesame oil in the instant pot. Add chopped chuck roast. Sprinkle the meat with peppercorns and cook for 3 minutes from each side. Then add coconut oil, salt, jalapeno, and chili peppers. Then add white onion and chicken broth. Cook the meat on manual mode (high pressure) for 40 minutes. When the time of cooking is finished, make a quick pressure release. Shred the meat gently.

Nutrition value/serving: calories 314, fat 17.9, fiber 0.5, carbs 1.6, protein 35

Keto Oxtail Goulash
Prep time: 15 minutes | Cooking time: 80 minutes | Servings: 5

Ingredients:
- 10 oz beef oxtail, chopped
- 2 oz celery root, chopped
- ½ carrot, chopped
- ½ cup onion, chopped
- 1 eggplant, chopped
- 3 oz fennel, chopped
- 1 cup beef broth
- 1 teaspoon salt
- 1 teaspoon ground black pepper
- 1 teaspoon dried oregano
- 2 teaspoons ground turmeric
- ½ teaspoon chili flakes
- 1 tablespoon sesame oil
- 2 tablespoons cream cheese

Directions:
Sprinkle the oxtails with salt and put in the instant pot. Add sesame oil and cook them on sauté mode for 4 minutes from each side. Then add celery root, carrot, onion, eggplant, fennel, ground black pepper, dried oregano, ground turmeric, and chili flakes. Mix up the ingredients with the help of the spoon. Then add beef broth and cream cheese Close the lid and cook the goulash for 65 minutes on manual mode (high pressure). When the time is over, allow the natural pressure release for 10 minutes.

Nutrition value/serving: calories 231, fat 12.2, fiber 4.8, carbs 10.7, protein 20.4

Italian Beef
Prep time: 15 minutes | Cooking time: 60 minutes | Servings: 8

Ingredients:
- 4-pound beef chuck, chopped
- 3 tablespoons almond butter
- ½ cup shallot, sliced
- 2 garlic cloves, sliced
- ½ cup pepperoncini peppers
- 1 cup chicken broth
- 1 teaspoon Italian seasonings
- ½ teaspoon chili powder
- 1 teaspoon Erythritol

Directions:
Melt almond butter on sauté mode and add sliced shallot and garlic cloves. Cook the vegetables for 5-6 minutes or until they are soft. After this, add chopped beef chuck, pepperoncini, Italian seasonings, and chili powder. Then add Erythritol and chicken broth. Close and seal the lid. Cook the beef on manual mode (high pressure) for 55 minutes. When the cooking time is finished, allow the natural pressure release for 15 minutes. Shred the meat with the help of the fork.

Nutrition value/serving: calories 474, fat 17.9, fiber 0.7, carbs 3.5, protein 71

Thyme Braised Beef
Prep time: 10 minutes | Cooking time: 45 minutes | Servings: 5

Ingredients:
- 1-pound beef loin
- 1 teaspoon dried thyme
- ½ teaspoon salt
- ½ cup butter
- ¼ cup cream cheese
- ½ cup of water

Directions:
Rub the beef loin with dried thyme and salt and put in the instant pot. Add butter and cream cheese. Add water. Close the lid and cook the beef for 45 minutes on manual mode (high pressure). When the meat is cooked, make the quick pressure release. Open the lid and transfer the meat on the chopping board. Chop the meat roughly and put it in the serving plates. Sprinkle the meat with cream cheese gravy.

Nutrition value/serving: calories 369, fat 30, fiber 0.1, carbs 0.5, protein 25.4

Butter Lamb

Prep time: 10 minutes | *Cooking time:* 3 hours | *Servings:* 3

Ingredients:
- 11 oz lamb fillet
- 1 teaspoon dried lemongrass
- ½ teaspoon salt
- ¼ cup coconut cream
- 2 tablespoons butter
- ½ cup beef broth
- ½ teaspoon ground paprika

Directions:
Melt butter in the instant pot on sauté mode. Chop the lamb fillet roughly and sprinkle it with dried lemongrass and ground paprika. Place the meat in the instant pot and cook on sauté mode for 2 minutes. Then flip the lamb on another side. Sprinkle it with salt. Add coconut cream and beef broth. Close and seal the lid. Cook the butter lamb for 3 hours on manual mode (low pressure).

Nutrition value/serving: calories 315, fat 20.4, fiber 0.6, carbs 1.6, protein 30.6

Coriander Leg of Lamb

Prep time: 10 minutes | *Cooking time:* 50 minutes | *Servings:* 4

Ingredients:
- 1-pound leg of lamb
- 1 tablespoon ground coriander
- 1 teaspoon salt
- 1 cup of water
- 1 tablespoon coconut oil

Directions:
Rub the leg of lamb with salt and ground coriander. Then place the coconut oil in the instant pot and melt it on sauté mode. Put the leg of lamb in the hot coconut oil. Cook the meat for 5 minutes from both sides. Then add water and close the lid. Cook the leg of lamb on manual mode (high pressure) for 40 minutes. When the time is over, make the quick pressure release.

Nutrition value/serving: calories 240, fat 11.7, fiber 0, carbs 0, protein 31.9

Dhansak Curry Meat

Prep time: 25 minutes | *Cooking time:* 45 minutes | *Servings:* 4

Ingredients:
- 1-pound beef sirloin, chopped
- 1 tablespoon nut oil
- ½ teaspoon curry powder
- ½ teaspoon ground paprika
- ½ teaspoon salt
- ½ teaspoon ground turmeric
- 1 teaspoon lemon juice
- 1 teaspoon minced ginger
- ½ cup of water
- ½ teaspoon garam masala
- 1 tomato, chopped
- 1 teaspoon dried cilantro

Directions:
Pour nut oil in the instant pot. Add chopped beef sirloin. Set sauté mode and cook the meat for 5 minutes. Stir it from time to time. After this, add curry powder, ground paprika, salt, turmeric, lemon juice, and minced ginger. Then add garam masala, tomato, and cilantro. Add water and close the lid. Cook the meat on manual mode (high pressure) for 40 minutes. When the time is over, allow the natural pressure release for 25 minutes.

Nutrition value/serving: calories 248, fat 10.6, fiber 0.5, carbs 1.4, protein 34.7

Mint Lamb Cubes
Prep time: 15 minutes | Cooking time: 50 minutes | Servings: 4

Ingredients:
- 1-pound lamb shoulder
- 1 teaspoon dried mint
- 1 teaspoon salt
- 1 teaspoon peppercorns
- 1 bay leaf
- 1 cup beef broth
- 1 teaspoon dried thyme

Directions:
Rub the lamb shoulder with salt and put it in the instant pot. Add dried mint, peppercorns, bay leaf, and dried thyme. Add beef broth and close the lid. Cook the meat on manual mode (high pressure) for 50 minutes. When the time of cooking is finished, allow the natural pressure release for 10 minutes. Then remove the lamb shoulder from the instant pot and slice it. Sprinkle the meat with the beef broth from the instant pot.

Nutrition value/serving: calories 224, fat 8.7, fiber 0.3, carbs 1, protein 33.2

Pork Chops in Sweet Sauce
Prep time: 10 minutes | Cooking time: 13 minutes | Servings: 2

Ingredients:
- 1 tablespoon Erythritol
- 1 teaspoon butter
- 1 tablespoon heavy cream
- ½ teaspoon ground nutmeg
- ¼ teaspoon salt
- ½ teaspoon cayenne pepper
- ½ tablespoon nut oil
- 2 pork chops
- 4 tablespoons water

Directions:
Sprinkle the pork chops with cayenne pepper, salt, and ground nutmeg. Then pour olive oil in the instant pot. Place the pork chops in the instant pot and cook them on sauté mode for 4 minutes. Then add water and flip the pork chops on another side. Cook the meat for 4 minutes more. Remove the meat from the instant pot. Add butter, heavy cream, and Erythritol. Cook the ingredients on sauté mode for 2-3 minutes or until the mixture is smooth. Add pork chops and coat in the sweet sauce. Sauté the meat for 3 minutes more.

Nutrition value/serving: calories 333, fat 28.2, fiber 0.2, carbs 0.7, protein 18.2

Kalua Pork
Prep time: 15 minutes | Cooking time: 70 minutes | Servings: 3

Ingredients:
- 9 oz pork shoulder
- 2 bacon slices, chopped
- ½ teaspoon of sea salt
- 1 teaspoon ground paprika
- ½ teaspoon liquid smoke
- ½ cup white cabbage, chopped
- ½ cup beef broth

Directions:
Place the chopped bacon in the instant pot and cook it on sauté mode for 5 minutes or until it is light brown. Chop the pork should and mix it up with sea salt and ground paprika. Add the meat in the instant pot. Add liquid smoke and beef broth. Close the lid and cook the meat on manual mode (high pressure) for 60 minutes. When the time is over, make the quick pressure release. Open the lid and add cabbage. Stir it well. Then close the lid again and cook the meal for 10 minutes on manual mode. Make the quick pressure release.

Nutrition value/serving: calories 328, fat 23.8, fiber 0.6, carbs 1.4, protein 25.6

Spoon Lamb

Prep time: 20 minutes | *Cooking time:* 65 minutes | *Servings:* 4

Ingredients:
- 12 oz leg of lamb, boneless, chopped
- ½ teaspoon salt
- ½ teaspoon ground black pepper
- ½ white onion, diced
- 2 oz celery stalk, chopped
- 1 teaspoon minced garlic
- 1 tablespoon lemon juice
- 1 teaspoon lemon zest, grated
- ½ teaspoon coriander seeds
- 1 tablespoon avocado oil
- 1 cup of water

Directions:
Pour avocado oil in the instant pot. Add chopped lamb and cook it on sauté mode for 5 minutes. Then stir the meat well and add ground black pepper and salt. Add minced garlic, lemon juice, lemon zest, and coriander seeds. Stir well and cook for 4 minutes more. Remove the meat mixture from the instant pot. Put onion and celery stalk in the instant pot. Put the meat mixture over the vegetables. Add water and close the lid. Cook the spoon lamb on manual (high pressure) for 55 minutes. When the time is over, allow the natural pressure release for 15 minutes. Mix up the meal with the help of the spoon gently.

Nutrition value/serving: calories 174, fat 6.7, fiber 0.8, carbs 2.5, protein 24.3

Rogan Josh

Prep time: 15 minutes | *Cooking time:* 35 minutes | *Servings:* 4

Ingredients:
- 1 tablespoon ghee
- 1 white onion, diced
- 1-pound beef shoulder
- 1 teaspoon minced garlic
- ½ teaspoon minced ginger
- 1 teaspoon chili pepper
- ½ teaspoon garam masala
- ½ teaspoon ground turmeric
- ½ teaspoon ground paprika
- ½ teaspoon ground cinnamon
- ½ teaspoon ground cloves
- ½ teaspoon ground cumin
- 1 cup of coconut milk
- 1 teaspoon tomato paste

Directions:
Put ghee in the instant pot and preheat it on sauté mode. Chop the beef shoulder into cubes and put in the hot ghee. Then add onion and stir the ingredients. Cook them for 5 minutes. Add minced garlic, ginger, chili pepper, garam masala, ground turmeric, paprika, cinnamon, ground cloves, and cumin. Stir well and sauté for 5 minutes more. Meanwhile, whisk together coconut milk and tomato paste. When the liquid is smooth, add it in the beef and mix up with the help of the spatula. Close and seal the lid. Cook the meal on manual (high pressure) for 25 minutes. When the cooking time is finished, allow the natural pressure release for 15 minutes. Mix up the meal well before serving.

Nutrition value/serving: calories 355, fat 25.7, fiber 2.5, carbs 7.5, protein 25.1

Chipotle Lamb Shank

Prep time: 25 minutes | *Cooking time:* 45 minutes | *Servings:* 4

Ingredients:
- 1-pound lamb shank
- 2 garlic cloves, diced
- 3 tablespoon apple cider vinegar
- ¼ cup crushed tomatoes
- 1 teaspoon dried parsley
- 1 teaspoon olive oil
- 4 chipotles in adobo
- 1 cup of water
- 1 teaspoon cayenne pepper

Directions:
Cut the lamb shank into 4 pieces and sprinkle with dried parsley and apple cider vinegar. Add olive oil and diced garlic. After this, sprinkle the meat with cayenne pepper. Mix it up and leave for 10-15 minutes to marinate. Then preheat the instant pot on sauté mode for 5 minutes. Add lamb pieces and all liquid from the meat (marinade). Cook the meat for 2 minutes and flip on another side. Cook it for 2 minutes more. After this, add crushed tomatoes, chipotles in adobo, and water. Close the lid and cook the meat on manual mode (high pressure) for 35 minutes. When the time of cooking is over, allow the natural pressure release for 15 minutes.

Nutrition value/serving: calories 245, fat 10.6, fiber 2.7, carbs 3.1, protein 33.4

White Pork Soup
Prep time: 15 minutes | Cooking time: 27 minutes | Servings: 2

Ingredients:
- ½ cup ground pork
- ½ shallot, diced
- 1 garlic clove, diced
- 1 teaspoon chili flakes
- 2 oz celery stalk, chopped
- 1 oz leek, chopped
- 1 tablespoon ghee
- ½ teaspoon salt
- ¼ teaspoon ground nutmeg
- 1 tablespoon cream cheese
- 1 cup of water

Directions:
Put ghee in the instant pot and melt it on sauté mode. When the ghee is melted, add ground pork, shallot, garlic clove, chili flakes, and salt. Sprinkle the ground pork with ground nutmeg and stir with the help of the spatula. Cook the meat on meat/stew mode for 10 minutes. Then stir it well and add celery stalk and leek. Add water and cream cheese and close the lid. Cook the soup on manual mode (high pressure) for 10 minutes. Then make the quick pressure release and open the lid. Let the soup rest for 15 minutes before serving.

Nutrition value/serving: calories 330, fat 24.6, fiber 0.8, carbs 5.4, protein 21.3

Lamb Pulao
Prep time: 15 minutes | Cooking time: 35 minutes | Servings: 4

Ingredients:
- 1 cup cauliflower, shredded
- 10 oz lamb loin, chopped
- ¼ cup crushed tomatoes
- ¼ onion, diced
- 1 tablespoon ghee
- ¼ teaspoon ground cardamom
- ¼ teaspoon cumin seeds
- ¼ teaspoon minced garlic
- ¼ teaspoon turmeric
- ¼ teaspoon ground coriander
- ½ cup chicken broth
- ½ teaspoon salt

Directions:
In the shallow bowl mix up together ground cardamom, cumin seeds, turmeric, salt, and ground coriander. Then preheat the instant pot on sauté mode for 2-3 minutes. Place the chopped lamb loin in the hot instant pot bowl and cook on sauté mode for 4 minutes. Then flip the meat on another side and sprinkle with spice mixture. Add ghee. Cook it for 5 minutes more. After this, add diced onion, crushed tomatoes, minced garlic, and chicken broth. Close and seal the lid. Cook the meat on manual mode (high pressure) for 20 minutes. Then make the quick pressure release and open the lid. Stir the meal well and add shredded cauliflower. Stir it again. Close the lid and cook the ingredients for 3 minutes on manual mode. When the cooking time is finished, make the quick pressure release.

Nutrition value/serving: calories 287, fat 22.9, fiber 1.1, carbs 3, protein 15.7

Meat&Cheese Pie

Prep time: 25 minutes | *Cooking time:* 45 minutes | *Servings:* 8

Ingredients:
- 6 oz ground beef
- 6 oz ground pork
- 3 oz Provolone cheese, grated
- 3 oz Mozzarella cheese, shredded
- 2 tablespoons butter
- 6 tablespoons almond flour
- 1 teaspoon coconut oil
- 1 teaspoon dried parsley
- ½ teaspoon salt
- 1 teaspoon tomato paste
- 1 tablespoon cream cheese
- 1 cup water, for cooking

Directions:
Make the dough: in the mixing bowl mix up butter and almond flour. Knead the ingredients. Then line the instant pot baking pan with baking paper. Pour water and insert the trivet in the instant pot. Roll up the dough into the circle and place it in the baking pan. Flatten the dough circle in the shape of the pie crust. After this, make the pie filling: In the bowl mix up together ground beef, pork, Provolone cheese, coconut oil, parsley, salt, tomato paste, and cream cheese. When the mixture is homogenous, put it over the pie crust and flatten well. Then top the meat filling with Mozzarella. Cover the surface of the pie with foil. Secure the edges. Place the baking pan with pie on the trivet and close the lid. Cook the meal on manual mode (high pressure) for 45 minutes. When the cooking time is finished, make the quick pressure release. Open the lid and immediately remove the baking pan with pie from the instant pot. Remove the foil and cool the pie to the room temperature. Then cut it into the servings.

Nutrition value/serving: calories 293, fat 21.2, fiber 2.3, carbs 5.3, protein 22.4

Burger Casserole

Prep time: 15 minutes | *Cooking time:* 44 minutes | *Servings:*4

Ingredients:
- 1 oz bacon, chopped
- 10 oz ground beef
- ¼ white onion, diced
- 1 teaspoon minced garlic
- 1 tablespoon cream cheese
- ¼ teaspoon mustard
- ¼ teaspoon salt
- 2 eggs, beaten
- 4 oz Cheddar, shredded
- 1/3 cup coconut cream
- 1 teaspoon chili powder
- 1 teaspoon avocado oil

Directions:
Put bacon in the instant pot and cook it on sauté mode for 4 minutes. Flip the bacon on another side after 2 minutes of cooking. When the bacon is cooked, transfer it in the mixing bowl. Then add the ground beef in the mixing bowl. After this, add diced onion, salt, mustard, minced garlic, eggs, chili powder, and cream cheese. Stir the ingredients. Brush the instant pot with avocado oil and arrange the meat mixture inside in the smooth layer. Top the beef layer with shredded Cheddar cheese. Then pour the coconut cream over the cheese and close the instant pot lid. Cook the casserole on manual mode (high pressure) for 40 minutes. When the time is over, allow the natural pressure release for 10 minutes.

Nutrition value/serving: calories 314, fat 17.5, fiber 0.9, carbs 3.4, protein 34.7

Cauliflower Shepherd's Pie

Prep time: 15 minutes | *Cooking time:* 20 minutes | *Servings:* 4

Ingredients:
- 1 cup cauliflower, chopped
- 1 teaspoon tomato paste
- 1 bell pepper, chopped
- 1 white onion, diced
- 1 teaspoon salt
- ½ cup Cheddar cheese, shredded
- ½ cup chicken broth
- ½ teaspoon ground paprika
- ½ teaspoon dried cilantro
- ½ teaspoon dried basil
- ½ teaspoon dried sage
- 1 teaspoon coconut oil
- ½ cup ground pork
- 1 cup water, for cooking

Directions:
Pour water and insert the steamer rack in the instant pot. Put the cauliflower in the steamer rack and close the lid. Cook the vegetables on manual (high pressure) for 4 minutes. Then make the quick pressure release and open the lid. Transfer the cauliflower in the bowl and mash it with the help of the potato masher. When you get cauliflower puree, add salt and ¼ cup of hot water from the instant pot. You should get a smooth and soft texture of cauliflower puree. After this, place the coconut oil in the instant pot and melt it on sauté mode. Then add bell pepper and white onion. Add ground paprika, cilantro, basil, sage, and ground pork. Mix up the meat mixture with the help of a spatula and sauté for 10 minutes. Stir it from time to time. Then add chicken broth and sauté the ingredients for 2 minutes more. After this, spread the cauliflower puree over the ground pork mixture and close the lid. Cook the meal on manual (high pressure) for 3 minutes. Then make the quick pressure release. Cool Shepherd's pie to room temperature.

Nutrition value/serving: calories 217, fat 14.3, fiber 1.8, carbs 6.9, protein 15.4

Big Mac Bites

Prep time: 10 minutes | *Cooking time:* 10 minutes | *Servings:* 2

Ingredients:
- ½ cup ground pork
- ¼ teaspoon white pepper
- ¼ teaspoon salt
- ½ cup lettuce iceberg
- 1 teaspoon flax meal
- 1 pickled cucumber, sliced
- 1 teaspoon coconut oil

Directions:
In the mixing bowl combine together ground pork with salt, flax meal, and white pepper. Then make 2 meatballs from ground pork mixture. Put the coconut oil in the instant pot and melt it on sauté mode. Then put the pork meatballs in the instant pot and cook them for 5 minutes from each side. After this, cool the cooked meatballs to the room temperature. Make the Big Mac bites: place the meatball on the plate and top it sliced cucumber, and lettuce. Pierce the ingredients with a toothpick. Repeat the same steps with the second meatball.

Nutrition value/serving: calories 265, fat 17.2, fiber 1.3, carbs 6.5, protein 21.5

Zoodle Pork Casserole

Prep time: 20 minutes | *Cooking time:* 45 minutes | *Servings:* 4

Ingredients:
- 1 zucchini, trimmed
- 7 oz ground pork
- 1 cup Cheddar cheese, shredded
- 1 teaspoon salt
- 1 tablespoon cream cheese
- 1 teaspoon chili flakes
- ½ teaspoon white pepper
- 1 teaspoon dried sage
- 1 cup water, for cooking

Directions:
Make the zoodles from the zucchini with the help of the spiralizer. In the mixing bowl combine together ground pork with salt, cream cheese, chili flakes, white pepper, and dried sage. Line the instant pot casserole mold with baking paper. Put the ground pork mixture in the casserole mold and flatten it gently with the help of the spatula. Then top it with spiralized zucchini and cream cheese. Sprinkle the casserole with shredded Cheddar cheese. Cover the surface of the casserole mold with foil. Secure the edges of it. Pour water and insert the trivet in the instant pot. Place the casserole mold over the trivet and close the lid. Cook the meal on manual mode (high pressure) for 45 minutes. When the cooking time is over, make the quick pressure release and open the lid. Cool the casserole little before serving.

Nutrition value/serving: calories 203, fat 12.1, fiber 0.7, carbs 2.4, protein 20.9

Ground Beef Skewers

Prep time: 20 minutes | *Cooking time:* 15 minutes | *Servings:* 6

Ingredients:
- 2 cups ground beef
- 1 small onion, minced
- 1 garlic clove, minced
- ½ teaspoon ground black pepper
- ½ teaspoon chili flakes
- ½ teaspoon salt
- ½ teaspoon ground paprika
- 1 teaspoon dried cilantro
- 1 egg, beaten
- 1 cup water, for cooking

Directions:
Mix up ground beef with minced onion, garlic clove, ground black pepper, chili flakes, salt, ground paprika, and dried cilantro. Add egg and stir the meat mixture until homogenous. Make 6 balls from the meat mixture and string them on the skewers. Flatten the meat evenly on the skewer. Pour water and insert the trivet in the instant pot. Line the trivet with baking paper and place the skewers with ground beef on it. Close and seal the lid. Cook the meal on manual mode (high pressure) for 15 minutes. Then allow the natural pressure release for 10 minutes. It is recommended to serve the ground beef skewers hot.

Nutrition value/serving: calories 103, fat 6.2, fiber 0.4, carbs 1.6, protein 9.8

Pastrami

Prep time: 2 days | Cooking time: 70 minutes | Servings: 4

Ingredients:
- 1 ½-corned beef
- 1 teaspoon Erythritol
- ½ teaspoon ground black pepper
- ½ teaspoon garlic powder
- ½ teaspoon onion powder
- 1 teaspoon ground paprika
- ¼ teaspoon salt
- 1 teaspoon ground coriander
- 1 teaspoon mustard
- 1 teaspoon liquid smoke
- 1 cup water, for cooking

Directions:
Pour water and insert the trivet in the instant pot. Place the corned beef on the trivet and close the lid. Cook the meat on Manual (high pressure) for 70 minutes. When the cooking time is finished, make the quick pressure release and transfer the meat on the plate. After this, in the shallow bowl mix up ground black pepper, garlic powder, onion powder, paprika, salt, and ground coriander. In the separated bowl whisk mustard with liquid smoke. Then brush the corned beef with mustard mixture and rub with the spice mixture generously. Place the meat in the fridge for at least 2 days.

Nutrition value/serving: calories 341, fat 24.8, fiber 0.4, carbs 1.3, protein 26.7

Pork Belly Salad

Prep time: 10 minutes | Cooking time: 8 minutes | Servings: 4

Ingredients:
- 7 oz pork belly, chopped
- ½ cup lettuce, chopped
- 1 teaspoon lemon juice
- 1 teaspoon avocado oil
- ¼ cup cherry tomatoes, halved
- 1 cucumber, chopped
- 1 oz Parmesan, grated
- ½ teaspoon coconut oil

Directions:
Preheat the instant pot on sauté mode for 4 minutes. Toss the chopped pork belly and coconut oil in the instant pot and cook it for 8 minutes – for 4 minutes from each side. Meanwhile, in the salad bowl mix up lettuce with cherry tomatoes and cucumber. Add lemon juice and avocado oil. Shake the salad well. Then top it with the cooked pork belly and grated Parmesan.

Nutrition value/serving: calories 273, fat 15.7, fiber 0.6, carbs 3.7, protein 25.8

Pork Salad with Kale

Prep time: 10 minutes | Cooking time: 15 minutes | Servings: 4

Ingredients:
- ½ cup ground pork
- 1 cup kale
- 1 teaspoon olive oil
- ½ teaspoon chili flakes
- ½ teaspoon onion powder
- 1 teaspoon cream cheese
- ¼ teaspoon salt
- 1 teaspoon peanuts, chopped
- ½ teaspoon sesame oil

Directions:
Pour sesame oil in the instant pot. Add ground pork. Start to cook the meat on sauté mode. After 3 minutes of cooking, stir the ground pork and add chili flakes, onion powder, and salt. Cook the ground pork for 10 minutes. Meanwhile, chop the kale roughly. Add kale in the instant pot and cook the mixture on sauté mode for 2 minutes. Transfer the ingredients in the salad bowl. Ad olive oil and peanuts. Stir the salad. The cooked salad should be served warm.

Nutrition value/serving: calories 148, fat 10.5, fiber 0.3, carbs 2.1, protein 10.8

Vegetable Meals

Garlic and Cheese Baked Asparagus

Prep time: 10 minutes | *Cooking time:* 6 minutes | *Servings:* 4

Ingredients:
- 9 oz asparagus
- 1 teaspoon garlic powder
- ½ cup heavy cream
- ¼ cup of water
- ½ cup Mozzarella, grated
- 1 teaspoon dried oregano
- ¼ teaspoon salt

Directions:
Chop the asparagus roughly. In the mixing bowl combine garlic powder with heavy cream, water, salt, and dried oregano. Then pour the liquid in the instant pot and preheat it on sauté mode for 5 minutes. After this, add chopped asparagus and Mozzarella. Close the lid and cook the meal on manual mode (high pressure) for 1 minute. When the time is over, make the quick pressure release.

Nutrition value/serving: calories 78, fat 63, fiber 1.6, carbs 3.8, protein 2.9

Brussels Sprouts in Heavy Cream

Prep time: 10 minutes | *Cooking time:* 6 minutes | *Servings:* 3

Ingredients:
- 6 oz Brussels sprouts
- 1/3 teaspoon salt
- ½ teaspoon ground black pepper
- 1 teaspoon butter
- ½ cup heavy cream

Directions:
Melt butter in sauté mode and add Brussels sprouts. Sprinkle them with salt and ground black pepper and cook on sauté mode for 3 minutes. Stir the vegetables and add heavy cream. Close the lid and cook the meal on manual mode (high pressure) for 3 minutes. When the cooking time is finished, allow the natural pressure release for 10 minutes. Stir the vegetables before serving.

Nutrition value/serving: calories 106, fat 8.9, fiber 2.2, carbs 5.9, protein 2.4

Wrapped Bacon Carrot

Prep time: 15 minutes | *Cooking time:* 4 minutes | *Servings:* 3

Ingredients:
- 2 large carrots, peeled
- 3 bacon slices
- ¾ teaspoon salt
- ¼ teaspoon ground turmeric
- 1 teaspoon avocado oil
- 1 cup water, for cooking

Directions:
Sprinkle the bacon slices with salt and ground turmeric. Pour avocado oil in the instant pot and heat it up on sauté mode for 2 minutes. Meanwhile, cut the carrots into 6 pieces. Cut the bacon into 6 pieces too. Wrap every carrot piece in the bacon and put in the hot oil in one layer. Cook the vegetables on sauté mode for 1 minute and then flip on another side. Cook the carrot for 1 minute more. Then transfer in the plate. Clean the instant pot and add water. Insert the trivet and put a carrot on it. Close and seal the lid. Cook the wrapped bacon carrot for 2 minutes. Then make the quick pressure release.

Nutrition value/serving: calories 102, fat 7.2, fiber 1.3, carbs 4.9, protein 5.4

Caprese Zoodles

Prep time: 15 minutes | *Cooking time:* 1 minute | *Servings:* 6

Ingredients:
- 1 zucchini, trimmed
- ½ cup cherry tomatoes, halved
- ½ cup mozzarella cheese, balls
- 1 teaspoon fresh basil, chopped
- 1 tablespoon lemon juice
- ¼ teaspoon white pepper
- 1 teaspoon sesame oil
- 1 cup water, for cooking

Directions:
Pour water in the instant pot and insert the steamer rack. With the help of the spiralizer make the noodles from the zucchini and put them in the steamer rack. Close and seal the lid and set the timer on "0". Cook the zucchini on high pressure. When the cooking time is finished, make the quick pressure release and open the lid. Transfer the zucchini noodles in the big salad bowl. Add cherry tomatoes, mozzarella balls, and basil. Then sprinkle the ingredients with lemon juice, white pepper, and sesame oil. Shake the meal gently.

Nutrition value/serving: calories 22, fat 1.3, fiber 0.6, carbs 1.9, protein 1.2

Cauliflower Florets Mix

Prep time: 10 minutes | *Cooking time:* 4 minutes | *Servings:* 3

Ingredients:
- ½ cup cauliflower florets
- ¼ cup broccoli florets
- 1 tablespoon hazelnuts
- ¼ teaspoon minced garlic
- 1 tablespoon avocado oil
- 1/3 teaspoon salt
- 1 cup water, for cooking

Directions:
Pour water and insert the steamer rack in the instant pot. Put the cauliflower florets and broccoli florets in the steamer. Close and seal the lid. Cook the vegetables on manual mode (steam mode) for 4 minutes. When the cooking time is finished, make the quick pressure release and open the lid. Cool the vegetables to the room temperature and transfer in the big bowl. Chop the hazelnuts and add in the vegetables. Then sprinkle the ingredients with minced garlic, avocado oil, and salt. Shake the well.

Nutrition value/serving: calories 23, fat 1.6, fiber 1, carbs 2, protein 0.8

Balsamic Brussels Sprouts

Prep time: 10 minutes | *Cooking time:* 7 minutes | *Servings:* 3

Ingredients:
- ¼ teaspoon Erythritol
- 1 teaspoon balsamic vinegar
- 2 tablespoons sesame oil
- ¼ teaspoon salt
- ¼ teaspoon chili flakes
- 8 oz Brussels sprouts
- 1 cup water, for cooking

Directions:
Pour water and insert the steamer rack in the instant pot. Put Brussels sprouts in the steamer rack and close the lid. Cook them on steam mode for 2 minutes. Then make the quick pressure release and open the lid. Transfer the vegetables in the bowl and clean the instant pot. Remove the steamer rack. Pour the sesame oil in the instant pot and heat it up on sauté mode for 3 minutes. Add cooked Brussels sprouts. Then sprinkle the vegetables with balsamic vinegar, chili flakes, and salt. Stir them and cook for 2 minutes.

Nutrition value/serving: calories 113, fat 9.3, fiber 2.8, carbs 6.9, protein 2.6

Tender Sautéed Vegetables
Prep time: 10 minutes | Cooking time: 8 minutes | Servings: 4

Ingredients:
- ½ cup radish, sliced
- 1 green bell pepper, chopped
- 1 zucchini, chopped
- 1 teaspoon tomato paste
- ½ teaspoon salt
- ½ teaspoon ground coriander
- 3 tablespoons avocado oil
- 1 cup water, for cooking

Directions:
In the shallow bowl mix up avocado oil and tomato paste. Pour water and insert the trivet in the instant pot. In the mixing bowl combine radish, bell pepper, and zucchini. Sprinkle the vegetables with salt and ground coriander. Then add tomato paste mixture. Stir the vegetables. After this, transfer them in the instant pot baking pan and cover with foil. Put the baking pan on the trivet and close the lid. Cook the vegetables on manual mode (high pressure) for 8 minutes. Then make the quick pressure release.

Nutrition value/serving: calories 35, fat 1.5, fiber 1.7, carbs 5.2, protein 1.2

Spaghetti Squash Nests
Prep time: 20 minutes | Cooking time: 5 minutes | Servings: 4

Ingredients:
- 12 oz spaghetti squash, peeled
- 1 egg, beaten
- ¼ teaspoon salt
- 1 tablespoon coconut flour
- ¼ teaspoon ground cumin
- 1 cup water, for cooking

Directions:
Grate the spaghetti squash and mix it up with egg, salt, coconut flour, and ground cumin. After this, fill the muffin molds with a grated squash mixture. Flatten the mixture in the shape of a nest Use the spoon for this step. Pour water and insert the steamer rack in the instant pot. Arrange the muffin molds with squash nests and close the lid. Cook the meal on manual (high pressure) for 5 minutes. Then make the quick pressure release. Remove the cooked squash nests from the muffin molds.

Nutrition value/serving: calories 50, fat 1.9, fiber 0.6, carbs 7, protein 2.2

Lemongrass Green Beans
Prep time: 10 minutes | Cooking time: 1 minute | Servings: 3

Ingredients:
- 8 oz green beans, chopped
- 1 teaspoon dried lemongrass
- 1 teaspoon lime juice
- ¼ teaspoon ground nutmeg
- 1 teaspoon butter, melted
- 1 cup water, for cooking

Directions:
Pour water and insert the steamer rack in the instant pot. Place the green beans and lemongrass in the rack and close the lid. Cook the vegetables on manual mode (high pressure) for 1 minute. Then make the quick pressure release. Transfer the green beans in the bowl. Add lime juice, ground nutmeg, and melted butter. Stir the vegetables well.

Nutrition value/serving: calories 37, fat 1.4, fiber 2.6, carbs 5.8, protein 1.4

Cucumbers and Zucchini Noodles

Prep time: 10 minutes | Cooking time: minute | Servings: 4

Ingredients:
- 2 cucumbers
- 1 zucchini, trimmed
- 1 teaspoon fresh dill, chopped
- 1 garlic clove, diced
- 1 teaspoon fresh parsley, chopped
- 1 tablespoon olive oil
- ¼ teaspoon chili powder
- 1 cup water, for cooking

Directions:
Make the noodles from zucchini and put them in the steamer rack. Pour water and insert the steamer rack in the instant pot. Close the lid. Cook the vegetable noodles for 1 minute on steam mode. Then make a quick pressure release and transfer the zucchini noodles in the salad bowl. Make the spirals from the cucumbers and add them to the zucchini. Then add dill, diced garlic, parsley, olive oil, and chili powder. Gently stir the ingredients.

Nutrition value/serving: calories 99, fat 0.7, fiber 4.4, carbs 22.8, protein 2.7

Eggs and Mushrooms Cups

Prep time: 10 minutes | Cooking time: 7 minutes | Servings: 4

Ingredients:
- 1 cup white mushrooms, grinded
- 2 eggs, beaten
- 2 tablespoons almond flour
- ¼ teaspoon salt
- ¼ teaspoon dried thyme
- 1 teaspoon cream cheese
- 1 teaspoon sesame oil
- 1 cup water, for cooking

Directions:
In the mixing bowl mix up grinded mushrooms, eggs, almond flour, salt, thyme, and cream cheese. Then brush the muffin molds with sesame oil. Put the mushroom mixture in the muffin molds. Then pour water and insert the trivet in the instant pot. Put the muffin molds on the trivet and close the lid. Cook the meal on manual mode (high pressure) for 7 minutes. Then make the quick pressure release. The meal tastes the best when it is cooled to the room temperature.

Nutrition value/serving: calories 128, fat 10.7, fiber 1.7, carbs 3.8, protein 6.4

Kale Skillet with Nuts

Prep time: 10 minutes | Cooking time: 1 minute | Servings: 4

Ingredients:
- 2 cups Italian dark leaf kale
- 1 teaspoon peanuts, chopped
- 1 teaspoon hazelnuts, chopped
- 1 teaspoon apple cider vinegar
- 1 tablespoon cream cheese
- ½ teaspoon salt
- 1 cup water, for cooking

Directions:
Pour water in the instant pot. Chop the kale roughly and put it in the steamer rack. Arrange the steamer rack in the instant pot and close the lid. Cook the kale on manual mode (steam mode) for 1 minute. Then make the quick pressure release. Transfer the kale in the bowl. Add apple cider vinegar, cream cheese, and salt. Then add hazelnuts and peanuts and mix up the meal well.

Nutrition value/serving: calories 35, fat 1.8, fiber 1.4, carbs 3.7, protein 2.3

Shredded Spaghetti Squash with Bacon

Prep time: 20 minutes | Cooking time: 8 minutes | Servings: 8

Ingredients:
- 4 oz bacon, chopped
- 1-pound spaghetti squash
- 1 tablespoon sesame oil
- 1 teaspoon salt
- 1 cup water, for cooking

Directions:
Pour water and place trivet in the instant pot. Wash and clean the spaghetti squash. Then cut it into halves and put in the trivet. Close the lid and cook it on manual mode (steam mode) for 8 minutes. Then allow the natural pressure release for 15 minutes. Then transfer the spaghetti squash in the plate. Shred it with the help of the fork. After this, transfer the shredded squash meat in the salad bowl. Clean the instant pot and remove the trivet. Add chopped bacon and cook it on sauté mode for 7 minutes. Stir it from time to time. Add the cooked bacon in the shredded spaghetti squash. Then add salt and sesame oil. Stir it.

Nutrition value/serving: calories 109, fat 7.9, fiber 0, carbs 4.1, protein 5.6

Green Peas Salad

Prep time: 10 minutes | Cooking time: 3 minutes | Servings: 2

Ingredients:
- ½ cup green peas, frozen
- ½ teaspoon fresh cilantro, chopped
- ½ teaspoon avocado oil
- ¼ teaspoon ground paprika
- ¾ teaspoon salt
- ½ cup white cabbage, shredded
- 1 cup water, for cooking

Directions:
Pour water and insert the steamer rack in the instant pot. Place the green peas in the steamer rack and close the lid. Cook it on the steam mode (high pressure) for 3 minutes. Allow the natural pressure release for 5 minutes. Transfer the cooked green peas in the bowl. Add cilantro, avocado oil, ground paprika, salt, and white cabbage. Stir the salad well.

Nutrition value/serving: calories 36, fat 0.4, fiber 2.4, carbs 6.5, protein 2.2

Cauliflower Risotto

Prep time: 10 minutes | Cooking time: 16 minutes | Servings: 4

Ingredients:
- 2 cups cauliflower, shredded
- 1 teaspoon coconut oil
- ¼ cup white onion, diced
- 6 oz white mushrooms, chopped
- ¼ teaspoon garlic powder
- ½ cup of organic almond milk
- 1/3 cup chicken broth
- 1 teaspoon coconut flour
- ½ teaspoon salt

Directions:
Put the coconut oil in the instant pot. Heat up it on sauté mode for 2 minutes. Then add onion, mushrooms, garlic powder, and salt. Stir it and sauté for 10 minutes. After this, add chicken broth and almond milk. Add cauliflower and mix up the risotto. Close the lid and cook it on manual mode (high pressure) for 4 minutes. Then make the quick pressure release. Stir the risotto well.

Nutrition value/serving: calories 46, fat 1.9, fiber 2.2, carbs 5.4, protein 3.1

Collard Greens with Cherry Tomatoes
Prep time: 15 minutes | Cooking time: 5 minutes | Servings: 4

Ingredients:
- 3 cups collard greens, chopped
- ½ cup cherry tomatoes, halved
- ½ red onion, diced
- 1 teaspoon avocado oil
- ½ teaspoon chili flakes
- ¼ oz Parmesan, grated
- 1 cup water, for cooking

Directions:
Pour water and insert the steamer rack in the instant pot. Place the chopped collard greens in the rack and close the lid. Cook the greens on manual (high pressure) for 5 minutes. When the cooking time is finished, allow the natural pressure release for 10 minutes. Transfer the cooked collard greens in the salad bowl. Add cherry tomatoes and diced red onion. Shake the ingredients gently. Then add chili flakes and avocado oil, and Parmesan. With the help of two spoons or spatulas, mix up the meal.

Nutrition value/serving: calories 26, fat 0.8, fiber 1.7, carbs 4.2, protein 1.7

Cauliflower Gratin
Prep time: 10 minutes | Cooking time: 25 minutes | Servings: 6

Ingredients:
- 2 cups cauliflower, chopped
- ½ cup mozzarella, shredded
- ½ cup coconut cream
- ½ cup of water
- 1 teaspoon butter
- ½ teaspoon salt
- 1 teaspoon dried oregano
- ½ teaspoon rosemary

Directions:
Grease the instant pot bowl with butter and put the chopped cauliflower inside. Flatten it in one layer if needed. Then in the mixing bowl mix up coconut cream with shredded mozzarella, salt, oregano, and dried rosemary. Pour the liquid over the cauliflower and close the lid. Cook the cauliflower gratin on meat/stew mode for 25 minutes.

Nutrition value/serving: calories 68, fat 5.9, fiber 1.4, carbs 3.2, protein 1.8

Scalloped Cabbage
Prep time: 15 minutes | Cooking time: 18 minutes | Servings: 6

Ingredients:
- 2 cups white cabbage, shredded
- 2 tablespoons almond meal
- ½ teaspoon salt
- 1 tablespoon ghee
- 1 teaspoon coconut flakes
- ½ cup Monterey Jack cheese, shredded
- ½ cup of organic almond milk

Directions:
Mix up white cabbage and salt. Stir the cabbage well and leave it for 5-10 minutes. Meanwhile, put the ghee in the instant pot. Melt it on sauté mode. Then add the almond meal and coconut flakes. Cook the ingredients on sauté mode for 2 minutes. Stir well and add almond milk. Then add cabbage and mix up. After this, top the cabbage with shredded cheese and close the lid. Cook the meal on manual (high pressure) for 15 minutes. Allow the natural pressure release for 10 minutes.

Nutrition value/serving: calories 72, fat 6.3, fiber 0.9, carbs 2, protein 3.1

Hash Brown Casserole

Prep time: 10 minutes | *Cooking time:* 20 minutes | *Servings:* 4

Ingredients:
- ½ cup cauliflower stalk, shredded
- 2 oz turnip, grated
- ½ cup Cheddar cheese, shredded
- ½ teaspoon onion powder
- ¼ teaspoon ground black pepper
- ¼ teaspoon white pepper
- ¼ teaspoon salt
- 1 teaspoon coconut oil
- 1 cup of coconut milk

Directions:
Place the coconut oil in the instant pot. Heat it up on sauté mode until the oil is melted. Add shredded cauliflower and turnip. Sprinkle the vegetables with onion powder, ground black pepper, and white pepper. Add salt and stir the vegetables. Cook them on sauté mode for 5 minutes. After this, add coconut milk and shredded Cheddar cheese. Close the lid and cook the casserole on meat/stew mode for 15 minutes.

Nutrition value/serving: calories 213, fat 20.1, fiber 1.9, carbs 5.4, protein 5.3

Stuffed Mushrooms

Prep time: 15 minutes | *Cooking time:* 4 minutes | *Servings:* 4

Ingredients:
- 1 cup cremini mushrooms, caps
- ¼ cup Mozzarella, shredded
- ¼ teaspoon ground nutmeg
- ¼ teaspoon salt
- 1 tablespoon chives, chopped
- 1 cup water, for cooking

Directions:
Trim the mushroom caps if needed. In the mixing bowl mix up shredded Mozzarella, ground nutmeg, salt, and chives. Fill the mushrooms with the cheese mixture. Pour water and insert the trivet in the instant pot. Then line the trivet with foil. Place the stuffed mushrooms on the trivet. Close and seal the lid. Cook the vegetables on manual mode (high pressure) for 4 minutes. Make the quick pressure release.

Nutrition value/serving: calories 11, fat 0.4, fiber 0.2, carbs 0.9, protein 1

Green Beans Salad

Prep time: 15 minutes | *Cooking time:* 4 minutes | *Servings:* 2

Ingredients:
- 1 cup green beans, chopped
- 3 oz goat cheese, crumbled
- 1 oz Feta cheese, crumbled
- ¼ teaspoon ground black pepper
- 1 shallot, peeled, sliced
- 1 teaspoon ghee
- ½ teaspoon chili flakes
- 1 cup water, for cooking

Directions:
Pour water and insert the steamer rack in the instant pot. Put the green beans in the steamer rack and close the lid. Cook the vegetables on manual (high pressure) for 4 minutes. Then allow the natural pressure release for 10 minutes and transfer the green beans in the bowl. Clean the instant pot and remove the steamer rack. Toss ghee in the instant pot and melt it on sauté mode. Add shallot and cook it until it is golden brown. Add the cooked shallot in the green beans. Then add crumbled Feta and goat cheese. After this, sprinkle the ingredients with chili flakes and ground black pepper. Mix up the salad well with the help of the spatula.

Nutrition value/serving: calories 22, fat 0.8, fiber 0.3, carbs 1.8, protein 2

Tuscan Mushrooms Sauce

Prep time: 20 minutes | Cooking time: 10 minutes | Servings: 3

Ingredients:
- 1 teaspoon almond butter
- ½ cup fresh spinach, chopped
- ½ cup white mushrooms, sliced
- 2 tablespoons flax meal
- 1 oz Parmesan, grated
- 1 cup coconut cream
- 1 teaspoon Tuscan seasonings
- ½ cup cherry tomatoes, chopped

Directions:

Heat up the almond butter in the instant pot on sauté mode. Put mushrooms in the hot almond butter and cook them for 3 minutes. After this, stir them and add spinach. Stir well. Sprinkle the vegetables with Tuscan seasonings and flax meal. After this, add coconut cream and cherry tomatoes. Close the lid and cook the sauce on manual (high pressure) for 5 minutes. Allow the natural pressure release for 10 minutes. Open the lid and add Parmesan. With the help of the spatula, mix up the meal until cheese is melted.

Nutrition value/serving: calories 279, fat 25.9, fiber 4.2, carbs 9.2, protein 8.1

Thyme Cauliflower Head

Prep time: 15 minutes | Cooking time: 3 minutes | Servings: 3

Ingredients:
- 1-pound cauliflower head, trimmed
- 1 teaspoon thyme
- 2 tablespoons avocado oil
- ¼ teaspoon minced garlic
- 1 cup water, for cooking

Directions:

Pour water in the instant pot and insert the steamer rack. Place the cauliflower head in the steamer rack and close the lid. Cook it on manual mode (high pressure) for 3 minutes. Then allow the natural pressure release for 5 minutes and transfer the cauliflower in the serving plate. In the shallow bowl whisk together avocado oil, minced garlic, and thyme. Brush the cooked cauliflower head with the thyme-oil mixture.

Nutrition value/serving: calories 51, fat 1.4, fiber 4.3, carbs 8.8, protein 3.2

Stuffed Spaghetti Squash

Prep time: 20 minutes | Cooking time: 9 minutes | Servings: 6

Ingredients:
- 1-pound spaghetti squash, cleaned, halved
- 5 oz seitan, chopped
- ¼ cup Cheddar cheese, shredded
- 2 eggs, beaten
- 1 tablespoon cream cheese
- ¼ cup heavy cream
- 1 teaspoon butter
- 1 bay leaf
- ½ teaspoon chili flakes
- ¼ teaspoon cayenne pepper
- ½ teaspoon salt
- 1 cup water, for cooking

Directions:

Scoop the squash meat from the spaghetti squash. Then grate the squash meat. In the mixing bowl mix up chopped seitan, grated spaghetti squash meat, shredded cheese, eggs, cream cheese, butter, heavy cream, chili flakes, cayenne pepper, and salt. Fill the spaghetti squash halves with the seitan filling. Wrap the spaghetti squash halves in foil. Then pour water in the instant pot. Add bay leaf. Then insert the trivet in the instant pot. Place the wrapped spaghetti squash on the trivet and close the lid. Cook the meal on manual (high pressure) for 9 minutes. When the cooking time is finished, make the quick pressure release and open the lid. Remove the foil from the spaghetti squash halves.

Nutrition value/serving: calories 187, fat 7.6, fiber 1.1, carbs 5.8, protein 21.5

Shallot Mushrooms

Prep time: 10 minutes | *Cooking time:* 25 minutes | *Servings:* 3

Ingredients:
- 1 cup cremini mushrooms, chopped
- 3 oz white mushrooms, chopped
- ½ cup shallot, sliced
- 1 tablespoon ghee
- 1 teaspoon Italian seasonings
- 1 teaspoon salt
- 1 teaspoon cream cheese

Directions:
Place the ghee in the instant pot and melt it on sauté mode. Add white mushrooms and cremini mushrooms. Cook the vegetables on sauté mode for 10 minutes. After this, add sliced shallot, cream cheese, salt, and Italian seasonings. Stir the ingredients well and close the lid. Sauté the meal for 15 minutes on sauté mode.

Nutrition value/serving: calories 78, fat 5.2, fiber 0.4, carbs 6.6, protein 2.3

Baked Kabocha Squash

Prep time: 10 minutes | *Cooking time:* 8 minutes | *Servings:* 3

Ingredients:
- 2 cups Kabocha squash, peeled, cubed
- ½ teaspoon Erythritol
- ½ teaspoon ground ginger
- ¼ teaspoon ground cinnamon
- 1 tablespoon butter, softened
- 1 cup heavy cream

Directions:
Sprinkle Kabocha squash with Erythritol, ground ginger, and ground cinnamon. Mix up the spices and squash and transfer in the instant pot. Add butter and heavy cream. Close and seal the lid and cook the meal on manual (high pressure) for 8 minutes. Then make the quick pressure release. Carefully transfer the cooked squash in the serving bowls.

Nutrition value/serving: calories 200, fat 18.7, fiber 1, carbs 7.7, protein 1.8

Sautéed Kohlrabi

Prep time: 10 minutes | *Cooking time:* 10 minutes | *Servings:* 3

Ingredients:
- 1 Serrano pepper, chopped
- 1 teaspoon ground ginger
- 1 tablespoon coconut oil
- 10 oz kohlrabi, chopped
- ½ cup chicken broth
- ½ teaspoon salt

Directions:
Preheat the instant pot on sauté mode for 3 minutes. Then add coconut oil and heat it up for 2 minutes. Add ground ginger and chopped Serrano. Cook the ingredients for 2 minutes. Then add kohlrabi and stir well. Add chicken broth and salt. Close and seal the lid. Cook the meal on manual (high pressure) for 3 minutes. Then allow the natural pressure release for 5 minutes.

Nutrition value/serving: calories 74, fat 4.9, fiber 3.6, carbs 6.6, protein 2.5

Butter Edamame Beans

Prep time: 5 minutes | *Cooking time:* 1 minute | *Servings:* 4

Ingredients:
- 1 cup mung beans
- 2 tablespoon butter
- ¼ teaspoon salt
- ¼ cup fresh parsley, chopped
- ½ teaspoon cayenne pepper
- 1 cup beef broth

Directions:
Pour beef broth in the instant pot. Add mung beans, butter, salt, parsley, and cayenne pepper. Close and seal the lid. Set time on 1 minute and cook the Edamame beans on manual (high pressure). Then make the quick pressure release.

Nutrition value/serving: calories 110, fat 8.2, fiber 2.2, carbs 4.4, protein 5.7

Marinated Tomatillos Paste
Prep time: 8 minutes | Cooking time: 10 minutes | Servings: 2

Ingredients:
- 1 cup tomatillos
- ½ teaspoon minced garlic
- 1 teaspoon fresh dill, chopped
- ¼ cup of water
- 1 tablespoon avocado oil
- ¼ teaspoon salt
- 1 teaspoon chili powder

Directions:
Finely chop the tomatillos. Heat up the instant pot. When it shows "Hot", add avocado oil and tomatillos. Cook them on sauté mode for 5 minutes. Then add salt, chili powder, and minced garlic. Add water and dill. Close the lid. Cook the ingredients on steam mode for 3 minutes. Then make the quick pressure release. With the help of the immersion blender grind the mixture into a paste.

Nutrition value/serving: calories 37, fat 1.8, fiber 2.1, carbs 5.5, protein 1

Tender Rutabaga
Prep time: 15 minutes | Cooking time: 9 minute | Servings: 4

Ingredients:
- 1-pound rutabaga, chopped
- ½ cup heavy cream
- 2 tablespoons cream cheese
- ½ teaspoon onion powder
- 1 teaspoon ground black pepper
- 1 cup water, for cooking

Directions:
Pour water in the instant pot. Insert the steamer rack. Put rutabaga in the steamer rack. Close the lid. Cook the rutabaga on manual (high pressure) for 9 minutes. Allow the natural pressure release for 5 minutes Transfer the cooked rutabaga in the big bowl. Bring the heavy cream to boil and add in the rutabaga. Then add cream cheese, onion powder, and ground black pepper. Stir the meal gently with the help of the spoon.

Nutrition value/serving: calories 112, fat 7.5, fiber 3, carbs 10.4, protein 2.1

Zucchini Goulash
Prep time: 5 minutes | Cooking time: 8 minutes | Servings: 4

Ingredients:
- 1 eggplant, chopped
- 2 small zucchini, chopped
- 1 white onion, chopped
- 1 turnip, chopped
- 1 cup chicken broth
- 1 teaspoon tomato paste
- 1 teaspoon fresh thyme
- 1 teaspoon salt
- 1 teaspoon sesame oil
- 1 teaspoon Italian seasonings

Directions:
Put all ingredients in the instant pot and close the lid. Set chili/meat mode (high pressure) and cook the goulash for 8 minutes. Then make the quick pressure release. It is recommended to serve the meal when it reaches room temperature.

Nutrition value/serving: calories 73, fat 1.9, fiber 6.2, carbs 13.8, protein 2.5

Cheddar Mushrooms

Prep time: 10 minutes | *Cooking time:* 15 minutes | *Servings:* 2

Ingredients:
- 1 cup cremini mushrooms, roughly chopped
- 1 tablespoon cream cheese
- ¼ cup of coconut milk
- 1 teaspoon ground cardamom
- ¼ teaspoon cumin seeds
- ½ teaspoon salt
- 1/3 cup Cheddar cheese, shredded

Directions:
In the mixing bowl mix up coconut milk, cream cheese, ground cardamom, cumin seeds, and salt. Heat up the instant pot. When it shows "HOT", add mushrooms and coconut milk mixture. Close the lid and cook the vegetables on sauté mode for 10 minutes. Then open the lid and stir them with the help of the spatula. Add cheese and close the lid. Cook the mushrooms for 5 minutes more.

Nutrition value/serving: calories 176, fat 15.3, fiber 1.2, carbs 4.3, protein 6.8

Garlic Eggplant Rounds

Prep time: 10 minutes | *Cooking time:* 10 minutes | *Servings:* 4

Ingredients:
- 2 eggplants
- 2 tablespoons ghee
- 1 teaspoon minced garlic
- 1 teaspoon salt
- ½ teaspoon cayenne pepper

Directions:
Trim the ends of the eggplants and slice them into the medium rounds. Then sprinkle the vegetables with salt and cayenne pepper. Shake well and leave them for 10 minutes to give the eggplants the opportunity to give juice. Meanwhile, preheat the instant pot. When it shows "HOT", place ghee inside. Melt it. Then put the eggplant rounds in the hot ghee in one layer. Cook the vegetables for 2 minutes from each side. Top the cooked eggplants with minced garlic.

Nutrition value/serving: calories 126, fat 6.9, fiber 9.7, carbs 16.5, protein 2.8

Vegetable Soup

Prep time: 10 minutes | *Cooking time:* 3 minutes | *Servings:* 6

Ingredients:
- 2 tablespoons cream cheese
- ½ cup heavy cream
- 4 cups of water
- 1 cup fresh spinach, chopped
- 1 cup celery stalk, chopped
- 1 zucchini, chopped
- ½ cup green peas
- 1 teaspoon salt
- 1 teaspoon ground black pepper
- ¼ teaspoon chili flakes

Directions:
Put all ingredients in the instant pot bowl. Close and seal the lid. Cook the soup on manual (high pressure) for 3 minutes. When the cooking time is finished, make the quick pressure release and leave the soup with the closed lid for 10 minutes.

Nutrition value/serving: calories 66, fat 5, fiber 1.5, carbs 4.1, protein 1.8

Cream of Celery

Prep time: 10 minutes | *Cooking time:* 15 minutes | *Servings:* 4

Ingredients:
- 1 white onion, diced
- 2 green bell peppers, chopped
- 1 cup celery stalk, chopped
- 1 teaspoon white pepper
- ¼ teaspoon salt
- ¼ cup heavy cream
- 1 cup beef broth
- 1 teaspoon ghee

Directions:
Put ghee in the instant pot and heat it up. Then add bell peppers and onion and cook the vegetables on sauté mode for 5 minutes. Stir them from time to time to avoid burning. Then add salt, white pepper, heavy cream, and chicken broth. Add celery stalk and close the lid. Cook the meal on manual mode (high pressure) for 10 minutes. When the cooking time is finished, make the quick pressure release.

Nutrition value/serving: calories 80, fat 4.4, fiber 1.9, carbs 8.6, protein 2.5

Steamed Rutabaga Mash

Prep time: 10 minutes | Cooking time: 5 minutes | Servings: 3

Ingredients:
- 1 teaspoon butter, softened
- ½ teaspoon salt
- 1 teaspoon ground turmeric
- ¼ teaspoon curry powder
- ¼ cup heavy cream, hot
- 2 cups rutabaga, chopped
- 1 cup water, for cooking

Directions:
Pour water and inset the steamer rack in the instant pot. Place the rutabaga in the steamer rack and close the lid. Cook it on manual mode (high pressure) for 5 minutes. Make the quick pressure release. With the help of the potato masher, mash cooked rutabaga. Add salt, butter, ground turmeric, curry powder, and heavy cream. Stir the mashed rutabaga until it is homogenous and will turn color into yellow.

Nutrition value/serving: calories 82, fat 5.3, fiber 2.5, carbs 8.4, protein 1.4

Fragrant Artichoke Hearts

Prep time: 10 minutes | Cooking time: 20 minutes | Servings: 4

Ingredients:
- 4 artichoke hearts
- ½ teaspoon fennel seeds
- ¼ teaspoon cumin seeds
- 1 tablespoon butter
- ¼ teaspoon salt
- ¼ teaspoon chili powder
- 1 cup water, for cooking

Directions:
Pour water in the instant pot. Place the artichoke hearts in the steamer rack. Arrange the rack in the instant pot and close the lid. Cook the vegetables on steam mode (high pressure) for 15 minutes. Then make the quick pressure release. Open the lid and transfer the artichoke heart in the bowl. Clean the instant pot. Heat it up and when the instant pot display shows "HOT", add butter. Melt it. Add fennel seeds, cumin seeds, salt, and chili powder. Bring the butter to boil and add artichoke hearts. Coat them in the hot butter and cook for 2 minutes on sauté mode.

Nutrition value/serving: calories 57, fat 3, fiber 2.2, carbs 7.3, protein 1.1

Steamed Broccoli Raab (Rabe)

Prep time: 10 minutes | Cooking time: 7 minutes | Servings: 2

Ingredients:
- 1 ½ cup broccoli rabe, chopped
- 1 teaspoon avocado oil
- 2 oz pancetta, chopped
- ½ teaspoon salt
- 1 teaspoon ground coriander
- ¼ garlic clove, diced
- ¼ cup chicken broth
- 1 cup water, for cooking

Directions:
Pour water and insert the steamer rack in the instant pot. Place the broccoli rabe in the steamer rack and close the lid. Set the timer to "0" and cook the greens on manual (high pressure). When the instant pot beeps, make a quick pressure release and transfer the broccoli rabe in the bowl. Shock the greens with cold water and dry little. Then clean the instant pot and discard the steamer rack. Pour avocado oil inside. Add pancetta. Cook it on sauté mode for 4 minutes. Stir it from time to time. Then sprinkle pancetta with salt, diced garlic, ground coriander, and add broccoli rabe. Stir the mixture well. Add chicken broth and cook it on sauté mode for 1 minute.

Nutrition value/serving: calories 177, fat 12.3, fiber 0.1, carbs 3, protein 12.7

Avocado Pie

Prep time: 20 minutes | *Cooking time:* 30 minutes | *Servings:* 6

Ingredients:
- 1 avocado, peeled, pitted
- 2 eggs, beaten
- ¼ cup Cheddar cheese, shredded
- 1 teaspoon cream cheese
- ½ teaspoon cayenne pepper
- ½ teaspoon ground paprika
- 1 teaspoon salt
- ½ cup almond flour
- 2 tablespoons butter, softened
- ½ teaspoon baking powder
- 1 teaspoon lemon juice
- 1 cup water, for cooking

Directions:
Make the pie crust: in the mixing bowl combine almond flour, baking powder, butter, and lemon juice. Knead the soft and non-sticky dough. Then roll it up. Line the instant pot round pan with baking paper and put the pie crust in it. Flatten it with the help of the hands if needed. Chop the avocado roughly and put it in the blender. Add eggs, cream cheese, cayenne pepper, ground paprika, and salt. Blend the mixture until smooth. After this, pour it over the pie crust. Top the filling with Cheddar cheese. Pour water and insert the trivet in the instant pot. Place the pan with pie on the trivet and close the lid. Cook the pie on manual mode (high pressure) for 30 minutes. When the time is over, make the quick pressure release and open the lid. Cool the pie well and then cut it into servings.

Nutrition value/serving: calories 159, fat 14.8, fiber 2.6, carbs 4, protein 4.3

Zucchini Pasta with Blue Cheese

Prep time: 15 minutes | *Cooking time:* 5 minutes | *Servings:* 2

Ingredients:
- 2 zucchini, trimmed
- 3 oz Blue cheese
- ¼ cup heavy cream
- ¼ teaspoon fresh basil, chopped
- ½ teaspoon salt
- 1 teaspoon butter

Directions:
Slice the zucchini into the pasta strips with the help of the potato peeler. Then put the butter in the instant pot and heat it up on sauté mode. When the butter is melted, add heavy cream, fresh basil, and salt. Then add zucchini paste and stir well. Cook the ingredients for 1 minute. Then crumble Blue cheese over the pasta. Cook the meal for 1 minute more.

Nutrition value/serving: calories 250, fat 20, fiber 2.2, carbs 8, protein 11.8

Lemon Artichoke

Prep time: 10 minutes | *Cooking time:* 21 minutes | *Servings:* 4

Ingredients:
- 4 medium artichokes, trimmed
- 4 teaspoons lemon juice
- 2 tablespoons avocado oil
- 1 teaspoon cayenne pepper
- 1 teaspoon minced garlic
- 1 teaspoon salt
- 1 cup water, for cooking

Directions:
In the shallow bowl mix up avocado oil, cayenne pepper, lemon juice, minced garlic, and salt. Whisk the liquid gently. Then brush every artichoke with avocado oil liquid and transfer the vegetables on the trivet. Pour water in the instant pot. Insert the trivet with artichokes in the instant pot and close the lid. Cook the vegetables on manual (high pressure) for 21 minutes. Then make the quick pressure release.

Nutrition value/serving: calories 73, fat 1.2, fiber 7.4, carbs 14.4, protein 4.4

Zucchini Boats

Prep time: 15 minutes | *Cooking time:* 12 minutes | *Servings:* 4

Ingredients:
- 2 medium zucchini
- 1 cup Mozzarella cheese, shredded
- 1 teaspoon tomato paste
- 2 teaspoons cream cheese
- ½ cup white mushrooms, chopped
- ½ teaspoon salt
- ½ teaspoon ground black pepper
- ½ teaspoon dried parsley
- ½ teaspoon dried oregano
- 1 teaspoon butter
- 1 cup water, for cooking

Directions:
Heat up butter on sauté mode. Add chopped white mushrooms, salt, ground black pepper, dried parsley, dried oregano, and cream cheese. Cook the ingredients on sauté mode for 5 minutes. After this, add tomato paste and stir the mixture with the help of the spatula until homogenous. Cook it for 3 minutes more. Meanwhile, cut the zucchini into halves and scoop the zucchini meat from them. Then fill the zucchini with mushrooms and top with Mozzarella cheese. Pour water and insert steamer rack in the instant pot. Place the zucchini boats in the steamer rack and close the lid. Cook the meal on manual (high pressure) for 4 minutes. Then make the quick pressure release. Very carefully transfer the zucchini boats in the serving plate.

Nutrition value/serving: calories 54, fat 3, fiber 1.4, carbs 4.4, protein 3.7

Zucchini Fettuccine

Prep time: 10 minutes | *Cooking time:* 5 minutes | *Servings:* 2

Ingredients:
- 1 large zucchini, trimmed
- 1 tablespoon coconut cream
- ¼ teaspoon minced garlic
- ¼ teaspoon ground ginger
- ¼ teaspoon ground black pepper
- ¾ teaspoon salt
- 1 teaspoon coconut oil

Directions:
Slice the zucchini into the ribs with the help of the vegetable peelers. Preheat the instant pot. When it shows "HOT", add coconut oil and melt it. Then add zucchini ribs (fettuccine), minced garlic, ground ginger, and ground black pepper. Stir the vegetables. After this, sprinkle them with coconut cream and close the lid. Cook the meal on sauté mode for 3 minutes.

Nutrition value/serving: calories 65, fat 4.4, fiber 2.1, carbs 6.3, protein 2.2

Keto Club Salad

Prep time: 15 minutes | *Cooking time:* 5 minutes | *Servings:* 6

Ingredients:
- 4 oz Cheddar cheese, cubed
- ½ cup cherry tomatoes, halved
- 2 cucumbers, chopped
- 4 eggs
- 1 tablespoon heavy cream
- 2 tablespoons coconut cream
- 1 teaspoon dried dill
- 1 teaspoon lemon juice
- ½ teaspoon salt
- 1 cup water, for cooking

Directions:
Pour water and insert the trivet in the instant pot. Place the eggs on the trivet and close the lid. Cook the eggs on manual (steam mode) for 5 minutes. Then make the quick pressure release and open the lid. Cool and peel the eggs. After this, place cheese, cherry tomatoes, and cucumbers in the salad bowl. Make the dressing: in the shallow bowl whisk together heavy cream, coconut cream, dried dill, salt, and lemon juice. Chop the eggs roughly and add them in the salad bowl. Then sprinkle it with dressing.

Nutrition value/serving: calories 157, fat 11.5, fiber 0.8, carbs 5.2, protein 9.4

Bell Pepper Pizza

Prep time: 10 minutes | *Cooking time:* 4 minutes | *Servings:* 2

Ingredients:

- 1 green bell pepper, halved, seeded
- 1 teaspoon cream cheese
- ¼ teaspoon tomato paste
- ¼ teaspoon dried basil
- 1/3 cup Mozzarella cheese, shredded
- 1 oz Parmesan, grated
- 1 cup water, for cooking

Directions:

In the mixing bowl mix up Parmesan, Mozzarella, and dried basil. In the shallow bowl whisk together cream cheese and tomato paste. Fill the bell pepper halves with cream cheese mixture and top with Mozzarella mixture. Place the pepper halves in the steamer rack. Then pour water in the instant pot. Insert the steamer rack and close the lid. Cook the pepper pizzas on manual (high pressure) for 4 minutes. Then make the quick pressure release.

Nutrition value/serving: calories 84, fat 4.6, fiber 0.8, carbs 5.4, protein 6.6

Peppers & Cheese Salad

Prep time: 15 minutes | *Cooking time:* 3 minutes | *Servings:* 5

Ingredients:

- ¼ cup Parmesan, grated
- ¼ cup Edam cheese, grated
- 4 bell peppers
- 1 tablespoon sesame oil
- 1 black olive, chopped
- ¼ teaspoon salt
- 1 tablespoon avocado oil

Directions:

Pour avocado oil in the instant pot. Pierce the bell peppers with the help of a knife and place in the instant pot. Cook the peppers on sauté mode for 3 minutes from each side. Then remove the vegetables from instant pot and peel them. Remove the seeds and cut the peppers into squares. Place them in the salad bowl. Add chopped olive, sesame oil, and salt. Mix up the peppers with the help of the spoon. Top the salad with Edam cheese and Parmesan cheese.

Nutrition value/serving: calories 136, fat 9, fiber 1.4, carbs 8, protein 7.4

Bok Choy Salad

Prep time: 10 minutes | *Cooking time:* 20 minutes | *Servings:* 4

Ingredients:

- 10 oz baby bok choy, trimmed
- ¼ teaspoon of sea salt
- 1 tablespoon peanut oil
- ½ teaspoon chili flakes
- ½ cup chicken broth
- 1 teaspoon olive oil
- 4 oz prosciutto, chopped

Directions:

Pour peanut oil in the instant pot and preheat it on sauté mode. When the oil is hot, add baby bok choy, sea salt, and chili flakes. Cook the vegetables for 3-4 minutes or until they are light brown. Add chicken broth and close the lid. Cook the bok choy on manual (high pressure) for 4 minutes. Then make the quick pressure release. Transfer the bok choy in the salad bowl. Add prosciutto and olive oil. Mix the salad.

Nutrition value/serving: calories 95, fat 6.4, fiber 0.7, carbs 2.1, protein 7.6

Avocado Pesto Zoodles

Prep time: 9 minutes | Cooking time: 5 minutes | Servings: 6

Ingredients:
- 1 avocado, peeled, pitted
- 2 medium zucchini, spiralized
- 3 tablespoons pesto sauce
- 1 teaspoon apple cider vinegar
- 1 teaspoon ground black pepper
- 1 teaspoon butter
- 3 tablespoons water

Directions:
Preheat the instant pot. When it shows "hot", add spiralized zucchini, apple cider vinegar, butter, and ground black pepper. Cook the zucchini on sauté mode for 2 minutes. Meanwhile, chop the avocado and put it in the blender. Add pesto and blend the mixture until smooth. Add avocado pesto over the zoodles and mix up well. Cook them for 1 minute more.

Nutrition value/serving: calories 119, fat 10.5, fiber 3.2, carbs 5.8, protein 2.2

Collard Wraps

Prep time: 10 minutes | Cooking time: 6 minutes | Servings: 4

Ingredients:
- 1 cup scallions, chopped
- 3 eggs
- 2 tablespoon cream cheese
- 1/3 teaspoon salt
- 1 teaspoon chili flakes
- 1 cup collard greens, only leaves
- 1 cup water, for cooking

Directions:
Cook the eggs: pour water and insert the steamer rack in the instant pot. Place the eggs on the rack and close the lid. Cook them in manual mode (high pressure) for 6 minutes. Then make the quick pressure release. Cool and peel the eggs. After this, chop the eggs and mix them up with the scallions. Add cream cheese, salt, and chili flakes. Trim the collard greens if needed. Spread the mixture over the collard greens leaves and wrap them.

Nutrition value/serving: calories 76, fat 5.2, fiber 1, carbs 2.9, protein 5.3

Portobello Toasts

Prep time: 8 minutes | Cooking time: 8 minutes | Servings: 2

Ingredients:
- 2 medium Portobello mushrooms caps
- 1 oz Parmesan, grated
- 2 tomato slices
- 2 teaspoons butter
- 1 cup water, for cooking

Directions:
Pour water and place the trivet in the instant pot. Line it with baking pan. Put the mushrooms on the trivet. Then put the butter in the mushrooms. After this, add sliced tomato and grated Parmesan. Close and seal the lid. Cook the mushroom toasts for 8 minutes on manual mode (high pressure). Then make the quick pressure release and open the lid. Cool the mushrooms to the room temperature and transfer in the serving plates.

Nutrition value/serving: calories 102, fat 6.9, fiber 1.2, carbs 4.1, protein 7.7

Spinach and Jarlsberg Pie

Prep time: 8 minutes | Cooking time: 10 minutes | Servings: 4

Ingredients:
- 5 eggs, beaten
- ¼ cup coconut flour
- ½ teaspoon ground black pepper
- 1 tablespoon cream cheese
- 5 oz Jarlsberg cheese, grated
- 1 cup spinach, chopped
- 1 tablespoon flax meal
- ½ teaspoon salt

Directions:
In the big bowl mix up eggs, coconut flour, ground black pepper, cream cheese, flax meal, and salt. Then pour liquid in the instant pot. Add spinach and cheese. Stir it gently with the help of the fork and close the lid. Cook the pie on meat/stew mode for 10 minutes (Make quick pressure release). Cool the pie completely and then cut into servings.

Nutrition value/serving: calories 255, fat 18.1, fiber 3.2, carbs 5.6, protein 17.6

Low Carb Falafel

Prep time: 10 minutes | Cooking time: 6 minutes | Servings: 2

Ingredients:
- ¼ cup cauliflower, shredded
- ¼ cup white onion, minced
- 1/3 garlic clove, minced
- 2 tablespoons almond flour
- 1 teaspoon flax meal
- ¼ teaspoon dried cilantro
- ¼ teaspoon cumin powder
- ¼ teaspoon salt
- 1 egg, beaten
- 1 tablespoon coconut oil

Directions:
In the mixing bowl mix up shredded cauliflower onion, garlic clove, almond flour, flax meal, dried cilantro, cumin powder, salt, and egg. Stir the mass until it is homogenous. Then make the balls from the mixture (falafel). Heat up an instant pot and put coconut oil inside. Melt it and add falafel. Cook it on sauté mode for 3 minutes from each side or until they are golden brown.

Nutrition value/serving: calories 148, fat 12.8, fiber 1.7, carbs 4.3, protein 5

Keto Ratatouille

Prep time: 10 minutes | Cooking time: 15 minutes | Servings: 4

Ingredients:
- 3 Mozzarella balls, sliced
- 1 eggplant, sliced
- 1 zucchini, sliced
- 1 tomato, sliced
- 1 tablespoon sesame oil
- 1 teaspoon salt
- 1 teaspoon ground turmeric
- 1 teaspoon fresh basil, chopped
- ½ cup chicken stock

Directions:
Place the sliced vegetables and Mozzarella in the instant pot one-by-one. Then sprinkle the ingredients with sesame oil, salt, ground turmeric, and fresh basil. Pour the chicken broth over the ratatouille and close the lid. Cook the meal on meat/stew mode for 15 minutes. Make the quick pressure release.

Nutrition value/serving: calories 133, fat .9.1, fiber 4.9, carbs 9.4, protein 5.8

Mushrooms and Tofu Scramble

Prep time: 10 minutes | Cooking time: 10 minutes | Servings: 4

Ingredients:
- ½ cup mushrooms, grinded
- ½ white onion, grinded
- ½ teaspoon salt
- 1 teaspoon butter
- 1 teaspoon ground ginger
- 4 eggs, beaten
- 3 oz tofu, crumbled

Directions:
Put butter in the instant pot and melt it on sauté mode. Add onion and mushrooms. Then sprinkle the vegetables with ground ginger and salt. Cook them for 5 minutes. Then stir well and add crumbled tofu. Cook the ingredients for 3 minutes more and add beaten eggs. Let the meal cooks for 2 minutes. Then scramble it with the help of the spatula and switch off the instant pot. Transfer the scramble in the serving plates.

Nutrition value/serving: calories 95, fat 6.3, fiber 0.6, carbs 2.6, protein 7.8

Sautéed Arugula Mash

Prep time: 5 minutes | *Cooking time:* 8 minutes | *Servings:* 2

Ingredients:
- 2 cups arugula, roughly chopped
- 1 tablespoon cream cheese
- 1 garlic clove, diced
- 1 teaspoon flax meal
- ½ teaspoon butter
- 2 oz Provolone cheese, grated
- ¼ teaspoon salt

Directions:
Put butter in the instant pot. Add cream cheese, flax meal, and diced garlic. Cook the ingredients on sauté mode for 1 minute. After this, add arugula and salt. Stir it well and cook for 2 minutes more. Then add cheese and stir the mixture until cheese is melted. Switch the instant pot mode to "keep warm" for 5 minutes.

Nutrition value/serving: calories 138, fat 10.8, fiber 0.7, carbs 2.3, protein 8.5

Masala Cauliflower

Prep time: 15 minutes | *Cooking time:* 6 minutes | *Servings:* 2

Ingredients:
- 1 ½ cup cauliflower florets
- 1 teaspoon garam masala
- ½ cup of coconut milk
- 1 teaspoon fresh cilantro, chopped
- 1 teaspoon butter
- ½ teaspoon salt

Directions:
Put all ingredients from the list above in the instant pot and close the lid. Cook the cauliflower on steam mode (high pressure) for 6 minutes. Then allow the natural pressure release for 10 minutes. Mash the cooked vegetables gently with the help of the spoon and transfer in the serving bowls.

Nutrition value/serving: calories 174, fat 16.3, fiber 3.2, carbs 7.3, protein 2.9

Pesto Zucchini Bake

Prep time: 10 minutes | *Cooking time:* 7 minutes | *Servings:* 4

Ingredients:
- 2 zucchini, sliced
- 2 tablespoons
- 1 cup Cheddar cheese, grated
- ½ cup heavy cream
- ½ teaspoon cayenne pepper

Directions:
Place ½ of all sliced zucchini in the instant pot. Flatten them in one layer. Then sprinkle them with Pesto sauce and ½ cup of Cheddar cheese. Top the cheese with the remaining zucchini. Add cayenne pepper, and remaining cheese. After this, pour the heavy cream over the ingredients and close the lid. Cook the meal on manual (high pressure) for 7 minutes. Then make the quick pressure release. Cool the meal for 10-15 minutes before serving.

Nutrition value/serving: calories 216, fat 18.4, fiber 1.3, carbs 4.7, protein 9.3

Baked Eggplant Mash

Prep time: 15 minutes | *Cooking time:* 20 minutes | *Servings:* 3

Ingredients:
- 2 cups eggplants, peeled, chopped
- 1 teaspoon ground cumin
- 1 teaspoon garlic powder
- ½ teaspoon minced ginger
- ½ teaspoon garam masala
- ½ teaspoon ground coriander
- 1 teaspoon ground paprika
- ½ teaspoon dried cilantro
- ¼ teaspoon ground black pepper
- 1 cup of water
- 1 tablespoon avocado oil

Directions:
Pour avocado oil in the instant pot. Add eggplants and cook them for 10 minutes on sauté mode. Stir the vegetables from time to time to avoid burning. After this, add ground cumin, garlic powder, minced ginger, garam masala, ground coriander, paprika, cilantro, and ground black pepper. Mix up the eggplants. Add water and close the lid. Cook the ingredients on manual (high pressure) for 10 minutes. Then allow the natural pressure release for 10 minutes. Open the lid and gently mash the soft eggplants with the help of the spoon.

Nutrition value/serving: calories 29, fat 1, fiber 2.6, carbs 5.2, protein 1

Garlic Okra

Prep time: 5 minutes | *Cooking time:* 20 minutes | *Servings:* 3

Ingredients:
- 2 cups okra, sliced
- 2 garlic cloves, minced
- 1 teaspoon lemon zest
- 1 tablespoon almond butter
- ¼ cup crushed tomatoes
- 1/3 cup beef broth
- ½ jalapeno pepper, sliced

Directions:
Put all ingredients in the instant pot and close the lid. Cook the okra on manual (high pressure) for 20 minutes. Then make the quick pressure release. Stir the cooked okra before serving.

Nutrition value/serving: calories 77, fat 3.3, fiber 3.5, carbs 8.8, protein 3.7

Cabbage Dippers

Prep time: 15 minutes | *Cooking time:* 4 minutes | *Servings:* 4

Ingredients:
- 4 prosciutto slices
- 8 oz white cabbage, roughly chopped into 4 pieces
- ¼ teaspoon cayenne pepper
- 1 teaspoon olive oil
- ¼ teaspoon dried basil
- 1 cup water, for cooking

Directions:
Pour water in the instant pot. Then insert the steamer rack inside. Rub the cabbage pieces with cayenne pepper and dried basil. Then sprinkle them with olive oil and place in the steamer rack. Close the lid and cook the cabbage on steam mode for 4 minutes. Make the quick pressure release. Then cool the cooked cabbage pieces to the room temperature and wrap in the prosciutto slices. Secure the cabbage dippers with the help of the toothpicks.

Nutrition value/serving: calories 55, fat 3, fiber 1.5, carbs 3.4, protein 4.5

Desserts
Chocolate Pudding
Prep time: 15 minutes | Cooking time: 10 minutes | Servings: 4

Ingredients:
- ½ cup heavy cream
- ½ cup of coconut milk
- 2 tablespoons cocoa powder
- ¼ cup Erythritol
- 2 tablespoons coconut flour
- 1 teaspoon gelatin
- 2 tablespoons water

Directions:
In the shallow bowl whisk together gelatin and water. Leave the mixture. Then pour heavy cream and coconut milk in the instant pot. Add cocoa powder and whisk the liquid until it is homogenous. Add Erythritol and coconut flour. Cook the liquid on sauté mode for 10 minutes. Stir it from time to time with the help of the spoon to avoid burning. When the time is over, cool the liquid for 10 minutes and add gelatin mixture. Stir it until gelatin is dissolved. Transfer the pudding in the serving cups.

Nutrition value/serving: calories 148, fat 13.6, fiber 2.7, carbs 5.6, protein 3.5

Pumpkin Pie Cups
Prep time: 10 minutes | Cooking time: 25 minutes | Servings: 4

Ingredients:
- 4 teaspoons coconut flour
- 4 teaspoons almond flour
- 2 teaspoons butter, softened
- ¼ teaspoon vanilla extract
- 2 teaspoons pumpkin puree
- 2 eggs, beaten
- 4 teaspoons Erythritol
- 4 tablespoons flax meal
- 1 tablespoon coconut cream
- 1 cup water, for cooking

Directions:
Mix up together coconut flour, almond flour, butter, and vanilla extract. Then fill the muffin molds with the dough. After this, in the mixing bowl combine together pumpkin puree, eggs Erythritol, flax meal, and coconut cream. Gently whisk the mixture and pour it over the dough. Pour water and insert the trivet in the instant pot. Place the muffin molds on the trivet and close the lid. Cook the pumpkin pie cups for 25 minutes on manual mode (high pressure). When the time is over, make the quick pressure release and open the lid. Cool the cooked dessert well.

Nutrition value/serving: calories 113, fat 8.9, fiber 3.2, carbs 4.5, protein 5.2

Keto Custard
Prep time: 10 minutes | Cooking time: 15 minutes | Servings: 2

Ingredients:
- ½ cup heavy cream
- 3 egg yolks
- ½ cup stevia powder
- ¼ teaspoon ground cardamom

Directions:
Pour heavy cream in the instant pot. Add ground cardamom. Cook the liquid on sauté mode until it starts to boil (appx 7-8 minutes). Stir it from time to time to avoid burning. Meanwhile, whisk together egg yolks with stevia powder until you get a fluffy mixture. Pour the egg yolk mixture in the heavy cream. Stir it constantly. When the liquid is homogenous, let it boil for 1 minute and switch off the instant pot. Pour the custard in the serving ramekins and let cool well.

Nutrition value/serving: calories 185, fat 17.9, fiber 0.1, carbs 1.9, protein 4.7

Pumpkin Spices Pudding
Prep time: 10 minutes | *Cooking time:* 15 minutes | *Servings:* 4

Ingredients:
- 1 cup coconut cream
- 4 tablespoons coconut flour
- 1 teaspoon pumpkin pie spices
- 1 teaspoon butter
- ½ cup of water
- 4 packets Splenda

Directions:
Pour coconut cream in the instant pot. Add Splenda, butter, and pumpkin pie spices. Cook the liquid on sauté mode until it starts to boil. Meanwhile, whisk together water with coconut flour. Pour the liquid in the boiling coconut cream. Whisk until homogenous. Switch off the instant pot. Pour the pudding in the serving cups and let it cool to room temperature.

Nutrition value/serving: calories 208, fat 17.3, fiber 7.4, carbs 13.6, protein 3.4

Molten Brownies Cups
Prep time: 15 minutes | *Cooking time:* 10 minutes | *Servings:* 5

Ingredients:
- 2 oz cocoa powder
- 4 tablespoons coconut butter
- 2 eggs
- 4 teaspoons Splenda
- 4 teaspoons coconut flour
- 1 teaspoon vanilla extract
- 1 cup water, for cooking

Directions:
Crack the eggs in the mixing bowl. Add cocoa powder, coconut butter, Splenda, and vanilla extract. Whisk the mass until it is smooth and homogenous. Then pour the mixture in the small baking cups. Cover every cup with foil. Pour water in the instant pot. Insert the trivet and place the cups on it. Close the lid and cook the molten brownies for 10 minutes on manual mode (high pressure). Then allow the natural pressure release for 10 minutes. Let the cooked dessert cool totally.

Nutrition value/serving: calories 151, fat 10.7, fiber 6.1, carbs 13.5, protein 5.3

Almond Tart
Prep time: 15 minutes | *Cooking time:* 20 minutes | *Servings:* 6

Ingredients:
- ½ cup almond flour
- 2 tablespoons almond butter
- ¼ teaspoon baking powder
- 1 egg, beaten
- ½ teaspoon ground cinnamon
- 1 tablespoon almond flakes
- ½ cup of organic almond milk
- 3 tablespoons coconut flour
- 2 tablespoons Erythritol
- 1 cup water, for cooking

Directions:
Make the tart crust: mix up together almond flour with almond butter, baking powder, and egg. Knead the dough. Then place the dough in the instant pot tart mold. Flatten it with the help of the fingertips in the shape of the tart crust. Pour water and insert the steamer rack in the instant pot. Place the tart mold on the rack and close the lid. Cook it on manual mode (high pressure) for 8 minutes. Then make a quick pressure release and remove the tart crust from it. Cool it well. After this, clean the instant pot and remove the steamer rack. Pour almond milk in the instant pot. Add coconut flour, Erythritol, and ground cinnamon. Bring the liquid to boil on sauté mode. Stir it constantly. Then switch off the instant pot. Pour the almond milk thick liquid over the pie crust and flatten well. Top the tart with almond flakes and refrigerate for at least 1 hour in the fridge.

Nutrition value/serving: calories 122, fat 10.4, fiber 2.8, carbs 5.2, protein 3.8

Chocolate Pudding Cake

Prep time: 20 minutes | *Cooking time:* 20 minutes | *Servings:* 8

Ingredients:
- 2 tablespoons flax meal
- 1 egg, beaten
- ½ cup almond flour
- 4 tablespoons butter, softened
- 1 tablespoon cocoa powder
- 1 cup heavy cream
- 2 tablespoons gelatin
- ¼ cup Erythritol
- 5 tablespoons water
- 1 cup water, for cooking

Directions:
Make the cake crust: mix up together flax meal with egg, almond flour, and butter. Knead the dough. Place it in the non-sticky instant pot cake mold and flatten well. Make the crust with edges. Then pour water and insert the steamer rack in the instant pot. Put the mold with cake crust in the instant pot and close the lid. Cook it on manual mode (high pressure) for 13 minutes When the time is over, make the quick pressure release and open the lid. Cool the cake crust well. Meanwhile, clean the instant pot and remove the rack from it. Pour heavy cream in the instant pot. Add cocoa powder and Erythritol. Cook the liquid on sauté mode for 7 minutes. Meanwhile, whisk water with gelatin together. When the time is over, add gelatin liquid in the cream mixture and switch off the instant pot. Stir the liquid until it is smooth. Then pour it in the bowl and cool to room temperature. Pour the thick liquid over the cake crust and refrigerate for 2 hours.

Nutrition value/serving: calories 135, fat 13.5, fiber 0.9, carbs 1.7, protein 3.4

Spice Pie

Prep time: 10 minutes | *Cooking time:* 45 minutes | *Servings:* 8

Ingredients:
- 1 cup coconut flour
- 2 tablespoons butter
- 2 tablespoons cream cheese
- ½ teaspoon ground cinnamon
- ¼ teaspoon ground turmeric
- ½ teaspoon ground cardamom
- ¼ teaspoon ground nutmeg
- 1 teaspoon vanilla extract
- 1 tablespoon peanuts, chopped
- 3 eggs, beaten
- 1 teaspoon pumpkin spices
- 3 tablespoons Splenda
- 1 cup water, for cooking

Directions:
Make the pie batter: whisk together coconut flour, butter, cream cheese, ground cinnamon, ground turmeric, cardamom, nutmeg, vanilla extract, peanuts, eggs, pumpkin spices, and Splenda. When the batter is prepared, pour it in the instant pot pie mold. Flatten the surface of the pie well. Pour water and insert the steamer rack in the instant pot. Place the pie on the steamer rack and close the lid. Cook the pie on manual mode (high pressure) for 45 minutes. When the time is over, make the quick pressure release and open the lid. Cool the pie to the room temperature and cut into the servings.

Nutrition value/serving: calories 98, fat 6.3, fiber 0.9, carbs 6.4, protein 2.9

Keto Cheesecake

Prep time: 25 minutes | *Cooking time:* 20 minutes | *Servings:* 6

Ingredients:
- ½ cup cream cheese
- 2 eggs, beaten
- 2 tablespoons whipped cream
- ¼ teaspoon vanilla extract
- 3 tablespoons Erythritol
- ½ cup almond flour
- 2 tablespoons butter, melted
- 1 cup water, for cooking

Directions:
Mix up almond flour with butter and knead the non-sticky dough. Then put the dough in the baking mold and flatten it in the shape of the pie crust. Pour water in the instant pot and insert the steamer rack. Place the pie crust in the instant pot and cook it on manual mode (high pressure) for 10 minutes. Make the quick pressure release and open the lid. After this, whisk together eggs with cream cheese, whipped cream, vanilla extract, and Erythritol. Pour the liquid over the pie crust and close the lid. Cook the cheesecake on manual mode (high pressure) for 10 minutes. When the time is over, make the quick pressure release and open the lid. Cool the cheesecake for 4 hours in the fridge.

Nutrition value/serving: calories 151, fat 14.8, fiber 0.3, carbs 1.3, protein 4

Butter Cake

Prep time: 15 minutes | *Cooking time:* 35 minutes | *Servings:* 6

Ingredients:
- ½ cup butter, softened
- 1 egg, beaten
- 1 teaspoon vanilla extract
- ½ teaspoon baking powder
- 1 teaspoon lemon juice
- 2 tablespoons cream cheese
- 1 tablespoon Erythritol
- 1 ½ cup almond flour
- 1 tablespoon Splenda
- 1 cup water, for cooking

Directions:
In the mixing bowl mix up together butter with egg, vanilla extract, baking powder, and lemon juice. Then add almond flour and Splenda. Knead the dough and place it in the baking pan. Flatten it well. Pour water and insert the trivet in the instant pot. Place the dough on the trivet and close the lid. Cook it on manual mode (high pressure) for 35 minutes. When the time is over, make the quick pressure release and open the lid. Whisk together Erythritol and cream cheese. Cool the cooked cake to the room temperature and spread with sweet cream cheese mixture. Cut it into the servings.

Nutrition value/serving: calories 330, fat 31.3, fiber 3, carbs 8.5, protein 7.3

Cinnamon Mini Rolls

Prep time: 15 minutes | *Cooking time:* 21 minutes | *Servings:* 10

Ingredients:
- 1 cup almond flour
- ¼ cup coconut flour
- 1 teaspoon baking powder
- 1 teaspoon apple cider vinegar
- 3 tablespoons butter, melted
- 1 tablespoon cream cheese
- ¼ cup Erythritol
- 1 tablespoon cinnamon
- 1 egg, beaten
- 1 teaspoon vanilla extract
- 1 cup water, for cooking

Directions:
In the bowl mix up almond flour, coconut flour, baking powder, and apple cider vinegar. Then add melted butter, cream cheese, egg, and vanilla extract. Knead the soft and non-sticky dough. Roll it up in the shape of a square. In the shallow bowl combine together Erythritol and ground cinnamon. Sprinkle the surface of dough square with ground cinnamon mixture and roll it into the log. Then cut the dough log on 10 pieces. Press ever cinnamon dough piece with the help of the hand palm. Pour water and insert the trivet in the instant pot. Line the trivet with baking paper and place the cinnamon rolls on it. Close the lid and cook the dessert for 21 minutes on manual mode (high pressure). When the time is finished, make a quick pressure release and open the lid. Cool the cooked cinnamon rolls for 5 minutes and remove from the instant pot

Nutrition value/serving: calories 72, fat 6, fiber 1.9, carbs 9.5, protein 1.7

Lava Cake

Prep time: 10 minutes | Cooking time: 15 minutes | Servings: 4

Ingredients:
- 1 tablespoon cocoa powder, unsweetened
- 1 teaspoon Erythritol
- 1/3 teaspoon baking powder
- 1 egg, beaten
- ¼ cup whipping cream
- 1 teaspoon butter
- 1 tablespoon almond meal
- ¼ teaspoon vanilla extract
- 1 cup water, for cooking

Directions:
In the big bowl whisk together egg and cocoa powder. Then add Erythritol and baking powder. Whisk the mixture for 2-3 minutes and add almond meal, vanilla extract, and whipping cream. Stir it until homogenous. Grease the instant pot baking mold with butter and place the cocoa mixture in it. Flatten it with the help of the spatula if needed. Pour water and insert the steamer rack in the instant pot. Place the baking mold with a cocoa mixture on the rack and close the lid. Cook the lava cake for 15 minutes on Manual mode (high pressure). Then make a quick pressure release and open the lid.

Nutrition value/serving: calories 59, fat 5.3, fiber 0.6, carbs 2.8, protein 2.1

Rhubarb Custard

Prep time: 20 minutes | Cooking time: 6 minutes | Servings: 4

Ingredients:
- 1/3 cup rhubarb, chopped
- 3 eggs, beaten
- 4 packets Splenda
- ½ teaspoon vanilla extract
- 1 cup heavy cream
- 2 tablespoons butter, melted
- 1 cup water, for cooking

Directions:
Whisk together eggs with Splenda. Then add vanilla extract and heavy cream. Add butter and whisk the mass until homogenous. Add chopped rhubarb and mix up the mixture with the help of the spoon. Then pour the mixture into 4 ramekins. Cover every ramekin with foil. Pour water and insert the trivet in the instant pot. Place the ramekins with rhubarb custard on the trivet and close the lid. Cook the meal on manual mode (high pressure) for 6 minutes. When the time is over, allow the natural pressure release for 10 minutes. Remove the foil from the ramekins and let them cool for 5-10 minutes before serving.

Nutrition value/serving: calories 205, fat 20.2, fiber 1.2, carbs 3.6, protein 4.9

Chocolate Mousse

Prep time: 15 minutes | Cooking time: 3 hours | Servings: 2

Ingredients:
- 2 egg, beaten
- ½ cup heavy cream
- 2 tablespoons cocoa powder
- 1 teaspoon Splenda
- 1 teaspoon butter
- 1 cup water, for cooking

Directions:
Pour heavy cream in the mixing bowl and whisk it until you get strong peaks. Add Splenda and cocoa powder. Whisk the mixture until smooth. After this, whisk the eggs in the separated bowl. Slowly start to add whisked eggs in the whipped cream mixture. Stir it until smooth. Grease the ramekins with butter. Pour the whipped cream mixture in the ramekins. Pour water and insert the steamer rack in the instant pot. Place the ramekins with mousse on the trivet and close the lid. Cook the mousse for 3 hours on Manual (low pressure).

Nutrition value/serving: calories 205, fat 18.1, fiber 1.6, carbs 6.1, protein 7.2

Cocoa-Vanilla Pudding

Prep time: 10 minutes | *Cooking time:* 10 minutes | *Servings:* 6

Ingredients:
- 1 teaspoon sugar-free maple syrup
- 2 oz hot water
- 1/3 teaspoon vanilla extract
- 9 oz coconut flour
- ¼ tablespoon cocoa powder
- 1/3 teaspoon baking powder
- 4 tablespoons butter, softened
- 2 tablespoons swerve
- 1 egg, beaten
- 1 cup water, for cooking

Directions:

Mix up maple syrup with vanilla extract, coconut flour, cocoa powder, baking powder, butter, and swerve, Add egg and stir the mixture with the help of the fork until smooth. Then transfer the mixture in the round baking mold. Pour water and insert the trivet in the instant pot. Place the mold with pudding on the trivet and close the lid. Cook the pudding on steam mode for 10 minutes. When the time is over, make a quick pressure release and remove the dessert from the instant pot.

Nutrition value/serving: calories 212, fat 11.7, fiber 12.8, carbs 20.4, protein 7.2

Keto Carrot Pie

Prep time: 20 minutes | *Cooking time:* 35 minutes | *Servings:* 6

Ingredients:
- 1 tablespoon walnuts, chopped
- 1 carrot, grated
- ½ cup almond butter
- 1 cup almond meal
- 3 tablespoons swerve
- 1 teaspoon psyllium husk powder
- 1 egg, beaten
- 1 teaspoon vanilla extract
- ½ teaspoon ground cinnamon
- ½ teaspoon baking powder
- 1 cup water, for steam mode

Directions:

Put all ingredients in the mixing bowl and stir them with the help of the spoon until you get a homogenous pie mixture. After this, transfer the pie mixture into the baking mold. Flatten the surface of the pie with the help of the spatula. Pour water and insert the steamer rack in the instant pot. Place the pie on the trivet and close the lid. Cook the carrot pie for 35 minutes on manual mode (high pressure). When the time is finished, allow the natural pressure release for 10 minutes and remove the pie from the instant pot.

Nutrition value/serving: calories 130, fat 10.2, fiber 3, carbs 6.7, protein 5

Pecan Pie

Prep time: 15 minutes | *Cooking time:* 15 minutes | *Servings:* 4

Ingredients:
- ½ cup coconut flour
- 1 tablespoon butter, melted
- 4 pecans, chopped
- 1 tablespoon Monk fruit powder
- 4 oz coconut milk
- 2 tablespoons almond butter
- 1 cup water, for cooking

Directions:

Make the pie crust: mix up together coconut flour and butter. Knead the non-sticky dough. Place the mixture in the instant pot mold and flatten it with the help of the fingertips in the shape of the pie crust. Pour water and insert the steamer rack in the instant pot. Place the mold with the pie crust on the rack and close the lid. Cook it on manual (high pressure) for 5 minutes. Then make a quick pressure release. Open the lid. In the mixing bowl whisk together milk, Monk fruit, and almond butter. When the mixture is smooth, pour it over the cooked pie crust. Top the pie with chopped pecans and close the lid. Cook the pecan pie for 10 minutes on manual mode (high pressure). When the time is over, make a quick pressure release. Cool the cooked pie well.

Nutrition value/serving: calories 297, fat 26.1, fiber 7.9, carbs 13.1, protein 5.9

Keto Crème Brulee

Prep time: 15 minutes | Cooking time: 8 minutes | Servings: 2

Ingredients:
- 1 tablespoon Erythritol
- 2 egg yolks
- 1 cup heavy cream
- ½ teaspoon vanilla extract
- 1 teaspoon Splenda
- 1 cup water, for cooking

Directions:
Whisk egg yolks and Splenda together until smooth. Then add heavy cream and vanilla extract. Whisk the mixture well and pour it into the ramekins. After this, cover every ramekin with foil. Pour water and insert the steamer rack in the instant pot. Place the ramekins on the rack and close the lid. Cook the crème Brulee on manual mode (high pressure) for 8 minutes. Then allow the natural pressure release for 10 minutes and remove the ramekins from the instant pot. Remove the foil and sprinkle the surface of crème Brulee with Erythritol. With the help of the kitchen torch, caramelize Erythritol.

Nutrition value/serving: calories 274, fat 26.7, fiber 0, carbs 4.4, protein 3.9

Lavender Pie

Prep time: 10 minutes | Cooking time: 40 minutes | Servings: 6

Ingredients:
- ½ cup blackberries
- 1 cup almond meal
- 2 tablespoons flax meal
- 1 teaspoon baking powder
- ½ teaspoon apple cider vinegar
- 3 eggs, beaten
- 1 teaspoon lavender extract
- 1/3 cup cream cheese
- 1/3 cup Erythritol
- 1 teaspoon butter, melted
- 1 cup water, for cooking

Directions:
In the big bowl combine together almond meal, flax meal, baking powder, apple cider vinegar, and eggs. Then add lavender extract, cream cheese, Erythritol, and melted butter. Stir the mixture In the end you should get a smooth thick batter. Pour it in the non-stick baking mold. Then insert the steamer rack and pour water in the instant pot. Place the mold with pie on the rack and close the lid. Cook the meal on manual mode (high pressure) for 40 minutes. When the time is over, make a quick pressure release and transfer the pie on the plate. Cool it to the room temperature and cut into the servings.

Nutrition value/serving: calories 145, fat 11.6, fiber 3.3, carbs 5.8, protein 6.8

Blueberry Parfait

Prep time: 15 minutes | Cooking time: 5 minutes | Servings: 4

Ingredients:
- ½ cup hazelnuts, chopped
- 1 teaspoon flax seeds
- 1 teaspoon chia seeds
- 1 teaspoon pumpkin seeds
- 1 teaspoon coconut oil
- 1 teaspoon liquid stevia
- 1 cup blueberries
- 1 tablespoon Erythritol
- 1 teaspoon water
- 4 tablespoons cream cheese

Directions:
Preheat the instant pot on sauté mode for 3 minutes. Meanwhile, in the mixing bowl combine together flax seeds, chia seeds, pumpkin seeds, and coconut oil. Add liquid stevia and stir it well. Then transfer the mixture in the instant pot and sauté it for 2 minutes. Stir it from constantly. Then transfer the mixture on the baking paper. Whisk together cream cheese with Erythritol and water. When you get a smooth and fluffy mixture, it is cooked. Crush the cooked hazelnut mixture. Then place a small amount of the hazelnut mixture in the glass jars. Add ½ tablespoon of cream cheese mixture and all blueberries in every glass. After this, top the blueberries with remaining hazelnut mixture and cream cheese.

Nutrition value/serving: calories 140, fat 11.5, fiber 2.6, carbs 8.2, protein 3

Pandan Custard
Prep time: 10 minutes | Cooking time: 25 minutes | Servings: 3

Ingredients:
- 1 teaspoon pandan extract
- 1 egg, beaten
- 4 tablespoons Truvia
- ½ cup of coconut milk
- 1 cup water, for cooking

Directions:
In the mixing bowl blend together pandan extract, egg, Truvia, and coconut milk. When the mixture is smooth, pour it in the ramekins. Then pour water in the instant pot and insert the rack. Place the ramekins on the rack and close the lid. Cook the custard on manual mode (high pressure) for 25 minutes. When the time is over, make a quick pressure release.

Nutrition value/serving: calories 113, fat 11, fiber 0.9, carbs 8.6, protein 2.8

Mug Cake
Prep time: 10 minutes | Cooking time: 18 minutes | Servings: 2

Ingredients:
- 4 teaspoons butter, softened
- 1 tablespoon cream cheese
- 1 teaspoon vanilla extract
- 2 tablespoons almond flour
- 2 teaspoons Erythritol
- ½ teaspoon baking powder
- 1 egg, beaten
- 1 cup water, for cooking

Directions:
In the mixing bowl, mix up together butter, cream cheese, vanilla extract, almond flour, Erythritol, baking powder, and egg. When the mixture is smooth, pour it into the mugs. Pour water in the instant pot and insert the trivet. Place the mugs on the trivet and close the lid. Cook the cakes on manual mode (high pressure) for 18 minutes. When the time is finished, make a quick pressure release and open the lid.

Nutrition value/serving: calories 2846, fat 25.6, fiber 3, carbs 7.2, protein 9.2

Coconut Cake
Prep time: 10 minutes | Cooking time: 30 minutes | Servings: 8

Ingredients:
- 1 cup of coconut oil
- ½ cup coconut flakes
- 1 teaspoon baking powder
- 2 eggs, beaten
- 1 tablespoon flax meal
- ¼ cup heavy cream
- 1 teaspoon butter, softened
- ½ cup Erythritol
- 1 teaspoon vanilla extract
- 1 cup water, for cooking

Directions:
Combine together coconut oil, coconut flakes, and baking powder. Add eggs, flax meal, heavy cream, and butter. After this, add Erythritol and vanilla extract. Stir the mixture with the help of the spoon until you get a smooth and thick batter. Then pour it in the non-stick baking mold. Pour water and insert the steamer rack in the instant pot. Place the baking mold with batter in the instant pot and close the lid. Cook the cake in manual mode (high pressure) for 30 minutes. When the time is over, make a quick pressure release and open the lid. Cool the cake well and after this, remove it from the baking mold and cut into the servings.

Nutrition value/serving: calories 291, fat 32.2, fiber 0.7, carbs 1.6, protein 1.8

Walnut pie

Prep time: 20 minutes | *Cooking time:* 5 minutes | *Servings:* 4

Ingredients:
- 1/3 cup walnuts
- ¼ cup hazelnuts
- 2 tablespoon butter, softened
- 4 tablespoons whipped cream
- 1 teaspoon coconut oil
- 1 oz dark chocolate
- 2 tablespoons swerve

Directions:
Place the walnuts and hazelnuts in the blender and blend until smooth. Add butter and blend for 30 seconds more or until you get the smooth homogenous texture of the mixture. Remove the mixture from the blender and place it in the baking mold. Flatten the mixture in the shape of the pie crust with the help of the fingertips. Place the crust in the freezer. After this, preheat the instant pot on sauté mode for 3 minutes. Add dark chocolate and coconut oil. Then add swerve and sauté the mixture until it is soft and homogenous (appx.for 5 minutes). Stir the mixture constantly to avoid burning. Then whisk together whipped cream and chocolate mixture. When it is smooth, pour the mixture over the frozen walnut pie crust and place it in the fridge. Let the pie rest for at least 3 hours.

Nutrition value/serving: calories 236, fat 22.6, fiber 1.4, carbs 6.5, protein 4.1

Keto Chip Cookies

Prep time: 10 minutes | *Cooking time:* 8 minutes | *Servings:* 6

Ingredients:
- 1 teaspoon xanthan gum
- 3 tablespoons butter, softened
- ½ teaspoon vanilla extract
- 1 egg, beaten
- 1/3 teaspoon baking powder
- 1 sugar-free chocolate chips
- 8 oz coconut flour
- 1 tablespoon Erythritol
- 1 cup water, for cooking

Directions:
In the big bowl combine together all ingredients except water for cooking. Knead the smooth dough and cut it into 6 pieces. Make the ball from every dough piece and press gently in the shape of a circle. Pour water and insert the steamer rack in the instant pot. Line the rack with baking paper and place the cookies on it in one layer. Close the lid and cook the chip cookies for 8 minutes on Manual mode (high pressure). When the time is over, make a quick pressure release and remove the cookies from the instant pot. Repeat the same step with remaining cookies.

Nutrition value/serving: calories 166, fat 10, fiber 8.4, carbs 15.2, protein 3.8

Keto Vanilla Crescent Cookies

Prep time: 15 minutes | *Cooking time:* 19 minutes | *Servings:* 7

Ingredients:
- 1/3 cup butter, softened
- 3 oz almond flour
- 1.5 oz almonds, grinded
- 2 ½ tablespoons stevia
- ½ teaspoon vanilla extract
- 1 tablespoon Erythritol
- 1 cup water, for cooking

Directions:
Knead the dough from almond flour, butter, almonds, stevia, and vanilla extract. Then roll the dough into the log shape and cut into 7 pieces. Make the shape of crescents. Pour water and insert the trivet in the instant pot. Line the trivet with baking paper and place the crescents on it. Cook the crescent cookies in the manual (high pressure) for 19 minutes. When the time is finished, make a quick pressure release. Sprinkle every crescent cookie in Erythritol.

Nutrition value/serving: calories 182, fat 17.8, fiber 2.1, carbs 3.9, protein 3.9

Vanilla Muffins

Prep time: 10 minutes | *Cooking time:* 15 minutes | *Servings:* 4

Ingredients:
- 4 tablespoons almond flour
- 1 tablespoon cream cheese
- 1 egg, beaten
- 1 teaspoon vanilla extract
- ¼ teaspoon baking powder
- ¼ teaspoon apple cider vinegar
- 4 teaspoons Erythritol
- 1 cup water, for cooking

Directions:
In the bowl combine together cream cheese, egg, vanilla extract, baking powder, apple cider vinegar, and Erythritol. When the mass is homogenous, add almond flour and stir until smooth. Pour water and insert the trivet in the instant pot. Fill the muffin molds with muffins batter and transfer on the trivet. Close the lid and cook the dessert on manual (high pressure) for 15 minutes. When the time is finished, make a quick pressure release and remove the muffins from the instant pot immediately.

Nutrition value/serving: calories 188, fat 16, fiber 3, carbs 6.4, protein 7.6

Fat Bomb Jars

Prep time: 8 minutes | *Cooking time:* 6 minutes | *Servings:* 4

Ingredients:
- 1 tablespoon coconut oil
- 1 pouch sugar-free chocolate chips
- ½ cup whipped cream
- 3 tablespoons almond butter
- ¼ teaspoon ground cardamom

Directions:
Toss the coconut oil in the instant pot and melt it on sauté mode. After this, add ground cardamom and chocolate chips. Melt the mixture and switch off the instant pot. After this, transfer the chocolate mixture into the bowl. Add whipped cream and almond butter. Stir the mixture until smooth and homogenous. With the help of the scooper place the mixture into the glass jars.

Nutrition value/serving: calories 172, fat 15.6, fiber 1.5, carbs 7, protein 3.1

Blueberry Clusters

Prep time: 10 minutes | *Cooking time:* 6 minutes | *Servings:* 6

Ingredients:
- 1.5 oz dark chocolate
- 1 tablespoon coconut oil
- 1/3 cup blueberries

Directions:
Toss coconut oil in the instant pot. Set sauté mode for 6 minutes and melt the oil. Add dark chocolate and stir well. Cook the mixture until it is homogenous. After this, line the baking tray with baking paper and arrange the blueberries on it into 6 circles. Then sprinkle every "blueberry circles" with melted chocolate mixture and let dry. Store the cooked clusters in the glass jar with the closed lid up to 2 days.

Nutrition value/serving: calories 67, fat 5.3, fiber 1.2, carbs 7.9, protein 0.6

Strawberry Cubes

Prep time: 10 minutes | *Cooking time:* 7 minutes | *Servings:* 4

Ingredients:
- 4 strawberries
- 1 tablespoon heavy cream
- 1 teaspoon butter
- 1 tablespoon cocoa powder

Directions:
Put the strawberries in the freezer for 5-10 minutes. Preheat the instant pot bowl on sauté mode for 3 minutes. Then add butter and melt it. Add heavy cream and cocoa powder. Whisk the mixture until smooth and turn off the instant pot. After this, let the chocolate mixture cool to room temperature. Dip every strawberry in the chocolate mixture and let to dry it for 3-4 minutes.

Nutrition value/serving: calories 28, fat 2.6, fiber 0.6, carbs 1.8, protein 0.4

Avocado Brownies

Prep time: 15 minutes | Cooking time: 14 minutes | Servings: 12

Ingredients:
- 1 avocado, peeled, pitted
- 1 tablespoon cocoa powder
- 1 tablespoon almond butter
- 1 teaspoon vanilla extract
- 1 egg, beaten
- 4 tablespoons almond flour
- ½ teaspoon baking powder
- 3 tablespoons Erythritol
- ½ teaspoon apple cider vinegar
- 1 cup water, for cooking

Directions:
Churn the avocado till the creamy texture. Add cocoa powder, almond butter, vanilla extract, and egg. Mix up the mixture until it is smooth. Then add almond flour, baking powder, Erythritol, and apple cider vinegar. Stir the mass well and pour in the instant pot baking mold. Flatten the surface and cover it with the foil. Pierce the foil with the help of the toothpick. Pour water and insert the trivet in the instant pot. Place the baking mold with a brownie on the trivet and close the lid. Cook the dessert for 14 minutes on manual mode (high pressure). When the time is finished, make a quick pressure release and remove the brownie. Discard the foil and cut the brownie into bars.

Nutrition value/serving: calories 103, fat 9.1, fiber 3, carbs 2.4, protein 3.1

Cheesecake Bites

Prep time: 15 minutes | Cooking time: 12 minutes | Servings: 2

Ingredients:
- 2 teaspoons cream cheese
- ¼ teaspoon vanilla extract
- 2 tablespoons peanut flour
- ¼ teaspoon coconut oil
- 1 egg, beaten
- 1 teaspoon Splenda
- 1 cup water, for cooking

Directions:
In the mixing bowl mix up cream cheese with vanilla extract, peanut flour, coconut oil, egg, and Splenda. When the mixture is smooth, transfer it in the muffin molds. Pour water and insert the trivet in the instant pot. Place the muffin molds on the trivet and close the lid. Cook the cheesecake bites on manual mode (high pressure) for 12 minutes. When the time is over, allow the natural pressure release for 10 minutes.

Nutrition value/serving: calories 76, fat 4.7, fiber 0.6, carbs 3.5, protein 4.3

Coconut Crack Bars

Prep time: 10 minutes | Cooking time: 8 minutes | Servings: 4

Ingredients:
- 1 cup unsweetened coconut flakes
- 4 tablespoons coconut oil
- 1 egg, beaten
- 2 tablespoons coconut flour
- 2 tablespoons monk fruit

Directions:
In the mixing bowl combine together 3 tablespoons of coconut oil, coconut flour, egg, and coconut flakes. Then add monk fruit and stir the mixture well with the help of the spoon. The prepared mixture should be homogenous. After this, toss the remaining coconut oil in the instant pot and heat it up on sauté mode. Meanwhile, make the small bars from the coconut mixture. Place them in the hot coconut oil in one layer and cook for 1 minute from each side. Dry the cooked coconut bars with a paper towel if needed.

Nutrition value/serving: calories 218, fat 21.2, fiber 3.3, carbs 6.1, protein 2.9

Keto Blondies

Prep time: 15 minutes | *Cooking time:* 30 minutes | *Servings:* 4

Ingredients:
- 2 oz almond flour
- 2 oz coconut flour
- ½ teaspoon baking powder
- 3 tablespoons Erythritol
- 1 egg, beaten
- 2 tablespoons almond butter, softened
- 1 teaspoon walnuts, chopped
- 1 cup water, for cooking

Directions:
Line the instant pot baking tray with baking paper. After this, in the mixing bowl combine together almond flour, coconut flour, baking powder, and Erythritol. Add egg, almond butter, and walnuts, With the help of the spoon stir the mass until homogenous. Then transfer it in the prepared baking tray and flatten well the surface of the dough. Pour water in the instant pot and insert the trivet. Place the tray on the trivet and close the lid. Cook the blondies for 30 minutes on manual mode (high pressure). When the time is over, make a quick pressure release. Cool the blondies to the room temperature and cut into serving bars.

Nutrition value/serving: calories 180, fat 14, fiber 4.9, carbs 9, protein 7.3

Low Carb Nutella

Prep time: 10 minutes | *Cooking time:* 5 minutes | *Servings:* 4

Ingredients:
- 3 oz hazelnuts
- 2 tablespoons coconut oil
- 1 teaspoon of cocoa powder
- 1 teaspoon Erythritol
- 2 tablespoons heavy cream

Directions:
Place coconut oil in the instant pot. Set sauté mode and heat it up for 3-4 minutes until the oil is melted. Then add Erythritol and cocoa powder. Whisk it well until homogenous. After this, add heavy cream. Stir the mixture until smooth and switch off the instant pot. After this, grind the hazelnuts. Add melted coconut oil mixture to the grinded hazelnuts. Stir well with the help of the spoon. Store Nutella in the fridge for up to 5 days.

Nutrition value/serving: calories 219, fat 22.6, fiber 2.2, carbs 4, protein 3.4

Cheesecake Fat Bombs

Prep time: 20 minutes | *Cooking time:* 30 minutes | *Servings:* 2

Ingredients:
- 1 egg yolk
- 2 tablespoons cream cheese
- 1 teaspoon swerve
- ¼ teaspoon vanilla extract
- 3 tablespoons heavy cream
- 1 teaspoon coconut flakes

Directions:
Whisk the egg yolk with swerve until smooth. Then add heavy cream and pour the liquid in the instant pot. Stir it until homogenous and cook on manual mode (low pressure) for 30 minutes. Meanwhile, mix up together cream cheese with vanilla extract, and coconut flakes. When the time is over and the egg yolk mixture is cooked, open the instant pot lid. Combine together cream cheese mixture with egg yolk mixture and stir until homogenous. Place the mixture in the silicone muffin molds and transfer in the freezer for 20 minutes. The cooked cheesecake fat bombs should be tender but not liquid.

Nutrition value/serving: calories 146, fat 14.4, fiber 0.1, carbs 2.4, protein 2.6

Peanut Butter Balls

Prep time: 10 minutes | *Cooking time:* 5 minutes | *Servings:* 2

Ingredients:
- 1 tablespoon peanuts
- 1 tablespoon butter
- 1 teaspoon Erythritol
- 4 tablespoons coconut flakes

Directions:
Set sauté mode on your instant pot for 5 minutes. Place the butter inside and melt it. Meanwhile, finely chop the peanuts. Add them in the melted butter. After this, add Erythritol and coconut flakes. Stir the mixture until homogenous. With the help of the scooper make 2 balls and chill them in the fridge.

Nutrition value/serving: calories 112, fat 11.4, fiber 1.3, carbs 2.3, protein 1.6

Cinnamon Muffins

Prep time: 10 minutes | *Cooking time:* 18 minutes | *Servings:* 4

Ingredients:
- 4 teaspoons cream cheese
- 1 teaspoon ground cinnamon
- 1 tablespoon butter, softened
- 1 egg, beaten
- 4 teaspoons almond flour
- ½ teaspoon baking powder
- 1 teaspoon lemon juice
- 2 scoops stevia
- ¼ teaspoon vanilla extract
- 1 cup of water, for cooking

Directions:
In the big bowl make the muffins batter: mix up together cream cheese, ground cinnamon, butter, egg, almond flour, baking powder, lemon juice, stevia, and vanilla extract. When the mixture is smooth and thick, pour it into the 4 muffin molds. Then pour the water in the instant pot and insert the trivet. Place the muffins on the trivet and close the lid. Cook them for 18 minutes on Manual mode (high pressure). When the time is over, make a quick pressure release and cool the cooked muffins well.

Nutrition value/serving: calories 216, fat 19.2, fiber 3.3, carbs 7, protein 7.7

Keto Fudge

Prep time: 10 minutes | *Cooking time:* 6 minutes | *Servings:* 5

Ingredients:
- ¾ cup of cocoa powder
- 1 oz dark chocolate
- 4 tablespoons butter
- 1 tablespoon ricotta cheese
- ¼ teaspoon vanilla extract

Directions:
Preheat the instant pot on sauté mode for 3 minutes. Place chocolate in the instant pot. Add butter and ricotta cheese. Then add vanilla extract and cook the ingredients until you get liquid mixture. Then add cocoa powder and whisk it to avoid the lumps. Line the glass mold with baking paper and pour the hot liquid mixture inside. Flatten it gently. Refrigerate it until solid. Then cut/crack the cooked fudge into the serving pieces.

Nutrition value/serving: calories 155, fat 13.8, fiber 4.6, carbs 10.7, protein 3.3

Fluffy Donuts
Prep time: 20 minutes | *Cooking time:* 14 minutes | *Servings:* 2

Ingredients:
- 1 tablespoon organic almond milk
- 1 egg, beaten
- ¼ teaspoon baking powder
- ¼ teaspoon apple cider vinegar
- 1 teaspoon ghee, melted
- 1 teaspoon vanilla extract
- 1 tablespoon Erythritol
- ¾ teaspoon xanthan gum
- 1 teaspoon flax meal
- 1 scoop stevia
- ¼ teaspoon ground nutmeg
- 1 tablespoon almond flour
- 1 cup water, for cooking

Directions:
Make the dough for the donut: in the big bowl mix up almond milk, egg, baking powder, apple cider vinegar, ghee, vanilla extract, Erythritol, xanthan gum, flax meal, and almond flour. With the help of the spoon stir the mixture gently. Then knead the non-sticky dough. Cut it into small pieces and put it in the silicone donut molds. Pour water and insert the trivet in the instant pot. Place the silicone molds with donuts on the trivet and close the lid. Cook the donuts on manual mode "high pressure" for 14 minutes. When the time is over, make a quick pressure release and open the lid. In the shallow bowl mix up together ground nutmeg and stevia. Sprinkle every donut with the stevia mixture.

Nutrition value/serving: calories 233, fat 18.9, fiber 5.4, carbs 9.3, protein 9.1

Coconut Muffins
Prep time: 15 minutes | *Cooking time:* 12 minutes | *Servings:* 6

Ingredients:
- ½ cup coconut flour
- 2 eggs, beaten
- ¼ cup Splenda
- ½ teaspoon vanilla extract
- 3 teaspoons coconut flakes
- ¼ cup heavy cream
- 1 teaspoon baking powder
- 1 teaspoon lemon zest, grated
- 1 cup water, for cooking

Directions:
Make the muffins batter: In the bowl whisk together coconut flour, eggs, Splenda, vanilla extract, coconut flour, heavy cream, baking powder, and lemon zest. Use the hand blender to make the batter smooth. Then pour water in the instant pot and insert the trivet. Pour muffins batter in the muffin molds. Then transfer the molds on the trivet and close the lid. Cook the desert on manual mode (high pressure) for 12 minutes. When the time is over, allow the natural pressure release for 5 minutes.

Nutrition value/serving: calories 48, fat 3.8, fiber 0.7, carbs 1.9, protein 2.2

Raspberry Pie
Prep time: 15 minutes | *Cooking time:* 25 minutes | *Servings:* 6

Ingredients:
- ¼ cup raspberries
- 1 tablespoon Erythritol
- 3 tablespoons butter, softened
- ¼ teaspoon baking powder
- ½ cup almond flour
- 1 tablespoon flax meal
- 1 teaspoon ghee, melted
- 1 cup water, for cooking

Directions:
Blend raspberries with Erythritol in the blender until smooth. Then in the mixing bowl combine together butter, baking powder, almond flour, flax meal, and knead the dough. Cut it into 2 pieces. Then put one piece of dough in the freezer. Meanwhile, roll up the remaining piece of dough in the shape of a circle. Grease the instant pot baking mold with ghee. Place the dough circle in the prepared baking mold. Then pour the blended raspberry mixture over it. Flatten it with the help of the spoon. Then grate the frozen piece of dough over the raspberries. Pour water and insert the trivet in the instant pot. Cover the pie with foil and put it on the trivet. Close the lid and cook the pie on manual mode (high pressure) for 25 minutes. When the time is finished, make a quick pressure release. Discard the foil from the pie and let it cool to the room temperature.

Nutrition value/serving: calories 118, fat 11.6, fiber 1.7, carbs 3, protein 2.4

Mint Cookies

Prep time: 10 minutes | Cooking time: 15 minutes | Servings: 4

Ingredients:
- ¼ cup Erythritol
- ½ teaspoon dried mint
- ¼ teaspoon mint extract
- 4 teaspoons cocoa powder
- 2 egg whites
- ¼ teaspoon baking powder
- ¼ teaspoon lemon juice
- 1 cup water, for cooking

Directions:
Whisk the egg whites gently and add dried mint. Then add Erythritol, mint extract, cocoa powder, baking powder, and lemon juice. Stir the mass until smooth. Pour water in the instant pot. Line the instant pot trivet with the baking paper. Place it in the instant pot. With the help of the scooper make 4 cookies and put them on the trivet. Close the lid and cook the cookies on manual mode (high pressure) for 15 minutes. When the time is over, make a quick pressure release. Open the lid and transfer the cookies on the plate or chopping board. Cool the cookies well.

Nutrition value/serving: calories 13, fat 0.3, fiber 0.6, carbs 1.3, protein 2.1

Coconut Clouds

Prep time: 10 minutes | Cooking time: 6 minutes | Servings: 2

Ingredients:
- 2 egg whites
- 4 tablespoons coconut flakes
- 1 tablespoon almond meal
- ¼ teaspoon ghee
- 1 teaspoon Erythritol

Directions:
Whisk the egg whites until strong peaks. Then slowly add the almond meal and coconut flakes. Add Erythritol and stir the mixture until homogenous with the help of the silicone spatula. Toss ghee in the instant pot and preheat it on sauté mode for 2 minutes. Then with the help of the spoon, make the clouds from egg white mixture and put them in the hot ghee. Close the lid and cook the dessert on sauté mode for 4 minutes.

Nutrition value/serving: calories 74, fat 5.4, fiber 1.3, carbs 2.4, protein 4.6

Shortbread Cookies

Prep time: 15 minutes | Cooking time: 14 minutes | Servings: 6

Ingredients:
- 1 egg, beaten
- ¾ teaspoon salt
- 1 tablespoon almond butter
- 1 teaspoon coconut oil
- ¼ teaspoon baking powder
- ¼ teaspoon apple cider vinegar
- 1 tablespoon Erythritol
- 5 oz coconut flour
- 1 cup water, for cooking

Directions:
Mix up egg with salt, almond butter, coconut flour, and baking powder. Add apple cider vinegar, coconut oil, and Erythritol. Knead the dough and make 6 balls from it. Then press the balls gently with the help of the hand palm and place in the non-sticky instant pot baking tray. Pour water and insert the trivet in the instant pot. Place the tray with cookies on the trivet and close the lid. Cook the cookies on manual mode (high pressure) for 14 minutes. When the time is over, make a quick pressure release and open the lid. Transfer the cooked cookies on the plate and let them cool well.

Nutrition value/serving: calories 135, fat 5.5, fiber 10.4, carbs 17.5, protein 4.9

Lime Bars

Prep time: 20 minutes | Cooking time: 10 minutes | Servings: 6

Ingredients:
- ½ cup coconut flour
- 2 teaspoons coconut oil
- ¼ teaspoon baking powder
- ½ tablespoon cream cheese
- 1/3 cup coconut cream
- 2 tablespoons lime juice
- 1 teaspoon lime zest, grated
- 2 tablespoons Erythritol
- 1 cup water, for cooking

Directions:
Knead the dough from coconut flour, coconut oil, baking powder, and cream cheese. When the mixture is soft and non-sticky, it is prepared. Then line the instant pot bowl with baking paper. Place the dough inside and flatten it in the shape of the pie crust (make the edges). Close the lid and cook it on sauté mode for 5 minutes. After this, switch off the instant pot. Make the filling: mix up coconut cream, lime juice, lime zest, and Erythritol. Then pour the liquid over the cooked pie crust and cook it on sauté mode for 5 minutes more. When the time is over, transfer the cooked meal in the freezer for 10 minutes. Cut the dessert into bars.

Nutrition value/serving: calories 88, fat 6, fiber 4.3, carbs 7.9, protein 1.7

Peppermint Cookies

Prep time: 20 minutes | Cooking time: 5 minutes | Servings: 2

Ingredients:
- ¼ teaspoon peppermint extract
- 2 tablespoons almond flour
- 1 teaspoon heavy cream
- ½ teaspoon butter, softened
- ¼ oz dark chocolate

Directions:
Preheat the instant pot on sauté mode for 3 minutes. Then add almond flour, butter, and heavy cream. Add peppermint extract and dark chocolate. Saute the mixture for 2 minutes. Stir well. Then line the tray with baking paper. With the help of the spoon make the cookies from the peppermint mixture and transfer on the prepared baking paper. Refrigerate the cookies for 20 minutes.

Nutrition value/serving: calories 199, fat 17.1, fiber 3.3, carbs 8.1, protein 6.2

Macadamia Cookies

Prep time: 15 minutes | Cooking time: 13 minutes | Servings: 4

Ingredients:
- 1 oz macadamia nuts, chopped
- ½ cup coconut flour
- 2 tablespoons butter
- 1 tablespoon Erythritol
- 1 egg, beaten
- 2 tablespoons flax meal
- 1 cup water, for cooking

Directions:
In the mixing bowl mix up macadamia nuts, coconut flour, butter, Erythritol, egg, and flax meal. Knead the non-sticky dough. Then cut the dough into the pieces and make balls from them. Pour water and insert the trivet in the instant pot. Line the trivet with baking paper and put the dough balls on it. Cook the cookies for 13 minutes on manual mode (high pressure). When the time is over, make a quick pressure release and transfer the cookies on the plate.

Nutrition value/serving: calories 193, fat 15.5, fiber 6.6, carbs 10.1, protein 4.8

Keto Pralines

Prep time: 10 minutes | Cooking time: 8 minutes | Servings: 6

Ingredients:
- ½ cup butter
- 5 tablespoons heavy cream
- 2 tablespoons Erythritol
- ¼ teaspoon xanthan gum
- 4 pecans, chopped

Directions:
Place the butter in the instant pot and melt it on sauté mode. Add heavy cream and Erythritol. Stir the mixture well and sauté for 2 minutes. After this, add xanthan gum and pecan. Stir well and cook the mixture for 3 minutes more. Line the baking tray with baking paper. With the help of the spoon, place the pecan mixture in the tray in the shape of circles. Refrigerate the pralines until they are solid.

Nutrition value/serving: calories 254, fat 26.6, fiber 3.5, carbs 4.2, protein 1.4

Blueberry Crisp

Prep time: 10 minutes | Cooking time: 6 minutes | Servings: 4

Ingredients:
- ¼ cup almonds, blended
- 1 teaspoon butter
- 1 teaspoon flax meal
- 1 tablespoon Erythritol
- ½ cup cream cheese
- ½ cup blueberries
- 1 oz peanuts, chopped

Directions:
Toss butter in the instant pot and melt it on sauté mode. Add almonds and flax meal. Cook the mixture on sauté mode for 4 minutes. Stir it constantly. After this, cool the mixture well. Whisk the cream cheese with Erythritol. Then put ½ of cream cheese mixture in the serving glasses. Add ½ part of the almond mixture and ½ part of blueberries. Repeat the same steps with remaining mixtures. Top the dessert with chopped peanuts.

Nutrition value/serving: calories 197, fat 17.8, fiber 2, carbs 6, protein 5.6

Chocolate and Bacon Bars

Prep time: 10 minutes | Cooking time: 8 minutes | Servings: 6

Ingredients:
- 2 oz dark chocolate, chopped
- 4 tablespoons heavy cream
- 1 bacon slice, chopped

Directions:
Place the bacon in the instant pot and cook it on sauté mode for 5 minutes or until it is crunchy. Then add heavy cream and dark chocolate. Stir the mixture well and cook for 2 minutes or until the chocolate is liquid. Then pour the mixture in the silicone bard mold and refrigerate until solid. Crack the dessert into the bars.

Nutrition value/serving: calories 102, fat 7.8, fiber 0.3, carbs 5.9, protein 2.1

Poppy Seeds Muffins

Prep time: 10 minutes | Cooking time: 13 minutes | Servings: 4

Ingredients:
- 2 eggs, beaten
- 2 tablespoons butter, melted
- ¼ cup Erythritol
- 1 teaspoon vanilla extract
- 1 teaspoon poppy seeds
- 1/3 cup coconut flour
- 1 cup water, for cooking

Directions:
Mix up together eggs, butter, Erythritol, vanilla extract, poppy seeds, and coconut flour. Pour the batter in the muffin molds. Pour water and insert the trivet in the instant pot. Place the muffin molds with batter on the trivet and close the lid. Cook the muffins on manual mode (high pressure) for 13 minutes. When the time is over, make a quick pressure release and transfer the muffins on the plate. Cool the dessert to the room temperature.

Nutrition value/serving: calories 129, fat 9.6, fiber 3.4, carbs 5.8, protein 4.3

Lemon Muffins

Prep time: 15 minutes | *Cooking time:* 10 minutes | *Servings:* 2

Ingredients:
- 1 tablespoon lemon juice
- 1 teaspoon lemon zest, grated
- ¼ teaspoon baking powder
- ½ cup almond meal
- ¼ cup heavy cream
- 2 teaspoons Splenda
- 1 cup water, for cooking

Directions:

Mix up together lemon juice, lemon zest, baking powder, almond meal, heavy cream, and Splenda. Fill the muffin molds with lemon mixture. Pour water and insert the steamer rack in the instant pot. Put the muffins on the steamer rack and close the lid. Cook the muffins on manual mode (high pressure) for 10 minutes. Then allow the natural pressure release for 5 minutes. Cool the cooked muffins well.

Nutrition value/serving: calories 212, fat 17.5, fiber 3.1, carbs 10.2, protein 5.4

Lime Chia Seeds Pudding

Prep time: 5 minutes | *Cooking time:* 30 minutes | *Servings:* 2

Ingredients:
- ½ cup coconut cream
- 1 oz chia seeds
- 1 tablespoon Erythritol
- ½ teaspoon vanilla extract
- 1 teaspoon lime zest, grated

Directions:

Put all ingredients in the instant pot bowl and stir with the help of the spoon. Close the lid and cook the pudding on manual mode (Low pressure) for 30 minutes. Then transfer the cooked pudding in the serving glasses.

Nutrition value/serving: calories 210, fat 18.7, fiber 6.3, carbs 9.6, protein 3.7

Phirni Kheer with Almonds

Prep time: 10 minutes | *Cooking time:* 65 minutes | *Servings:* 3

Ingredients:
- ½ cup whipped cream
- ½ teaspoon ground cardamom
- ½ cup of organic almond milk
- 1 scoop stevia
- ¼ cup coconut flour
- ¼ teaspoon vanilla extract

Directions:

Pour whipped cream and almond milk in the instant pot. Add ground cardamom, coconut flour, and vanilla extract. Add stevia and stir the liquid well. Cook the mixture on sauté mode for 5 minutes. Stir it from time to time. Then switch the instant pot on manual mode (low pressure). Cook the meal for 1 hour. Stir the cooked kheer well and pour into the serving glasses.

Nutrition value/serving: calories 114, fat 8.5, fiber 3.8, carbs 6.9, protein 2.1

Tagalong Bars

Prep time: 10 minutes | *Cooking time:* 15 minutes | *Servings:* 8

Ingredients:
- 1 cup almond flour
- ¾ teaspoon baking powder
- ¼ teaspoon vanilla extract
- 1 teaspoon Erythritol
- ¼ cup peanut butter
- 2 tablespoons coconut oil
- 1 cup water, for cooking

Directions:

Make the dough: mix up almond flour with baking powder, vanilla extract, Erythritol, and coconut oil. In the end, you should get a non-sticky soft dough. Line the instant pot trivet with baking paper and put the dough on it. Then flatten it well and cover with the second baking paper sheet. Pour water in the instant pot. Place the trivet with the dough in the instant pot and close the lid. Cook the dessert on manual mode (high pressure) for 15 minutes. When the time is over, make a quick pressure release and transfer the cooked dough on the plate. Spread the surface of the dough with peanut butter and cut it into the bars.

Nutrition value/serving: calories 97, fat 9.2, fiber 0.9, carbs 2.6, protein 2.8

Keto Marshmallows

Prep time: 30 minutes | Cooking time: 10 minutes | Servings: 30

Ingredients:
- 6 oz water
- 1 oz gelatin
- 1 cup xylitol
- Cooking spray

Directions:
Pour 2 oz of water in the bowl. Sprinkle gelatin over the water and stir. Leave the gelatin mixture for 5-10 minutes. Meanwhile, set the sauté mode on your instant pot. Pour the remaining water in the instant pot and bring it to boil (appx.6 minutes). Then add xylitol and stir it well until it is dissolved. Cook the liquid for 2 minutes more and switch off the instant pot. Start to whisk the liquid with the help of the hand blender for 3 minutes. Then add gelatin mixture and whisk the mass until it is thick and white. Then spray the baking mold with cooking spray. Pour the white sweet mixture in the mold and flatten it. Let the marshmallow rest for 20-30 minutes. When the marshmallow mixture is solid, cut it into serving bars.

Nutrition value/serving: calories 8, fat 0, fiber 0, carbs 1.3, protein 0.8

Tiger Butter

Prep time: 10 minutes | Cooking time: 15 minutes | Servings: 5

Ingredients:
- 1 oz dark chocolate, chopped
- 2 tablespoons peanut butter
- 3 tablespoons almond butter
- 1 tablespoon coconut butter
- 2 tablespoons Erythritol
- 2 tablespoons heavy cream
- ½ teaspoon vanilla extract

Directions:
Set the sauté mode and adjust 10 minutes. Put the peanut butter, almond butter, and coconut butter in the instant pot and melt it. Stir it from time to time during melting. Then add Erythritol and vanilla extract, and stir it well until it is dissolved. Then pour the butte liquid in the silicone square mold. Put the chocolate in the instant pot. Add heavy cream. Cook the ingredients on sauté mode for 4-5 minutes or until you get a liquid chocolate mixture. Then sprinkle the butter mixture with the chocolate mixture (make the swirls on the butter surface). Refrigerate the tiger butter until it is solid.

Nutrition value/serving: calories 167, fat 14.3, fiber 2, carbs 7.4, protein 4.4

Coffee Panna Cotta

Prep time: 30 minutes | Cooking time: 10 minutes | Servings: 4

Ingredients:
- 1 teaspoon instant coffee
- 1 ½ cup of coconut milk
- 2 tablespoons gelatin
- ½ teaspoon vanilla extract
- 1 tablespoon Erythritol

Directions:
Pour 1 cup of coconut milk in the instant pot. Preheat it on sauté mode for 4 minutes. Stir it from time to time with the help of the spoon. Meanwhile, mix up together remaining coconut milk with gelatin. When the coconut milk is warm but not hot, add vanilla extract and Erythritol. Stir the liquid until Erythritol is dissolved. Then switch off the instant pot. Add gelatin liquid in the warm coconut milk and stir well until gelatin is dissolved. Pour the coconut milk liquid into the ramekins and refrigerate for 30 minutes. When the panna cotta is solid, sprinkle it with instant coffee.

Nutrition value/serving: calories 220, fat 21.5, fiber 2, carbs 5.1, protein 5.1

Almond Milk Pudding with Nuts

Prep time: 15 minutes | *Cooking time:* 9 minutes | *Servings:* 3

Ingredients:
- 1 cup organic almond milk
- 3 teaspoons Splenda
- 1 tablespoon gelatin
- 3 teaspoons peanuts, chopped

Directions:

Whisk together gelatin and 3 tablespoons of almond milk. Pour all remaining milk in the instant pot. Add Splenda and cook it on sauté mode for 5 minutes. Stir the liquid from time to time. Then add gelatin mixture and stir until gelatin is dissolved. Switch off the instant pot. Pour the pudding into the ramekins and pour with peanuts. Let the pudding rest for 15-20 minutes in the fridge before serving.

Nutrition value/serving: calories 58, fat 2.5, fiber 0.3, carbs 4.5, protein 3.1

CONCLUSION

This book is a wonderful guide in the world of delicious and easy meals. After reading the last recipe you already understood that a keto diet is simple to follow if you have an instant pot. There is a lot of questions about why this kitchen equipment is so special. The answer is obvious: it is a multi cook which can implement in life your bravest culinary desires. The standard models of Instant pot include slow cooker, rice cooker, yogurt maker; they also have steam, saute, stew, and warm modes. Nevertheless, you are not restricted only by these specific sets of cooking regimes. It is possible to adjust the timer for any meal. Time goes and scientists develop new instant pot models. For instance, the newest type of instant pot is more functional in comparison with its old mates. It includes air fryer, roast, broil, and reheat modes. Some of the kitchen machines are equipped with rotate mode for rotisserie-style cooking.

Below you can find some tips which will help to use instant pot more efficiently:

1. Such vegetables as broccoli, zucchini, some type of mushrooms, kale, and Brussels sprouts can be overcooked fastly; to avoid it, it is recommended to use quick pressure release to release the steam and minimum time for cooking (maximum 5-6 minutes).

2. For tender, juicy, and fragrant meat chunks while using Steam mode – add spices and vegetables in water for steaming.

3. Connect the instant pot to your phone via Bluetooth. It will save your time and make the process of cooking more comfortable.

4. Remaining fat can be easily removed. All you need is to pour warm water and a small amount of liquid dishwasher in the instant pot bowl and then wash it with the sponge.

The instant pot is the perfect combination of healthy and tasty meals.

This cookbook was created to make your life easier. There are only benefits of it. The book is a perfect solution for freshmen and profi in cooking and wonderful inspirator for keto lovers!

Recipe Index

ALMOND
Butter Crepes, 13
Egg Benedict Sandwich, 29
Breakfast Kale Bread, 30
Green Beans Casserole, 62
Zucchini, 63
Salmon Pie, 97
Keto Cereal Bowl, 13
Keto Vanilla Crescent Cookies, 186
Blueberry Crisp, 194
Keto Oatmeal, 24
Parmesan Chicken Balls, 31
Chicken Paprika, 43
Parmesan Onion Rings, 64
Cauliflower Gnocchi, 66
Cheddar Tots with Broccoli, 67
Broccoli Nuggets, 69
Oregano Fennel Steaks, 70
Baked Green Beans, 73
Garlic Bread, 74
Zucchini Fries in Bacon, 76
Oregano Keto Bread Rounds, 77
Cheese Almond Meal Bites, 78
Popcorn Chicken, 81
Aromatic Swedish Meatballs, 83
Salmon and Kohlrabi Gratin, 105
Turkey Stuffed Mushrooms, 132
Scalloped Cabbage, 164
Lava Cake, 182
Keto Carrot Pie, 183
Lavender Pie, 184
Coconut Clouds, 192
Lemon Muffins, 195

ALMOND BUTTER
Bacon Eggs with Chives, 18
Sweet Porridge, 27
Salmon Balls, 32
Beef Cabbage Soup, 36
Keto Lunch Bowl, 41
Asiago Cauliflower Rice, 70
Tender Jicama Fritters, 78
Keto Queso Dip, 80
Brazilian Fish Stew, 96
Beef and Squash Ragu, 147
Italian Beef, 150
Tuscan Mushrooms Sauce, 166
Garlic Okra, 177
Almond Tart, 179
Keto Carrot Pie, 183
Pecan Pie, 183
Fat Bomb Jars, 187
Avocado Brownies, 188
Keto Blondies, 189
Shortbread Cookies, 192

Tiger Butter, 196

ALMOND FLAKES
Almond Tart, 179

ALMOND MILK
Sweet Porridge, 27
Zuppa Toscana, 55
Cauliflower Cheese, 61
Oregano Fennel Steaks, 70
Chocolate Shake, 94
Beef & Cabbage Stew, 148
Cauliflower Risotto, 163
Scalloped Cabbage, 164
Almond Tart, 179
Fluffy Donuts, 191
Phirni Kheer with Almonds, 195
Almond Milk Pudding with Nuts, 197

ANCHOVIES
Ancho Chili, 53

ANISE
Taiwanese Braised Pork Belly, 141

ARTICHOKES
Warm Antipasto Salad, 72
Fragrant Artichoke Hearts, 170
Lemon Artichoke, 171

ARUGULA
Frittata with Greens, 21
Bacon Salad with Eggs, 28
Sautéed Arugula Mash, 176

ASPARAGUS
Herbed Asparagus, 65
Steamed Asparagus, 68
Spiced Asparagus, 75
Bacon Bites with Asparagus, 76
Butter Chicken Stew, 127
Garlic and Cheese Baked Asparagus, 159

AVOCADO
Breakfast Avocado Bombs, 17
Avocado Boats with Omelet, 19
Breakfast Stuffed Avocado, 25
Classic Breakfast Casserole, 28
Cobb Salad, 41
Avocado Chicken Salad, 55
Keto Guacamole Deviled Eggs, 86
Bacon Avocado Bombs, 88
Edamame Hummus, 90
Tuna Salad, 98
Shrimp Salad with Avocado, 101

Chicken Stuffed Avocado, 129
Avocado Pie, 171
Avocado Pesto Zoodles, 174
Avocado Brownies, 188

AVOCADO OIL
Green Hash, 16
Breakfast Avocado Bombs, 17
Ham Roll, 18
Breakfast Sausages, 34
Chicken Enchilada Soup, 39
Lobster Salad, 41
Pork Roast with Sauerkraut, 52
Bacon Brussels Sprouts, 58
Fried Cauliflower Slices, 59
Zucchini, 63
Turnip Cubes, 65
Cilantro-Kale Salad, 65
Vegetable Fritters, 68
Jalapeno Popper Bread, 73
Turnip Fries, 81
Aromatic Swedish Meatballs, 83
Heart of Palm Dip, 85
Hot Tempeh, 87
Bacon-Wrapped Shrimps, 90
Marinated Olives, 91
Chicharrones, 91
Cauliflower PopCorn, 93
Salmon in Fragrant Sauce, 100
Shrimp Tacos, 101
Crab Melt with Zucchini, 103
Baked Snapper, 104
Paprika Salmon Skewers, 106
Parmesan Scallops, 106
Mussels Mariniere, 108
Tuna Rolls, 109
Halibut Ceviche, 113
Parchment Fish, 113
Poached Cod, 114
Chicken Tonnato, 116
Paprika Chicken Wings, 116
Hoagie Bowl, 119
Chicken Zucchini Enchiladas, 122
Balsamic Roast Chicken, 123
Chicken Divan Casserole, 125
Chicken Crust Pizza, 128
Blackened Chicken, 133
Ground Turkey Chili, 134
Chicken Moussaka, 136
Rosemary Barbecue Pork Chops, 138
Char Siu, 140
Chili Spare Ribs, 140
Taiwanese Braised Pork Belly, 141
Korean Style Pork Ribs, 141
Sage Pork Loin, 143
Pork and Celery Curry, 146
Beef Tips, 147

Prosciutto and Eggs Salad, 149
Spoon Lamb, 153
Burger Casserole, 155
Pork Belly Salad, 158
Wrapped Bacon Carrot, 159
Cauliflower Florets Mix, 160
Tender Sautéed Vegetables, 161
Green Peas Salad, 163
Collard Greens with Cherry Tomatoes, 164
Thyme Cauliflower Head, 166
Marinated Tomatillos Paste, 168
Steamed Broccoli Raab (Rabe), 170
Lemon Artichoke, 171
Peppers & Cheese Salad, 173
Baked Eggplant Mash, 177

BACON
Breakfast Stuffed Avocado, 25
Provolone Chicken Soup, 35
Keto "Potato" Soup, 36
Bacon Chowder, 37
Creamy Cauliflower Soup, 39
Sour Cauliflower Salad, 43
Clam Chowder, 47
Tuscan Soup, 54
Bacon Brussels Sprouts, 58
Spinach Mash with Bacon, 58
Jalapeno Popper Bread, 73
Bacon Bites with Asparagus, 76
Seafood Bisque, 107
Chicken Cheese Calzone, 127
Burger Casserole, 155
Shredded Spaghetti Squash with Bacon, 163
Bacon Egg Cups, 16
Breakfast Avocado Bombs, 17
Bacon Eggs with Chives, 18
Bacon Tacos, 19
Morning Bacon Bombs, 23
Egg Sandwich, 23
Bacon Salad with Eggs, 28
Kalua Chicken, 46
Pork Roast with Sauerkraut, 52
Gouda Vegetable Casserole, 72
Bacon Onion Rings, 76
Bacon Avocado Bombs, 88
Bacon Sushi, 88
Bacon-Wrapped Shrimps, 90
Chocolate Bacon, 93
Wrapped Chicken Cubes, 95
Shrimp Salad with Avocado, 101
Bacon-Wrapped Cod, 111
Crab Rangoon Fat Bombs, 112
Tuna and Bacon Cups, 113
Caesar Salad, 118
BLT Chicken Wrap, 119
Bacon-Wrapped Chicken Tenders, 130
Chicken Fricassee, 135

Ground Meat Stew, 144
Kalua Pork, 152
Wrapped Bacon Carrot, 159
Chocolate and Bacon Bars, 194

BEANS (EDAMAME)
Edamame Hummus, 90
Turkey Soup, 135

BEANS (GREEN)
Crustless Egg Pie, 32
Green Beans with Ham, 50
Green Beans Casserole, 62
Cayenne Pepper Green Beans, 68
Sichuan Style Green Beans, 71
Baked Green Beans, 73
Crunchy Green Beans, 82
Chicken Moussaka, 136
Lemongrass Green Beans, 161
Green Beans Salad, 165

BEANS (MUNG)
Butter Edamame Beans, 167

BEANS (SNAP)
Beef Curry Soup, 52

BEEF
Meat Sandwich, 13
Zucchini Meat Cups, 16
Minced Beef Pancakes, 17
Breakfast Taco Omelet, 22
Chili Casserole, 26
Breakfast Spaghetti Squash Casserole, 27
Nutritious Taco Skillet, 29
Keto Taco Soup, 38
Southwestern Chili, 47
Parsley Meatloaf, 47
Corned Beef with Cabbage, 51
Reuben Soup, 54
Zuppa Toscana, 55
Aromatic Swedish Meatballs, 83
Keto Nachos, 89
Cheese Meatballs with Greens, 95
Ground Meat Stew, 144
Hoisin Meatballs, 145
Beef Tips, 147
Beef & Cabbage Stew, 148
Tender Salisbury Steak, 148
Meat&Cheese Pie, 155
Burger Casserole, 155
Ground Beef Skewers, 157
Pastrami, 158
Beef Cabbage Soup, 36
Asian Style Zucchini Soup, 38
Hot Sausages Soup, 46
Fajita Soup, 46

200

Lunch Pot Roast, 49
Lazy Meat Mix, 51
Beef Curry Soup, 52
Low Carb Zucchini and Eggplant Soup, 56
Taco Shells, 86
Korean Style Pork Ribs, 141
Hoisin Meatballs, 145
Beef and Squash Ragu, 147
Beef Loin with Acorn Squash, 147
Keto Oxtail Goulash, 150
Keto Oxtail Goulash, 150
Italian Beef, 150
Thyme Braised Beef, 150
Butter Lamb, 151
Dhansak Curry Meat, 151
Mint Lamb Cubes, 152
Kalua Pork, 152
Rogan Josh, 153
Butter Edamame Beans, 167
Cream of Celery, 169
Garlic Okra, 177
Beet Cubes with Pecans, 73

BELL PEPPER
Paprika Eggs in Pepper Holes, 15
Keto Shakshuka, 22
Egg Muffins, 23
Classic Breakfast Casserole, 28
Spinach Casserole, 33
Jalapeno Soup, 35
Chicken Enchilada Soup, 39
Tuscan Soup, 54
Mexican Style Keto Rice, 60
Low Carb Fall Vegetables, 67
Chicken Cacciatore, 122
Chicken & Snap Pea Salad, 124
Chicken Scarpariello, 125
Cauliflower Shepherd's Pie, 156

BELL PEPPER (GREEN)
Keto Lunch Bowl, 41
Stuffed Pepper Halves with Omelet, 15
Hot Sausages Soup, 46
Fajita Soup, 46
Keto Nachos, 89
Fajita Chicken Casserole, 136
Peppers & Cheese Salad, 173
Brazilian Fish Stew, 96
Crab Melt with Zucchini, 103
Chicken Zucchini Enchiladas, 122
Chicken Moussaka, 136
Tender Sautéed Vegetables, 161
Bell Pepper Pizza, 173
Cream of Celery, 169

BELL PEPPER (RED)
Baked Snapper, 104

Marinated Red Bell Peppers, 69

BLACKBERRIES
Blackberry Pork Chops, 146
Lavender Pie, 184

BLUEBERRIES
Blueberry Muffins, 31
Blueberry Parfait, 184
Blueberry Clusters, 187
Blueberry Crisp, 194

BOK CHOY
Breakfast Egg Hash, 19
Sausages & Vegetable Stew, 40
Bok Choy Salad, 173

BROCCOLI
Mini Frittatas, 29
Chicken Fritters, 31
Broccoli Toast Spread, 33
Keto Lunch Bowl, 41
Cheddar Soup, 49
Cheddar Tots with Broccoli, 67
Broccoli Nuggets, 69
Fish Pie, 111
Fajita Chicken Casserole, 136
Ground Meat Stew, 144
Broccoli Soup, 56
Steamed Broccoli, 67
Parmesan Broccoli Head, 74
Crab&Broccoli Casserole, 112
Zingy Fish, 115
Chicken Divan Casserole, 125
Cauliflower Florets Mix, 160
Steamed Broccoli Raab (Rabe), 170

BRUSSELS SPROUTS
Mashed Brussel Sprouts, 59
Brussels Sprouts Casserole, 57
Bacon Brussels Sprouts, 58
Brussels Sprouts in Heavy Cream, 159
Balsamic Brussels Sprouts, 160

BUTTER
Meat Sandwich, 13
Butter Crepes, 13
Soft Eggs, 14
Bacon Egg Cups, 16
Spiced Hard-Boiled Eggs, 17
Breakfast Egg Hash, 19
Cauliflower Toast, 20
Breakfast Taco Omelet, 22
Oregano Egg en Cocotte, 24
Morning Pudding, 25
Layered Casserole, 25

Breakfast Hot Cacao, 26
Zucchini Cheese Fritters, 26
Egg Benedict Sandwich, 29
Egg Scramble, 30
Crustless Egg Pie, 32
Broccoli Toast Spread, 33
Butternut Squash Soup, 37
Tortilla Soup, 37
Bone Broth Soup, 40
Sausages & Vegetable Stew, 40
Chicken Paprika, 43
Warm Radish Salad, 43
Zoodle Soup, 45
Fajita Soup, 46
Southwestern Chili, 47
Parsley Meatloaf, 47
Meat & Collard Greens Bowl, 48
Lunch Pot Roast, 49
Spiral Ham, 50
Coconut Soup, 50
Corned Beef with Cabbage, 51
Manhattan Chowder, 53
Zuppa Toscana, 55
Broccoli Soup, 56
Rosemary&Butter Mushrooms, 57
Mashed Cauliflower, 58
Soft Spinach with Dill, 60
Butter Spaghetti Squash, 61
Green Beans Casserole, 62
Turnip Creamy Gratin, 63
Parmesan Onion Rings, 64
Sweet Baby Carrot, 64
Herbed Asparagus, 65
Cauliflower Gnocchi, 66
Low Carb Fall Vegetables, 67
Broccoli Nuggets, 69
Butter Shirataki Noodles, 70
Spaghetti Squash Mac&Cheese, 71
Baked Green Beans, 73
Spiced Asparagus, 75
Soul Bread, 77
Spiced Chicken Carnitas, 78
Zucchini Parsley Tots, 79
Keto Jalapeno Bread, 80
Parmesan Cauliflower Tots, 83
Kale Wraps, 83
Bread Twists, 84
Butter Coffee, 84
Pesto Wings, 87
Keto Taquitos, 89
Keto Spanakopita Pie Slices, 92
Wrapped Chicken Cubes, 95
Salmon Pie, 97
Pesto Salmon, 97
Seafood Omelet, 101
Butter Scallops, 103
Butter Cod Loin, 104

Tuscan Shrimps, 106
Parmesan Scallops, 106
Lobster Bisque, 107
Tarragon Lobster, 107
Dill Halibut, 110
Spinach and Tilapia Casserole, 111
Fish Pie, 111
Mackerel Pate, 112
Parchment Fish, 113
Salmon with Lemon, 115
Garlic Chicken Drumsticks, 116
Chicken with Blue Cheese Sauce, 117
Chicken Stroganoff, 126
Pecan Chicken, 126
Chicken Cheese Calzone, 127
Butter Chicken Stew, 127
Chicken Cauliflower Rice, 128
Chicken Stuffed Avocado, 129
Chicken Cordon Bleu, 129
Chicken Liver Pate, 131
Coconut Chicken Cubes, 131
Blackened Chicken, 133
Keto Ham, 139
Korean Style Pork Ribs, 141
Pork and Turnip Cake, 141
Spinach and Fennel Pork Stew, 143
Ham and Cheese Dinner Casserole, 146
Blackberry Pork Chops, 146
Onion Baby Back Ribs, 148
Cumin Kielbasa, 149
Thyme Braised Beef, 150
Butter Lamb, 151
Pork Chops in Sweet Sauce, 152
Meat&Cheese Pie, 155
Brussels Sprouts in Heavy Cream, 159
Lemongrass Green Beans, 161
Cauliflower Gratin, 164
Stuffed Spaghetti Squash, 166
Baked Kabocha Squash, 167
Butter Edamame Beans, 167
Steamed Rutabaga Mash, 170
Fragrant Artichoke Hearts, 170
Avocado Pie, 171
Zucchini Pasta with Blue Cheese, 171
Zucchini Boats, 172
Avocado Pesto Zoodles, 174
Portobello Toasts, 174
Mushrooms and Tofu Scramble, 175
Sautéed Arugula Mash, 176
Masala Cauliflower, 176
Pumpkin Pie Cups, 178
Pumpkin Spices Pudding, 179
Spice Pie, 180
Keto Cheesecake, 181
Butter Cake, 181
Cinnamon Mini Rolls, 181
Lava Cake, 182

Rhubarb Custard, 182
Chocolate Mousse, 182
Cocoa-Vanilla Pudding, 183
Pecan Pie, 183
Lavender Pie, 184
Mug Cake, 185
Coconut Cake, 185
Walnut pie, 186
Keto Chip Cookies, 186
Keto Vanilla Crescent Cookies, 186
Strawberry Cubes, 187
Peanut Butter Balls, 190
Cinnamon Muffins, 190
Keto Fudge, 190
Raspberry Pie, 191
Peppermint Cookies, 193
Macadamia Cookies, 193
Keto Pralines, 194
Blueberry Crisp, 194
Poppy Seeds Muffins, 194

BUTTERNUT
Butternut Squash Soup, 37
Butternut Squash Fries, 81

CABBAGE
Sour Cauliflower Salad, 43
Corned Beef with Cabbage, 51
Winter Soup, 54
Winter Soup, 54
Thyme Purple Cabbage Steaks, 66
Cabbage Chips, 77

CABBAGE (SAVOY)
Sausages & Vegetable Stew, 40

CABBAGE (WHITE)
Cabbage Hash Browns, 14
Bacon Tacos, 19
Beef Cabbage Soup, 36
Cobb Salad, 41
White Cabbage in Cream, 60
Turmeric Cabbage Rice, 63
Shrimp Tacos, 101
Beef & Cabbage Stew, 148
Kalua Pork, 152
Green Peas Salad, 163
Cabbage Dippers, 177

CARB TORTILLAS
Tortilla Soup, 37
Keto Taquitos, 89
Cheese Melt, 98
Shrimp Tacos, 101
BLT Chicken Wrap, 119

CARROT

Zucchini Meat Cups, 16
Bone Broth Soup, 40
Tuscan Soup, 54
Sweet Baby Carrot, 64
Chicken Lettuce Rolls, 132
Turkey Bolognese Sauce, 132
Chicken Fricassee, 135
Chicken Steamed Balls, 135
Keto Oxtail Goulash, 150
Keto Carrot Pie, 183
Wrapped Bacon Carrot, 159

CAULIFLOWER
Cauliflower Bake, 20
Cauliflower Toast, 20
Morning Bacon Bombs, 23
Cauliflower Fritters, 27
Keto "Potato" Soup, 36
Creamy Cauliflower Soup, 39
Sour Cauliflower Salad, 43
Clam Chowder, 47
Tuscan Soup, 54
Zuppa Toscana, 55
Cauliflower Mac&Cheese, 57
Mashed Cauliflower, 58
Cauliflower Rice, 59
Mexican Style Keto Rice, 60
Cauliflower Cheese, 61
Cauli-Tatoes, 61
Cauliflower Gnocchi, 66
Smashed Cauliflower with Goat Cheese, 66
Vegetable Fritters, 68
Roasted Cauliflower Steak, 68
Asiago Cauliflower Rice, 70
Cauliflower Tortillas, 71
Side Dish Cauliflower Ziti, 74
Parmesan Cauliflower Tots, 83
Crab Spread, 90
Mussels Casserole, 102
Chicken Cauliflower Rice, 128
South American Garden Chicken, 136
Lamb Pulao, 154
Cauliflower Shepherd's Pie, 156
Cauliflower Risotto, 163
Cauliflower Gratin, 164
Low Carb Falafel, 175
Fried Cauliflower Slices, 59
Cauliflower Salad with Provolone Cheese, 75
Cauliflower PopCorn, 93
Cauliflower Florets Mix, 160
Hash Brown Casserole, 165
Thyme Cauliflower Head, 166
Masala Cauliflower, 176

CELERY
Hot Sausages Soup, 46
Seafood Bisque, 107

Lobster Bisque, 107
Breakfast Egg Hash, 19
Chicken Salad, 33
Buffalo Chicken Soup, 40
Lobster Salad, 41
Southwestern Chili, 47
Clam Chowder, 47
Manhattan Chowder, 53
Gouda Vegetable Casserole, 72
Chicken Celery Boats, 89
Tuna Salad, 98
Cajun Crab Casserole, 103
Fish Pie, 111
Ground Chicken Mix, 130
Turkey Soup, 135
Chicken Fricassee, 135
South American Garden Chicken, 136
Ground Meat Stew, 144
Pork and Celery Curry, 146
Keto Oxtail Goulash, 150
Spoon Lamb, 153
White Pork Soup, 154
Vegetable Soup, 169
Cream of Celery, 169

CHEESE (ASIAGO)
Asiago Cauliflower Rice, 70
Asiago Chicken Drumsticks, 128

CHEESE (BLUE)
Chicken with Blue Cheese Sauce, 117
Zucchini Pasta with Blue Cheese, 171

CHEESE (CHEDDAR)
Burger Casserole, 155
Zucchini Meat Cups, 16
Green Hash, 16
Breakfast Avocado Bombs, 17
Bacon Tacos, 19
Cauliflower Toast, 20
Sausage Casserole, 21
Layered Casserole, 25
Chili Casserole, 26
Cauliflower Fritters, 27
Mini Casserole in Jars, 32
Keto "Potato" Soup, 36
Tortilla Soup, 37
Creamy Cauliflower Soup, 39
Egg & Cheese Salad with Dill, 42
Cheddar Soup, 49
Reuben Soup, 54
Broccoli Soup, 56
Squash Casserole, 62
Turnip Creamy Gratin, 63
Cheddar Tots with Broccoli, 67
Eggplant Gratin, 72
Jalapeno Popper Bread, 73

Oregano Keto Bread Rounds, 77
Tender Jicama Fritters, 78
Cheese Almond Meal Bites, 78
Bread Twists, 84
Keto Taquitos, 89
Keto Spanakopita Pie Slices, 92
Keto Cheetos, 92
Cheese Melt, 98
Mussels Casserole, 102
Cajun Crab Casserole, 103
Spinach and Tilapia Casserole, 111
Crab Rangoon Fat Bombs, 112
Crab&Broccoli Casserole, 112
Hoagie Bowl, 119
Chicken Zucchini Enchiladas, 122
Chicken Crust Pizza, 128
Chicken Stuffed Avocado, 129
Fajita Chicken Casserole, 136
Ham and Cheese Dinner Casserole, 146
Cauliflower Shepherd's Pie, 156
Zoodle Pork Casserole, 157
Hash Brown Casserole, 165
Stuffed Spaghetti Squash, 166
Cheddar Mushrooms, 169
Avocado Pie, 171
Keto Club Salad, 172
Pesto Zucchini Bake, 176
Paprika Eggs in Pepper Holes, 15
Cheese Chips, 84
Lime Salmon Burger, 99

CHEESE (COTIJA)
Shrimp Tacos, 101
CHEESE (EDAM)
Spaghetti Squash Mac&Cheese, 71
Peppers & Cheese Salad, 173

CHEESE (FETA)
Feta and Zucchini Bowl, 64
Breakfast Crustless Quiche, 22
Cobb Salad, 41
Greek Chicken, 121

CHEESE (GOAT)
Smashed Cauliflower with Goat Cheese, 66
Cheese Meatballs with Greens, 95
Spinach Stuffed Chicken, 124
Green Beans Salad, 165

CHEESE (GOUDA)
Breakfast Crustless Quiche, 22
Gouda Vegetable Casserole, 72

CHEESE (JARLSBERG)
Keto Jalapeno Bread, 80
Ham and Cheese Dinner Casserole, 146
Cumin Kielbasa, 149

Spinach and Jarlsberg Pie, 174

CHEESE (MEXICAN)
Nutritious Taco Skillet, 29
Keto Queso Dip, 80

CHEESE (MONTEREY JACK)
Classic Breakfast Casserole, 28
Brussels Sprouts Casserole, 57
Cheesy Radish, 65
Crab Melt with Zucchini, 103
Scalloped Cabbage, 164

CHEESE (MOZZARELLA)
Stuffed Pepper Halves with Omelet, 15
Ham Roll, 18
Mason Jar Omelet, 20
Cheese Egg Balls, 21
Zucchini Cheese Fritters, 26
Breakfast Spaghetti Squash Casserole, 27
Aromatic Lasagna with Basil, 35
Sliced Zucchini Casserole, 62
Zucchini, 63
Mini Cheese Pepperoni Pizza, 80
Mini Margharita Pizzas in Mushroom Caps, 86
Keto Crackers, 95
Tuna and Bacon Cups, 113
Chicken Divan Casserole, 125
Cayenne Pepper Chicken Meatballs, 126
Chicken Cheese Calzone, 127
Chicken Crust Pizza, 128
Turkey Stuffed Mushrooms, 132
Garlic and Cheese Baked Asparagus, 159
Cauliflower Gratin, 164
Stuffed Mushrooms, 165
Warm Antipasto Salad, 72
Keto Ratatouille, 175
Side Dish Cauliflower Ziti, 74
Keto Breadsticks, 82
Chicken Caprese Casserole, 118
Pizza Stuffed Chicken, 119
Mozzarella Chicken Fillets, 120
Chicken with Black Olives, 137
Meat&Cheese Pie, 155
Caprese Zoodles, 160
Zucchini Boats, 172
Bell Pepper Pizza, 173

CHEESE (PARMESAN)
Avocado Boats with Omelet, 19
Cauliflower Bake, 20
Hot Jalapeno Poppers Mix, 24
Breakfast Stuffed Avocado, 25
Mini Frittatas, 29
Parmesan Chicken Balls, 31
Kale Soup, 39
Parsley Meatloaf, 47

Cheesy Pork Rinds, 52
Kale&Parmesan Bowl, 60
Cauliflower Cheese, 61
Parmesan Onion Rings, 64
Cauliflower Gnocchi, 66
Spaghetti Squash Mac&Cheese, 71
Garlic Bread, 74
Parmesan Broccoli Head, 74
Zucchini Fries in Bacon, 76
Cabbage Chips, 77
Parmesan Tomatoes Slices, 79
Parmesan Cauliflower Tots, 83
Fish Casserole, 97
Seafood Omelet, 101
Cod in Cream Sauce, 105
Parmesan Scallops, 106
Salmon under Parmesan Blanket, 108
Garlic Chicken Drumsticks, 116
Caesar Salad, 118
BLT Chicken Wrap, 119
Coconut Chicken Tenders, 123
Chicken Stroganoff, 126
Parmesan Pork, 138
Parmesan Pork Tenderloins, 139
Pork Belly Salad, 158
Collard Greens with Cherry Tomatoes, 164
Tuscan Mushrooms Sauce, 166
Bell Pepper Pizza, 173
Peppers & Cheese Salad, 173
Portobello Toasts, 174

CHEESE (PROVOLONE)
Provolone Chicken Soup, 35
Cauliflower Mac&Cheese, 57
Spinach Mash with Bacon, 58
Broccoli Nuggets, 69
Baked Green Beans, 73
Cauliflower Salad with Provolone Cheese, 75
Zucchini Parsley Tots, 79
Heart of Palm Dip, 85
Keto Nachos, 89
Cheese Pops, 93
Salmon and Kohlrabi Gratin, 105
Tuscan Shrimps, 106
Meat&Cheese Pie, 155
Sautéed Arugula Mash, 176
Bruschetta Chicken, 120

CHEESE (RICOTTA)
Aromatic Lasagna with Basil, 35
Butternut Squash Soup, 37
Side Dish Cauliflower Ziti, 74
Tuna Salad, 98
Skagenrora, 102
Crab Melt with Zucchini, 103
Crab&Broccoli Casserole, 112
Chicken Tonnato, 116

Chicken Lettuce Rolls, 132
Keto Fudge, 190

CHEESE (SWISS)
Turkey Bolognese Sauce, 132
Chicken Cordon Bleu, 129

CHIA SEEDS
Sweet Porridge, 27
Low-Carb Flaxseed Brule, 28
Lime Chia Seeds Pudding, 195

CHICKEN
Cauliflower Toast, 20
Layered Casserole, 25
Parmesan Chicken Balls, 31
Chicken Fritters, 31
Kale Wraps, 83
Ranch Poppers, 88
Cayenne Pepper Chicken Meatballs, 126
Chicken Crust Pizza, 128
Herbed Whole Chicken, 129
Ground Chicken Mix, 130
Keto Chicken Burger, 131
Chicken Lettuce Rolls, 132
Blackened Chicken, 133
Chicken Steamed Balls, 135
Ground Meat Stew, 144
Bacon Tacos, 19
Hot Jalapeno Poppers Mix, 24
Crustless Egg Pie, 32
Chicken Salad, 33
Provolone Chicken Soup, 35
Egg Soup, 36
Bacon Chowder, 37
Butternut Squash Soup, 37
Tortilla Soup, 37
Tortilla Soup, 37
Asian Style Zucchini Soup, 38
Chili Verde, 38
Chicken Enchilada Soup, 39
Creamy Cauliflower Soup, 39
Buffalo Chicken Soup, 40
Keto Lunch Bowl, 41
Cobb Salad, 41
Chicken Paprika, 43
Warm Radish Salad, 43
Crack Chicken, 44
Salsa Chicken, 44
Smoky Pulled Pork, 45
Chicken & Dumplings Soup, 45
Chicken & Dumplings Soup, 45
Zoodle Soup, 45
Fajita Soup, 46
Kalua Chicken, 46
Southwestern Chili, 47
Meat & Collard Greens Bowl, 48

Chicken & Mushroom Bowl, 49
Cheddar Soup, 49
Corned Beef with Cabbage, 51
Lazy Meat Mix, 51
Shredded Chicken Salad, 51
Manhattan Chowder, 53
Tuscan Soup, 54
Reuben Soup, 54
Avocado Chicken Salad, 55
Lettuce Chicken Salad, 55
Zuppa Toscana, 55
Broccoli Soup, 56
Rosemary&Butter Mushrooms, 57
Cauliflower Rice, 59
Mexican Style Keto Rice, 60
Sliced Zucchini Casserole, 62
Herbed Asparagus, 65
Butter Shirataki Noodles, 70
Asiago Cauliflower Rice, 70
Spiced Chicken Carnitas, 78
Spiced Chicken Carnitas, 78
Popcorn Chicken, 81
Mini Chicken Skewers, 82
Aromatic Swedish Meatballs, 83
Taco Shells, 86
Pesto Wings, 87
Keto Taquitos, 89
Wrapped Chicken Cubes, 95
Brazilian Fish Stew, 96
Mussel Chowder, 105
Seafood Bisque, 107
Lobster Bisque, 107
Mussels Mariniere, 108
Chicken Tonnato, 116
Paprika Chicken Wings, 116
Garlic Chicken Drumsticks, 116
Chicken Provencal, 117
Chicken Provencal, 117
Chicken with Blue Cheese Sauce, 117
Flying Jacob Casserole, 117
Chicken Caprese Casserole, 118
Cajun Chicken Salad, 118
Cajun Chicken Salad, 118
Caesar Salad, 118
BLT Chicken Wrap, 119
Pizza Stuffed Chicken, 119
Pizza Stuffed Chicken, 119
Chicken Patties, 120
Mozzarella Chicken Fillets, 120
Mozzarella Chicken Fillets, 120
Bruschetta Chicken, 120
Greek Chicken, 121
Chicken Rendang, 121
Chicken Zucchini Enchiladas, 122
Chicken Cacciatore, 122
Chicken Cacciatore, 122
Coconut Chicken Tenders, 123

Balsamic Roast Chicken, 123
Chicken & Snap Pea Salad, 124
Spinach Stuffed Chicken, 124
Chicken Scarpariello, 125
Chicken Scarpariello, 125
Chicken Divan Casserole, 125
Orange Chicken, 125
Chicken Stroganoff, 126
Pecan Chicken, 126
Chicken Cheese Calzone, 127
Butter Chicken Stew, 127
Chicken Cauliflower Rice, 128
Chicken Cauliflower Rice, 128
Asiago Chicken Drumsticks, 128
Chicken Stuffed Avocado, 129
Chicken Cordon Bleu, 129
Bacon-Wrapped Chicken Tenders, 130
Chicken and Spinach Bowl, 130
Chicken Liver Pate, 131
Coconut Chicken Cubes, 131
Anniversary Chicken, 133
Ajiaco, 134
Ethiopian Spicy Doro Wat Soup, 134
Ethiopian Spicy Doro Wat Soup, 134
Turkey Soup, 135
Chicken Fricassee, 135
South American Garden Chicken, 136
Fajita Chicken Casserole, 136
Fajita Chicken Casserole, 136
Chicken with Black Olives, 137
Indian Chicken Korma, 137
Garlic Pork Loin, 138
Spinach and Fennel Pork Stew, 143
Tender Pork Satay, 145
Beef and Squash Ragu, 147
Tender Salisbury Steak, 148
Mississippi Roast, 149
Italian Beef, 150
Lamb Pulao, 154
Cauliflower Shepherd's Pie, 156
Cauliflower Risotto, 163
Sautéed Kohlrabi, 167
Zucchini Goulash, 168
Steamed Broccoli Raab (Rabe), 170
Bok Choy Salad, 173
Keto Ratatouille, 175

CHILI FLAKES
Meat Sandwich, 13
Meat Muffins with Quail Eggs, 14
Spiced Hard-Boiled Eggs, 17
Fluffy Eggs, 18
Morning Bacon Bombs, 23
Egg Scramble, 30
Spinach Casserole, 33
Egg Soup, 36
Keto Taco Soup, 38

Cobb Salad, 41
Italian Style Salad, 42
Salsa Chicken, 44
Zoodle Soup, 45
Pepper Pork Chops, 48
Cheddar Soup, 49
Lettuce Chicken Salad, 55
Zuppa Toscana, 55
Feta and Zucchini Bowl, 64
Roasted Cauliflower Steak, 68
Sichuan Style Green Beans, 71
Parmesan Broccoli Head, 74
Cauliflower Salad with Provolone Cheese, 75
Spiced Asparagus, 75
Kale Wraps, 83
Bacon-Wrapped Shrimps, 90
Egg Yolk Spread, 94
Spicy Mackerel, 100
Seafood Omelet, 101
Salmon Salad, 104
Butter Cod Loin, 104
Tuna Cakes, 108
Salmon under Parmesan Blanket, 108
Fish Sticks, 109
Bacon-Wrapped Cod, 111
Cajun Chicken Salad, 118
Chicken Patties, 120
Greek Chicken, 121
Balsamic Roast Chicken, 123
Orange Chicken, 125
Butter Chicken Stew, 127
Chicken Lettuce Rolls, 132
Turkey Bolognese Sauce, 132
Anniversary Chicken, 133
Turkey Soup, 135
Fajita Chicken Casserole, 136
Chili Spare Ribs, 140
Ground Meat Stew, 144
Keto Oxtail Goulash, 150
White Pork Soup, 154
Zoodle Pork Casserole, 157
Ground Beef Skewers, 157
Pork Salad with Kale, 158
Balsamic Brussels Sprouts, 160
Collard Greens with Cherry Tomatoes, 164
Green Beans Salad, 165
Stuffed Spaghetti Squash, 166
Vegetable Soup, 169
Bok Choy Salad, 173
Collard Wraps, 174

CHILI PEPPER (GREEN)
Taco Shells, 86

CHIVES
Fluffy Eggs, 18
Bacon Eggs with Chives, 18

Oregano Egg en Cocotte, 24
Wontons, 30
Egg Soup, 36
Asian Style Zucchini Soup, 38
Crack Chicken, 44
Seafood Soup, 53
Garlic Bread, 74
Cauliflower Salad with Provolone Cheese, 75
Kale Wraps, 83
Keto Guacamole Deviled Eggs, 86
Cheese Meatballs with Greens, 95
Lime Salmon Burger, 99
Seafood Omelet, 101
Cod in Cream Sauce, 105
Lobster Bisque, 107
Crab Rangoon Dip, 110
Korean Style Pork Ribs, 141
Stuffed Mushrooms, 165

CHOCOLATE
Chocolate Bacon, 93
Walnut pie, 186
Blueberry Clusters, 187
Keto Fudge, 190
Peppermint Cookies, 193
Chocolate and Bacon Bars, 194
Tiger Butter, 196
Keto Chip Cookies, 186
Fat Bomb Jars, 187

CLAMS
Clam Chowder, 47
Manhattan Chowder, 53

COCONUT
Sweet Porridge, 27

COCONUT AMINOS
Lunch Pot Roast, 49
Salty Nuts Mix, 85

COCONUT BUTTER
Molten Brownies Cups, 179
Tiger Butter, 196

COCONUT CREAM
Pecan Chicken, 126
Chicken Cheese Calzone, 127
Chicken Crust Pizza, 128
Curry Pork Sausages, 142
Pork and Celery Curry, 146
Butter Lamb, 151
Burger Casserole, 155
Cauliflower Gratin, 164
Tuscan Mushrooms Sauce, 166
Zucchini Fettuccine, 172
Keto Club Salad, 172

Pumpkin Pie Cups, 178
Pumpkin Spices Pudding, 179
Lime Bars, 193
Lime Chia Seeds Pudding, 195

COCONUT FLAKES
Keto Oatmeal, 24
Tender Jicama Fritters, 78
Crunchy Green Beans, 82
Cauliflower PopCorn, 93
Cheese Pops, 93
Chocolate Shake, 94
Fish Sticks, 109
Coated Coconut Shrimps, 114
Chicken Rendang, 121
Coconut Chicken Cubes, 131
Scalloped Cabbage, 164
Coconut Cake, 185
Coconut Crack Bars, 188
Cheesecake Fat Bombs, 189
Peanut Butter Balls, 190
Coconut Muffins, 191
Coconut Clouds, 192

COCONUT MILK
Butter Crepes, 13
Keto Oatmeal, 24
Morning Pudding, 25
Sweet Porridge, 27
Mini Frittatas, 29
Coconut Soup, 50
Beef Curry Soup, 52
Seafood Soup, 53
Cauliflower Mac&Cheese, 57
Rosemary&Butter Mushrooms, 57
Turmeric Cabbage Rice, 63
Pumpkin Spices Latte, 85
Fish Saag, 96
Brazilian Fish Stew, 96
Curry Fish, 99
Skagenrora, 102
Mussels Mariniere, 108
Crab&Broccoli Casserole, 112
Chicken Rendang, 121
Chicken Divan Casserole, 125
Chicken Stroganoff, 126
Fajita Chicken Casserole, 136
Rogan Josh, 153
Hash Brown Casserole, 165
Cheddar Mushrooms, 169
Masala Cauliflower, 176
Chocolate Pudding, 178
Pecan Pie, 183
Pandan Custard, 185
Coffee Panna Cotta, 196

COCONUT OIL

Keto Cereal Bowl, 13
Butter Crepes, 13
Cabbage Hash Browns, 14
Minced Beef Pancakes, 17
Bacon Tacos, 19
Mason Jar Omelet, 20
Frittata with Greens, 21
Keto Shakshuka, 22
Chili Casserole, 26
Classic Breakfast Casserole, 28
Nutritious Taco Skillet, 29
Blueberry Muffins, 31
Mini Casserole in Jars, 32
Spinach Casserole, 33
Green Egg Bites, 34
Jalapeno Soup, 35
Bacon Chowder, 37
Asian Style Zucchini Soup, 38
Keto Taco Soup, 38
Cobb Salad, 41
Italian Style Salad, 42
Clam Chowder, 47
Chicken & Mushroom Bowl, 49
Beef Curry Soup, 52
Ancho Chili, 53
Low Carb Zucchini and Eggplant Soup, 56
Green Beans Casserole, 62
Turmeric Cabbage Rice, 63
Cheddar Tots with Broccoli, 67
Oregano Fennel Steaks, 70
Eggplant Gratin, 72
Oregano Keto Bread Rounds, 77
Cheese Almond Meal Bites, 78
Popcorn Chicken, 81
Crunchy Green Beans, 82
Salty Nuts Mix, 85
Bacon Sushi, 88
Keto Nachos, 89
Keto Cheetos, 92
Fish Casserole, 97
Salmon Pie, 97
Fried Salmon, 100
Salmon Salad, 104
Mussel Chowder, 105
Tuscan Shrimps, 106
Seafood Bisque, 107
Salmon Poppers, 109
Fish Pie, 111
Light Shrimp Pad Thai, 114
Coated Coconut Shrimps, 114
Chicken Provencal, 117
Bruschetta Chicken, 120
Chicken Cacciatore, 122
Ground Chicken Mix, 130
Chicken Lettuce Rolls, 132
Turkey Bolognese Sauce, 132
Anniversary Chicken, 133

Curry Pork Sausages, 142
Beef & Cabbage Stew, 148
Mississippi Roast, 149
Coriander Leg of Lamb, 151
Meat&Cheese Pie, 155
Cauliflower Shepherd's Pie, 156
Big Mac Bites, 156
Pork Belly Salad, 158
Cauliflower Risotto, 163
Hash Brown Casserole, 165
Sautéed Kohlrabi, 167
Zucchini Fettuccine, 172
Low Carb Falafel, 175
Blueberry Parfait, 184
Coconut Cake, 185
Walnut pie, 186
Fat Bomb Jars, 187
Blueberry Clusters, 187
Cheesecake Bites, 188
Coconut Crack Bars, 188
Low Carb Nutella, 189
Shortbread Cookies, 192
Lime Bars, 193
Tagalong Bars, 195

COD
Fish Casserole, 97
Curry Fish, 99
Butter Cod Loin, 104
Bacon-Wrapped Cod, 111
Poached Cod, 114

CRAB
Crab Salad, 42
Crab Spread, 90
Seafood Omelet, 101
Cajun Crab Casserole, 103
Crab Melt with Zucchini, 103
Crab Rangoon Dip, 110
Crab Rangoon Fat Bombs, 112
Crab&Broccoli Casserole, 112
Steamed Crab Legs, 115

CREAM
Cinnamon Pancakes, 15
Avocado Boats with Omelet, 19
Mason Jar Omelet, 20
Cauliflower Bake, 20
Frittata with Greens, 21
Cheese Egg Balls, 21
Breakfast Crustless Quiche, 22
Breakfast Taco Omelet, 22
Oregano Egg en Cocotte, 24
Hot Jalapeno Poppers Mix, 24
Breakfast Hot Cacao, 26
Classic Breakfast Casserole, 28
Egg Scramble, 30

Crustless Egg Pie, 32
Spinach Casserole, 33
Chicken Salad, 33
Bacon Chowder, 37
Keto Taco Soup, 38
Kale Soup, 39
Cobb Salad, 41
Crab Salad, 42
Chicken Paprika, 43
Fajita Soup, 46
Clam Chowder, 47
Chicken & Mushroom Bowl, 49
Cheddar Soup, 49
Shredded Chicken Salad, 51
Cheesy Pork Rinds, 52
Tuscan Soup, 54
Winter Soup, 54
Reuben Soup, 54
Avocado Chicken Salad, 55
Broccoli Soup, 56
Brussels Sprouts Casserole, 57
Spinach Mash with Bacon, 58
Fried Cauliflower Slices, 59
Mashed Brussel Sprouts, 59
White Cabbage in Cream, 60
Green Beans Casserole, 62
Turnip Creamy Gratin, 63
Cheesy Radish, 65
Eggplant Gratin, 72
Side Dish Cauliflower Ziti, 74
Keto Queso Dip, 80
Aromatic Swedish Meatballs, 83
Butter Coffee, 84
Heart of Palm Dip, 85
Garlic Aioli, 87
Chocolate Shake, 94
Wrapped Chicken Cubes, 95
Salmon Pie, 97
Shrimp Salad with Avocado, 101
Shrimp Tacos, 101
Mussels Casserole, 102
Cajun Crab Casserole, 103
Cod in Cream Sauce, 105
Salmon and Kohlrabi Gratin, 105
Mussel Chowder, 105
Tuscan Shrimps, 106
Lobster Bisque, 107
Dill Halibut, 110
Spinach and Tilapia Casserole, 111
Fish Pie, 111
Flying Jacob Casserole, 117
Caesar Salad, 118
Hoagie Bowl, 119
BLT Chicken Wrap, 119
Greek Chicken, 121
Chicken Zucchini Enchiladas, 122
Chicken Divan Casserole, 125

Chicken Lettuce Rolls, 132
Chicken Fricassee, 135
Chicken Moussaka, 136
Chicken with Black Olives, 137
Parmesan Pork, 138
Parmesan Pork Tenderloins, 139
Ground Meat Stew, 144
Blackberry Pork Chops, 146
Onion Baby Back Ribs, 148
Pork Chops in Sweet Sauce, 152
Brussels Sprouts in Heavy Cream, 159
Stuffed Spaghetti Squash, 166
Baked Kabocha Squash, 167
Tender Rutabaga, 168
Vegetable Soup, 169
Cream of Celery, 169
Steamed Rutabaga Mash, 170
Zucchini Pasta with Blue Cheese, 171
Keto Club Salad, 172
Pesto Zucchini Bake, 176
Chocolate Pudding, 178
Keto Custard, 178
Chocolate Pudding Cake, 180
Rhubarb Custard, 182
Chocolate Mousse, 182
Keto Crème Brulee, 184
Coconut Cake, 185
Strawberry Cubes, 187
Low Carb Nutella, 189
Cheesecake Fat Bombs, 189
Coconut Muffins, 191
Peppermint Cookies, 193
Keto Pralines, 194
Chocolate and Bacon Bars, 194
Lemon Muffins, 195
Tiger Butter, 196
Sausages & Vegetable Stew, 40
Garlic and Cheese Baked Asparagus, 159
Keto Cheetos, 92

CREAM CHEESE
Morning Bacon Bombs, 23
Egg Muffins, 23
Hot Jalapeno Poppers Mix, 24
Breakfast Stuffed Avocado, 25
Layered Casserole, 25
Green Egg Bites, 34
Provolone Chicken Soup, 35
Keto "Potato" Soup, 36
Keto Taco Soup, 38
Creamy Cauliflower Soup, 39
Egg & Cheese Salad with Dill, 42
Crab Salad, 42
Sour Cauliflower Salad, 43
Crack Chicken, 44
Salsa Chicken, 44
Fajita Soup, 46

Shredded Chicken Salad, 51
Cheesy Pork Rinds, 52
Seafood Soup, 53
Cauliflower Mac&Cheese, 57
Spinach Mash with Bacon, 58
Kale&Parmesan Bowl, 60
White Cabbage in Cream, 60
Cauli-Tatoes, 61
Squash Casserole, 62
Parmesan Onion Rings, 64
Cauliflower Gnocchi, 66
Smashed Cauliflower with Goat Cheese, 66
Gouda Vegetable Casserole, 72
Garlic Bread, 74
Soul Bread, 77
Paprika Deviled Eggs, 79
Keto Queso Dip, 80
Keto Breadsticks, 82
Taco Shells, 86
Mini Margharita Pizzas in Mushroom Caps, 86
Keto Guacamole Deviled Eggs, 86
Pesto Wings, 87
Bacon Avocado Bombs, 88
Bacon Sushi, 88
Chicken Celery Boats, 89
Crab Spread, 90
Keto Spanakopita Pie Slices, 92
Egg Yolk Spread, 94
Keto Crackers, 95
Cheese Melt, 98
Seafood Omelet, 101
Seafood Bisque, 107
Salmon Poppers, 109
Crab Rangoon Dip, 110
Spinach and Tilapia Casserole, 111
Mackerel Pate, 112
Tuna and Bacon Cups, 113
Coated Coconut Shrimps, 114
Chicken Caprese Casserole, 118
Caesar Salad, 118
Chicken Patties, 120
Coconut Chicken Tenders, 123
Chicken Cheese Calzone, 127
Asiago Chicken Drumsticks, 128
Chicken Stuffed Avocado, 129
Ground Chicken Mix, 130
Coconut Chicken Cubes, 131
Turkey Stuffed Mushrooms, 132
Turkey Soup, 135
Rosemary Barbecue Pork Chops, 138
Pork&Mushrooms Ragout, 144
Beef Tips, 147
Cumin Kielbasa, 149
Keto Oxtail Goulash, 150
Thyme Braised Beef, 150
White Pork Soup, 154
Meat&Cheese Pie, 155

Burger Casserole, 155
Zoodle Pork Casserole, 157
Pork Salad with Kale, 158
Eggs and Mushrooms Cups, 162
Kale Skillet with Nuts, 162
Stuffed Spaghetti Squash, 166
Shallot Mushrooms, 167
Tender Rutabaga, 168
Cheddar Mushrooms, 169
Vegetable Soup, 169
Avocado Pie, 171
Zucchini Boats, 172
Bell Pepper Pizza, 173
Collard Wraps, 174
Spinach and Jarlsberg Pie, 174
Sautéed Arugula Mash, 176
Spice Pie, 180
Keto Cheesecake, 181
Butter Cake, 181
Cinnamon Mini Rolls, 181
Lavender Pie, 184
Blueberry Parfait, 184
Mug Cake, 185
Vanilla Muffins, 187
Cheesecake Bites, 188
Cheesecake Fat Bombs, 189
Cinnamon Muffins, 190
Lime Bars, 193
Blueberry Crisp, 194

CUCUMBERS
Cilantro-Kale Salad, 65
Bacon Sushi, 88
Greek Chicken, 121
Big Mac Bites, 156
Pork Belly Salad, 158
Lobster Salad, 41
Cucumbers and Zucchini Noodles, 162
Keto Club Salad, 172

EGGPLANT
Bone Broth Soup, 40
Low Carb Zucchini and Eggplant Soup, 56
Low Carb Fall Vegetables, 67
Eggplant Gratin, 72
Keto Oxtail Goulash, 150
Zucchini Goulash, 168
Keto Ratatouille, 175
Aromatic Lasagna with Basil, 35
Chicken Moussaka, 136
Garlic Eggplant Rounds, 169
Baked Eggplant Mash, 177

EGGS
Meat Sandwich, 13
Keto Cereal Bowl, 13
Butter Crepes, 13
Soft Eggs, 14
Cabbage Hash Browns, 14
Meat Muffins with Quail Eggs, 14
Cinnamon Pancakes, 15
Paprika Eggs in Pepper Holes, 15
Stuffed Pepper Halves with Omelet, 15
Bacon Egg Cups, 16
Green Hash, 16
Spiced Hard-Boiled Eggs, 17
Minced Beef Pancakes, 17
Fluffy Eggs, 18
Bacon Eggs with Chives, 18
Avocado Boats with Omelet, 19
Breakfast Egg Hash, 19
Mason Jar Omelet, 20
Sausage Casserole, 21
Frittata with Greens, 21
Cheese Egg Balls, 21
Breakfast Crustless Quiche, 22
Breakfast Taco Omelet, 22
Keto Shakshuka, 22
Egg Muffins, 23
Egg Sandwich, 23
Oregano Egg en Cocotte, 24
Morning Pudding, 25
Breakfast Stuffed Avocado, 25
Zucchini Cheese Fritters, 26
Cauliflower Fritters, 27
Bacon Salad with Eggs, 28
Classic Breakfast Casserole, 28
Low-Carb Flaxseed Brule, 28
Mini Frittatas, 29
Egg Benedict Sandwich, 29
Nutritious Taco Skillet, 29
Wontons, 30
Breakfast Kale Bread, 30
Egg Scramble, 30
Blueberry Muffins, 31
Chicken Fritters, 31
Crustless Egg Pie, 32
Spinach Casserole, 33
Chicken Salad, 33
Green Egg Bites, 34
Egg Soup, 36
Cobb Salad, 41
Egg & Cheese Salad with Dill, 42
Sour Cauliflower Salad, 43
Parsley Meatloaf, 47
Cauliflower Gnocchi, 66
Vegetable Fritters, 68
Broccoli Nuggets, 69
Cauliflower Tortillas, 71
Jalapeno Popper Bread, 73
Garlic Bread, 74
Zucchini Fries in Bacon, 76
Oregano Keto Bread Rounds, 77
Soul Bread, 77

Tender Jicama Fritters, 78
Cheese Almond Meal Bites, 78
Paprika Deviled Eggs, 79
Keto Jalapeno Bread, 80
Crunchy Green Beans, 82
Keto Breadsticks, 82
Parmesan Cauliflower Tots, 83
Aromatic Swedish Meatballs, 83
Bread Twists, 84
Keto Guacamole Deviled Eggs, 86
Bacon Avocado Bombs, 88
Keto Spanakopita Pie Slices, 92
Keto Cheetos, 92
Cauliflower PopCorn, 93
Cheese Pops, 93
Egg Yolk Spread, 94
Keto Crackers, 95
Tuna Salad, 98
Seafood Omelet, 101
Cajun Crab Casserole, 103
Tuna Cakes, 108
Salmon Poppers, 109
Fish Sticks, 109
Fish Pie, 111
Tuna and Bacon Cups, 113
Light Shrimp Pad Thai, 114
Coated Coconut Shrimps, 114
Flying Jacob Casserole, 117
Chicken Patties, 120
Coconut Chicken Tenders, 123
Pecan Chicken, 126
Cayenne Pepper Chicken Meatballs, 126
Chicken Cheese Calzone, 127
Chicken Crust Pizza, 128
Turkey Stuffed Mushrooms, 132
Ethiopian Spicy Doro Wat Soup, 134
Chicken Fricassee, 135
Pork and Turnip Cake, 141
Hoisin Meatballs, 145
Ham and Cheese Dinner Casserole, 146
Tender Salisbury Steak, 148
Prosciutto and Eggs Salad, 149
Burger Casserole, 155
Ground Beef Skewers, 157
Spaghetti Squash Nests, 161
Eggs and Mushrooms Cups, 162
Stuffed Spaghetti Squash, 166
Avocado Pie, 171
Keto Club Salad, 172
Collard Wraps, 174
Spinach and Jarlsberg Pie, 174
Low Carb Falafel, 175
Mushrooms and Tofu Scramble, 175
Pumpkin Pie Cups, 178
Keto Custard, 178
Molten Brownies Cups, 179
Almond Tart, 179

Chocolate Pudding Cake, 180
Spice Pie, 180
Keto Cheesecake, 181
Butter Cake, 181
Cinnamon Mini Rolls, 181
Lava Cake, 182
Rhubarb Custard, 182
Chocolate Mousse, 182
Cocoa-Vanilla Pudding, 183
Keto Carrot Pie, 183
Keto Crème Brulee, 184
Lavender Pie, 184
Pandan Custard, 185
Mug Cake, 185
Coconut Cake, 185
Keto Chip Cookies, 186
Vanilla Muffins, 187
Avocado Brownies, 188
Cheesecake Bites, 188
Coconut Crack Bars, 188
Keto Blondies, 189
Cheesecake Fat Bombs, 189
Cinnamon Muffins, 190
Fluffy Donuts, 191
Coconut Muffins, 191
Mint Cookies, 192
Coconut Clouds, 192
Shortbread Cookies, 192
Macadamia Cookies, 193
Poppy Seeds Muffins, 194

ERYTHRITOL
Cinnamon Pancakes, 15
Keto Oatmeal, 24
Morning Pudding, 25
Breakfast Hot Cacao, 26
Low-Carb Flaxseed Brule, 28
Blueberry Muffins, 31
Spiral Ham, 50
Sweet Baby Carrot, 64
Chocolate Shake, 94
Fried Salmon, 100
Salmon in Fragrant Sauce, 100
Crab Rangoon Dip, 110
Chicken & Snap Pea Salad, 124
Keto Ham, 139
Char Siu, 140
Pork&Mushrooms Ragout, 144
Blackberry Pork Chops, 146
Italian Beef, 150
Pork Chops in Sweet Sauce, 152
Pastrami, 158
Balsamic Brussels Sprouts, 160
Baked Kabocha Squash, 167
Chocolate Pudding, 178
Pumpkin Pie Cups, 178
Almond Tart, 179

Chocolate Pudding Cake, 180
Keto Cheesecake, 181
Butter Cake, 181
Cinnamon Mini Rolls, 181
Lava Cake, 182
Keto Crème Brulee, 184
Lavender Pie, 184
Blueberry Parfait, 184
Mug Cake, 185
Coconut Cake, 185
Keto Chip Cookies, 186
Keto Vanilla Crescent Cookies, 186
Vanilla Muffins, 187
Avocado Brownies, 188
Keto Blondies, 189
Low Carb Nutella, 189
Peanut Butter Balls, 190
Fluffy Donuts, 191
Raspberry Pie, 191
Mint Cookies, 192
Coconut Clouds, 192
Shortbread Cookies, 192
Lime Bars, 193
Macadamia Cookies, 193
Keto Pralines, 194
Blueberry Crisp, 194
Poppy Seeds Muffins, 194
Lime Chia Seeds Pudding, 195
Tagalong Bars, 195
Tiger Butter, 196
Coffee Panna Cotta, 196

FENNEL
Ground Chicken Mix, 130
Spinach and Fennel Pork Stew, 143
Keto Oxtail Goulash, 150
Beef Cabbage Soup, 36
Sausages & Vegetable Stew, 40
Oregano Fennel Steaks, 70
Heart of Palm Dip, 85
Marinated Olives, 91
Pork and Celery Curry, 146

GARAM MASALA
Spinach Saag, 48
Fish Saag, 96
Tandoori Salmon, 98
Indian Chicken Korma, 137
Dhansak Curry Meat, 151
Rogan Josh, 153
Masala Cauliflower, 176
Baked Eggplant Mash, 177
GHEE
Mini Frittatas, 29
Lemon Carnitas, 44
Chicken & Dumplings Soup, 45
Hot Sausages Soup, 46

Spinach Saag, 48
Reuben Soup, 54
Lettuce Chicken Salad, 55
Ethiopian Spicy Doro Wat Soup, 134
South American Garden Chicken, 136
Fajita Chicken Casserole, 136
Indian Chicken Korma, 137
Rogan Josh, 153
White Pork Soup, 154
Lamb Pulao, 154
Scalloped Cabbage, 164
Green Beans Salad, 165
Shallot Mushrooms, 167
Garlic Eggplant Rounds, 169
Cream of Celery, 169
Fluffy Donuts, 191
Raspberry Pie, 191
Coconut Clouds, 192

HALIBUT
Brazilian Fish Stew, 96
Dill Halibut, 110
Halibut Ceviche, 113

HAM
Ham Roll, 18
Green Beans with Ham, 50
Warm Antipasto Salad, 72
Hoagie Bowl, 119
Ham and Cheese Dinner Casserole, 146
Chicken Cordon Bleu, 129

HAZELNUTS
Cauliflower Florets Mix, 160
Kale Skillet with Nuts, 162
Blueberry Parfait, 184
Walnut pie, 186
Low Carb Nutella, 189

KABOCHA SQUASH
Beef and Squash Ragu, 147
Baked Kabocha Squash, 167

KALE
Keto Shakshuka, 22
Breakfast Kale Bread, 30
Mini Casserole in Jars, 32
Beef Cabbage Soup, 36
Kale Soup, 39
Tuscan Soup, 54
Kale&Parmesan Bowl, 60
Cilantro-Kale Salad, 65
Salmon Salad, 104
Chicken Cacciatore, 122
Pork Salad with Kale, 158
Kale Skillet with Nuts, 162
Tuna Rolls, 109

LAMB
Coriander Leg of Lamb, 151
Spoon Lamb, 153
Butter Lamb, 151
Mint Lamb Cubes, 152
Chipotle Lamb Shank, 153
Lamb Pulao, 154

LEEK
Layered Casserole, 25
Bacon Brussels Sprouts, 58
Seafood Bisque, 107
Tuna Rolls, 109
Chicken Provencal, 117
Mozzarella Chicken Fillets, 120
Ground Turkey Chili, 134

LEMON
Lemon Carnitas, 44
Avocado Chicken Salad, 55
Cauliflower Tortillas, 71
Mini Chicken Skewers, 82
Seafood Bisque, 107
Parchment Fish, 113
Salmon with Lemon, 115
Caesar Salad, 118
Spoon Lamb, 153
Garlic Okra, 177
Coconut Muffins, 191
Lemon Muffins, 195

LEMON JUICE
Butter Crepes, 13
Bacon Salad with Eggs, 28
Breakfast Kale Bread, 30
Tortilla Soup, 37
Cobb Salad, 41
Chicken Paprika, 43
Sour Cauliflower Salad, 43
Warm Radish Salad, 43
Lemon Carnitas, 44
Pepper Pork Chops, 48
Coconut Soup, 50
Shredded Chicken Salad, 51
Avocado Chicken Salad, 55
Fried Cauliflower Slices, 59
Soft Spinach with Dill, 60
Thyme Purple Cabbage Steaks, 66
Cauliflower Tortillas, 71
Spiced Asparagus, 75
Spiced Chicken Carnitas, 78
Keto Jalapeno Bread, 80
Popcorn Chicken, 81
Heart of Palm Dip, 85
Keto Guacamole Deviled Eggs, 86
Edamame Hummus, 90

Marinated Olives, 91
Cauliflower PopCorn, 93
Brazilian Fish Stew, 96
Tuna Salad, 98
Tandoori Salmon, 98
Salmon in Fragrant Sauce, 100
Shrimp Tacos, 101
Shrimp Cocktail, 102
Salmon and Kohlrabi Gratin, 105
Paprika Salmon Skewers, 106
Tarragon Lobster, 107
Mussels Mariniere, 108
Mackerel Pate, 112
Halibut Ceviche, 113
Chicken Tonnato, 116
BLT Chicken Wrap, 119
Greek Chicken, 121
Orange Chicken, 125
Ethiopian Spicy Doro Wat Soup, 134
South American Garden Chicken, 136
Greek Style Pork Chops, 142
Pork&Mushrooms Ragout, 144
Prosciutto and Eggs Salad, 149
Dhansak Curry Meat, 151
Spoon Lamb, 153
Pork Belly Salad, 158
Caprese Zoodles, 160
Avocado Pie, 171
Lemon Artichoke, 171
Keto Club Salad, 172
Butter Cake, 181
Cinnamon Muffins, 190
Mint Cookies, 192
Lemon Muffins, 195

LEMONGRASS
Coconut Soup, 50
Fried Salmon, 100
Baked Snapper, 104
Chicken Rendang, 121
Butter Lamb, 151

LETTUCE
Bacon Salad with Eggs, 28
Cobb Salad, 41
Lettuce Chicken Salad, 55
Warm Antipasto Salad, 72
Taco Shells, 86
Shrimp Salad with Avocado, 101
Cajun Chicken Salad, 118
Caesar Salad, 118
Hoagie Bowl, 119
BLT Chicken Wrap, 119
Prosciutto and Eggs Salad, 149
Lemon Carnitas, 44
Avocado Chicken Salad, 55
Keto Chicken Burger, 131

Chicken Lettuce Rolls, 132

LIME
Lime Salmon Burger, 99
Salmon in Fragrant Sauce, 100
Bacon-Wrapped Cod, 111
Lime Bars, 193
Lime Chia Seeds Pudding, 195

LIME JUICE
Crab Salad, 42
Mexican Style Keto Rice, 60
Garlic Aioli, 87
Lime Salmon Burger, 99
Skagenrora, 102
Chicken Fricassee, 135
Lime Bars, 193

LOBSTER
Lobster Salad, 41
Lobster Bisque, 107
Tarragon Lobster, 107

MACADAMIA NUTS
Macadamia Cookies, 193

MACKEREL
Spicy Mackerel, 100
Mackerel Pate, 112

MUSHROOMS
Bacon Chowder, 37
Brussels Sprouts Casserole, 57
Low Carb Fall Vegetables, 67
Chicken Provencal, 117
Chicken Fricassee, 135
Pork&Mushrooms Ragout, 144
Mushrooms and Tofu Scramble, 175

MUSHROOMS (BELLA)
Chicken Stroganoff, 126

MUSHROOMS (BUTTON)
Green Beans Casserole, 62
MUSHROOMS (CREMINI)
Asian Style Zucchini Soup, 38
Chicken & Mushroom Bowl, 49
Chicken Cacciatore, 122
Stuffed Mushrooms, 165
Shallot Mushrooms, 167
Cheddar Mushrooms, 169

MUSHROOMS (PORTOBELLO)
Mini Margharita Pizzas in Mushroom Caps, 86
Portobello Toasts, 174

MUSHROOMS (WHITE)

Coconut Soup, 50
Winter Soup, 54
Rosemary&Butter Mushrooms, 57
Gouda Vegetable Casserole, 72
Fish Casserole, 97
Mozzarella Chicken Fillets, 120
Turkey Stuffed Mushrooms, 132
Tender Salisbury Steak, 148
Eggs and Mushrooms Cups, 162
Cauliflower Risotto, 163
Tuscan Mushrooms Sauce, 166
Shallot Mushrooms, 167
Zucchini Boats, 172

MUSSELS
Mussels Casserole, 102
Mussel Chowder, 105

NUT OIL
Chicken Rendang, 121
Dhansak Curry Meat, 151
Pork Chops in Sweet Sauce, 152

NUTMEG
Crustless Egg Pie, 32
Creamy Cauliflower Soup, 39
Chicken Paprika, 43
Green Beans with Ham, 50
Corned Beef with Cabbage, 51
Avocado Chicken Salad, 55
Fried Cauliflower Slices, 59
Herbed Asparagus, 65
Keto Spanakopita Pie Slices, 92
Cauliflower PopCorn, 93
Fried Salmon, 100
Tuna Rolls, 109
Fish Sticks, 109
Tuna and Bacon Cups, 113
Paprika Chicken Wings, 116
Chicken Stuffed Avocado, 129
Fajita Chicken Casserole, 136
Parmesan Pork Tenderloins, 139
Sage Pork Loin, 143
Pork Chops in Sweet Sauce, 152
White Pork Soup, 154
Lemongrass Green Beans, 161
Stuffed Mushrooms, 165
Spice Pie, 180
Fluffy Donuts, 191

NUTS
Sliced Zucchini Casserole, 62

OKRA
Pork&Mushrooms Ragout, 144
Garlic Okra, 177

ONION
Cabbage Hash Browns, 14
Meat Muffins with Quail Eggs, 14
Mini Casserole in Jars, 32
Kale Soup, 39
Chicken & Dumplings Soup, 45
Southwestern Chili, 47
Lazy Meat Mix, 51
Manhattan Chowder, 53
Tuscan Soup, 54
Side Dish Cauliflower Ziti, 74
Mussel Chowder, 105
Cayenne Pepper Chicken Meatballs, 126
South American Garden Chicken, 136
Chicken Moussaka, 136
Ground Meat Stew, 144
Keto Oxtail Goulash, 150
Chicken Cauliflower Rice, 128
Ground Beef Skewers, 157

ONION (GREEN)
Bacon Avocado Bombs, 88
Shrimp Tacos, 101

ONION (RED)
Classic Breakfast Casserole, 28
Chicken Salad, 33
Crab Salad, 42
Tuna Salad, 98
Skagenrora, 102
Seafood Bisque, 107
Halibut Ceviche, 113
Hoagie Bowl, 119
Chicken & Snap Pea Salad, 124
Chicken and Spinach Bowl, 130

ONION (WHITE)
Breakfast Egg Hash, 19
Keto Shakshuka, 22
Chili Casserole, 26
Nutritious Taco Skillet, 29
Provolone Chicken Soup, 35
Aromatic Lasagna with Basil, 35
Butternut Squash Soup, 37
Chicken Enchilada Soup, 39
Creamy Cauliflower Soup, 39
Buffalo Chicken Soup, 40
Lemon Carnitas, 44
Clam Chowder, 47
Green Beans with Ham, 50
Beef Curry Soup, 52
Reuben Soup, 54
Zuppa Toscana, 55
Broccoli Soup, 56
Green Beans Casserole, 62
Turmeric Cabbage Rice, 63
Parmesan Onion Rings, 64

Asiago Cauliflower Rice, 70
Gouda Vegetable Casserole, 72
Bacon Onion Rings, 76
Aromatic Swedish Meatballs, 83
Fish Saag, 96
Brazilian Fish Stew, 96
Cajun Crab Casserole, 103
Tuscan Shrimps, 106
Lobster Bisque, 107
Mussels Mariniere, 108
Tuna Rolls, 109
Fish Pie, 111
Parchment Fish, 113
Light Shrimp Pad Thai, 114
Chicken Rendang, 121
Chicken Zucchini Enchiladas, 122
Chicken Stroganoff, 126
Chicken Liver Pate, 131
Turkey Bolognese Sauce, 132
Ajiaco, 134
Ground Turkey Chili, 134
Ethiopian Spicy Doro Wat Soup, 134
Garlic Pork Loin, 138
Parmesan Pork Tenderloins, 139
Pork and Turnip Cake, 141
Hoisin Meatballs, 145
Tender Pork Satay, 145
Beef Tips, 147
Tender Salisbury Steak, 148
Mississippi Roast, 149
Spoon Lamb, 153
Rogan Josh, 153
Burger Casserole, 155
Cauliflower Shepherd's Pie, 156
Cauliflower Risotto, 163
Zucchini Goulash, 168
Cream of Celery, 169
Low Carb Falafel, 175
Mushrooms and Tofu Scramble, 175
Onion Baby Back Ribs, 148

ORANGE
Zingy Fish, 115
Orange Chicken, 125

ORANGE JUICE
Orange Chicken, 125

PANCETTA
Manhattan Chowder, 53
Chicken Provencal, 117
Steamed Broccoli Raab (Rabe), 170

PASTE (CURRY)
Coconut Soup, 50
Curry Fish, 99
Curry Pork Sausages, 142

Pork and Celery Curry, 146

PEANUT
Shrimp Salad with Avocado, 101
Flying Jacob Casserole, 117
Indian Chicken Korma, 137
Pork Salad with Kale, 158
Kale Skillet with Nuts, 162
Spice Pie, 180
Peanut Butter Balls, 190
Blueberry Crisp, 194
Almond Milk Pudding with Nuts, 197

PEANUT BUTTER
Tender Pork Satay, 145
Tagalong Bars, 195
Tiger Butter, 196

PEANUT OIL
Bok Choy Salad, 173

PEAS (GREEN)
Salmon Pie, 97
Fish Pie, 111
Chicken & Snap Pea Salad, 124
Green Peas Salad, 163
Vegetable Soup, 169

PECAN
Bacon Salad with Eggs, 28
Cilantro-Kale Salad, 65
Kale&Parmesan Bowl, 60
Beet Cubes with Pecans, 73
Salty Nuts Mix, 85
Pecan Chicken, 126

PEPPER (BANANA)
Seafood Soup, 53
Hoagie Bowl, 119

PEPPER (CAYENNE)
Bacon Salad with Eggs, 28
Classic Breakfast Casserole, 28
Keto "Potato" Soup, 36
Bacon Chowder, 37
Chili Verde, 38
Pepper Pork Chops, 48
Spinach Saag, 48
Chicken & Mushroom Bowl, 49
Manhattan Chowder, 53
Winter Soup, 54
Spinach Mash with Bacon, 58
Low Carb Fall Vegetables, 67
Cayenne Pepper Green Beans, 68
Keto Taquitos, 89
Cheese Pops, 93
Lime Salmon Burger, 99

Fried Salmon, 100
Shrimp Tacos, 101
Cajun Crab Casserole, 103
Salmon under Parmesan Blanket, 108
Bacon-Wrapped Cod, 111
Spinach and Tilapia Casserole, 111
Parchment Fish, 113
Coated Coconut Shrimps, 114
Chicken with Blue Cheese Sauce, 117
BLT Chicken Wrap, 119
Greek Chicken, 121
Balsamic Roast Chicken, 123
Pecan Chicken, 126
Cayenne Pepper Chicken Meatballs, 126
Herbed Whole Chicken, 129
Chicken and Spinach Bowl, 130
Keto Chicken Burger, 131
Ground Turkey Chili, 134
Pork Chops in Sweet Sauce, 152
Chipotle Lamb Shank, 153
Stuffed Spaghetti Squash, 166
Butter Edamame Beans, 167
Garlic Eggplant Rounds, 169
Avocado Pie, 171
Lemon Artichoke, 171
Pesto Zucchini Bake, 176
Cabbage Dippers, 177

PEPPER (CHILI)
Chili Casserole, 26
Fajita Soup, 46
Beef Curry Soup, 52
Warm Antipasto Salad, 72
Side Dish Cauliflower Ziti, 74
Flying Jacob Casserole, 117
Chicken Rendang, 121
Chicken Zucchini Enchiladas, 122
Chicken Scarpariello, 125
Ground Turkey Chili, 134
Jalapeno Pulled Pork, 140
Mississippi Roast, 149

PEPPER (JALAPENO)
Jalapeno Soup, 35
Keto Taco Soup, 38
Chicken Enchilada Soup, 39
Fajita Soup, 46
Ancho Chili, 53
Jalapeno Popper Bread, 73
Spiced Chicken Carnitas, 78
Salmon in Fragrant Sauce, 100
Salmon Poppers, 109
Halibut Ceviche, 113
Jalapeno Pulled Pork, 140
Korean Style Pork Ribs, 141
Mississippi Roast, 149
Garlic Okra, 177

Hot Jalapeno Poppers Mix, 24
Keto Jalapeno Bread, 80

PEPPER (POBLANO)
Tortilla Soup, 37

PEPPER (SERRANO)
Sautéed Kohlrabi, 167

PORK
Wontons, 30
Mini Casserole in Jars, 32
Jalapeno Soup, 35
Aromatic Lasagna with Basil, 35
Meat & Collard Greens Bowl, 48
Aromatic Swedish Meatballs, 83
Pork and Turnip Cake, 141
Ground Meat Stew, 144
White Pork Soup, 154
Meat&Cheese Pie, 155
Big Mac Bites, 156
Zoodle Pork Casserole, 157
Pork Salad with Kale, 158
Chili Verde, 38
Lemon Carnitas, 44
Smoky Pulled Pork, 45
Pepper Pork Chops, 48
Lazy Meat Mix, 51
Pork Roast with Sauerkraut, 52
Winter Soup, 54
Chicharrones, 91
Rosemary Barbecue Pork Chops, 138
Kalua Pork, 138
Parmesan Pork, 138
Garlic Pork Loin, 138
Fragrant Pork Belly, 139
Parmesan Pork Tenderloins, 139
Jalapeno Pulled Pork, 140
Char Siu, 140
Chili Spare Ribs, 140
Taiwanese Braised Pork Belly, 141
Kalua Pig, 142
Greek Style Pork Chops, 142
Sage Pork Loin, 143
Spinach and Fennel Pork Stew, 143
Garlic Smoky Ribs, 143
Pork&Mushrooms Ragout, 144
Mesquite Ribs, 144
Keto Pork Posole, 145
Tender Pork Satay, 145
Blackberry Pork Chops, 146
Pork and Celery Curry, 146
Onion Baby Back Ribs, 148
Pork Chops in Sweet Sauce, 152
Kalua Pork, 152
Pork Belly Salad, 158

PORK RINDS
Salmon Balls, 32
Broccoli Toast Spread, 33
Parsley Meatloaf, 47
Cheesy Pork Rinds, 52
Salmon Poppers, 109

PORK SAUSAGES
Dog Nuggets, 92
Curry Pork Sausages, 142

PROSCIUTTO
Prosciutto Shrimp Skewers, 99
Prosciutto and Eggs Salad, 149
Bok Choy Salad, 173
Cabbage Dippers, 177

PUMPKIN
Zucchini Parsley Tots, 79
South American Garden Chicken, 136
Pumpkin Spices Latte, 85
Pumpkin Pie Cups, 178
Pumpkin Spices Pudding, 179
Spice Pie, 180
Blueberry Parfait, 184

RADISH
Warm Radish Salad, 43
Lettuce Chicken Salad, 55
Rosemary Radish Halves, 64
Cheesy Radish, 65
Taco Shells, 86
Cajun Chicken Salad, 118
Keto Pork Posole, 145
Tender Sautéed Vegetables, 161

RASPBERRIES
Raspberry Pie, 191

RUTABAGA
Tender Rutabaga, 168
Steamed Rutabaga Mash, 170

SALMON
Salmon Balls, 32
Seafood Soup, 53
Salmon Pie, 97
Pesto Salmon, 97
Tandoori Salmon, 98
Lime Salmon Burger, 99
Fried Salmon, 100
Salmon in Fragrant Sauce, 100
Salmon Salad, 104
Cod in Cream Sauce, 105
Salmon and Kohlrabi Gratin, 105
Paprika Salmon Skewers, 106
Salmon under Parmesan Blanket, 108

Salmon Poppers, 109
Parchment Fish, 113
Salmon with Lemon, 115

SALSA
Southwestern Chili, 47

SALSA (HOT)
Salsa Chicken, 44

SALSA (VERDE)
Chili Verde, 38

SAUCE (BBQ)
Rosemary Barbecue Pork Chops, 138
Char Siu, 140

SAUCE (BUFFALO)
Buffalo Chicken Soup, 40

SAUCE (ENCHILADA)
Chicken Zucchini Enchiladas, 122

SAUCE (HOISIN)
Hoisin Meatballs, 145

SAUCE (MARINARA)
Keto Shakshuka, 22
Breakfast Spaghetti Squash Casserole, 27
Aromatic Lasagna with Basil, 35
Mini Cheese Pepperoni Pizza, 80

SAUCE (OYSTER)
Wontons, 30

SAUCE (PESTO)
Pesto Wings, 87
Pesto Salmon, 97
Chicken Caprese Casserole, 118
Avocado Pesto Zoodles, 174

SAUSAGES
Classic Breakfast Casserole, 28
Mini Frittatas, 29
Spinach Casserole, 33
Kale Soup, 39
Sausages & Vegetable Stew, 40
Hot Sausages Soup, 46
Tuscan Soup, 54
Zuppa Toscana, 55
Chicken Scarpariello, 125

SCALLIONS
Cheese Meatballs with Greens, 95
Seafood Bisque, 107
Chicken Cauliflower Rice, 128
Ajiaco, 134

Hoisin Meatballs, 145
Collard Wraps, 174

SCALLOPS
Butter Scallops, 103
Parmesan Scallops, 106

SEABASS
Coriander Seabass, 110

SHALLOT
Taiwanese Braised Pork Belly, 141
Korean Style Pork Ribs, 141
Keto Pork Posole, 145
Italian Beef, 150
White Pork Soup, 154
Green Beans Salad, 165
Shallot Mushrooms, 167

SHRIMPS
Italian Style Salad, 42
Seafood Soup, 53
Bacon-Wrapped Shrimps, 90
Prosciutto Shrimp Skewers, 99
Shrimp Salad with Avocado, 101
Shrimp Tacos, 101
Shrimp Cocktail, 102
Skagenrora, 102
Tuscan Shrimps, 106
Seafood Bisque, 107
Light Shrimp Pad Thai, 114
Coated Coconut Shrimps, 114

SOUR CREAM
Crab Salad, 42
Shredded Chicken Salad, 51

SPAGHETTI SQUASH
Breakfast Spaghetti Squash Casserole, 27
Butter Spaghetti Squash, 61
Squash Casserole, 62
Spaghetti Squash Mac&Cheese, 71
Spaghetti Squash Nests, 161
Shredded Spaghetti Squash with Bacon, 163
Stuffed Spaghetti Squash, 166

SPINACH
Green Hash, 16
Frittata with Greens, 21
Breakfast Crustless Quiche, 22
Spinach Casserole, 33
Green Egg Bites, 34
Bacon Chowder, 37
Crab Salad, 42
Hot Sausages Soup, 46
Spinach Saag, 48
Spinach Mash with Bacon, 58

Soft Spinach with Dill, 60
Keto Spanakopita Pie Slices, 92
Fish Saag, 96
Tuscan Shrimps, 106
Spinach and Tilapia Casserole, 111
Spinach Stuffed Chicken, 124
Chicken and Spinach Bowl, 130
Spinach and Fennel Pork Stew, 143
Tuscan Mushrooms Sauce, 166
Vegetable Soup, 169
Spinach and Jarlsberg Pie, 174
Egg Benedict Sandwich, 29

SPLENDA
Pumpkin Spices Pudding, 179
Molten Brownies Cups, 179
Spice Pie, 180
Butter Cake, 181
Rhubarb Custard, 182
Chocolate Mousse, 182
Keto Crème Brulee, 184
Cheesecake Bites, 188
Coconut Muffins, 191
Lemon Muffins, 195
Almond Milk Pudding with Nuts, 197

STEVIA
Sweet Porridge, 27
Light Shrimp Pad Thai, 114
Blueberry Parfait, 184
Keto Vanilla Crescent Cookies, 186
Cinnamon Muffins, 190
Fluffy Donuts, 191
Phirni Kheer with Almonds, 195
Keto Custard, 178

STRAWBERRIES
Strawberry Cubes, 187

SYRUP (MAPLE)
Cocoa-Vanilla Pudding, 183

TARRAGON
Tarragon Lobster, 107

TILAPIA
Fish Sticks, 109
Spinach and Tilapia Casserole, 111

TOMATO PASTE
Keto Shakshuka, 22
Chili Casserole, 26
Nutritious Taco Skillet, 29
Keto Taco Soup, 38
Chicken Enchilada Soup, 39
Chicken Paprika, 43
Smoky Pulled Pork, 45

Southwestern Chili, 47
Lazy Meat Mix, 51
Side Dish Cauliflower Ziti, 74
Mini Chicken Skewers, 82
Fish Saag, 96
Brazilian Fish Stew, 96
Lobster Bisque, 107
Cajun Chicken Salad, 118
Pizza Stuffed Chicken, 119
Butter Chicken Stew, 127
Turkey Bolognese Sauce, 132
Ethiopian Spicy Doro Wat Soup, 134
Jalapeno Pulled Pork, 140
Chili Spare Ribs, 140
Beef & Cabbage Stew, 148
Tender Salisbury Steak, 148
Rogan Josh, 153
Meat&Cheese Pie, 155
Cauliflower Shepherd's Pie, 156
Tender Sautéed Vegetables, 161
Zucchini Goulash, 168
Zucchini Boats, 172
Bell Pepper Pizza, 173

TOMATO SAUCE
Mini Margharita Pizzas in Mushroom Caps, 86

TOMATOES
Fajita Soup, 46
Bacon Tacos, 19
Spinach Casserole, 33
Jalapeno Soup, 35
Ancho Chili, 53
Sliced Zucchini Casserole, 62
Warm Antipasto Salad, 72
Halibut Ceviche, 113
Hoagie Bowl, 119
Keto Chicken Burger, 131
Chicken Moussaka, 136
Indian Chicken Korma, 137
Dhansak Curry Meat, 151
Keto Ratatouille, 175
Portobello Toasts, 174
Breakfast Crustless Quiche, 22
Tortilla Soup, 37
Manhattan Chowder, 53
Parmesan Tomatoes Slices, 79
Chicken Cacciatore, 122
Ground Turkey Chili, 134
Chipotle Lamb Shank, 153
Lamb Pulao, 154
Garlic Okra, 177

TOMATOES (CHERRY)
Italian Style Salad, 42
Salmon Salad, 104
Chicken Caprese Casserole, 118

Bruschetta Chicken, 120
Pork Belly Salad, 158
Caprese Zoodles, 160
Collard Greens with Cherry Tomatoes, 164
Tuscan Mushrooms Sauce, 166
Keto Club Salad, 172

TUNA
Tuna Salad, 98
Cheese Melt, 98
Tuna Cakes, 108
Tuna Rolls, 109
Tuna and Bacon Cups, 113
Chicken Tonnato, 116
Tuna Steak Skewers, 91

TURKEY
Turkey Bolognese Sauce, 132
Turkey Stuffed Mushrooms, 132
Ground Turkey Chili, 134
Chicken Moussaka, 136
Hoagie Bowl, 119
Turkey Soup, 135

TURKEY SAUSAGE
Breakfast Sausages, 34

TURNIP
Winter Soup, 54
Cheesy Radish, 65
Turnip Fries, 81
Turkey Soup, 135
Pork and Turnip Cake, 141
Beef and Squash Ragu, 147
Beef Tips, 147
Hash Brown Casserole, 165
Zucchini Goulash, 168

WALNUTS
Keto Cereal Bowl, 13
Sweet Porridge, 27
Salty Nuts Mix, 85
Light Shrimp Pad Thai, 114
Keto Carrot Pie, 183
Walnut pie, 186

Keto Blondies, 189

WHIPPED CREAM
Low-Carb Flaxseed Brule, 28
Lobster Salad, 41
Soul Bread, 77
Fish Casserole, 97
Crab Rangoon Dip, 110
Butter Chicken Stew, 127
Keto Cheesecake, 181
Walnut pie, 186
Fat Bomb Jars, 187
Phirni Kheer with Almonds, 195
Lava Cake, 182

ZUCCHINI
Zucchini Meat Cups, 16
Zucchini Cheese Fritters, 26
Asian Style Zucchini Soup, 38
Zoodle Soup, 45
Lunch Pot Roast, 49
Low Carb Zucchini and Eggplant Soup, 56
Sliced Zucchini Casserole, 62
Squash Casserole, 62
Zucchini, 63
Feta and Zucchini Bowl, 64
Low Carb Fall Vegetables, 67
Zucchini Fries in Bacon, 76
Zucchini Parsley Tots, 79
Ranch Poppers, 88
Crab Melt with Zucchini, 103
Mussel Chowder, 105
Chicken Zucchini Enchiladas, 122
Zoodle Pork Casserole, 157
Caprese Zoodles, 160
Tender Sautéed Vegetables, 161
Cucumbers and Zucchini Noodles, 162
Zucchini Goulash, 168
Vegetable Soup, 169
Zucchini Pasta with Blue Cheese, 171
Zucchini Boats, 172
Zucchini Fettuccine, 172
Avocado Pesto Zoodles, 174
Keto Ratatouille, 175
Pesto Zucchini Bake, 176

Copyright 2020 by Victoria Green All rights reserved.

All rights Reserved. No part of this publication or the information in it may be quoted from or reproduced in any form by means such as printing, scanning, photocopying or otherwise without prior written permission of the copyright holder.

Disclaimer and Terms of Use: Effort has been made to ensure that the information in this book is accurate and complete, however, the author and the publisher do not warrant the accuracy of the information, text and graphics contained within the book due to the rapidly changing nature of science, research, known and unknown facts and internet. The Author and the publisher do not hold any responsibility for errors, omissions or contrary interpretation of the subject matter herein. This book is presented solely for motivational and informational purposes only.